LISA YUSKAVAGE

ARIEL LEVY
BARRY SCHWABSKY
LENA DUNHAM
JASON SCHMIDT

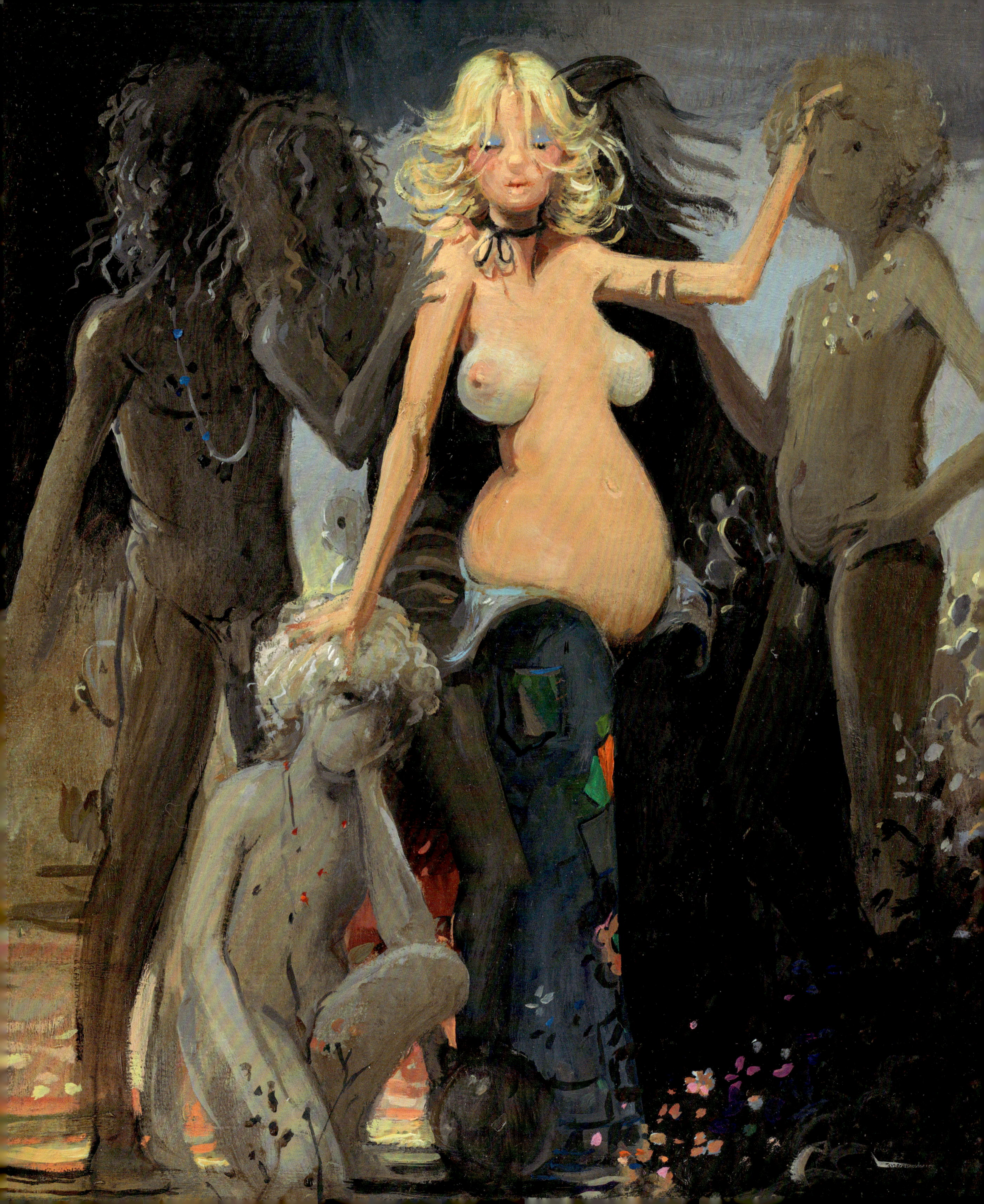

A LITTLE DÉJA VU, 2017–18
OIL ON LINEN
38 X 32 CM

CONTENTS

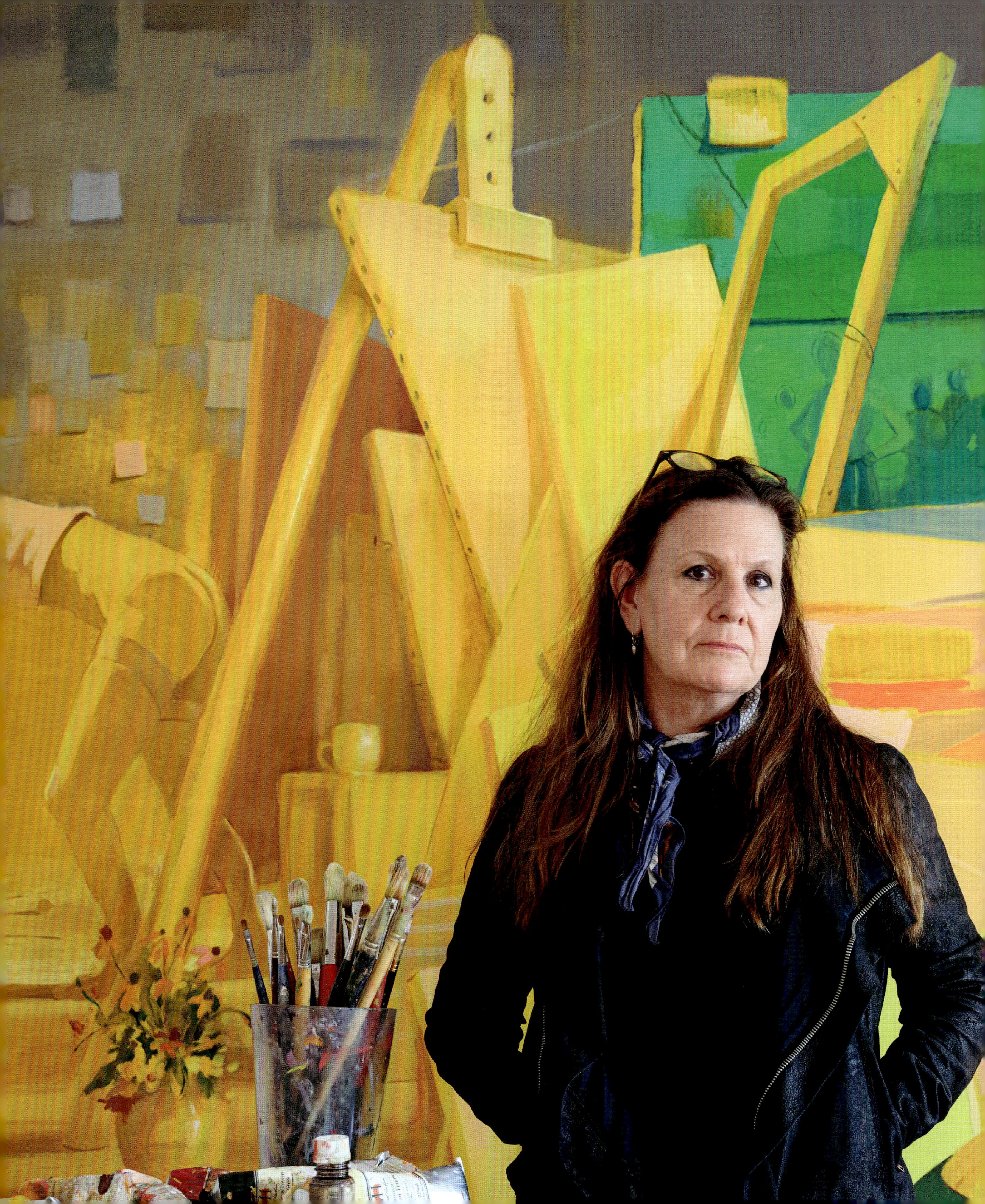

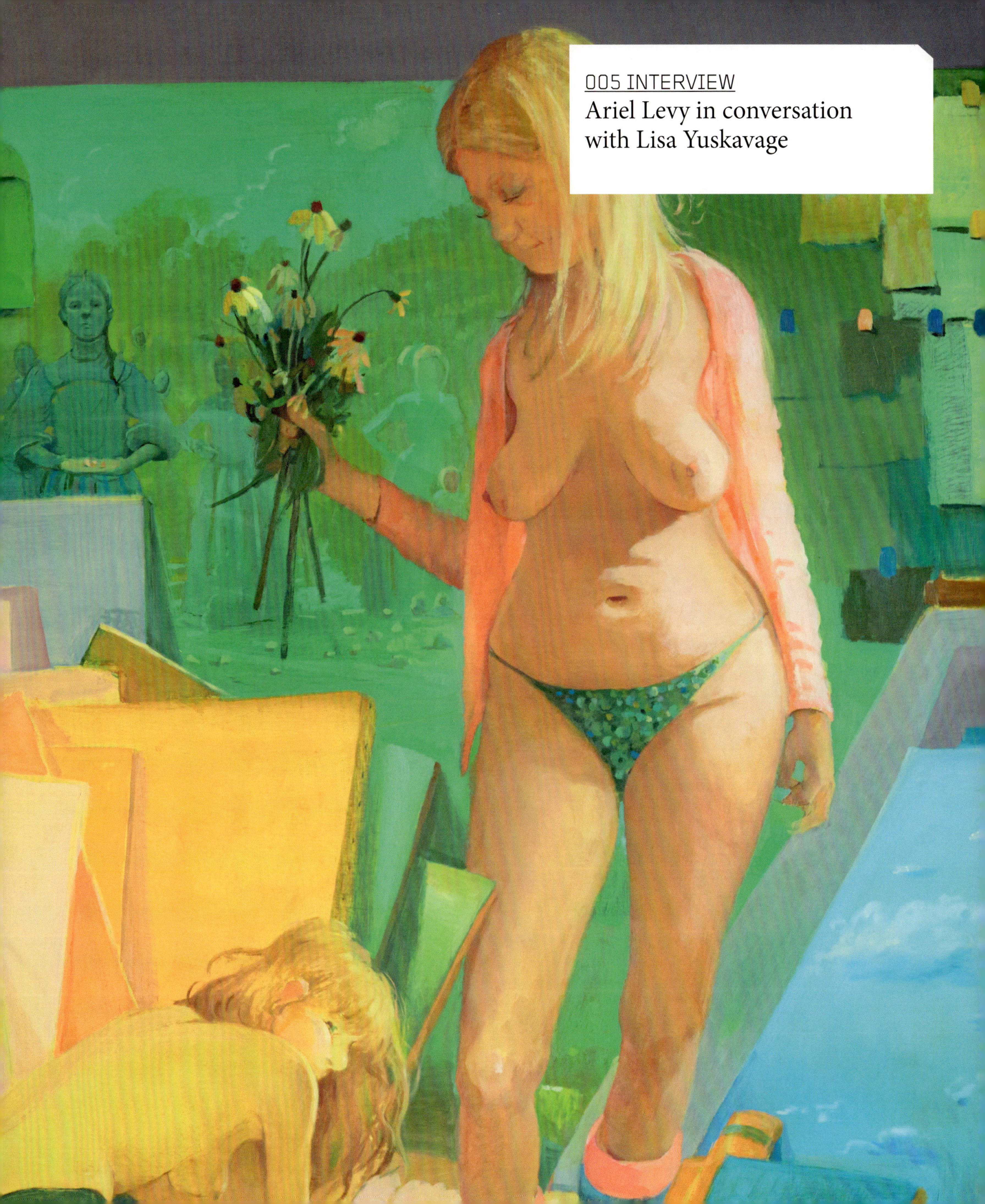

005 INTERVIEW

Ariel Levy in conversation with Lisa Yuskavage

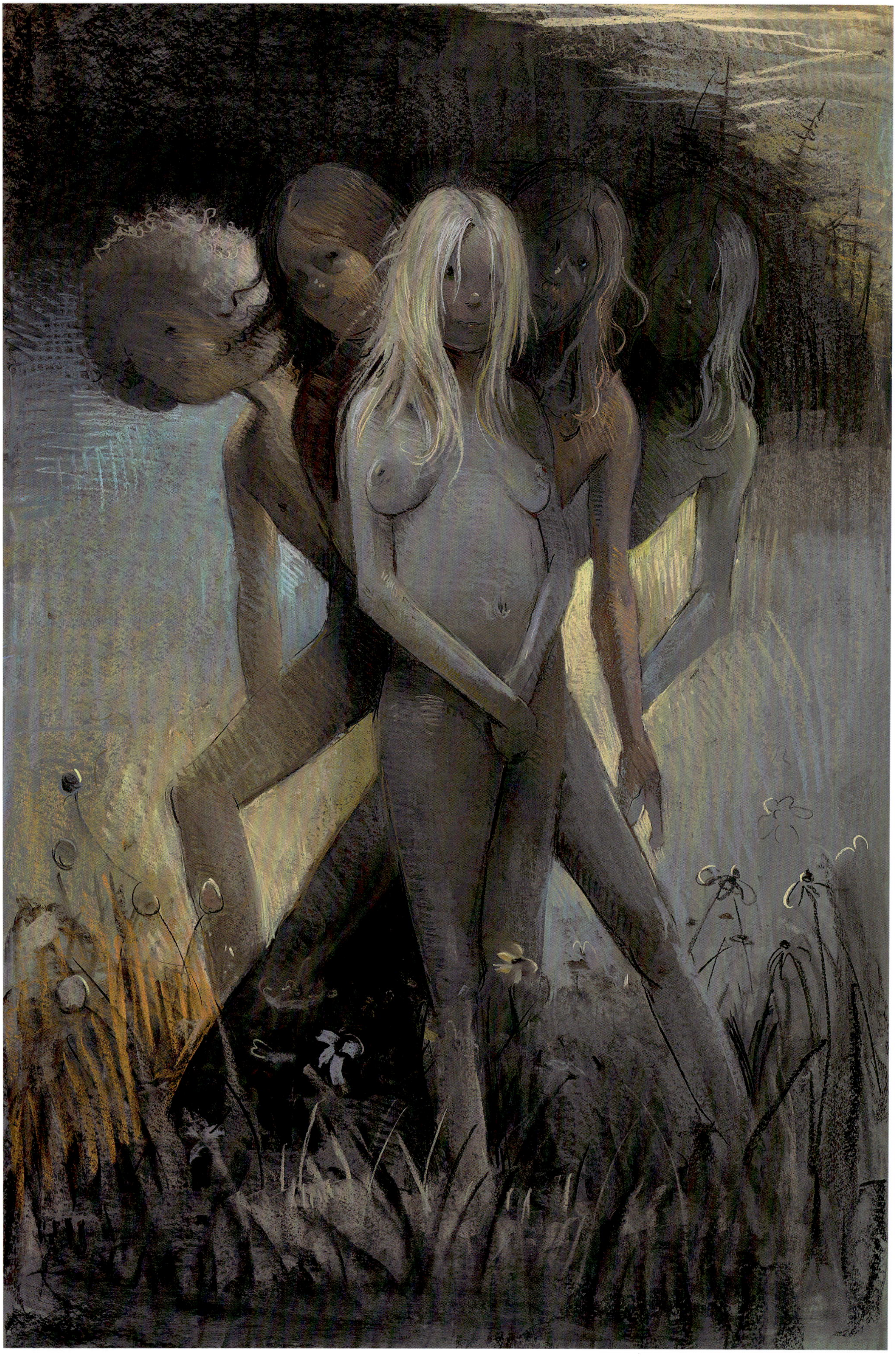

HIPPIES, 2013
MONOPRINT WITH HAND
ADDITIONS IN PASTEL
107 X 109 CM

previous pages:
LISA YUSKAVAGE,
NEW YORK, 2024

ARIEL LEVY: *Lisa, do you think the culture has caught up to you? It's almost like the young have taught the old how to see your work.*

LISA YUSKAVAGE: I think that young people were not burdened by modernist orthodoxy, that they didn't bring certain burdens of Puritanism to looking at what I was doing. I was naively surprised that anyone would see my work as misogynist. I mean, I know that I was pushing certain kinds of buttons, but it's sort of like Philip Roth being seen as a self-hating Jew.

LEVY: *As if Sabbath's Theater was a mission statement instead of a work of fiction.*

YUSKAVAGE: I don't believe that the job of the artist is to create a warm chocolate-chip cookie for the audience. I'm not trying to create Arcadia.

What am I trying to create? is maybe the question. I believe paintings at their best are very complex things, images that can be very contradictory, and sort of unpack themselves slowly over time. The work of someone like Philip Guston, for instance – who was friends with Roth at a very critical time in both of their careers. They were both hiding out for different reasons: one because of failure; and one because of success. And they recognized each other, what they were trying to do in their work.

I was thinking a lot about this idea that what makes an artist really vital, especially as they get older, is that they've drunk from the well and have a very deep relationship with not just art history, but history in itself. I think writers who have a profound knowledge of the visual world and the world of pictures have a much richer verbal acuity.

PIEFACE, 2008
OIL ON LINEN
122 X 102 CM

And I think highly of painters who read a lot – it's got obvious benefits. It isn't just staying in your lane. It's being a cultured person. And I think the deeper that pond, as you get older, there's an endless supply of oxygen.

LEVY: *Fuel.*

YUSKAVAGE: Yes, fuel of whatever nature. The key is to have a seemingly endless supply so you can keep on going, and you're just constantly having ideas that keep moving you forwards.

LEVY: *You've said to me before that the point is to find subject matter that 'unlocks' you.*

YUSKAVAGE: Yes, it's almost like the *Alice in Wonderland* keys. Because I do think we all have these imaginations that don't unlock under any old circumstances. There was a point when I was very young – and I don't know how I knew to do this, it was before I made almost any work that we'd recognize as *my* work – I laid out my 35 millimeter slides on the light table, and I thought, 'Out of every twenty paintings here, one just jumps out as a serious winner in the group. The rest are kind of, you know...'

LEVY: *They don't have that same mojo.*

YUSKAVAGE: They just didn't. And I was really trying to analyze the situation. Like, what is it that made these pictures work? I put them all out and it was sort of like that children's song...

LEVY: *Which one of these is not like the other?*

YUSKAVAGE: But the opposite. What did they have in common? So I took out a notebook and I just sat there trying to recall details of what was happening when I made the stand-outs. I asked myself, 'Where were you? Were you painting at night? Were you painting in the morning? Were you listening to music? Were you hungry?' And I realized that I'm not a person who can paint under crazy circumstances like some artists. Nothing out of the ordinary. Nothing too exciting.

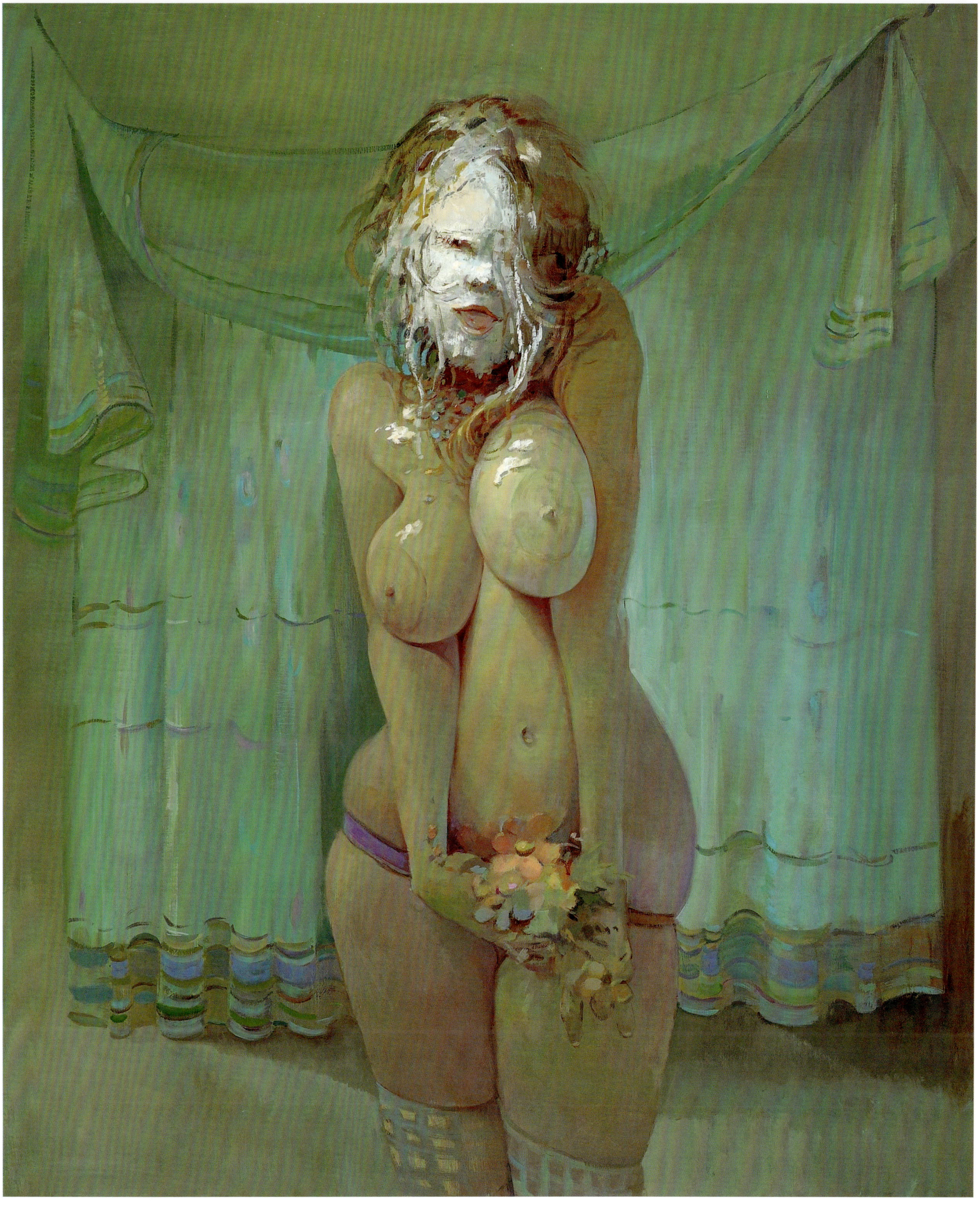

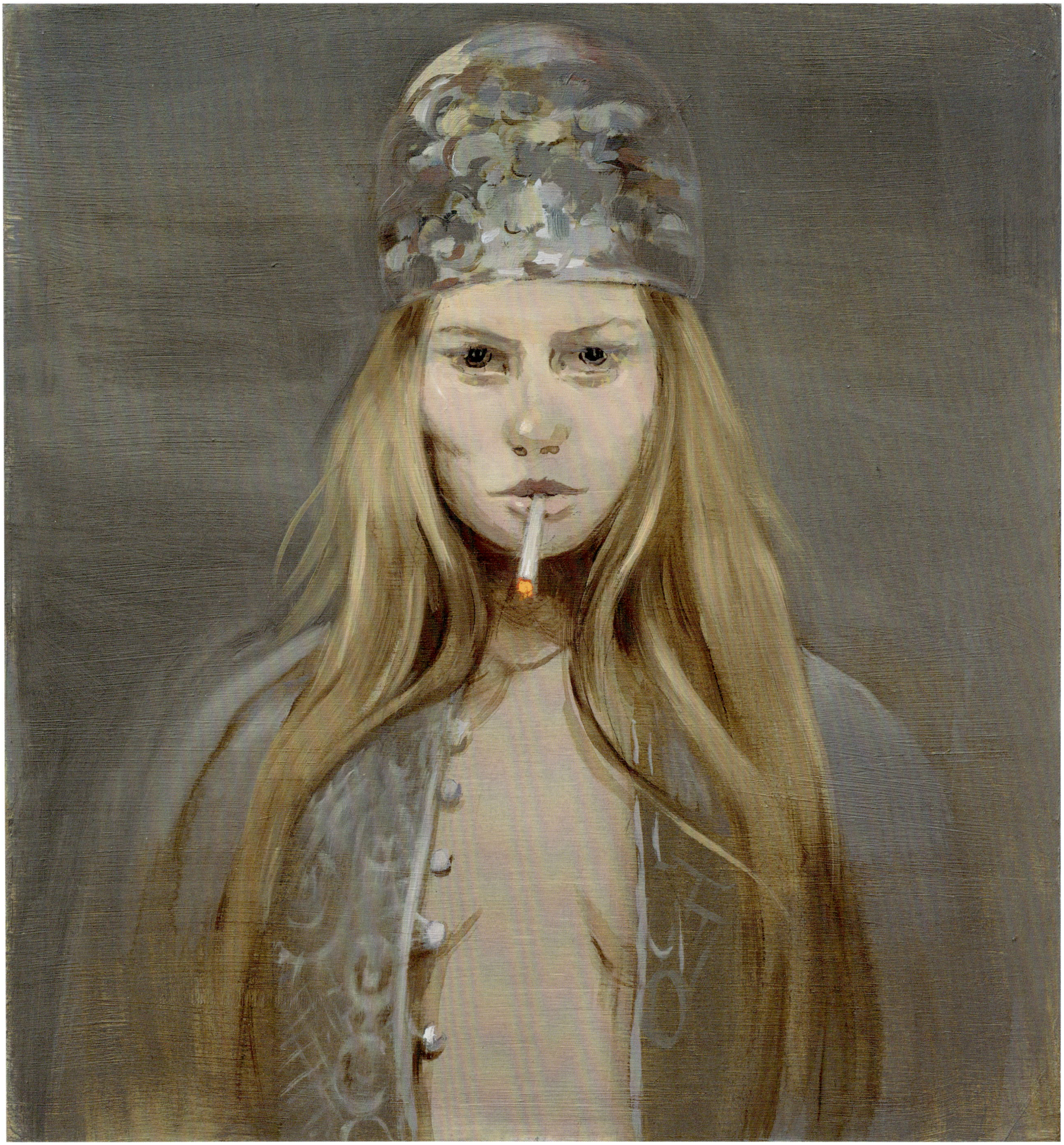

right,
THE FUCK YOU PAINTING,
2020
OIL ON LINEN
31 X 29 CM

opposite,
STONED, 2016
OIL AND GRAPHITE
ON LINEN
42 X 40 CM

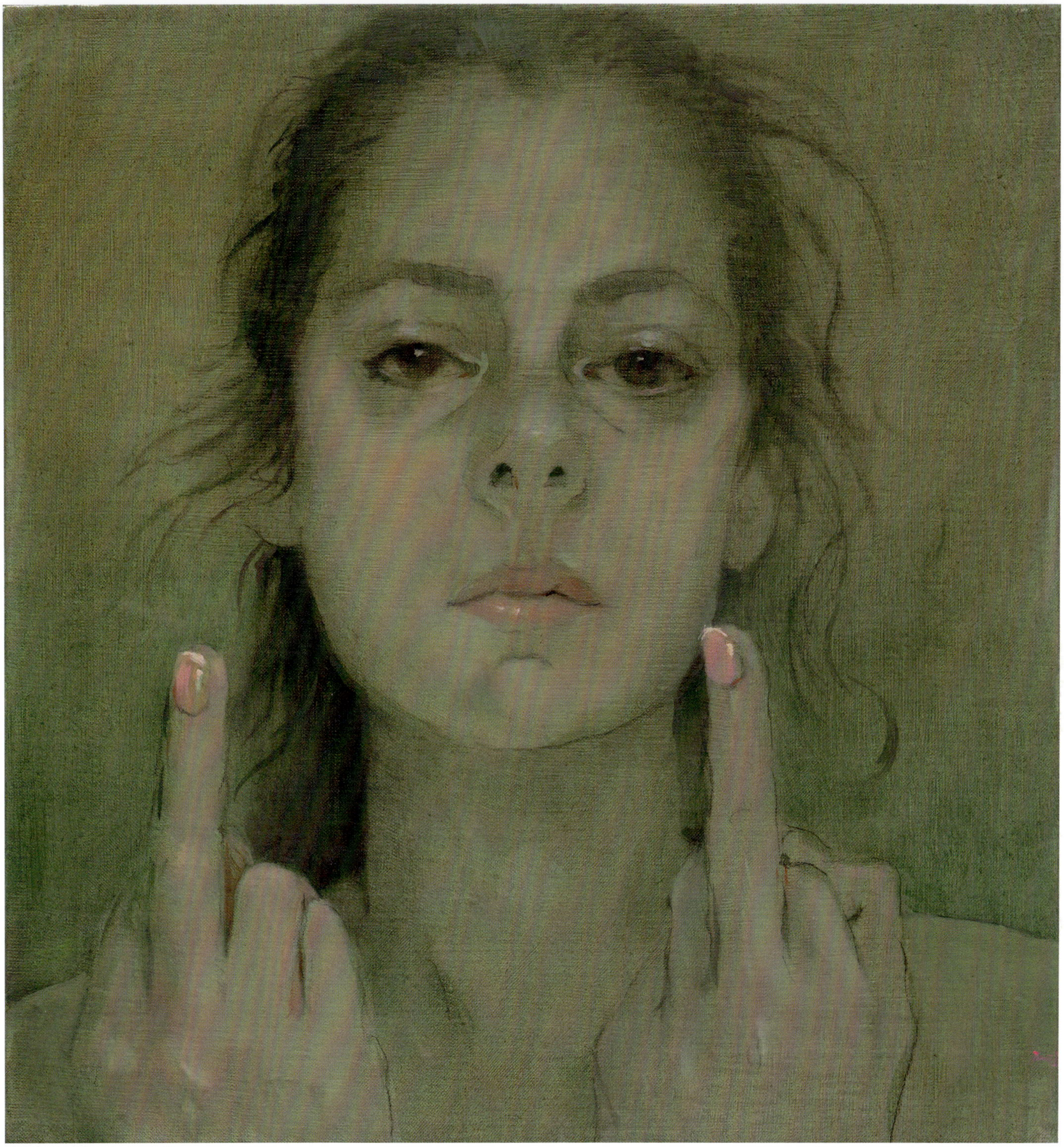

LEVY: *So the conditions are important.*

YUSKAVAGE: Yes, and my state of mind.

LEVY: *It sounds like there were columns.*

YUSKAVAGE: There were columns. I was looking at everything that went into this. It's like, 'No, you're not high, you're not drunk, you're not painting in the middle of the night, you're not being extreme'. I actually think everyone's Venn diagram of what works for them is so unique. I really do my best work between ten and eleven in the morning and six and seven in the evening. And not on a full stomach. But not starving, either.

LEVY: *Well, it almost seems like you need to be able to forget about your mortal body, your material casing: you can't be hungry, you can't be tired, you can't be drunk. You need to be able to just exist without being distracted by…*

YUSKAVAGE: The body. It needs to be well enough, and exercised just enough, not more. Also, the *mind* has to be well enough.

It really works to analyze what's correct when things connect. When it works. And then you just get rid of the things that don't work. If you can't paint a hand, don't ever put one in your work. Get rid of it! Paint around it. That's not a thing you have to do. What I love about being an artist is that every time we approach making an artwork, we're creating the rules of our own game; it's a brand new game. *You're* creating how the game is won or lost. And for years, people would tell me that I was losing the game. And I thought, 'But you're judging me by somebody else's rules!' I had to be strong enough of mind to remember that.

LEVY: *What was in the column where you assessed the work, not the painter? Visually, what did the standouts have in common?*

YUSKAVAGE: I noticed that in the good ones, I really gave into rendering using light. That wasn't something that was in vogue in contemporary art at the time.

LEVY: *It was unacceptable because that was the antithesis of modernism.*

YUSKAVAGE: Yes. And I decided I didn't give a fuck. I was just doing what I wanted to do. And then I really kind of stopped thinking about my teachers. Because I was actually…

LEVY: *Not in school anymore.*

YUSKAVAGE: But the problem is that even when they're not in school, there are people who continue to be ruled by the yeses and nos, and they never take the shackles off. I see that in people's work. It's like they're very shackled by the rules of society. But the studio is not society! I said to myself, 'This is a safe place to run amok. Take the mental shackles off.' I was basically allowing much more of my id in to play. And I gave into my painting abilities. I stopped sitting on my hands.

LEVY: *You leaned into your gifts.*

NEL'ZAH'S, 2012
OIL ON LINEN
46 X 40 CM

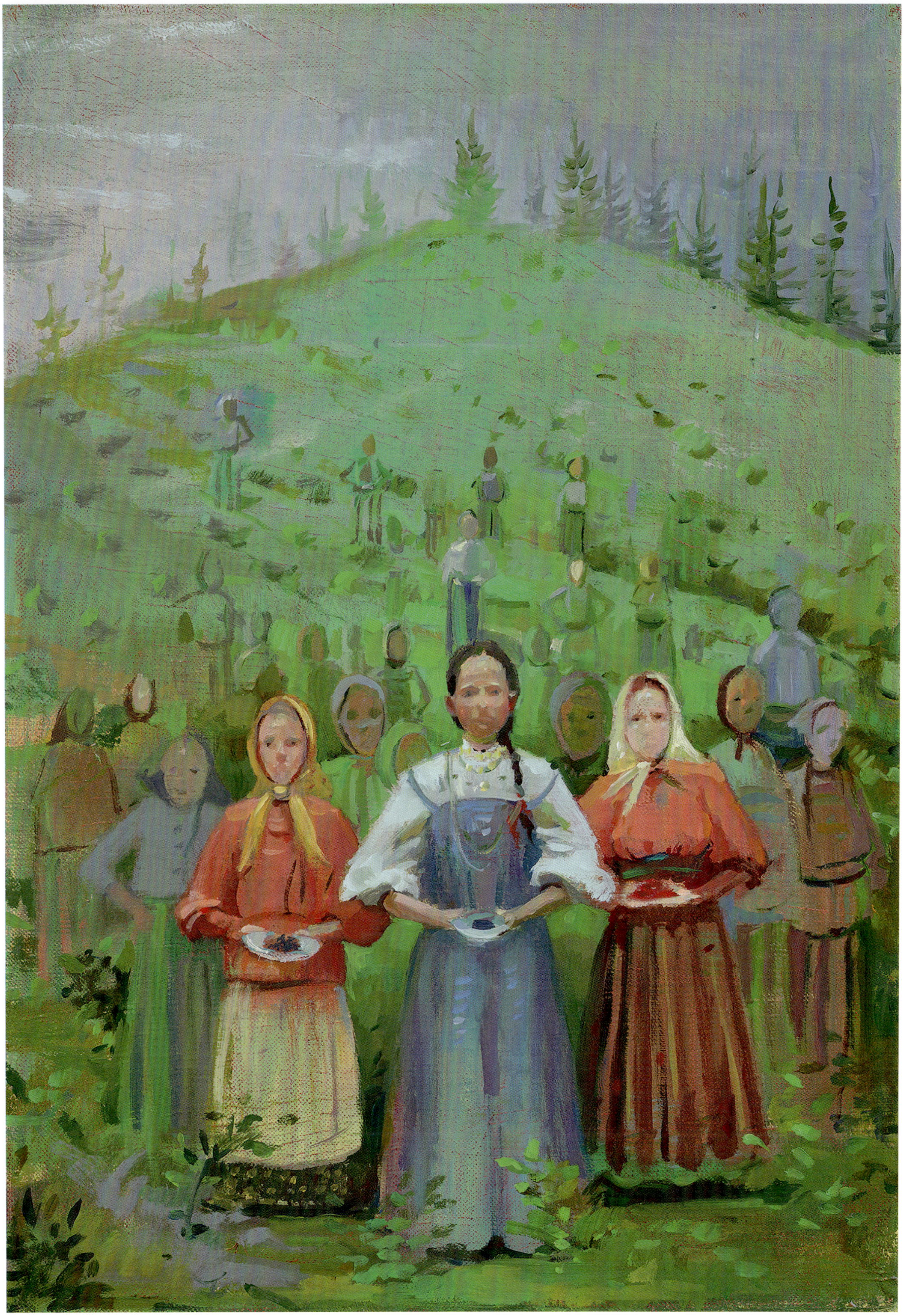

LITTLE FARM, 2012
OIL ON LINEN
26 X 35 CM

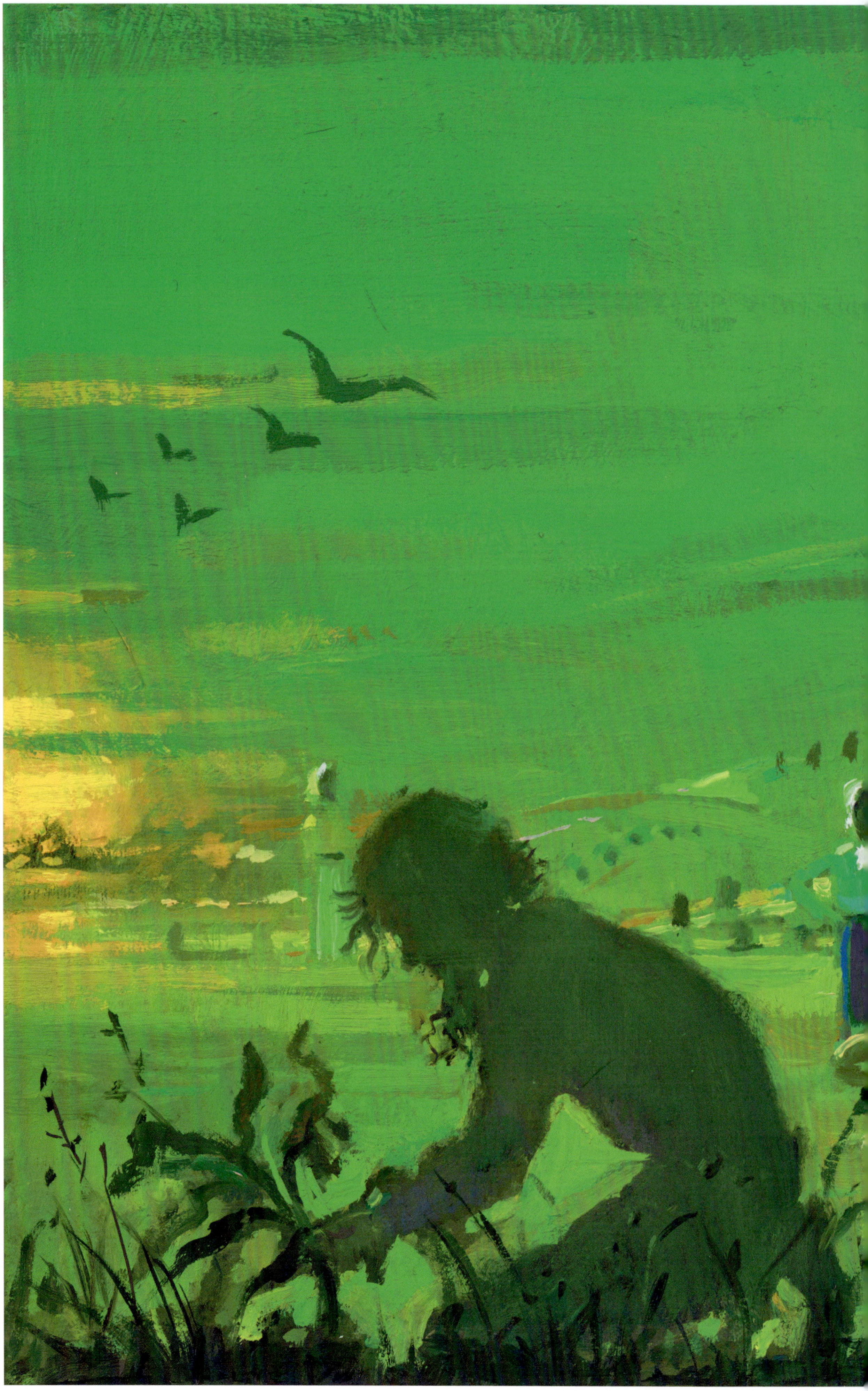

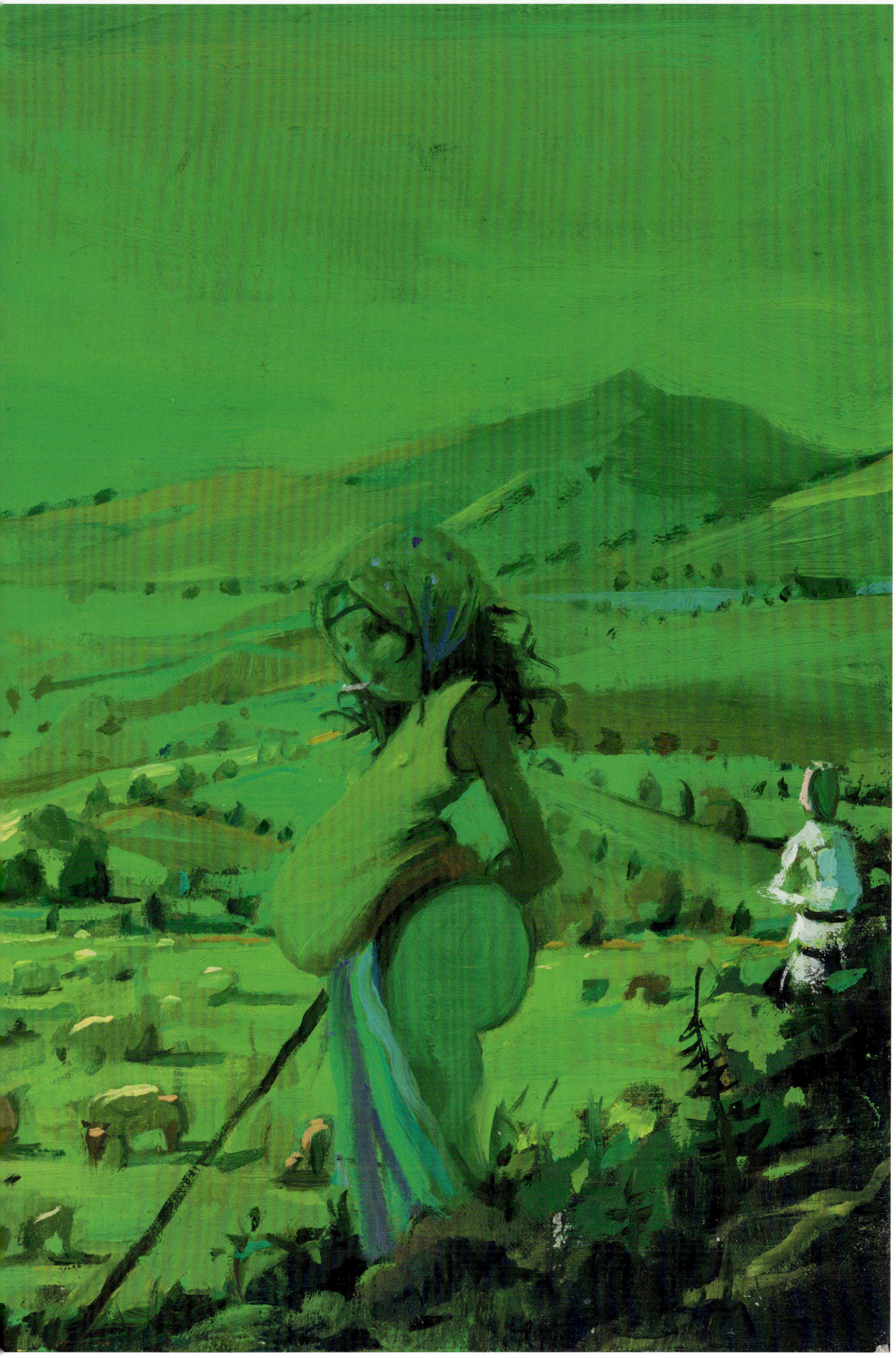

ACT TWO: LOLA AND BAD BABY, 2022
OIL ON LINEN
40 X 45 CM

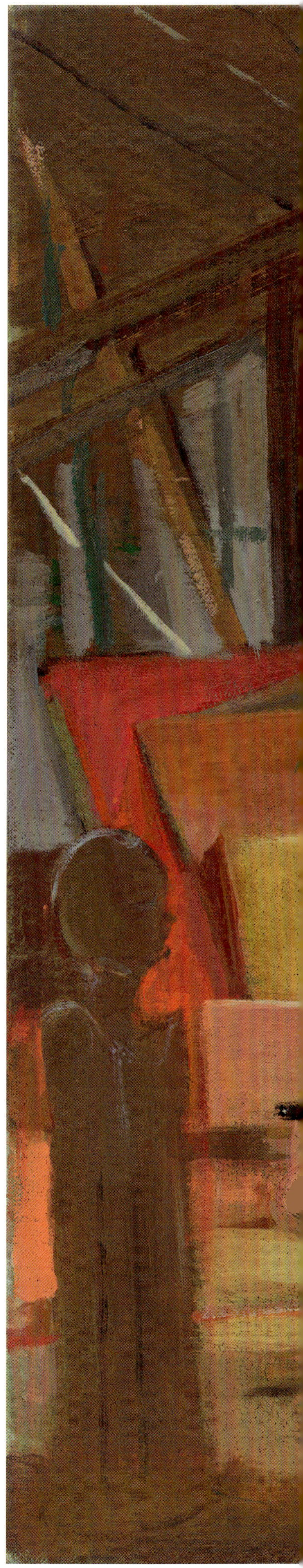

YUSKAVAGE: Yes, I leaned into my gifts, and also I started to have fun! I stopped worrying about, 'No, Lisa, no'. I stopped listening to the judgemental, dowdy schoolmarms I'd internalized.

LEVY: *The Nel'Zahs! Tell that story, please, I love it.*

YUSKAVAGE: Matvey and I got married in 1992, and because of the fall of the Soviet Union, we took our so-called honeymoon in sunny Eastern Europe, Moscow in particular. Matvey never thought he could go back after he emigrated in 1980, so it was an interesting trip to take for us at that time. Everywhere we went, in museums and shops all over town, these old babushka-wearing women in housecoats and slippers and a perma-frown kept aggressively shuffling up to me and shouting 'NEL'ZAH! NEL'ZAH!' And I asked Matvey, 'Why do they keep saying that to me?'

'They're saying "Don't! Don't!"', he told me.

I said, 'Don't what?' And he responded, 'Whatever it is you were thinking about doing'.

LEVY: *And then these scolding peasants, the embodiments of every 'No! Don't!' you've ever received, started showing up in your paintings, looking down from on high at all the trouble you were making. I'm thinking of the blow-up doll paintings where they look like they're about to burst and all their orifices are threatening to evaginate.*

YUSKAVAGE: I mean, those were pretty insane paintings to make. Where did those things come from? I wonder what I was even looking at? When I think about making those paintings now, I have no idea; they might as well be painted by somebody else because they're so out there. The critic Christian Viveros-Fauné called *Rorschach Blot* '*The Scream* for the third-wave feminist'.

LEVY: *That's hilarious. I guess it's not just that the art world has come around to you in their sophisticated way. The culture at large is also so much more saturated with pornographic depictions of women. The way you've described it to me in the past is that you had a lot of information from the culture about what it means to be a woman, from looking at advertising, from listening to your dad and other men where you grew up talk about women. You told me you'd find these pictures of naked ladies hidden in the nooks and crannies around your neighbourhood, like behind car chassis and the tanks of toilets.*

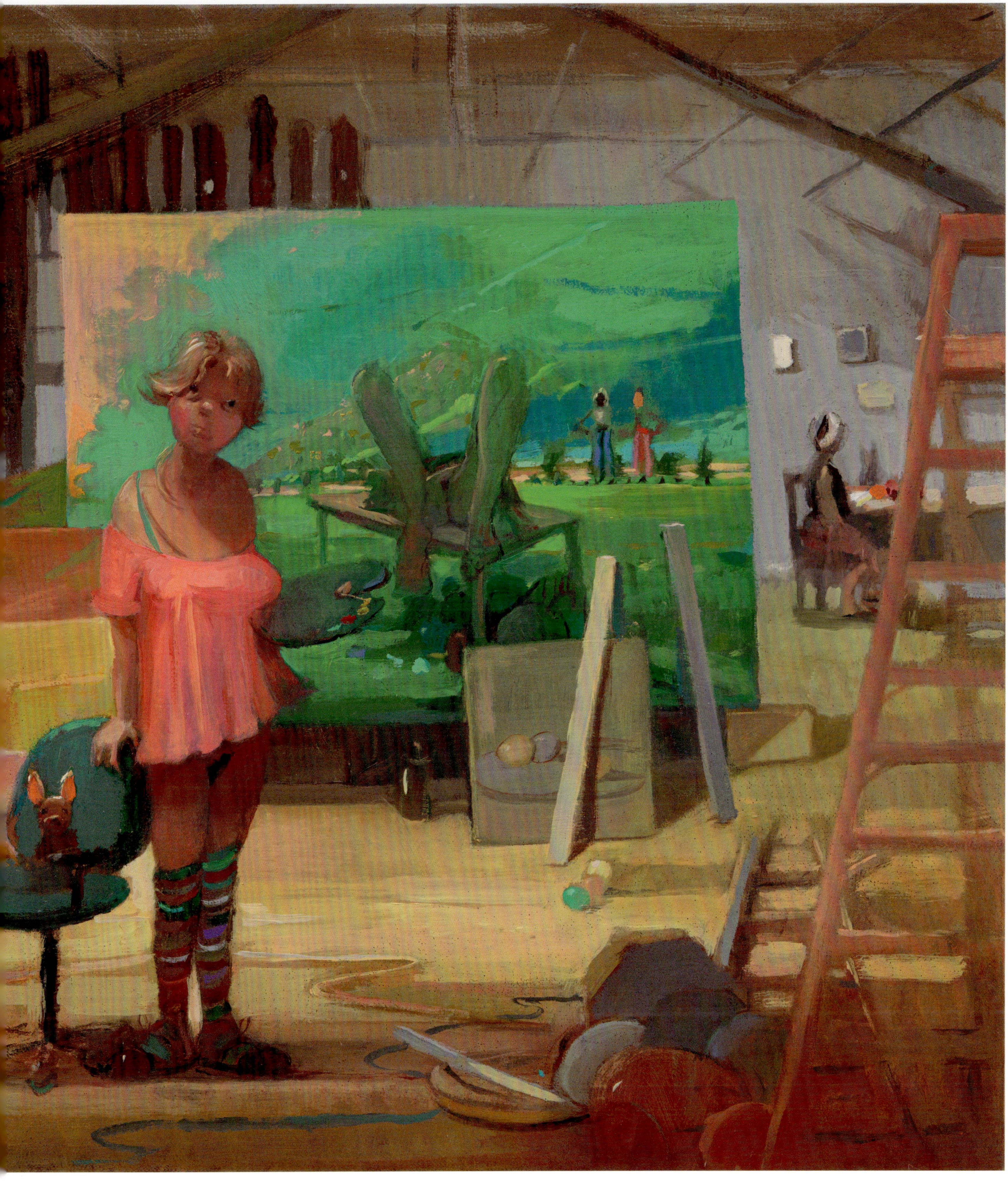

RAPTURE #2, 1993
WATERCOLOUR ON PAPER
56 X 57 CM

But those kinds of images of women, they're so ubiquitous now, you barely even notice that you're seeing them. There was no internet when you started out, for example.

YUSKAVAGE: Yes. And I think a lot of younger painters, queer artists in particular, started really taking on the body and sex in painting, and pushing it to their own extreme. And it just became, as you say, ubiquitous. It's just like, you're not alone in this project of putting something like that out there.

I don't give that many talks anymore, but a young lady stood up at a talk in Tampa a couple years ago and asked me, 'Do you feel like it's incumbent upon an artist to be honest?' Something like that. And I said, 'Well, yeah, but most artists aren't prepared for the response. It's a problem.'

LEVY: *I listened to that talk. She said, 'Is there such a thing as artistic freedom?' And you said, 'Yeah, there is…'*

YUSKAVAGE: 'But you better be ready for the response, which might be quite unpleasant.'

LEVY: *Don't expect people to thank you.*

YUSKAVAGE: I think that a lot of artists in their studios – and I can totally imagine this, because I've probably done this myself, but I fortunately didn't stay in this state – but you feel like you're doing something *good for humanity*. And then, you take this beautiful gift, which is probably why I called that early painting *The Gifts*, and you're like, 'Look at what I'm giving you.'

LEVY: *'Enjoy my precious creation'.*

YUSKAVAGE: 'Look at what I've given the world. Look at what I'm doing. Mommy, daddy, look! Isn't this a wonderful thing?' Because you really, really mean to do well, and then SURPRISE! You get your ass whooped. And that's very confusing. And then what do you do? And that was why I thought that that question was so wonderful, because it was just like, yes! I do believe in artistic freedom! But you've got to be ready for potential blowback. Or worse, the dead silence. That's what comes to most of us for an extended period. I had the idea that it would be fun to post scans of all my gallery rejection letters when I was on Instagram, and people were so ecstatic about it: 'Oh my God, *YOU'VE* been rejected'. And I'm like, 'Of course I've been rejected'. But I didn't

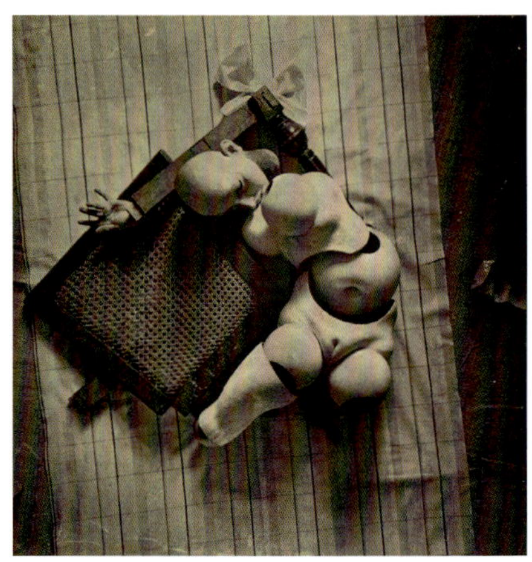

HANS BELLMER
THE DOLL (LA POUPÉE), 1935
GELATIN SILVER PRINT OVER-PAINTED WITH WHITE GOUACHE
66 X 64 CM

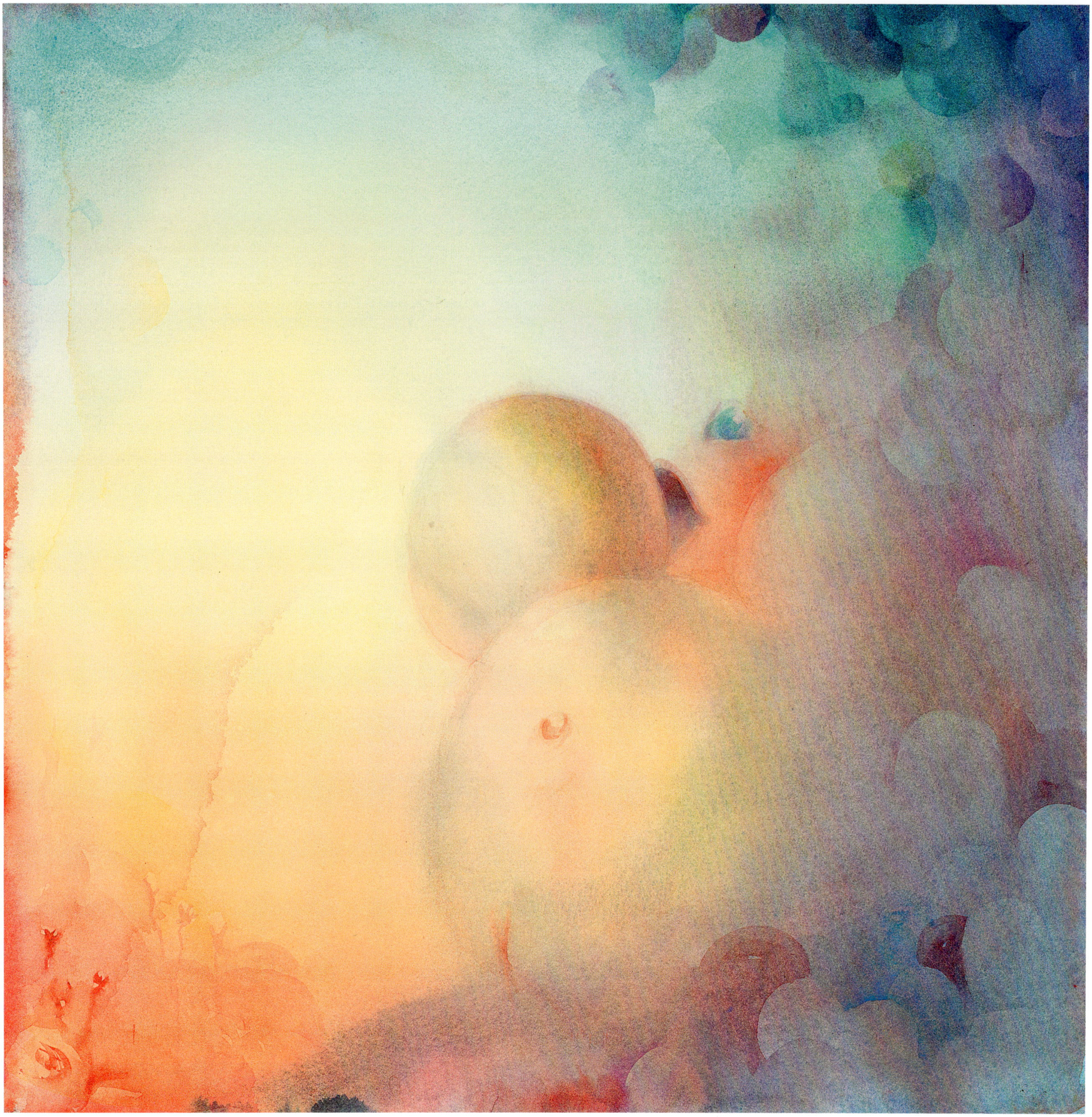

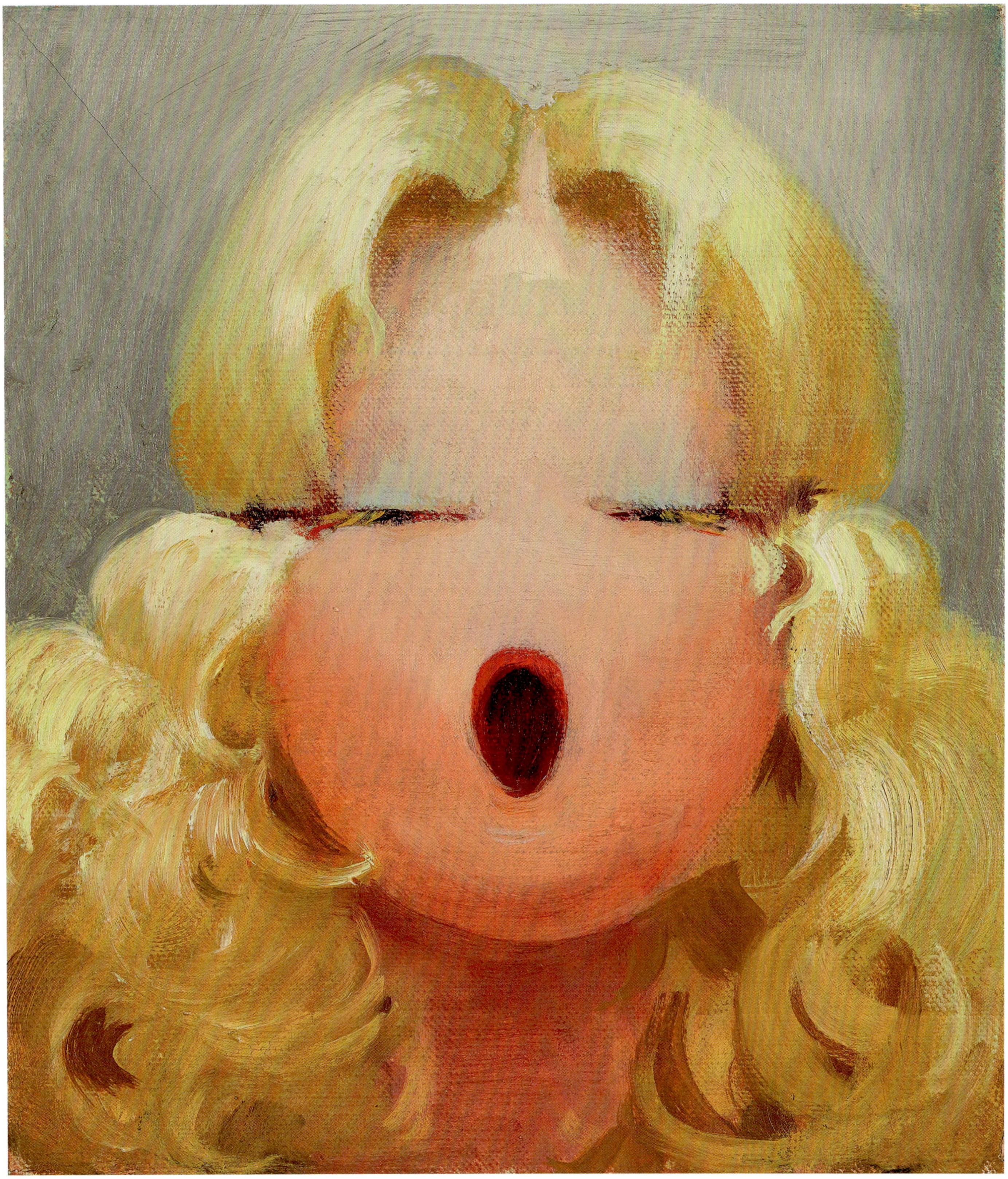

left,
OH, 1995
OIL ON LINEN
23 X 20 CM

opposite,
STUDY FOR BLONDE WITH OVENMITT, 1995
PASTEL ON PAPER
56 X 76 CM

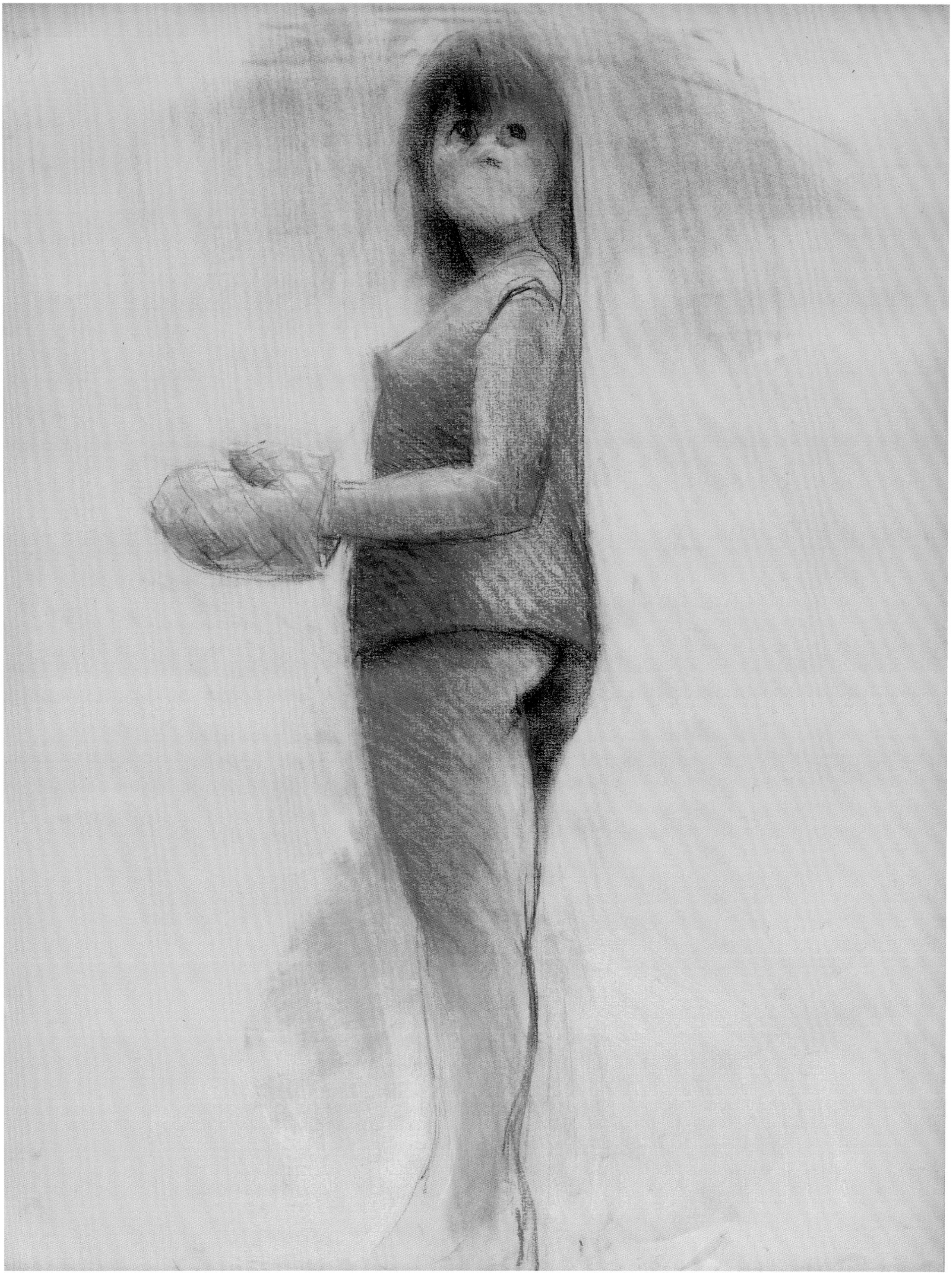

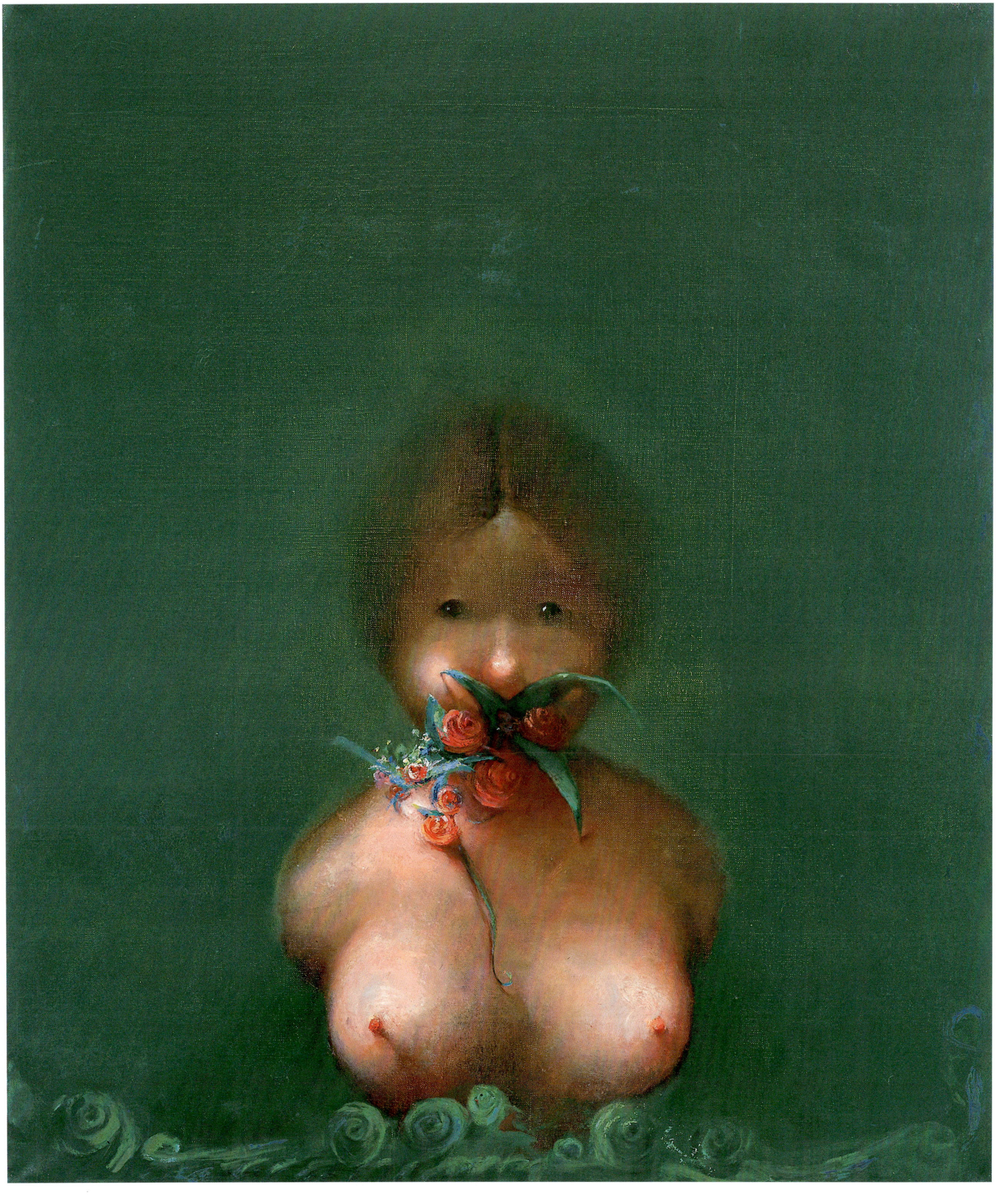

THE ONES THAT SHOULDN'T: THE GIFTS, 1991
OIL ON LINEN
76 X 66 CM

quit. I didn't make it into 'the dark, negative forces against me'. I remember knowing that it was vital not to turn into a bitter asshole. Speaking of state of mind: that's not conducive to creativity at a high level. I just went back to work. When I was making the blow-up dolls, I was trying to truly *reach* with colour and roundness. And they just lent themselves to that. I remember I was like, 'Lisa, is that really something you're going to do?' And then I saw Hans Bellmer's photographs of the doll. And there was something about that doll that was just so insane. The way he stacked it and reused the belly, this orb, with these two ball sockets at the bottom – and that the ball sockets could turn into breasts *or* hip sockets. It's a really clever object, the way he made it. I remember reading that a lot of artists and intellectuals were so into that doll when it was first made, that they were writing love letters to it. Which I was like, OK, I can't go for that …

LEVY: *Take it easy, gentlemen.*

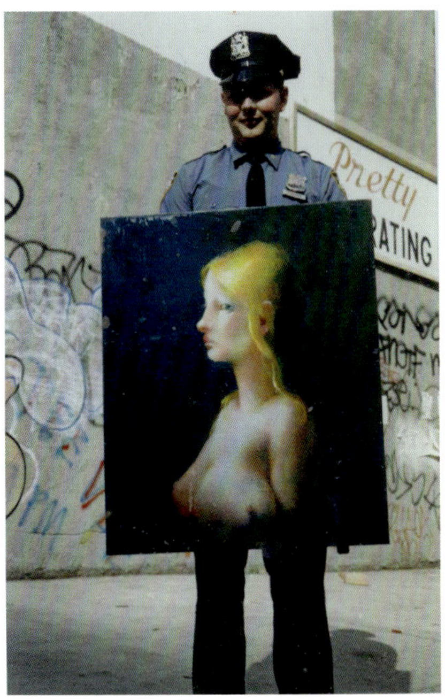

UNREALIZED ARTFORUM PROJECT, 1993
PHOTOGRAPH BY KEVIN LANDERS

YUSKAVAGE: I didn't want to marry the fucking thing, but I loved the way it looked. I just couldn't take my eyes off it. This visual *thing* was so intoxicating! It definitely had a hold on me and I wanted to make art using it. And it did turn into *Big Blonde Jerking Off*, and *Rorschach Blot*, and a number of other paintings. And interestingly, I'm recycling a lot of that period of work into the new paintings I'm making now, trying to find a way to acknowledge how important that work was to me. These are imagined studios I'm making – these studios are obviously not real studios.

LEVY: *The new paintings are like the behind-the-scenes, almost, of the studios we saw in your last body of work. It's even more surreal. It's like the back-of-the-house of an invented, impossible world that you've already created for us.*

YUSKAVAGE: Yes. One of them, I was calling it *Discarded Masterpieces*, and I keep on thinking about the way in which your memories – and the way you flip through remembering things – are forms of discarded masterpieces. I mean, obviously there are these rectangular forms in the picture, some of which have things rendered on them, like clouds or these peasant figures. And then there are models in the room, and then there's this tumbling bunch of colour-field-flat-things – paintings, we assume. And I was just thinking that it's almost like going through your own history, and there's some things that you discarded, and that you want to bring back.

LEVY: *Going through that file of cards in your mind.*

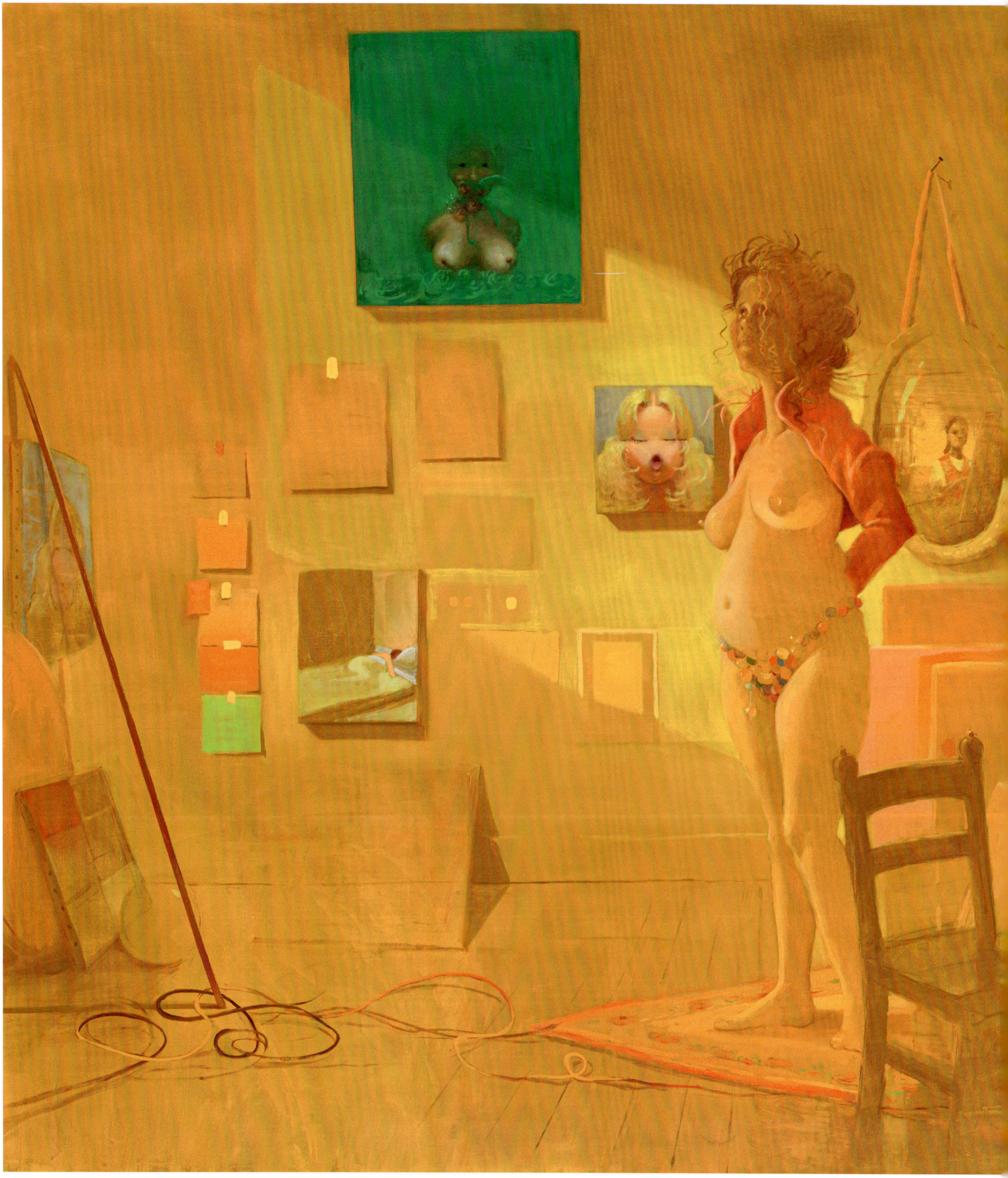

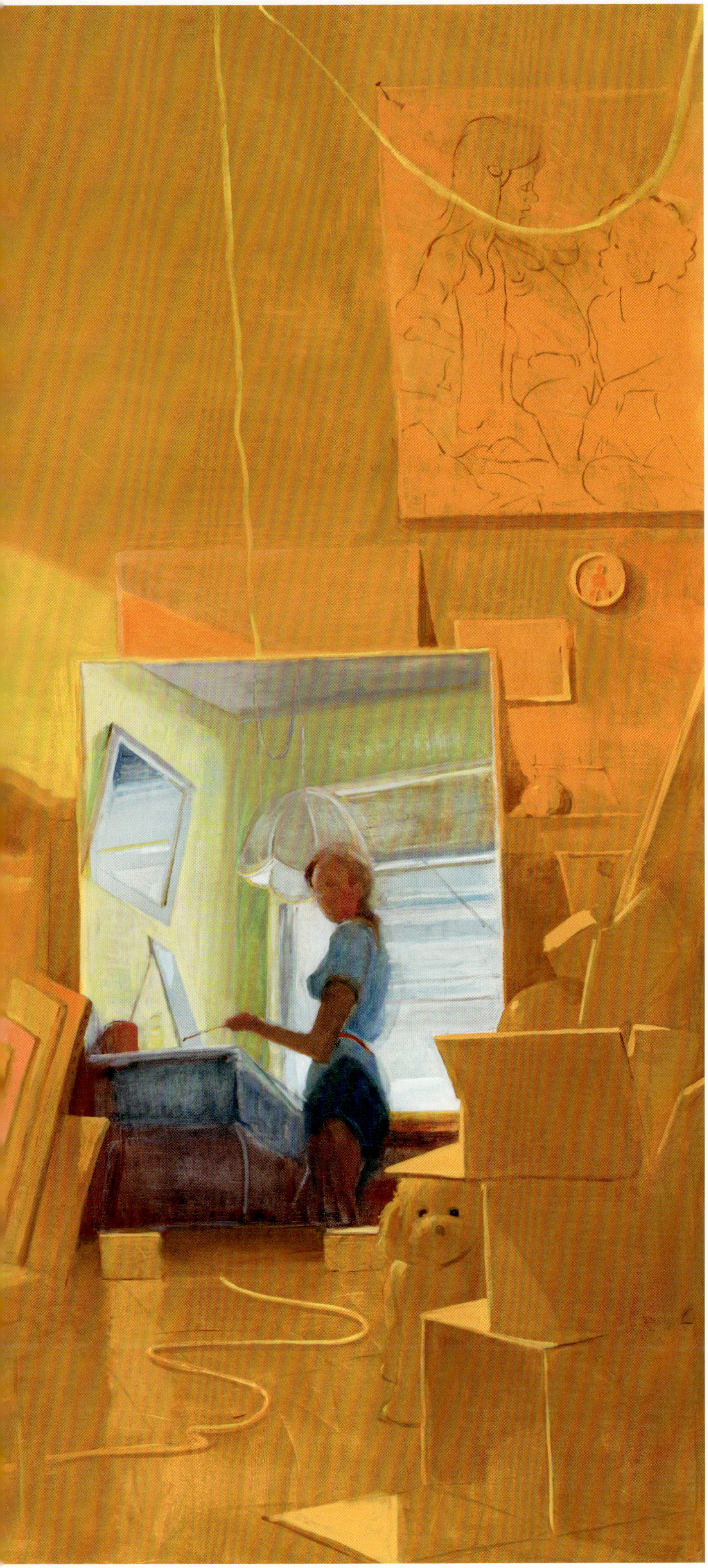

left,
GOLDEN STUDIO, 2023
OIL AND CHARCOAL ON LINEN
218 X 305 CM

below,
SELF PORTRAIT, 1983
OIL ON MASONITE
33 X 28 CM

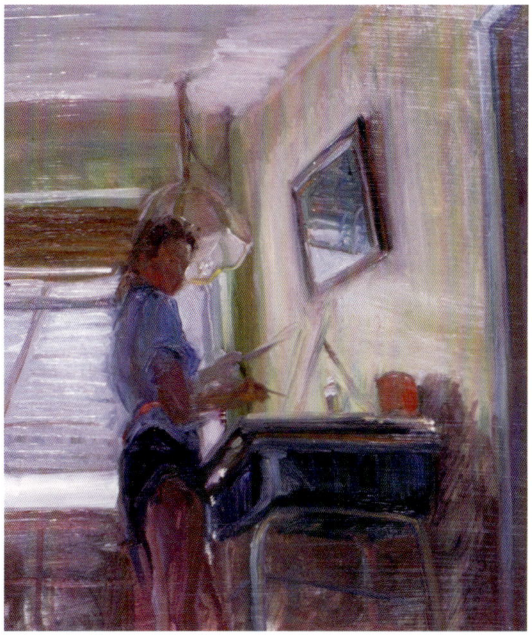

OUTSKIRTS, 2011
OIL ON LINEN
218 X 305 CM

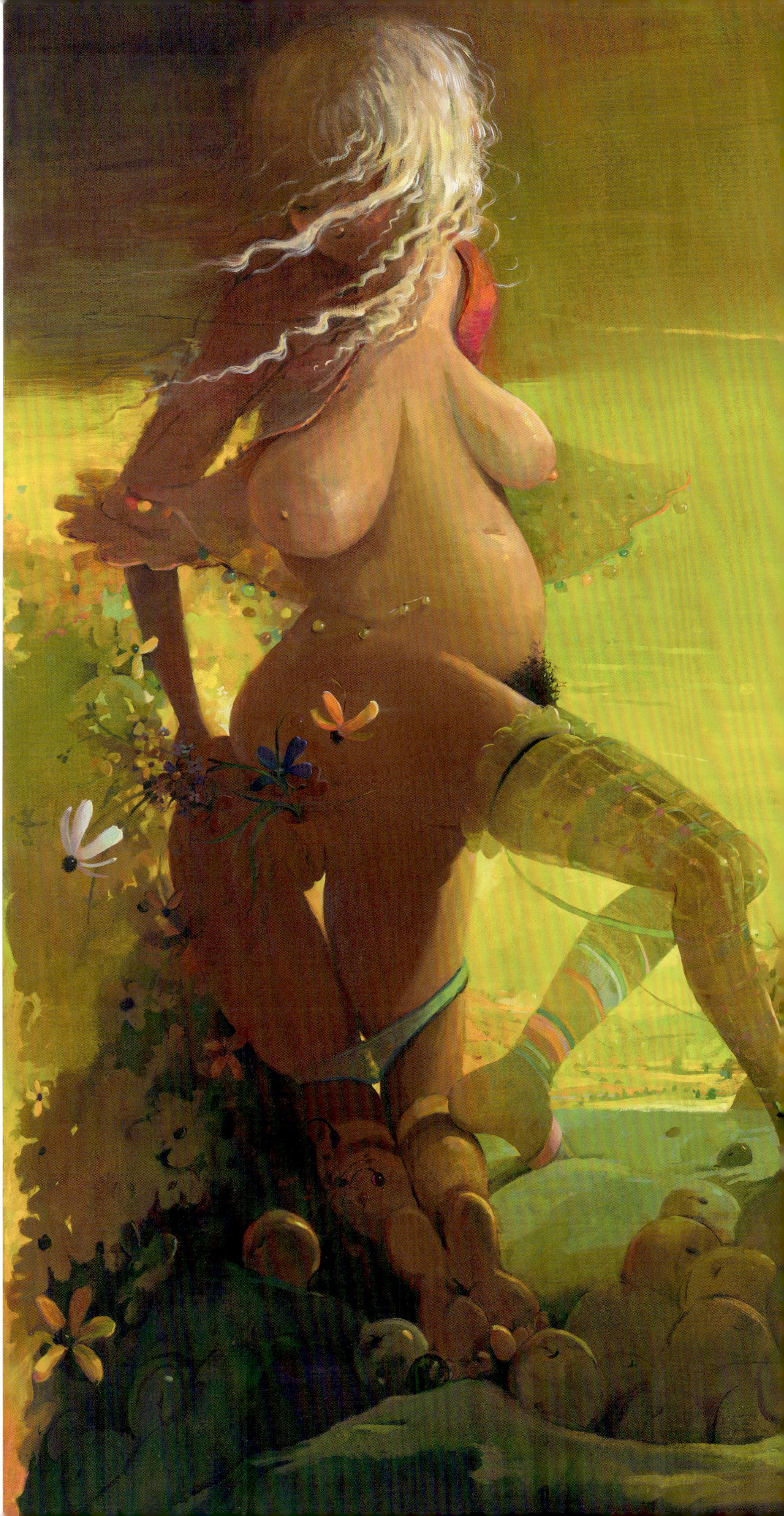

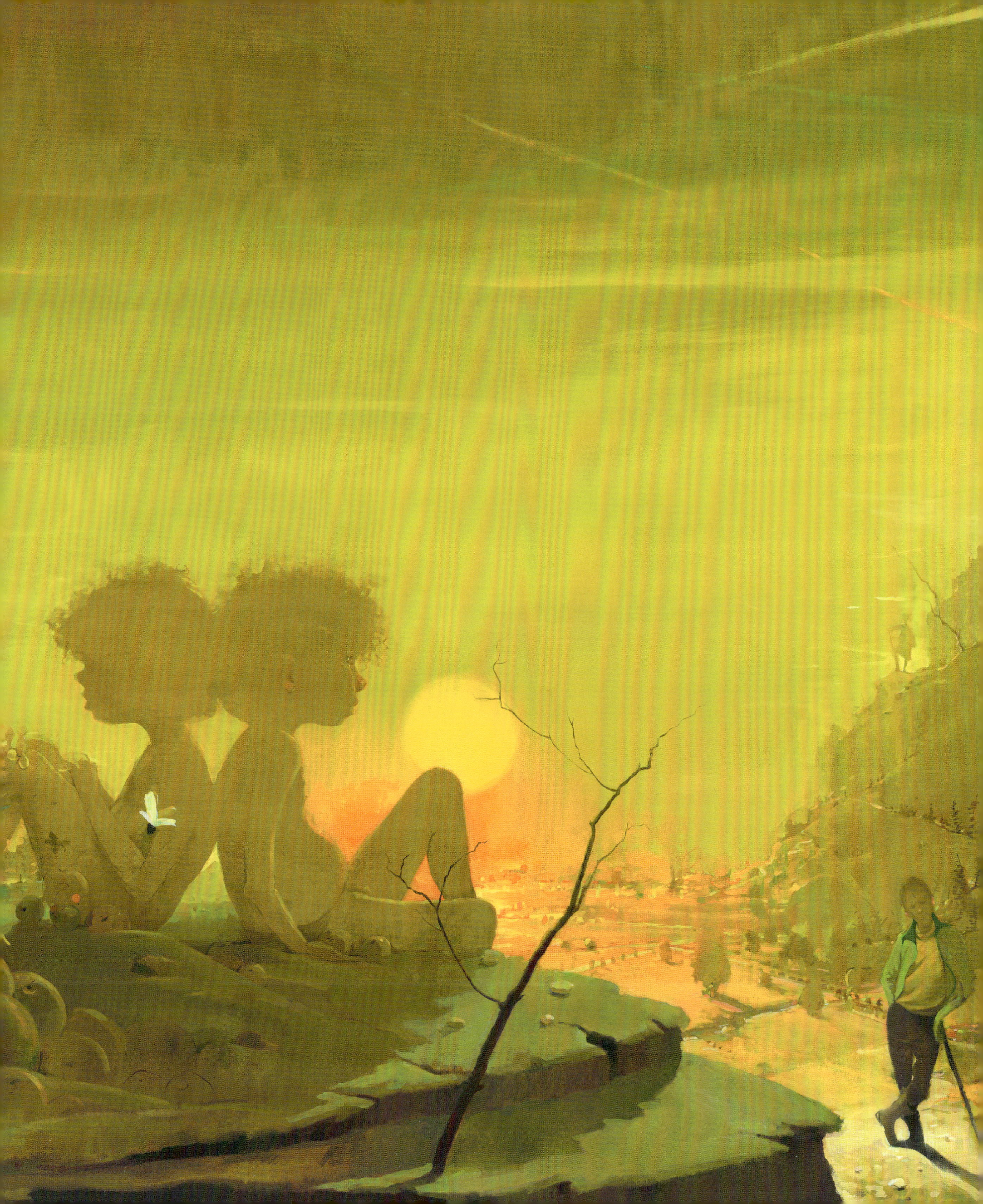

BIG LITTLE LAURA, 1998
OIL ON LINEN
193 X 244 CM

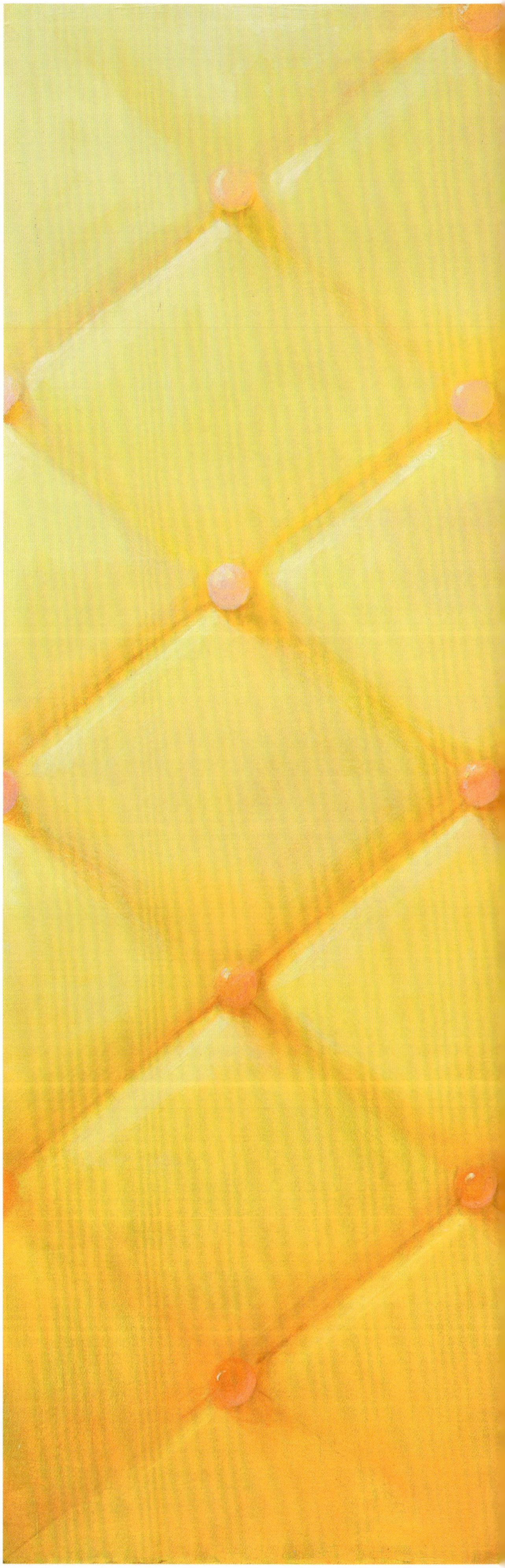

YUSKAVAGE: Yes. I also like the clashing of languages in this work, because there's a flatness alongside rendered things. The new process that I'm using to make these paintings is a very important piece of the puzzle. I'm laying fields down, fields of saturated colour, with a palette knife, and I'm covering the entire surface with a field of colour, and then pulling the images out of that field of colour. That's been going on now for a while.

LEVY: *That reminds me of what Kerry James Marshall told me about your paintings. He was talking about how the colour calls out to the viewer in this irresistible way: you're pulled into the colour to see what's happening in there.*

YUSKAVAGE: The fields that I'm laying down, letting them dry and then having to summon the painting out from that, it really is a very different way of making a painting, especially a figurative painting. And it's very intoxicating to me. It's part of the reason why I'm so interested in what I'm doing now, because I've found a way to paint that's so unique to me.

LEVY: *Talk about it for a minute.*

YUSKAVAGE: There's just been this search that I've had for so many years: how to create colour as air or atmosphere. So I've been experimenting in many media: watercolour, pastel. Even when I was making prints, I really wanted to make a coloured atmosphere, which doesn't come naturally to that medium. Over the time of experimenting and working with all these different processes, I stumbled upon ways to carry pieces of what I'd learned from each into working in oil paint. I now build a painting like it's a pastel or watercolour: it's an overall approach, colour from the bottom to the top, and showing through in layers. I often think of how the ground colour will impact the final image, and in most paintings there are untouched areas of ground representing something. So when I talk about rendering, I think one of the more interesting things in my paintings is how I create a sense of air out of colour.

Morandi – and Vuillard, in the small paintings – are extraordinary examples of people who painted paintings that are on that perfect precipice of rendering, but also not illustrating, and building something out of coloured light. That's an example of what really turns me on. But how to make that on a scale, and in a way that's obviously from a woman in the twenty-first century, telling a story that's very different from their stories? I'm not living in Bologna with my mom and my sister telling the story that Morandi's telling.

Vuillard, interestingly enough, also lived with his mother and his sister. I think what's very important is state of mind, and that's probably why they stayed home, setting aside all other things to allow for ultimate focus. You think about somebody like Picasso

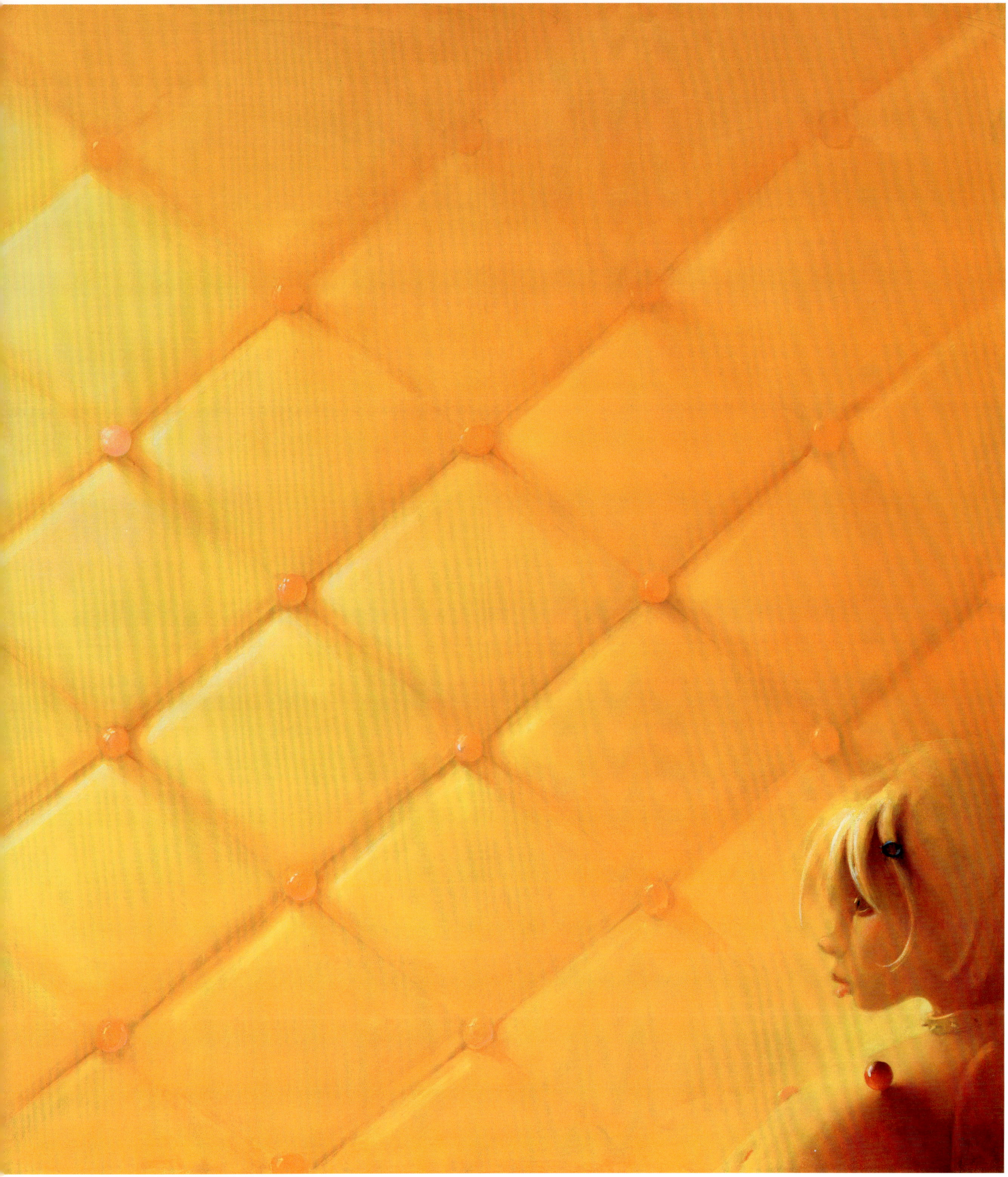

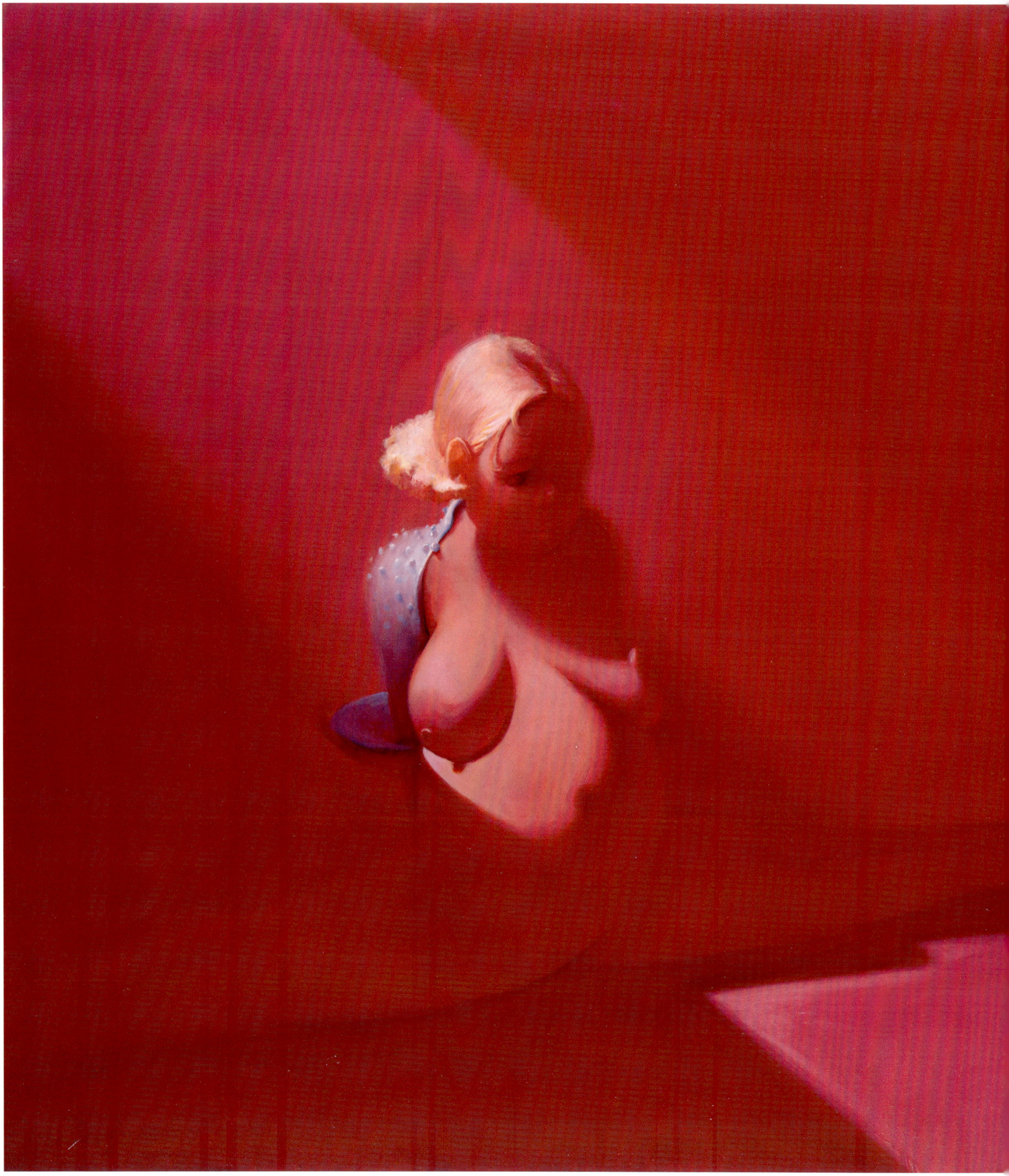

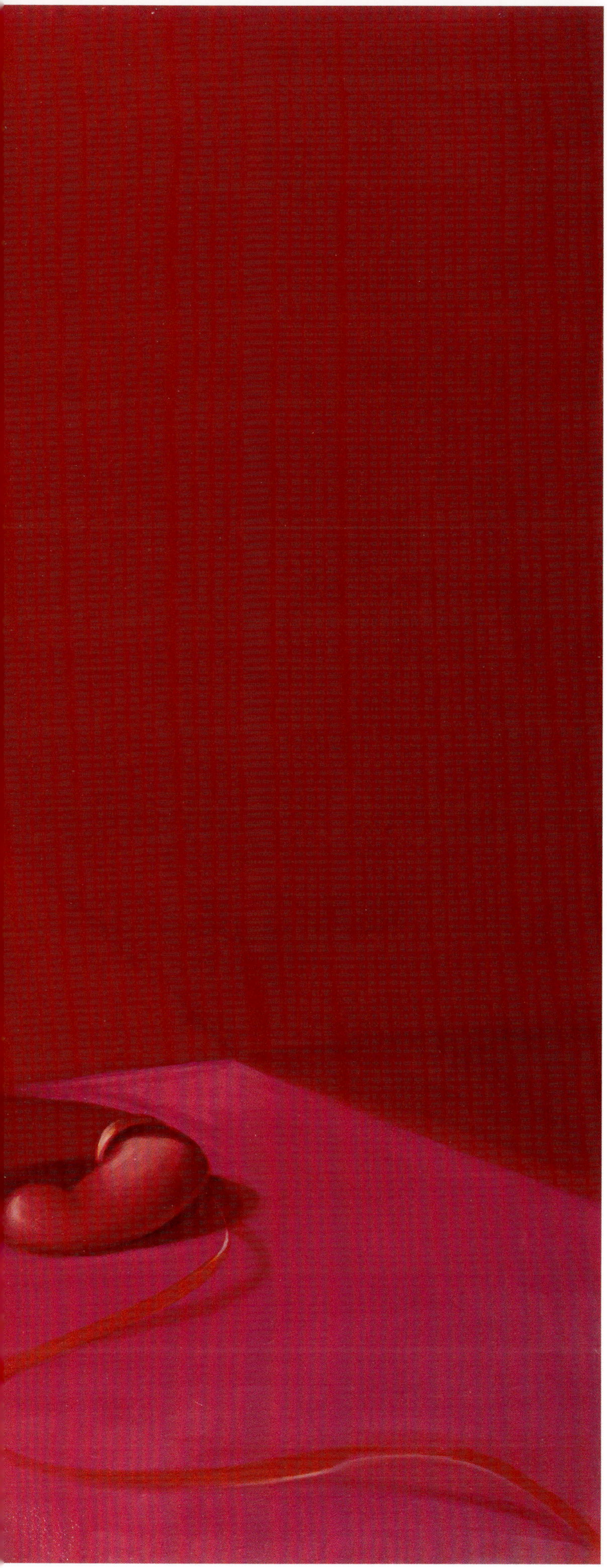

NOW YOU CAN DANCE, 1998
OIL ON LINEN
163 X 214 CM

RESEARCH IMAGE FOR NOW YOU CAN DANCE, 1998
POLAROID PHOTOGRAPH

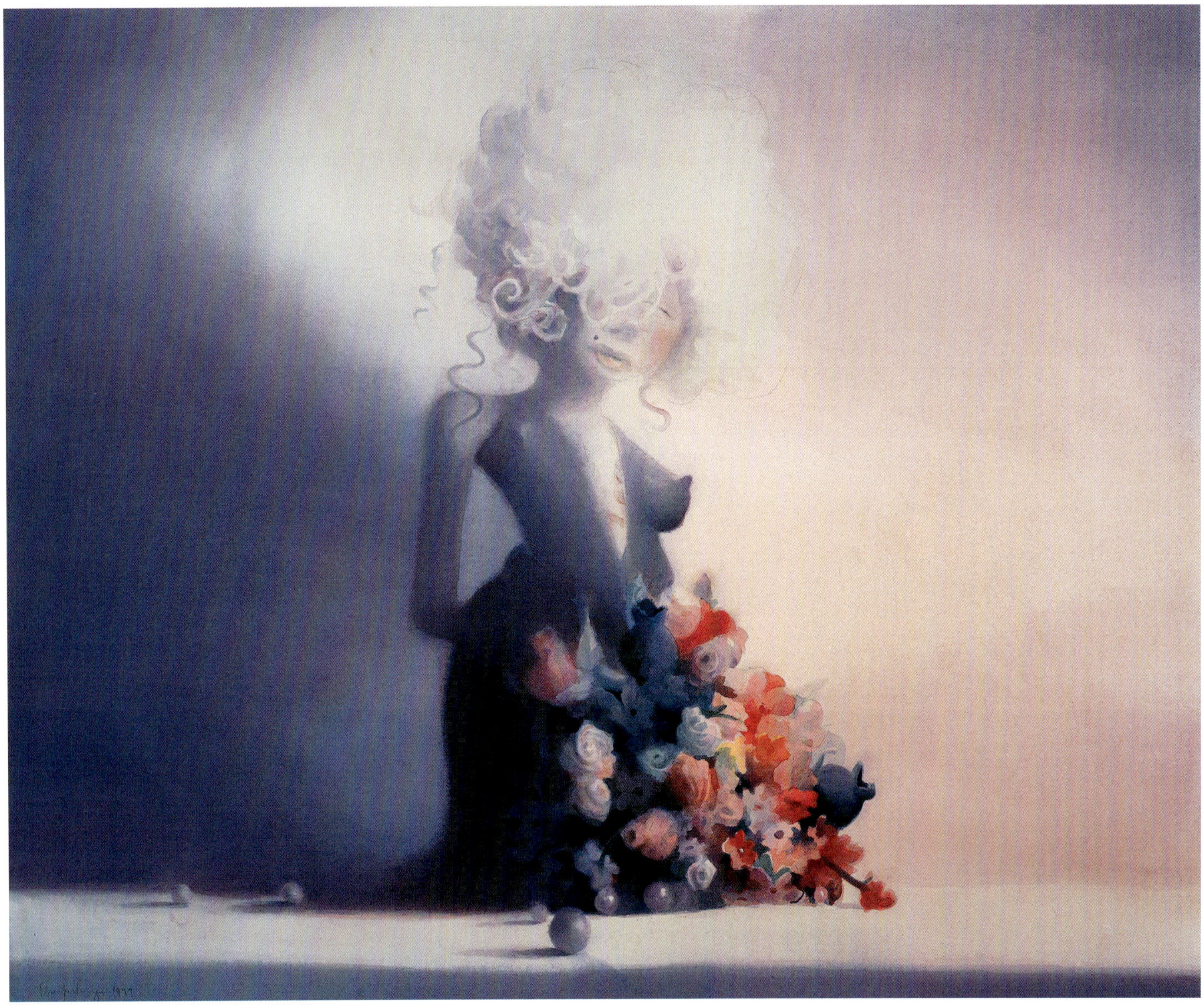

left,
STILL LIFE WEARING A WIG, 1999
WATERCOLOUR ON PAPER
93 X 114 CM

opposite,
STRIPED SCARF, 2013
OIL ON LINEN
25 X 20 CM

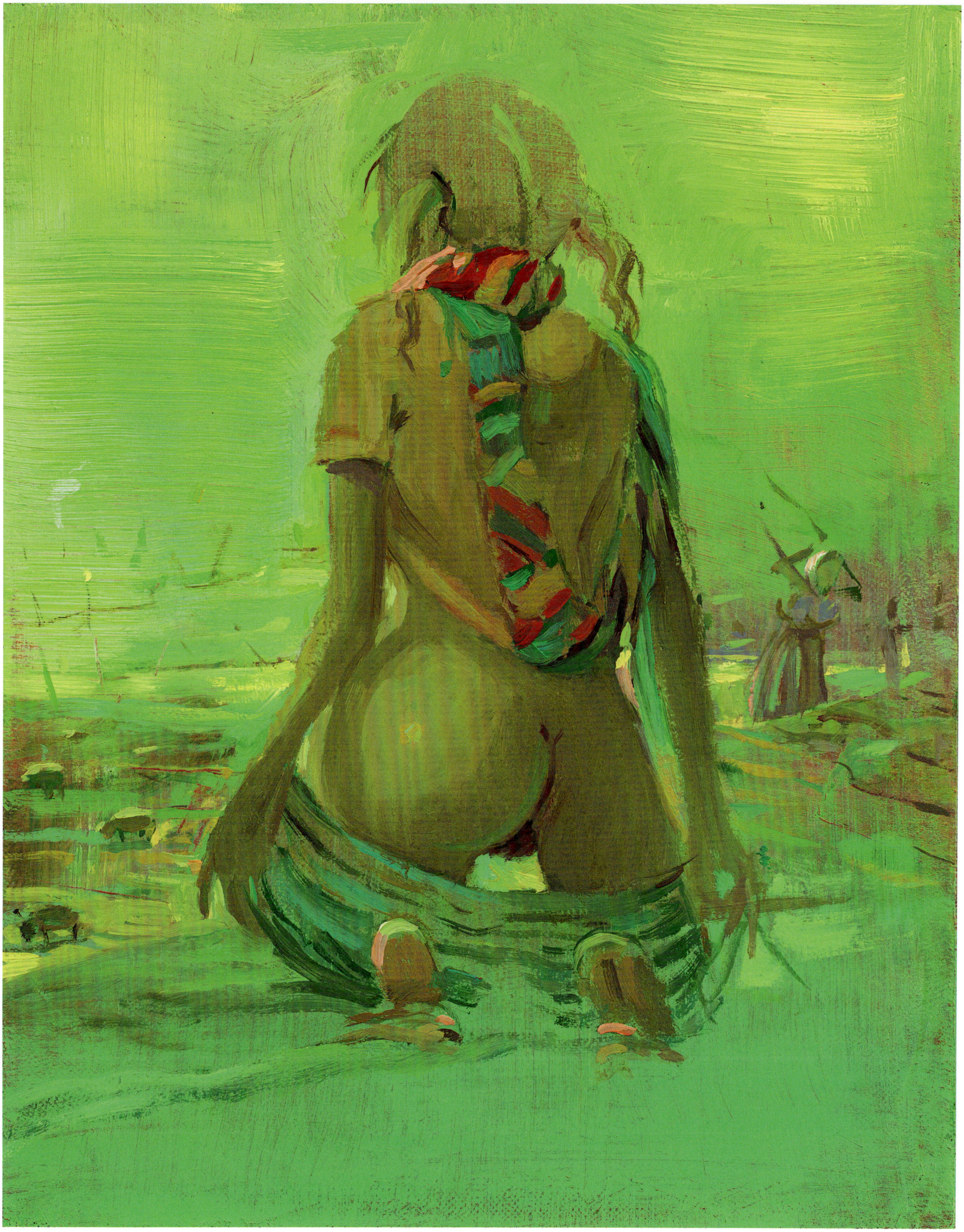

FIREPLACE, 2010
OIL ON LINEN
196 X 165 CM

and the presumption of how cruel he was to everybody. He was able to do damage and not look back. Other people just decided not to ever get involved; they didn't have big appetites; they just decided to stick close to home. Each of us as artists has to figure out how to stay extraordinarily focused to be able to accomplish whatever it is we're trying to do; to be able to get to that point where you can hear the voices.

I didn't think this when I was younger, but I actually really do believe that I don't do this alone. I am not trying to say it's a mystical hand of God thing, but I do think that there's a way in which if you're quiet enough, you can hear – perhaps it's your own inner voice, but I call it the voices of the angels. I've always loved that painting by Caravaggio where the angel is giving St Matthew instructions, and he's pulling back his finger saying, 'Okay, number one...' It's a very funny image, because St Matthew isn't writing the scriptures on his own. The angel is actually floating down in a cornucopia and telling him what to do. I think that Caravaggio must have known what it's like to need an angel. My point is, you can't control what your childhood was, but as an artist, you have to protect and control how you advance through life, to get to the point where you can hear what you need to do. Because there are times when I really, I got nothing. Zero ideas. And I have to hear it, and I follow it, and then it opens up into a whole new world. But it's very faint sometimes. It's like, you asked me once about having kids and it's just hard if you are dealing with a lot of...

LEVY: *Practicalities. Logistics. Distractions. Needs.*

YUSKAVAGE: Yes. I just think it's a very interesting problem: how do you stay connected to what it is that feeds your creativity? And for somebody like you, you probably wouldn't have been able to stay creative if you hadn't fulfilled your wish to be a mom.

LEVY: *That might be true. I mean, now we'll never know.*

YUSKAVAGE: You may have withered on the vine! For one person, it's one thing, for another person, another thing. And anyway, she's not going to be screaming for your attention much longer; you'll be screaming for her attention pretty soon. She's going to be flipping you off pretty soon.

LEVY: *My daughter is three, Lisa. Give her a little credit: she's already flipping me off.*

YUSKAVAGE: We all have different things that we need to do in order to go forth and make our work – whatever it takes to be able to tune out whatever the noise is. Van Gogh didn't have to contend with iPhones. I mean apparently, sometimes he did hear voices, but imagine if he also got texts! The question is, how do you keep focused? Is that something you ask yourself?

LEVY: *I don't know that I think of it in those terms specifically; I think, 'What can I write now that will be exciting for me and different from what I already know how to do?' Which I guess is just another way of saying the same thing.*

YUSKAVAGE: There's something about the large size that I moved into in the past five years that's made me just totally intoxicated with my work again in a way that I haven't been. I'm not poo-pooing what I did before, but now, I've lost contact with the real world.

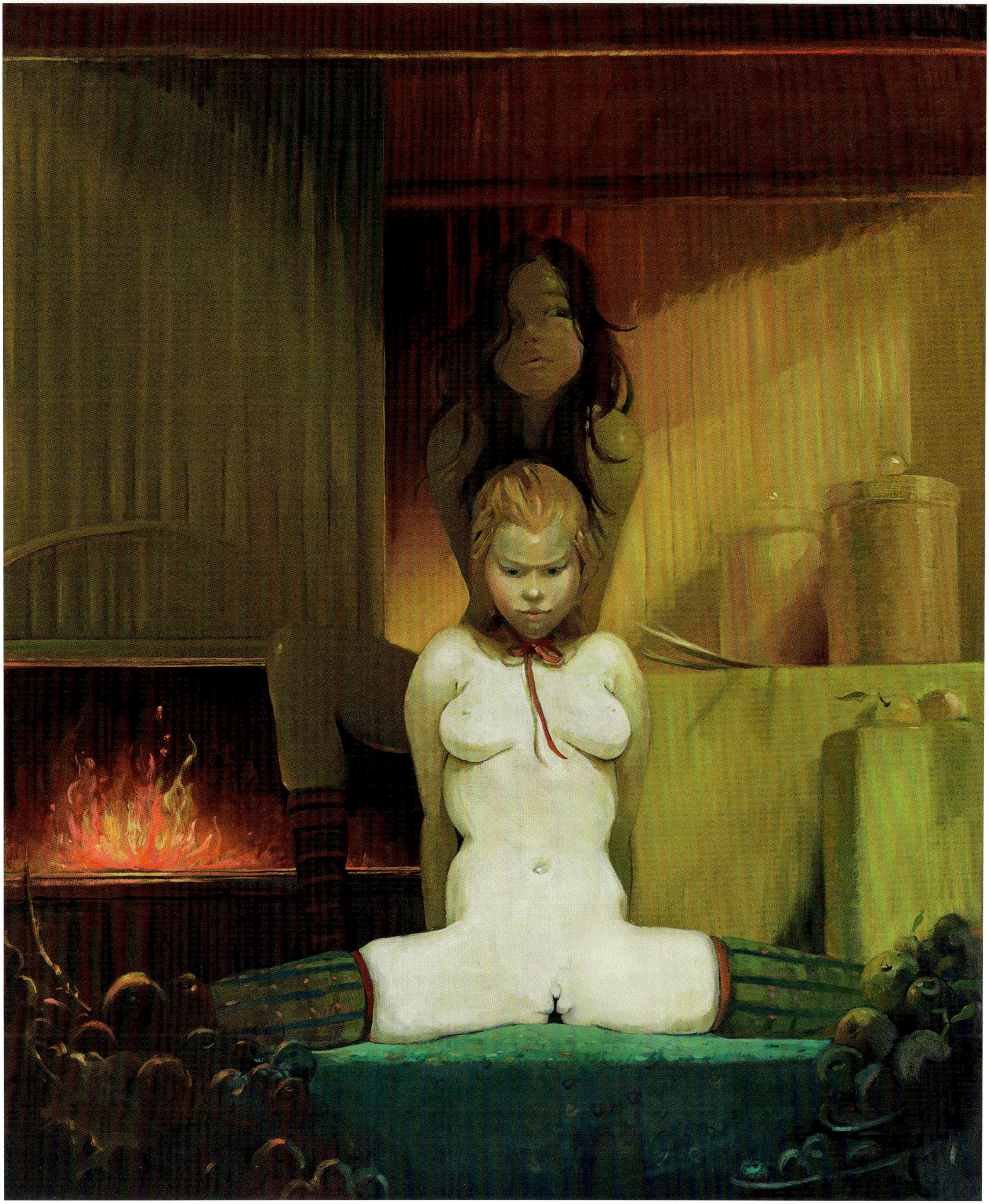

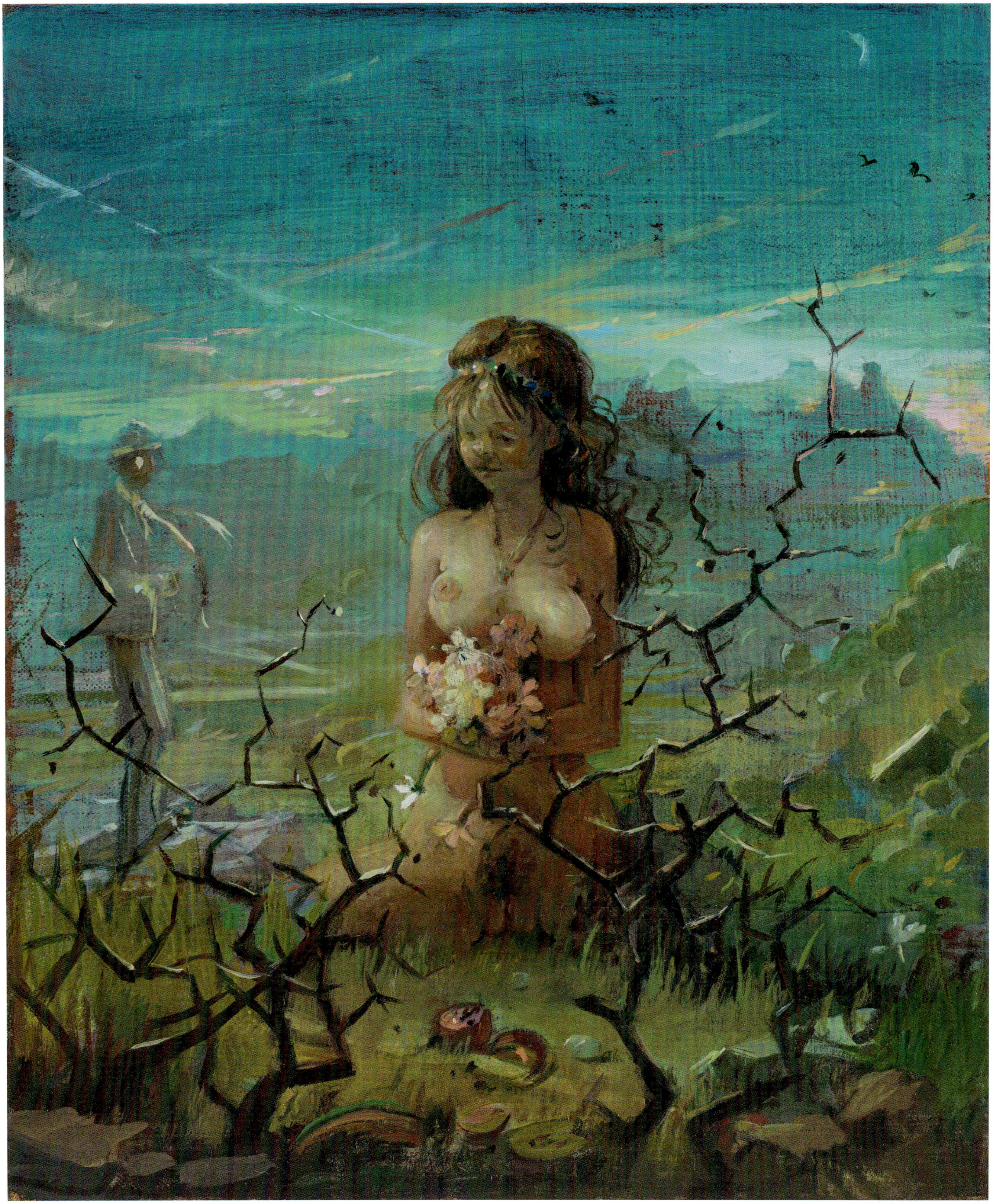

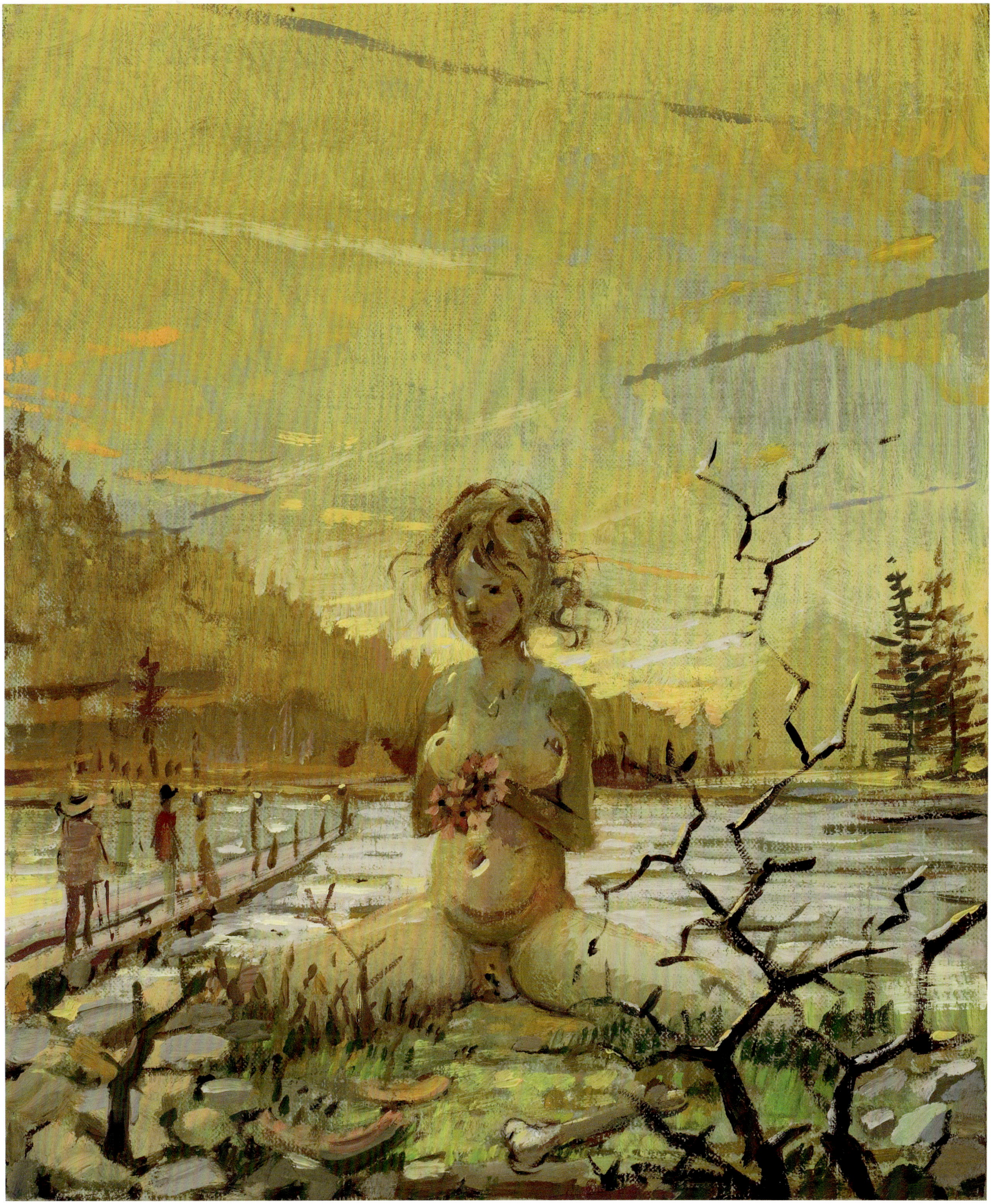

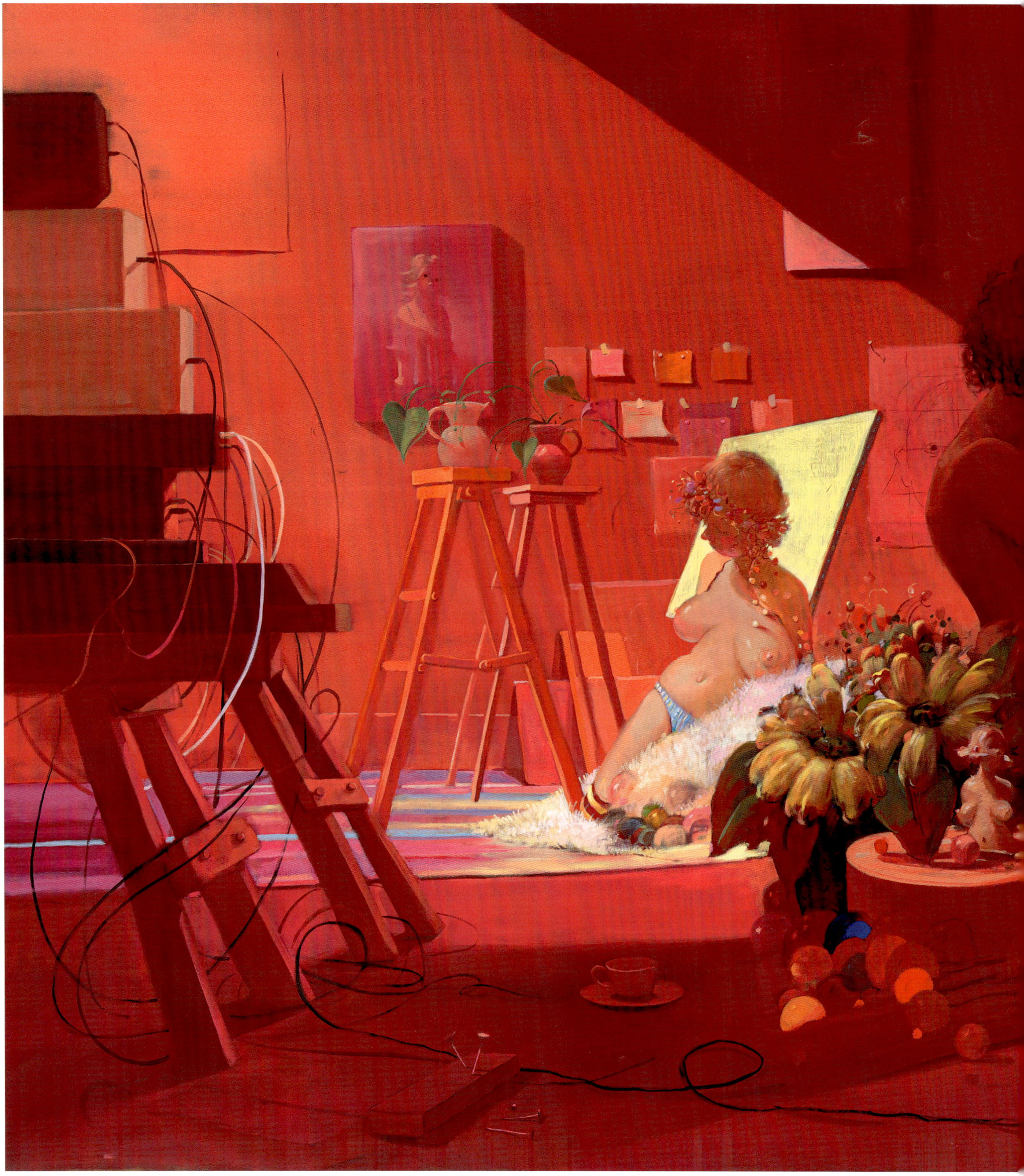

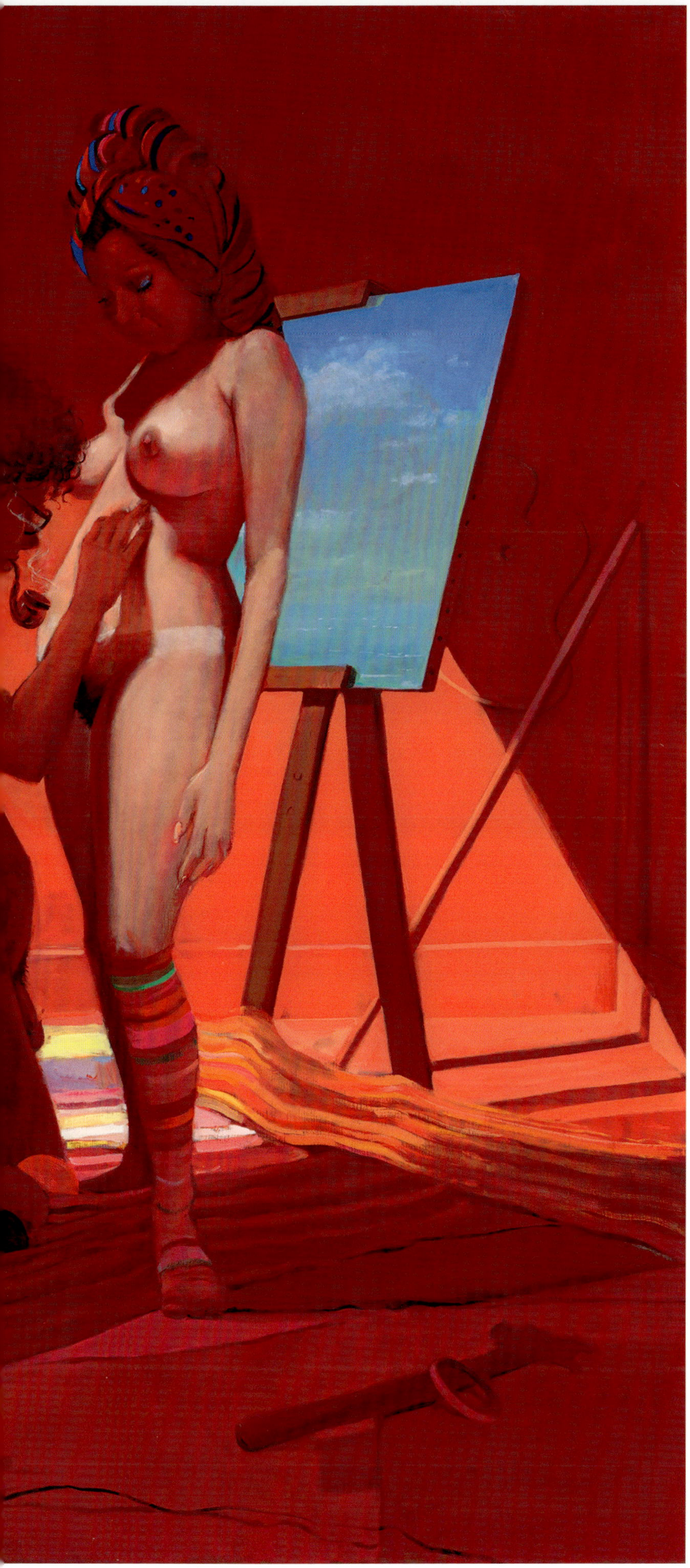

left,
NIGHT CLASSES AT THE DEPARTMENT OF PAINTING DRAWING AND SCULPTURE,
2018–20
OIL ON LINEN
218 X 305 CM

previous pages, from left,
TOURIST, 2008
OIL ON LINEN
33 X 28 CM

WEE TRAVELLERS, 2008
OIL ON LINEN
33 X 28 CM

LEVY: *It's almost like you need that big of a canvas to contain all that you know and want to do at this stage of your life.*

YUSKAVAGE: Well also, as a figurative painter, size really matters. The one-to-one human scale is understood by every single person who looks at a picture: everyone knows what size a real head is. I enjoy making small paintings, too, because they're almost like my logistical team. And I get to muck about in different ways and have different experiences at different scales.

LEVY: *So now that you're working with these massive canvases, does it make your habit of ordering a second, back-up canvas when you start a new painting more challenging?*

YUSKAVAGE: I don't make a ton of paintings every year, so it's not like this is hundreds and hundreds of paintings, but I give myself room to trip up and then start over and know that I'm not going to have a nasty underpainting that's going to be constantly threatening the results of what's going on in the next painting. The first time I ever ordered a second canvas, I think was when I made a painting called *Travellers*. I made a little painting of it, and I really liked the little painting. And so I started a larger painting of it and it started to go south super-fast. I was apoplectic. What went wrong? I realized, 'Okay, just be cool. The idea is good enough. I like the idea, but just start again.' So there's a second version of the painting on a small scale that I like, called *Wee Travellers*. In the meantime, I called the manufacturer, Simon Liu, where I get my canvases, and I said, 'Beg, borrow, or steal, but please get me a canvas here as quickly as possible'. It's not that easy to get stuff quickly, because there's only a few of them and a lot of us. So it could take a month and you pay a premium, and by the time it gets to you, you put a ground on it and that takes a month to dry. So now you've set yourself back by quite a bit of time. By the time I came back to working on this canvas again, I was off by a couple of months. I'd moved on to other things. So after that, moving forwards, I've always ordered at least two canvases, because I realized it takes too long to have this waiting process, where you have to give yourself space to be able to make the error, go in the wrong direction, and then…

LEVY: *Work from there, with the knowledge you've gained.*

YUSKAVAGE: Another artist might say, why wouldn't you have just sanded it down? Or why wouldn't you have just painted over it? And I have very important reasons for that, which is that this particular painting was getting a little too slick. I had a problem with the medium and somehow it got unpleasantly rubbery. And I think that, had I painted over it, the painting would've cracked. It was a conservation decision on my part. Now, maybe it's my working-class roots, but I make really well-made paintings.

RENDEZVOUS BEHIND THE ARTIST'S STUDIO, 2023
OIL ON LINEN
244 X 305 CM

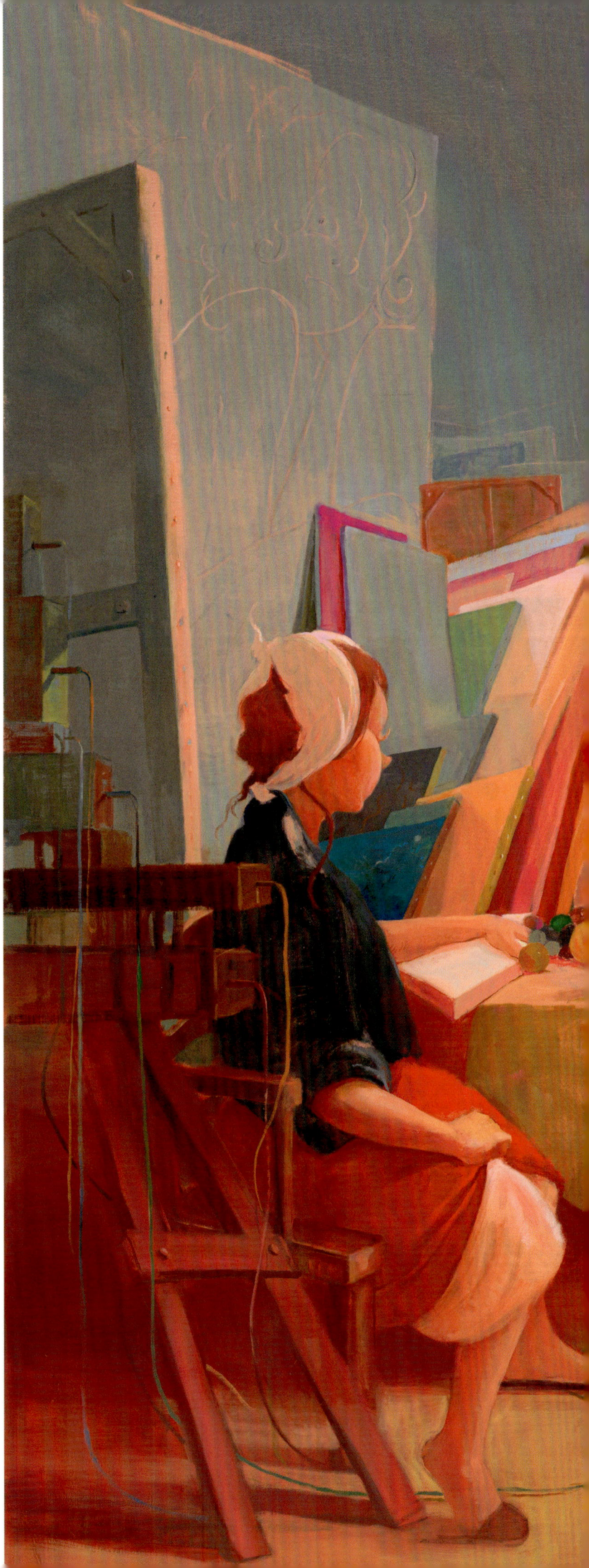

LEVY: *You make things that are built to last.*

YUSKAVAGE: Exactly.

LEVY: *Like the awning your father put on the house where you grew up in Juniata Park that was still there when we went to Philadelphia last spring for your* New Yorker *profile.*

YUSKAVAGE: Which shocked me. That bad boy is still shading somebody's bedroom! It's very important to me that, if I want to paint over an old painting, then so be it. For example, there's a painting that the Art Institute of Chicago owns, called *Night Classes at the Department of Painting, Drawing and Sculpture*, that I started as a grisaille painting. It was a painting that was huge. And I was like, 'Why in the world would this ever be interesting as a grey painting?' And I got crazy about it. I went away and I thought about it and I decided… well, I had an angel intervene actually. A voice in my head just came to me, 'This is a studio painting, it should be red'. And I thought, 'Are you fucking with me, angel? Are you saying I'm going to even remotely touch on *The Red Studio*?' And then there was, 'Have fun!'

Then I realized the task at hand was to run to the nearest art-supply store and buy all their Old Holland Cadmium Red Purple and begin to trowel on the colour over the underpainting and cancel out the grisaille. On my website, I even share images of the stages. There's a word called pentimenti: it's an Italian word for what you see coming from underneath and I could still glimpse some of what was under there.

LEVY: *Like a palimpsest.*

YUSKAVAGE: I felt instant relief once I did that. I sort of killed it, but I was also performing a drastic lifesaving operation. That was very intentional. It's not like I don't use, at times, what's underneath. Grisaille is very dry, it won't crack when you put a cadmium over it, because paintings are made to be fat over lean. And that certainly was a fat layer over a lean layer. That painting will hold up. I think what really brought it to life is that there's a shaft of light, and that colour isn't what you would think the light colour of cadmium red-purple would be. It's actually a salmon colour, an almost orange colour, going warmer and much richer. I tried a whole bunch of different things and then that just lit it up. Once I did that, the whole thing became a real space, it felt like, with real inhabitants and all of the objects. It left no doubt in my mind how much more interesting this was than that grey thing I left behind. That painting was so damn big, when I started with the red I didn't yet have the second canvas, but I did order one.

LEVY: *And then, if you'd chosen to, you would have been able to recreate the whole bloody thing? You could just take it from the top?*

YUSKAVAGE: Honestly, most of the time things go in the way they're supposed to go. With the painting that was at the Metropolitan Museum, *Bonfire*, I was painting that figure on the canvas that was ultimately on the far left, and I was working on that

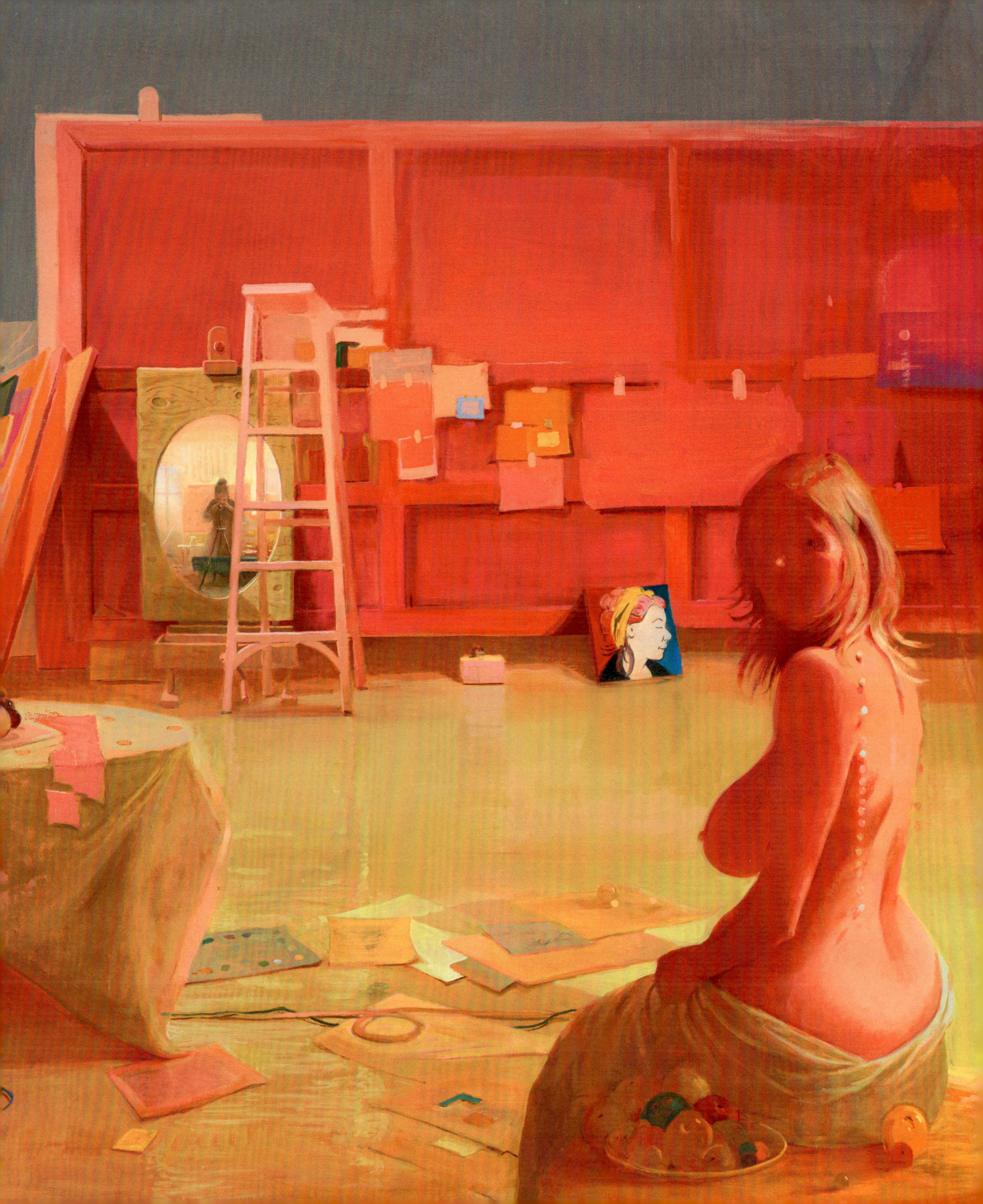

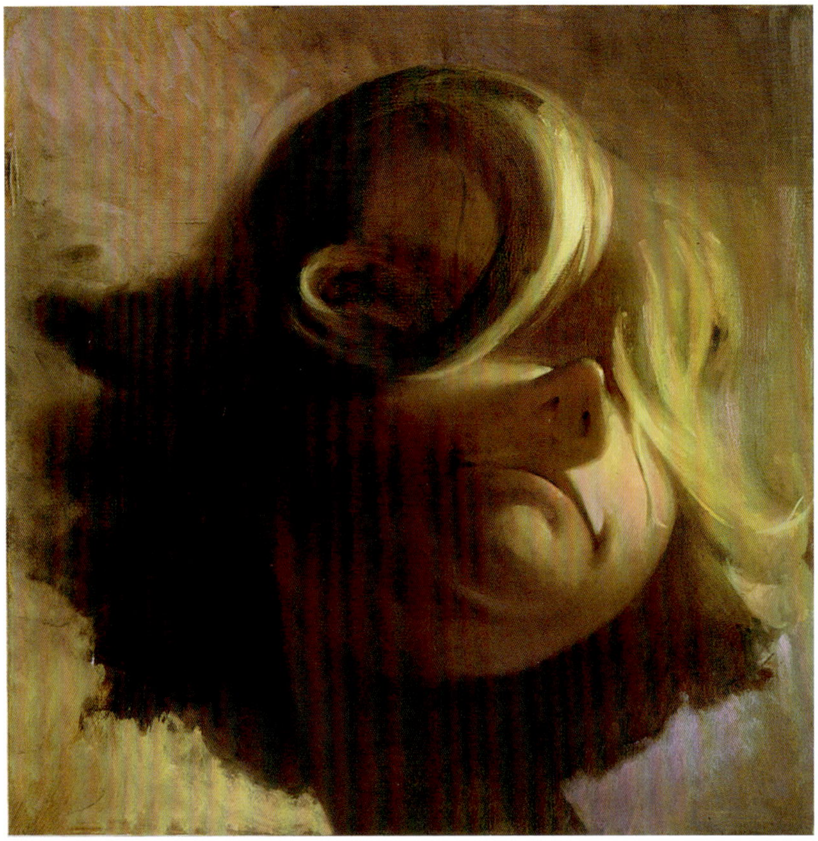

left,
ASSPICKER'S HEAD,
1996–97
OIL ON LINEN
91 X 91 CM

right,
DISCARDED
MASTERPIECES, 2023
OIL ON LINEN
58 X 71 CM

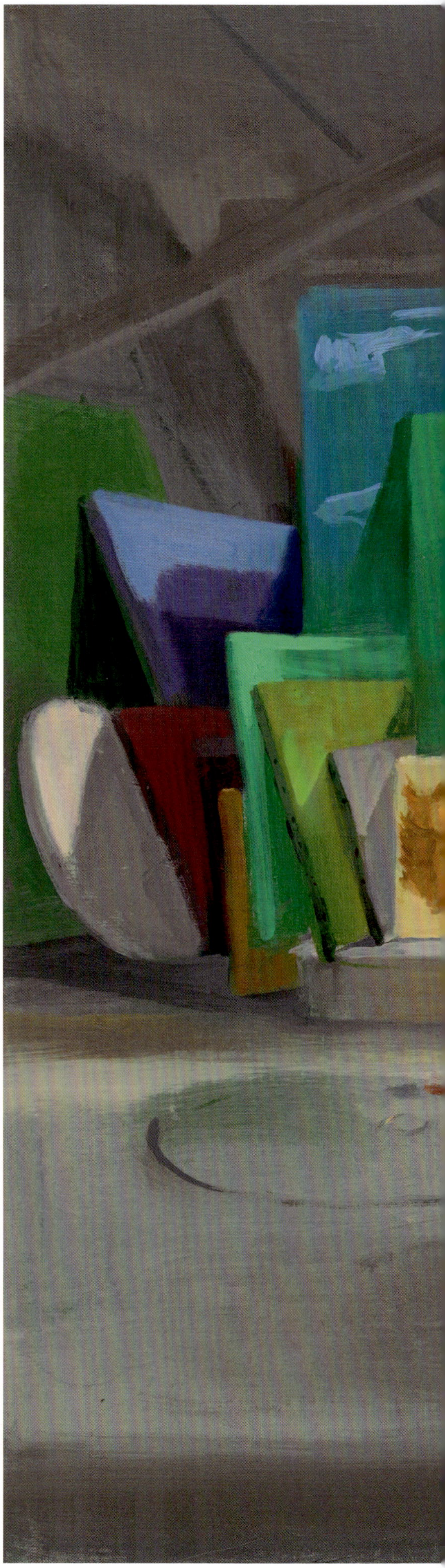

painting, and I had the other canvas tucked away in my storage, just in case. But then this kind of weird voice said to me, 'This painting is not complete. It needs a bookend.' So just because I had that second canvas at the ready, I made that painting as a diptych. The use of the double canvas sort of began to have a life of its own. The thing is that, as I got older, I became more and more committed to my ideas. What I'm not committed to is floundering and thrashing.

LEVY: *Which is a perfect segue to the image I came in with tonight: talk to me about swimming to the bottom of the pool and swimming up with a weight when you were training to be a lifeguard.*

YUSKAVAGE: I think I was using that as a metaphor of what it's like to start a painting versus what it's like to be in the middle and end of a painting.

LEVY: *Give it to us.*

YUSKAVAGE: You're a writer. What's it like to start something? What's it like to be in the middle? And what's it like to be at the end? It's so much fun at the end, and it's so fucking hard in the beginning.

LEVY: *Ah, but the end!*

YUSKAVAGE: You finally get to enjoy it, and it's taken away.

LEVY: *It's like sex. The minute you're where you want to be, you're like, 'Well, now we're done'.*

YUSKAVAGE: So then you've got to find your next thing. But you have to realize it's going to happen again. It's going to be the same goddamn problem.

LEVY: *Every time.*

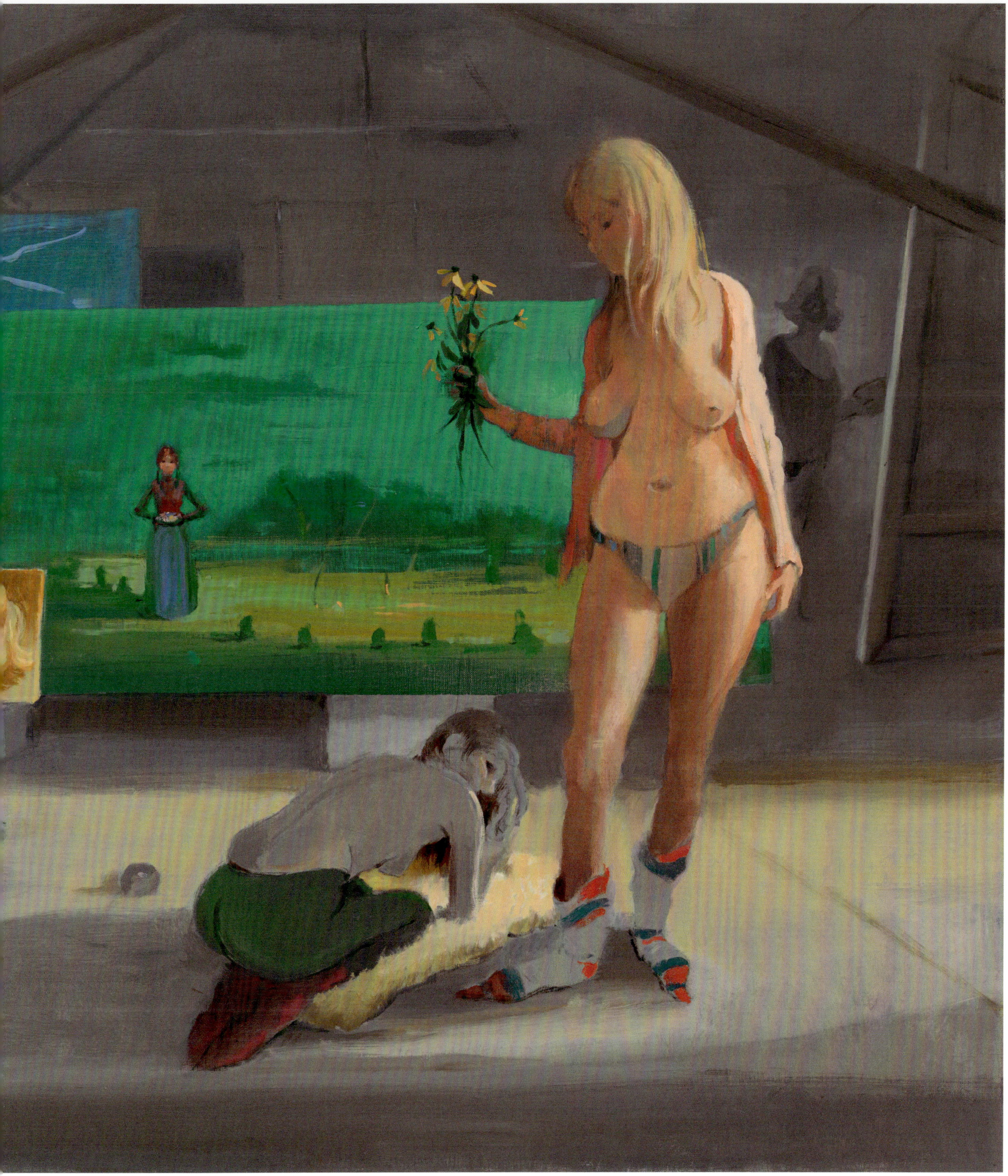

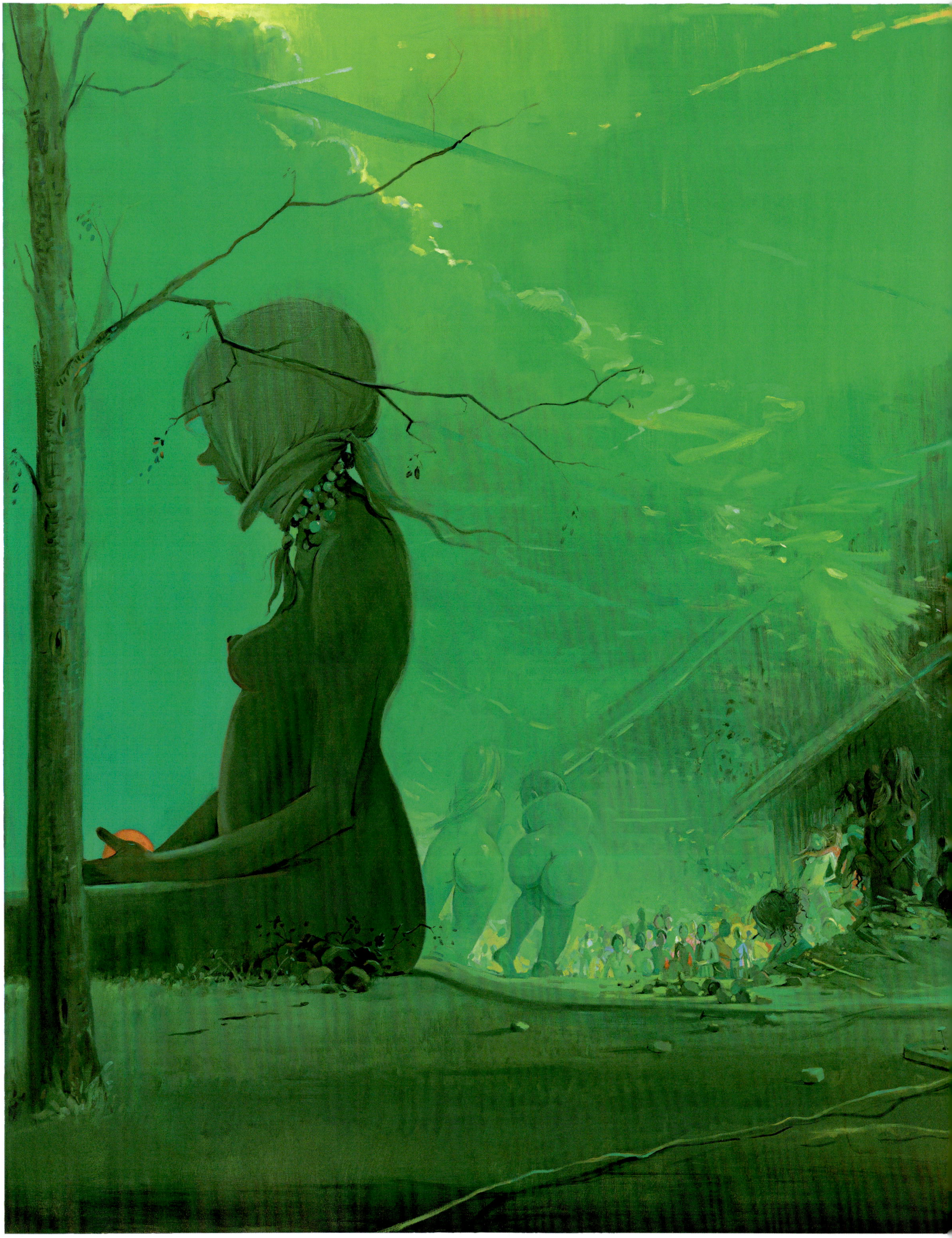

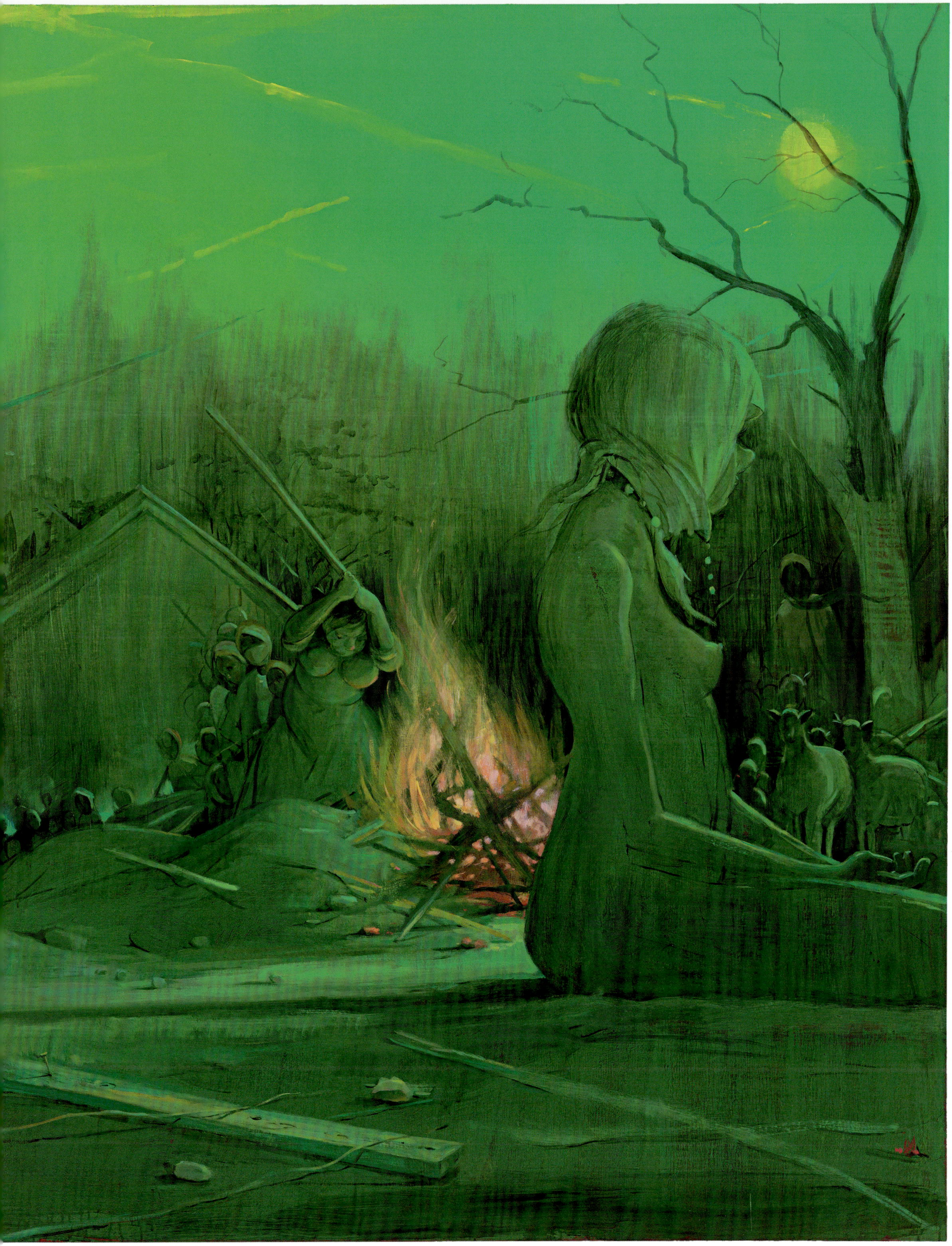

previous pages,
BONFIRE, 2013–15
OIL ON LINEN
208 X 338 CM

opposite,
YELLOW STUDIO, 2021
OIL ON LINEN
178 X 196 CM

YUSKAVAGE: Same pain. That's the way it is. The work of starting something is, I think, the serious artistic doubt. What I think I will say to you, Ariel, is only a wonderful writer would have that kind of self-doubt. So what I can actually say to myself, because I'll say it to you, is that if you don't have artistic doubt, there's something wrong with you. Doubt is an important piece of the state of mind for making stuff.

LEVY: *And it's real every time.*

YUSKAVAGE: OK, back to the pool question. I was trained to be a lifeguard in the 1970s at the YMCA and they threw a cinder block into the deep end of the pool. I think it was nine and a half or ten feet deep. And we had to dive down and retrieve it, the idea being that if there's a lifeless body at the bottom of the pool, you need to be able to swim back up with it, with one hand, kicking against gravity. Anytime I'm trying to get a painting off the ground, I always remember that feeling of almost drowning, trying to bring that damn cinder block up.

LEVY: *And the idea that it's a dead body and you're trying to drag it up to life!*

YUSKAVAGE: Well, I think it's easier to pull a painting out of the ether than swim with a cinder block, let alone a dead body, but I'm ready for anything.

LEVY: *Sure, but when you're making a new thing, you're trying to convince it not to die, or rather to come to life in the first place. 'All right, what do I have to put on this canvas? How do I proceed to create a world that mysteriously seems alive, and the atmosphere has a smell? How do I make this thing not be dead?'*

YUSKAVAGE: And then it's weird the way suddenly, it falls into place. The middle of it, it becomes like, 'Is it happening? Am I getting lucky?' And then, it's the downhill. You're like, 'Oh my God, it's happening. I don't want it to end.'

LEVY: *At the beginning, you're like, 'The joke's on me. I don't know why I thought I could make living things.' The middle's baffling. And then, all of a sudden, you're on a toboggan.*

YUSKAVAGE: But I will say that, if you do it often enough, you get used to the pain, the discomfort.

LEVY: *It becomes undeniable. It becomes recognizable.*

YUSKAVAGE: Not that I lift weights, but I know I'm supposed to, and apparently it stops hurting as much if you do it often enough.

LEVY: *So I'm told. Once in a blue moon, have you had the experience of being like, 'Wow, that was easy?'*

YUSKAVAGE: Me?

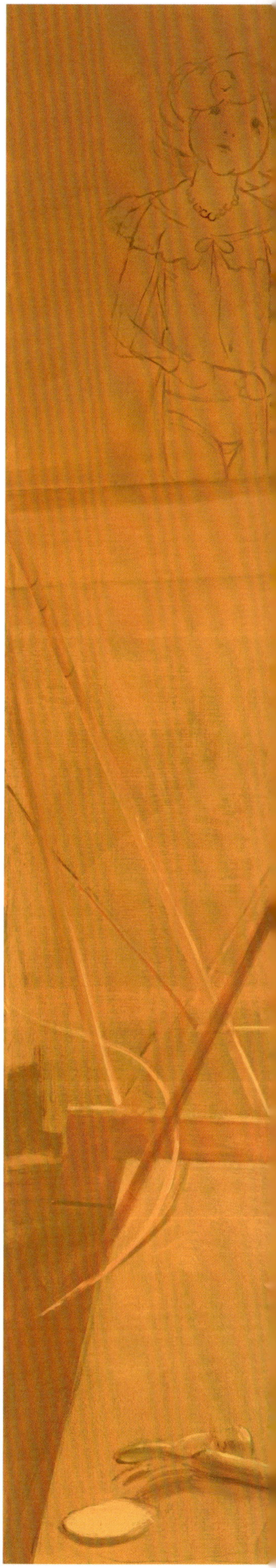

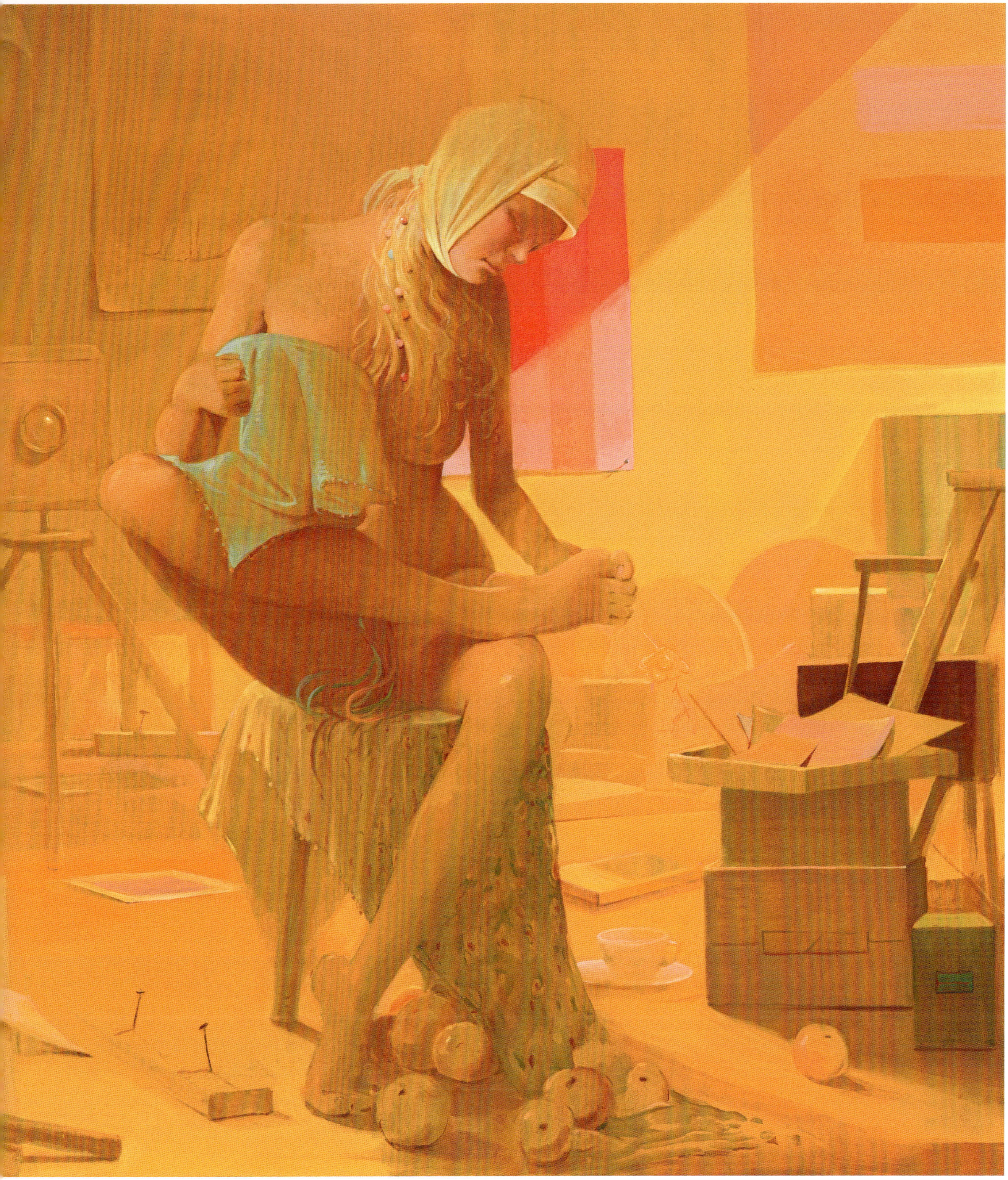

PEACOCK INFESTATION IN THE GARRET, 2024
OIL ON LINEN
64 X 77 CM

LEVY: *Once or twice, in the whole time, where you think, 'Well, that happened. That didn't hurt.'*

YUSKAVAGE: Well, maybe. I find it hard to trust those things.

LEVY: *Of course. You're like, 'I'm Catholic. I want to see some suffering.'*

YUSKAVAGE: I just make them so hard out of the gate, that, in the beginning, I'm like, 'Whoa, there's no way this is going to work'.

LEVY: *Right.*

YUSKAVAGE: So that, in the end, I feel really good, but it's almost like there's more wind beneath my wings, because I can't believe I did it. It's really all about how I smash things together, all of my ideas, and force them to work. I've realized that one of the things that I get the most excited about is synthesizing: trying to find a way to make things hang together is really where I'm inventing. And colour – not the colour that we see in this world, but the colour that had never existed until *I made it* exist.

It always jerks me awake a little bit when somebody uses the expression, 'My painting practice', because I don't feel like I'm practising. I feel like I'm actually not practising. There's so much muscularity in what I'm working with, that 'practice' doesn't feel right.

LEVY: *Right. If I wrestle this alligator to the ground, don't call it practice.*

YUSKAVAGE: Yes, I'm punching the shit out of that alligator.

LEVY: *If there comes a day where I'm riding that alligator down the beach and I look comfortable, I fucking earned it.*

YUSKAVAGE: Practising is for somebody else. It's like, 'You practice. I'm making something happen over here.'

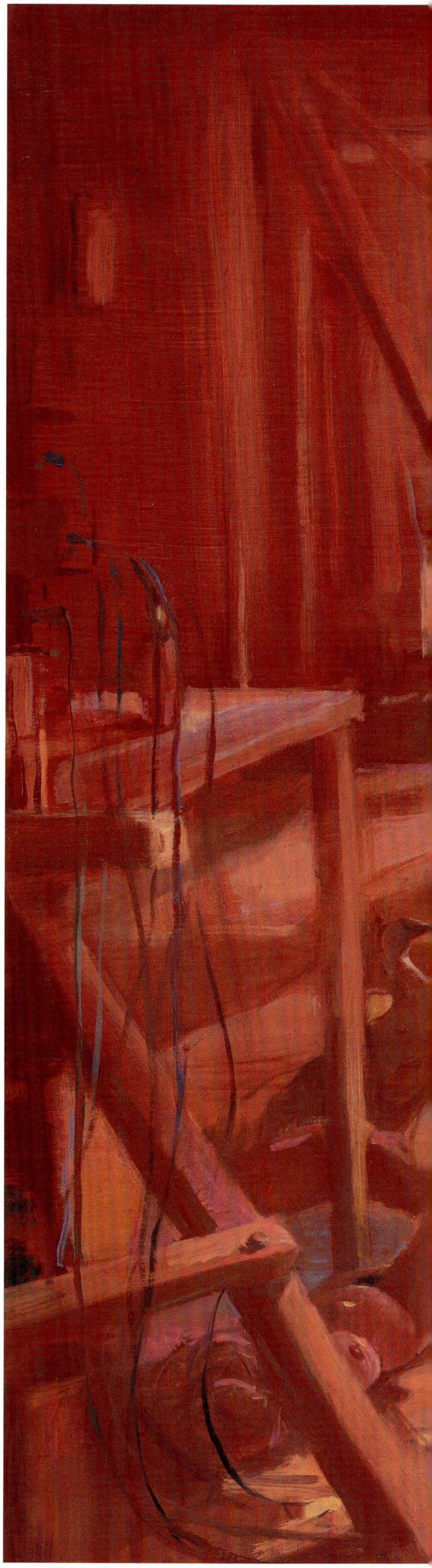

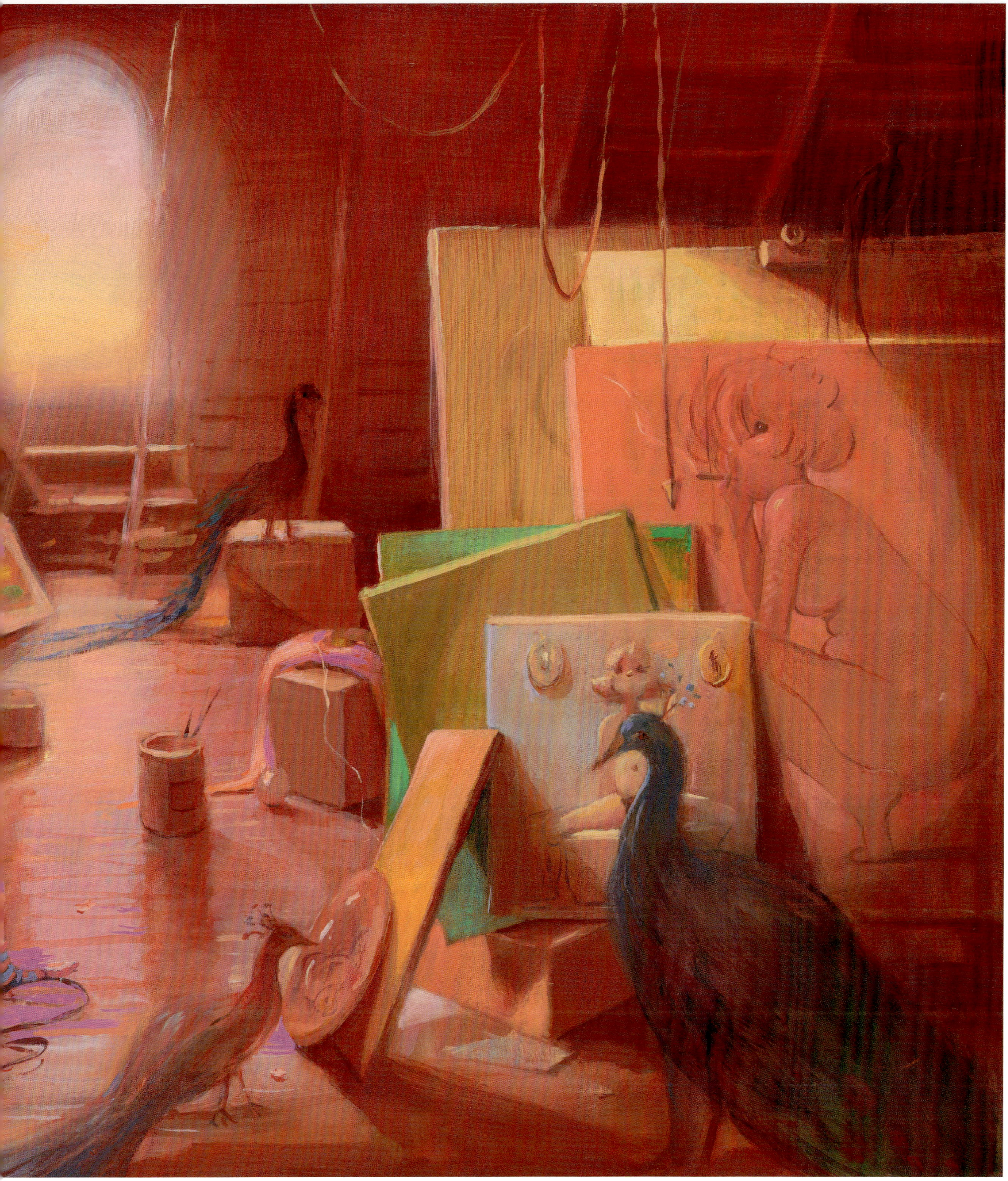

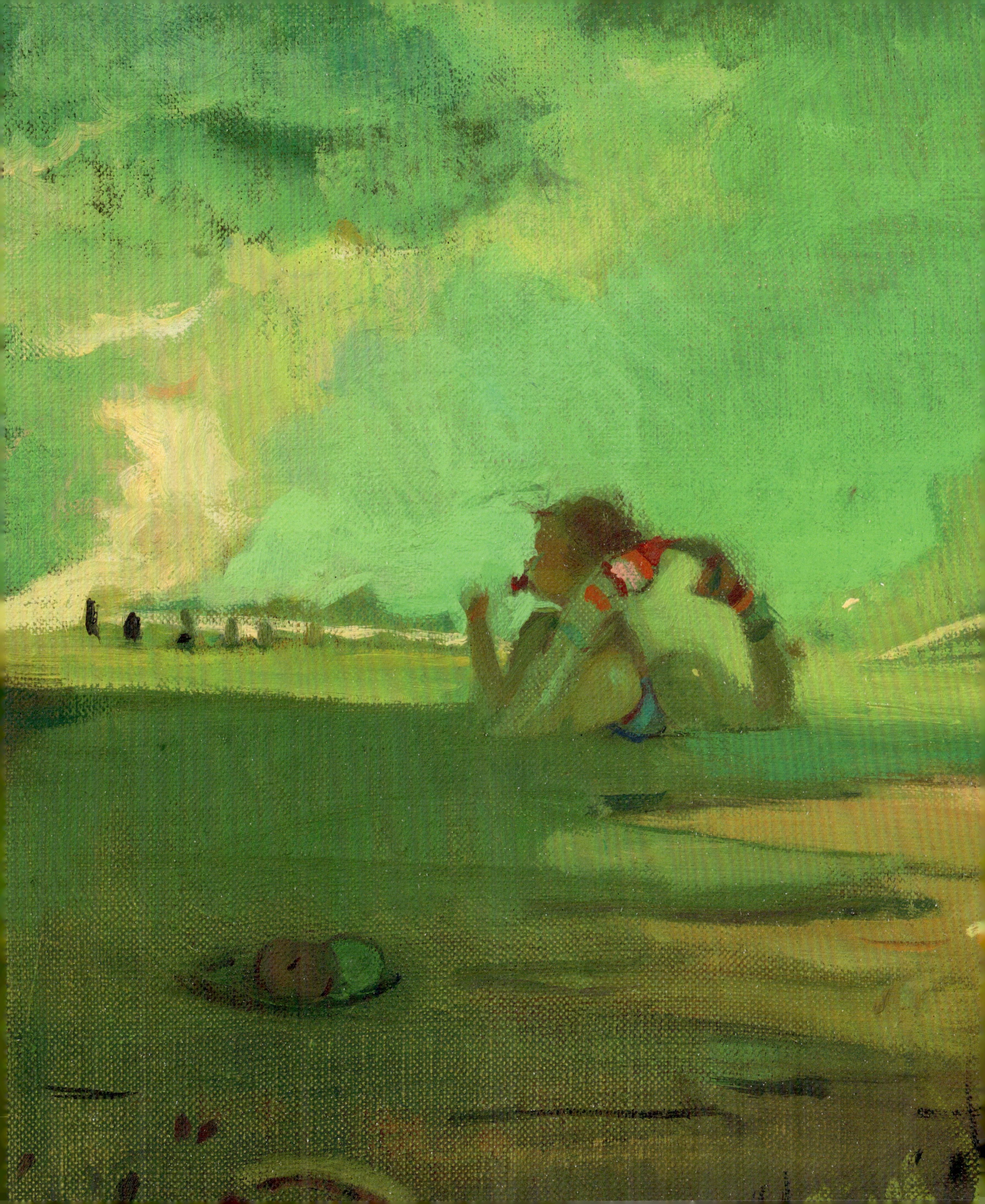

And how did you feel about that?

Barry Schwabsky

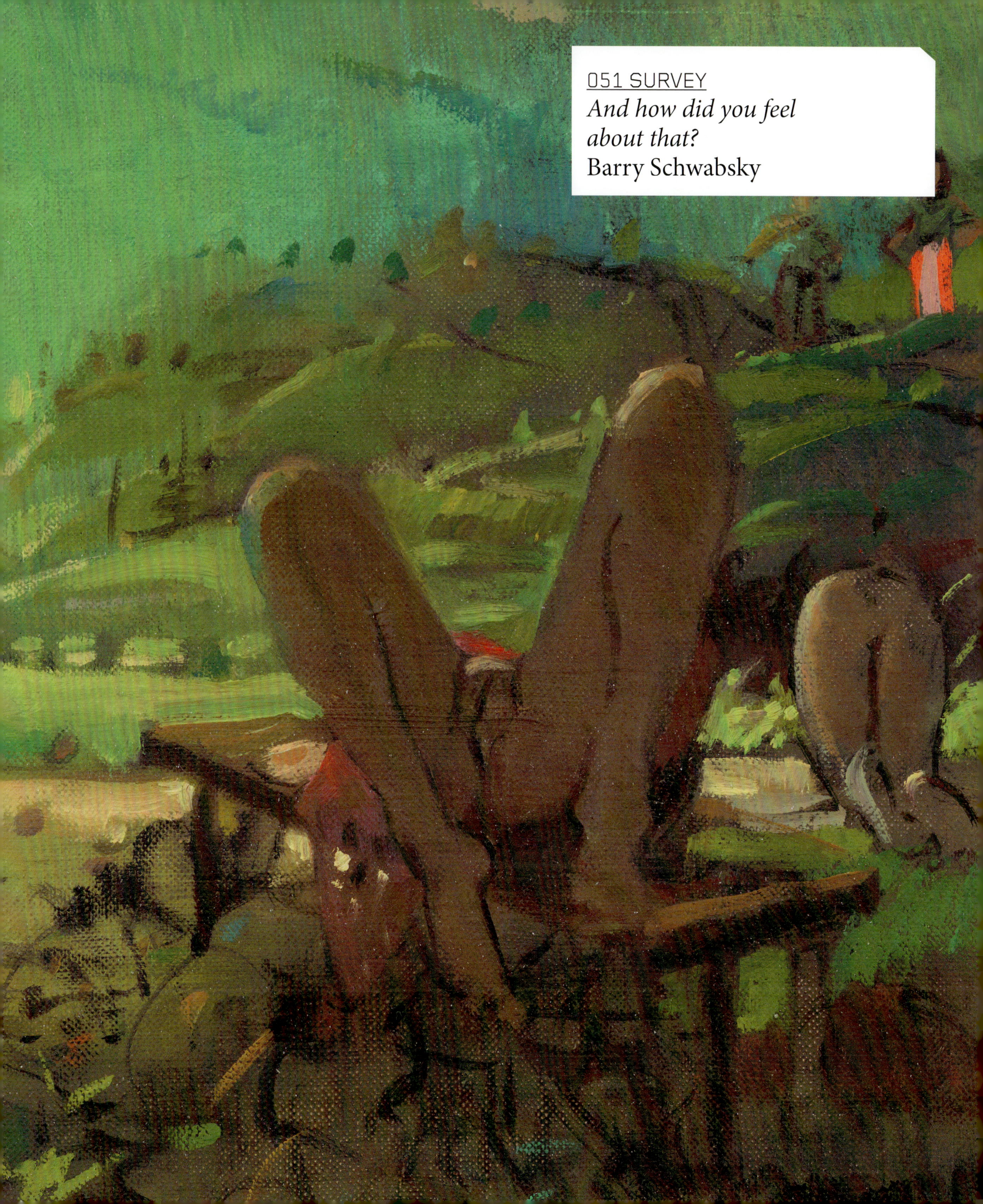

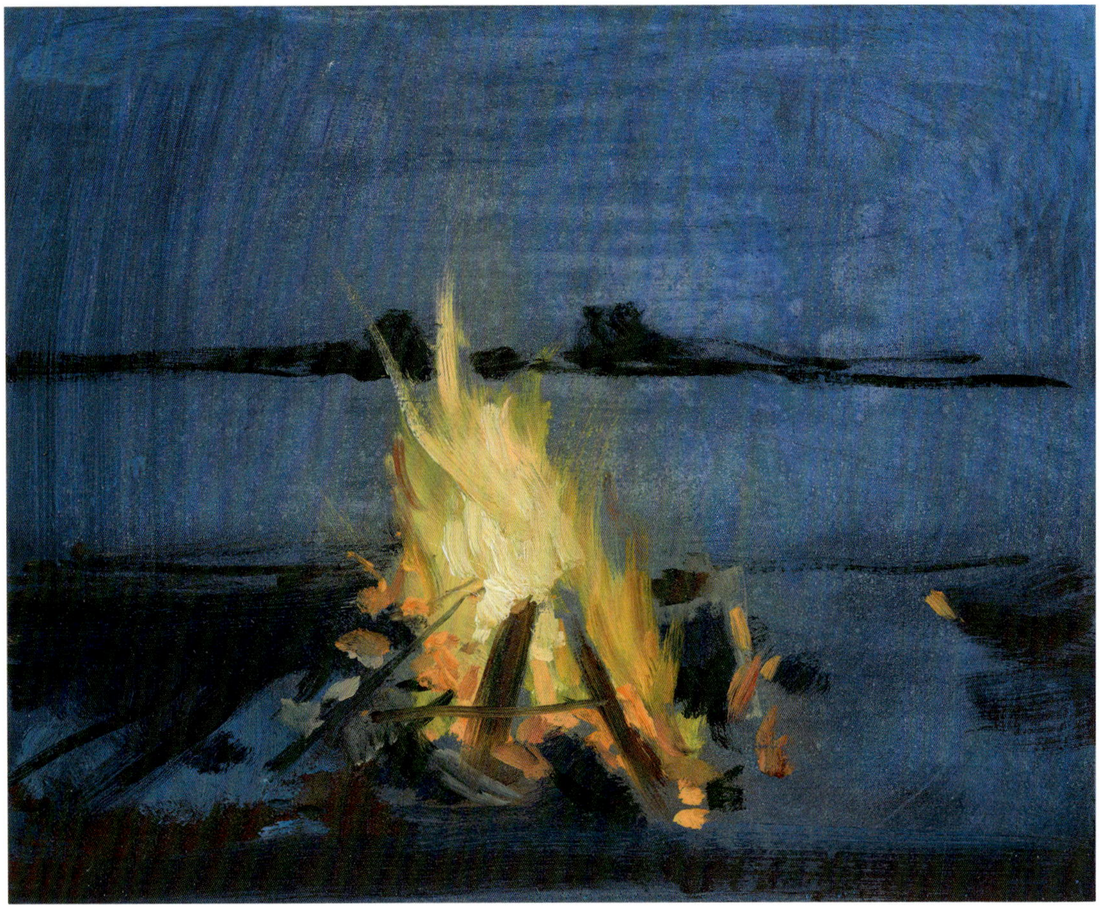

left,
BEACH FIRE, 2012
OIL ON WOOD PANEL
21 X 26 CM

previous pages,
GIVEN AND NEL'ZAHS,
2010
OIL ON LINEN
28 X 39 CM

opposite,
MASTER CLASS, 2021
OIL ON LINEN
213 X 83 CM

The first time I wrote about Lisa Yuskavage's paintings, in an exhibition review published back in 1993, I came to this conclusion: 'To analyze them thoroughly would probably be something like psychoanalyzing oneself in public.'[1] Writing a brief review, of course, I'd given myself an out: I wasn't claiming to explore the works thoroughly, just to give a first immediate response to an oeuvre that was still in an early phase and which until that point had been little seen or discussed. But what was already clear was that Yuskavage's art works by way of the wrong, that is, the inappropriate, the unseemly, maybe even the indecent. Or like something that sticks in your throat: say that it went down the wrong way. But at this point in my life, and in my love affair with Yuskavage's paintings, I'm willing to consider that there's nothing wrong with either me or her art. I'm willing to state positively that there is something wonderfully if unfamiliarly right about it, and it's perfectly right to feel that.

Still, having reviewed Yuskavage's exhibitions periodically since then, and at the start of a longer consideration of her now much more extensive and no less provocative production, I am aware that I might at the same time appear to be putting myself on the proverbial couch. With that in mind, I beg the reader and (potential) surrogate shrink to remember that I intend this essay to be entirely about the art and its maker, and to kindly file away any diagnostic observations about the author as matter for consideration on some other occasion *sine die* – and for now to allow me to persist in my dream of aesthetic disinterestedness. What I want to talk about, and what I want you to think about, in other words, is not why a certain critic is so passionate about Yuskavage's art, but about what it is within that art that might earn such fervency.

Of course, another way to look at Yuskavage's work would be to publicly psychoanalyze not oneself or even the work but rather *her*. After all, as she herself has observed of art generally, 'The work carries markers of the artist's inner life – be it Carroll Dunham's or Giovanni Bellini's – for us to connect to', and all the more so today: 'Since contemporary artists are not hired by, say, the Vatican, we have the freedom to ask ourselves what we believe in and then to assert that belief'.[2] So art is necessarily confessional, and in a more deliberate way than might have been the case in the past. But it's confessional in a funny way – indirect. 'Some people confuse art with autobiography', Yuskavage has said. 'It's a shame, and a limiting way to view art'.[3] An artist's subjectivity is part of their work's means, not its end.

Besides, to conduct a one-sided psychoanalysis – a wrong-sided analysis moreover, since it's supposed to be the analyst who does all the talking – would of course be a highly unethical thing to do, *if* I were a psychoanalyst; but as I am not one, I have no relevant professional code of ethics to violate. But anyway, would it really be worth doing?

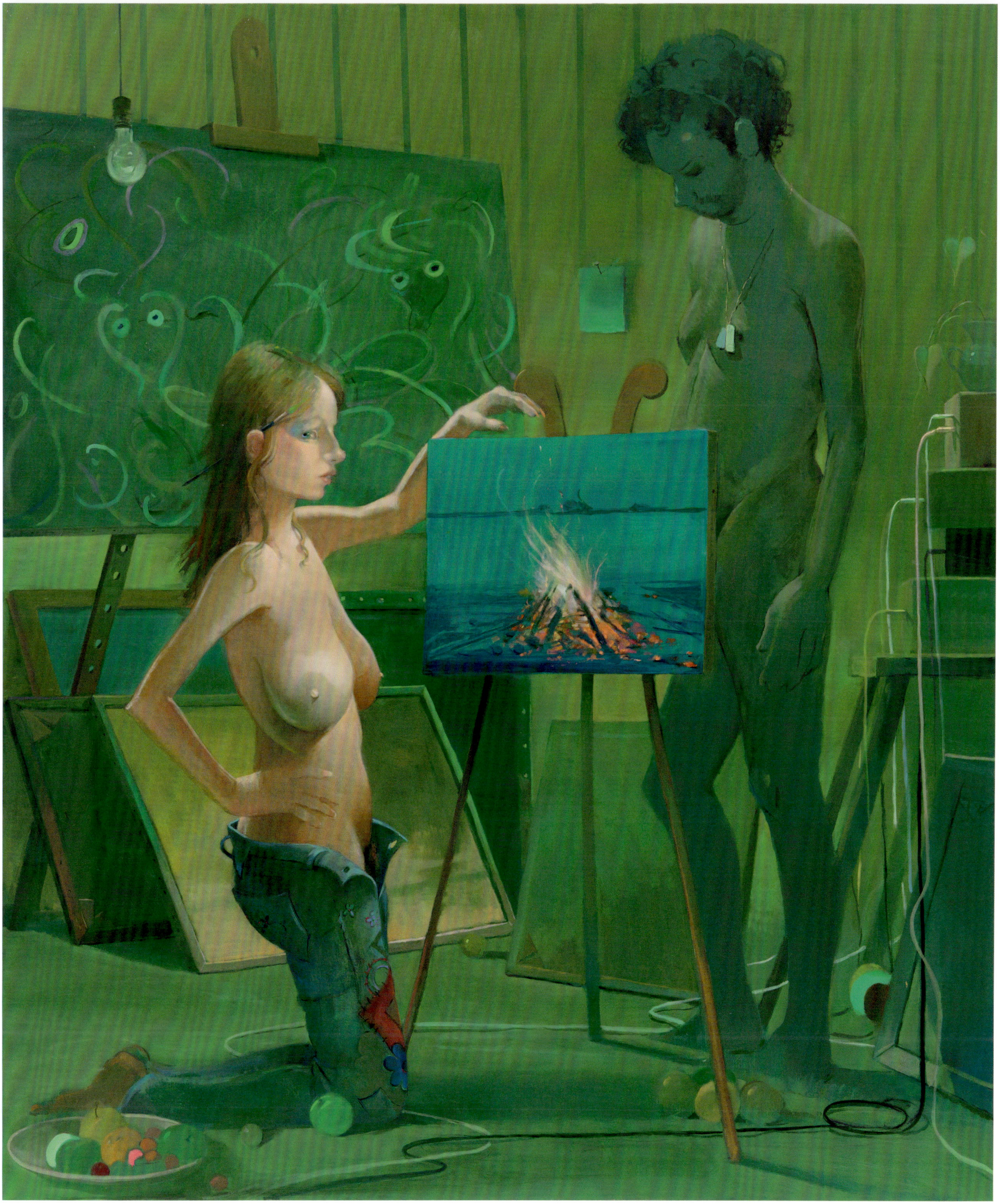

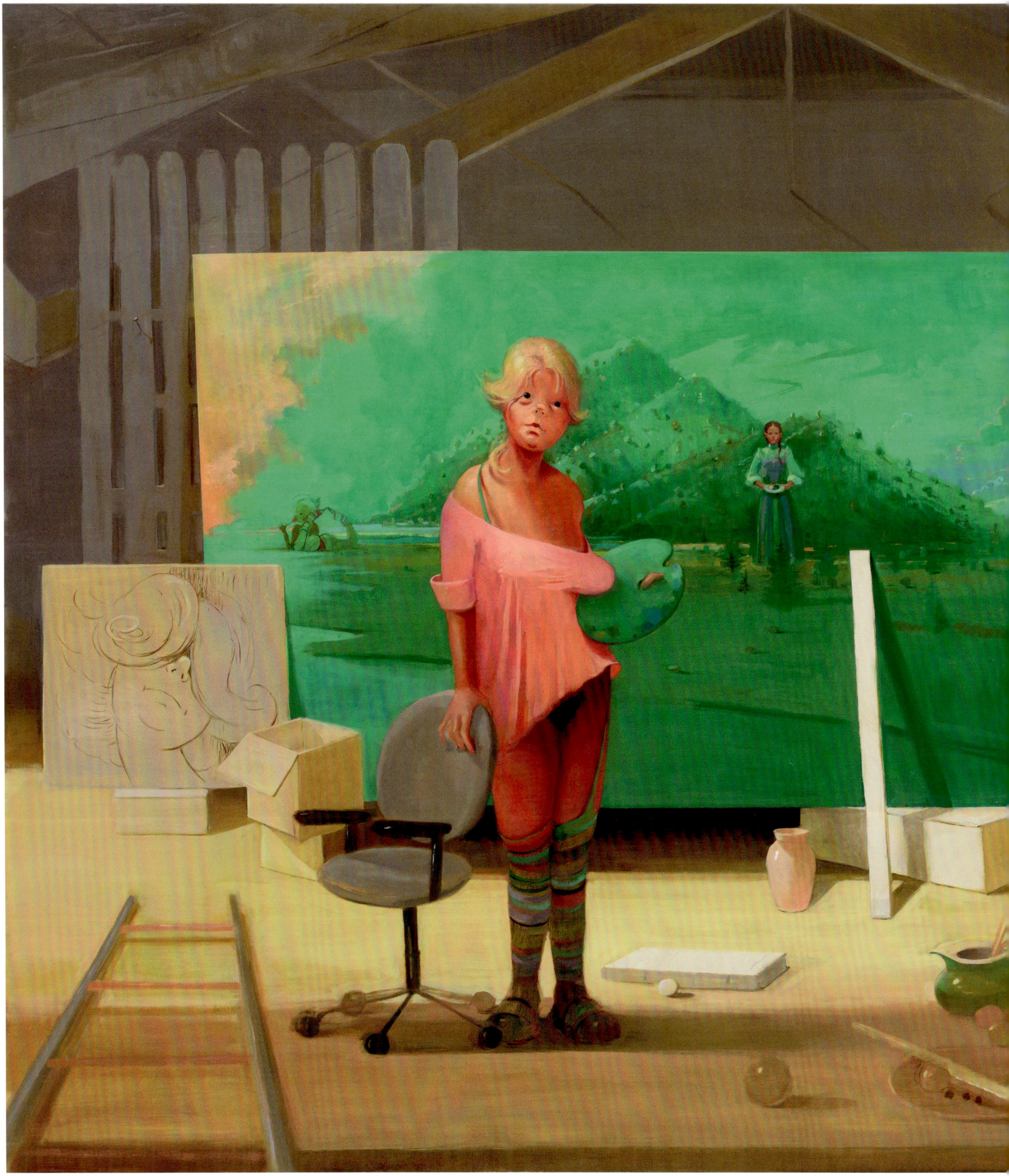

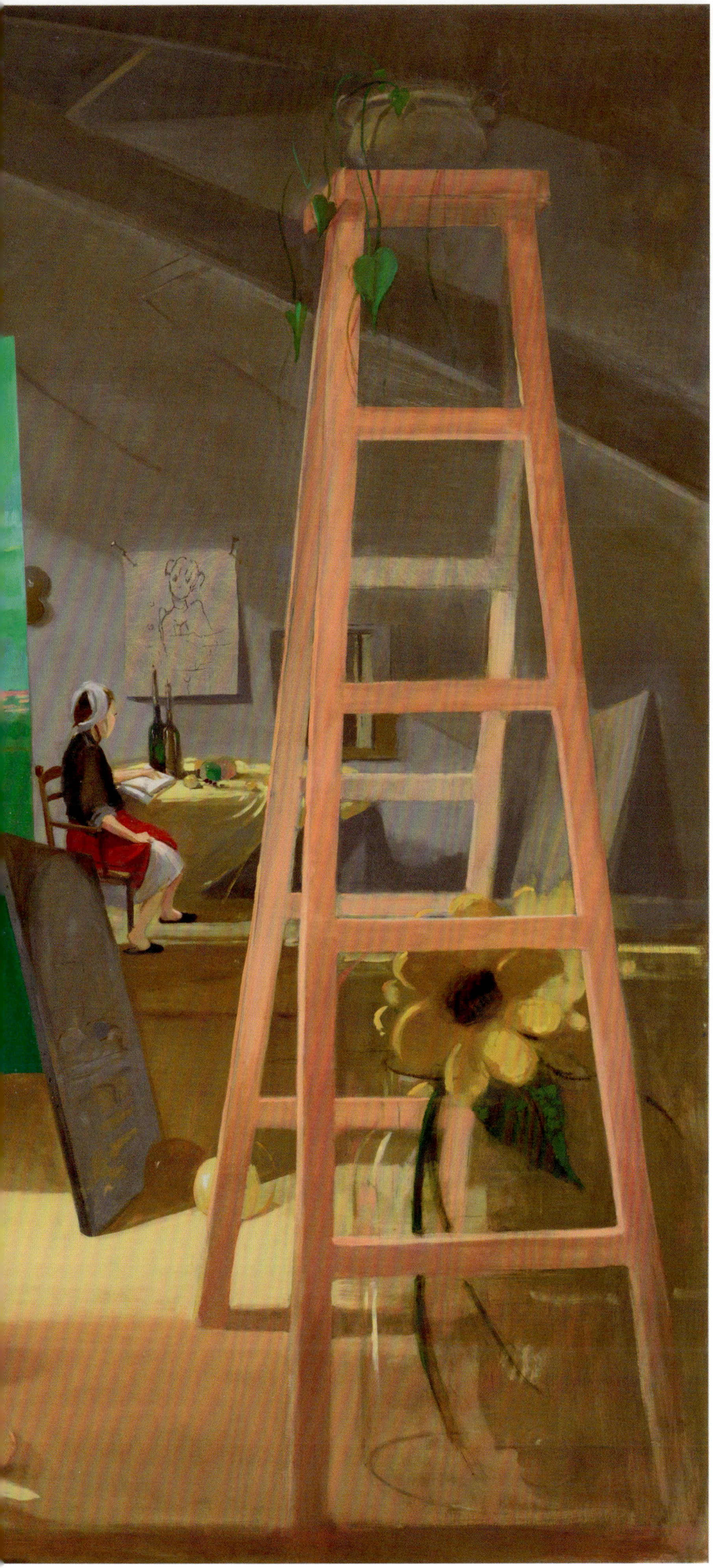

THE ARTIST'S STUDIO, 2022
OIL AND CHARCOAL ON LINEN
218 X 305 CM

This art is so forthright in laying its anxieties and ambivalences on the table that the couch might enable few revelations – little more than a reiteration of the self-evident. Remember, Yuskavage says she wants to base her art on an assertion of what she believes in. And assertions only become psychoanalytically interesting when they're really evasions. Where her work concurs with the psychoanalytic attitude is in implying that the real sources of feeling go back deep, to the remote past. There's a self we travel long and far to get away from but it always turns out to be with us and we're always somehow heading back to it. Perhaps it is more important that Yuskavage's paintings address that self than that they come from and return to it, but both things are true.

My high school girlfriend told me that when you dream, all the characters in the dream are different aspects of you. She must have read that somewhere, maybe in some self-help book, but the moment she said it, I was sure it was true and I still believe that today. What she and I say about dreams, Yuskavage says about paintings: 'The truth is, all of these paintings represent aspects of me: the vulnerable, the aggressive, the enraged, the duality of the twins in *Bonfire*. It's all there: I'm the dude that looks like Jesus. I want to drop trou and have a big cock hang out. I'd love that.'[4] Another way to put this is to say that Yuskavage is fully invested in everything she paints. And that includes, not only the figures, but the clothes they wear (including the 'trou' that gets dropped), the rooms and landscapes, the people, the still-life objects around them, and so on. That's the unity of the painting, which is always evident in its form, and it is communicated above all through colour. And that colour seems to address me personally – to call me by name. Or at least to address something nameless within me that I have to recognize as part of myself.

*

Time, in painting, moves in all sorts of different ways. It puts the past into the present. I had meant to start at the beginning – the artist's childhood in working-class Juniata Park, Philadelphia; Catholic primary school and rejection of the church; public high school and first inklings of the desire to be an artist; study at the Tyler School of Art (BFA, 1984) and the Yale School of Art (MFA, 1986) – where her contemporaries included John Currin, Sean Landers, and Richard Phillips, as well her Russian-born future husband Matvey Levenstein – followed by a solo debut which Yuskavage realized she couldn't stand behind, that she felt was inauthentic, etc. But no: I want to start my chronicle of Yuskavage's art at what is, for now, the end, with some of her most recent paintings. Think of it like

opposite,
THE ONES THAT DON'T WANT TO: BAD BABY, 1991
OIL ON LINEN
87 X 76 CM

a film noir that starts at the conclusion of the story and gradually reveals what led to that denouement through a series of flashbacks.

It makes sense, doesn't it? Artists make paintings of their studio when they need to take stock, pause, look forwards but especially backwards and see where they find themselves, where they've come from, what they've made of themselves. Gustave Courbet, of course, is the paradigmatic case: *The Painter's Studio: A real allegory summing up seven years of my artistic and moral life* (1855). In a *New Yorker* profile, centered on the 2023 Paris show in which she exhibited her studio paintings, Yuskavage is shown visiting the Musée d'Orsay to feast her eyes on Courbet's masterpiece. 'He's painting a landscape, with a nude model watching him – it's so dreamlike,' she says. 'It's got all the figures from his previous paintings. Time is folding in and out'.[5] Those folds… I can't help but recall Stéphane Mallarmé – excuse me for pointing this out but might this not be the first time that name has been cited in relation to Yuskavage's paintings? – and his vision of the city of Bruges, where '*Comme furtive d'elle et visible je sens / Que se dévêt pli selon pli la pierre veuve*' (as furtively and visibly I sense / its widowed stone undress fold by fold).[6] Folds mean concealing and revealing, veiling and unveiling. That's what paintings do with time, and what time does with paintings, and that's tied in with their ability to conjure all substances by way of a single substance. As Frances Richard wrote in 2007, in what I still think is one of the most accurately evocative passages written about Yuskavage's work, 'She blurs a ninth-month belly or grotesque breast into a nobbly pear, a fake pearl, or a hot sfumato that describes no tangible thing at all. All are envisioned as temporary clumps of the same shimmering, morphing stuff, in which even aggressive physicality evanesces.'[7]

In Yuskavage's studio paintings, multiple points in the development of her art converge and waft around each other. More often than directly quoting past works, as Henri Matisse did in his *Red Studio* (1911), she evokes them in a general way, perhaps approaching them asymptotically. That's because Matisse's painting is (like Courbet's, but in a different way) a work of direct autobiography. Yuskavage deflects her self-representation as an artist: the painter she shows us is not exactly herself, nor is the depicted studio what you'd see if you made the pilgrimage to her actual workspace in the Gowanus section of Brooklyn. But the artworks glimpsed in the fictional studio? Let's see.

The painting *The Artist's Studio* (2022) – I might as well start with the one with the bluntest title – shows a painter, female, standing in a vast space filled with golden light. Behind her, sitting on two big blocks but not leaning on any wall one can see, is a large, apparently unfinished, bright green landscape with a single demurely garbed female figure holding out a dish of … something, who knows what … standing in the middle distance and, harder to make out and a little further back on the far left, another female figure in what might almost be some perverse sort of yoga pose, prone, with her belly on the ground but her head up in the air, sucking a lollypop, and her legs bent at the knee so that her stripe-socked toes touch high in the air. This painting within the painting is a sort of Yuskavage synthesis: the virid landscape with its three mountain peaks, one in front of the other in the midst of a plain, recalls the setting of more than one work in the artist's oeuvre, but perhaps most notably the grand, eighteen-foot-wide 2011 *Triptych*. And in fact, that tousle-headed lolly licker is taken from *Triptych*, though also resembling the blonde in Yuskavage's 1995 trio of small square portrait-like depictions of heads, *Blonde Brunette and Redhead*, while the standing figure is one of several that one spies further in the background of that earlier painting, all dressed similarly in ankle-length dresses, like repressed nineteenth-century farm girls. What *In the Studio* is missing from *Triptych* is its central motif, which is reminiscent of a different Courbet painting from his famous Studio: his infamous crotch-shot stunner *L'Origine du monde* (1866) – a title usually translated as 'The Origin of the World', but (since *monde* means "people" just as much as it means "world") is perhaps better rendered as 'The Origin of Everyone' or even 'Where People Come From'. In Yuskavage's version, the woman in question, well shaved, is sprawled over a rustic-looking wooden bench; all we can see of her is her legs and what's between them.

The multiple temporalities of painting always include at least two: the time when it is seen and thought about, and the time, often extended and therefore inherently already multiple, in which it was made. There are also times referred to or evoked: in *Triptych*, the imagined distant era of repressed and puritanical (yet powerfully, commandingly upright) women bearing provender on the

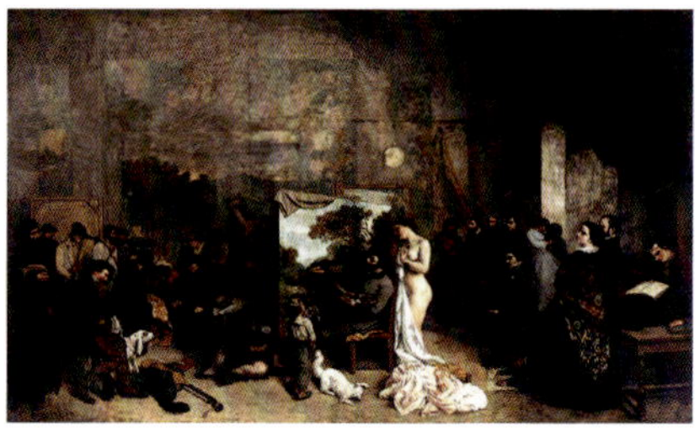

GUSTAVE COURBET
THE ARTIST'S STUDIO,
1854–55
OIL ON CANVAS
361 X 598 CM

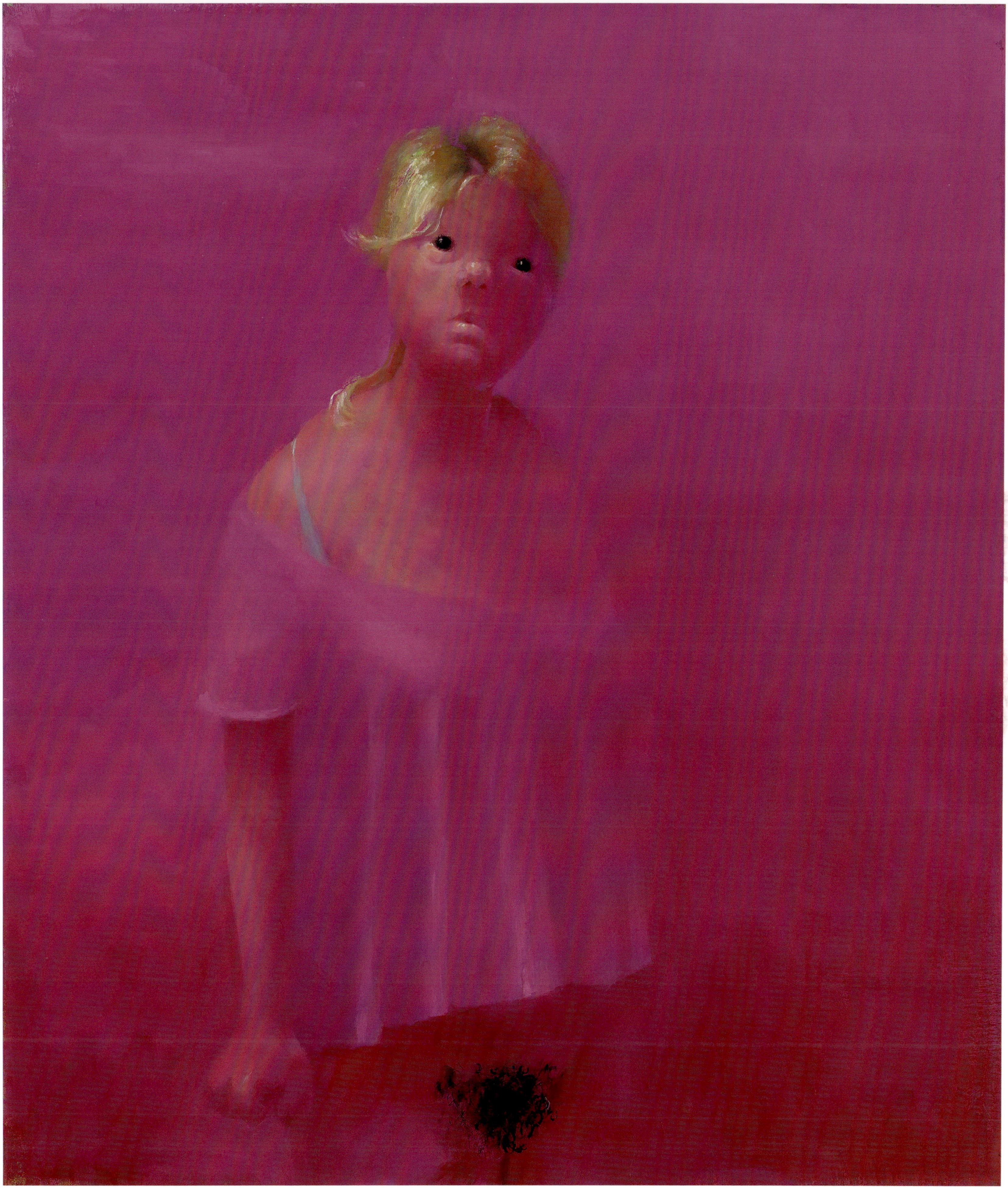

TRIPTYCH, 2010–11
OIL ON LINEN
196 X 534 CM

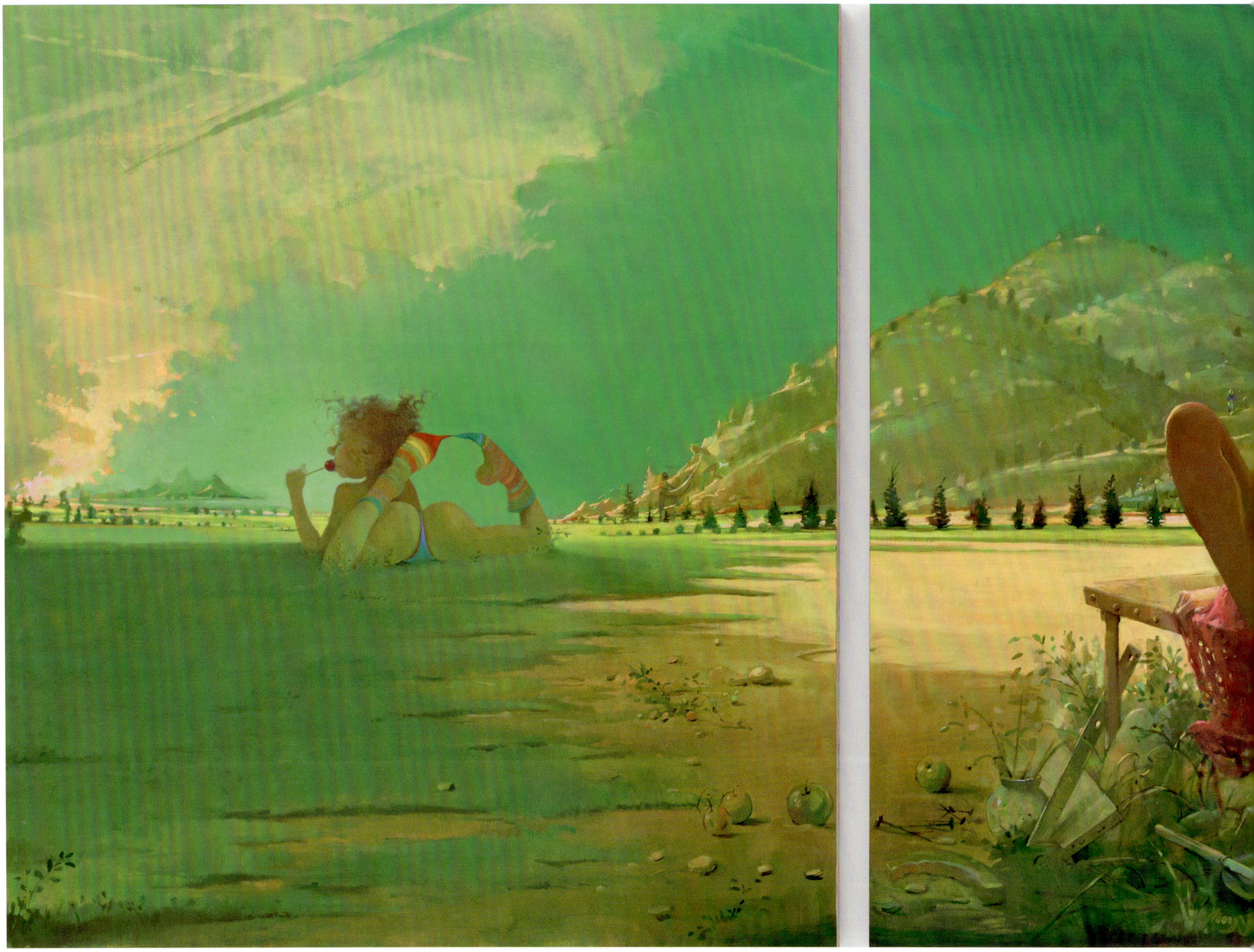

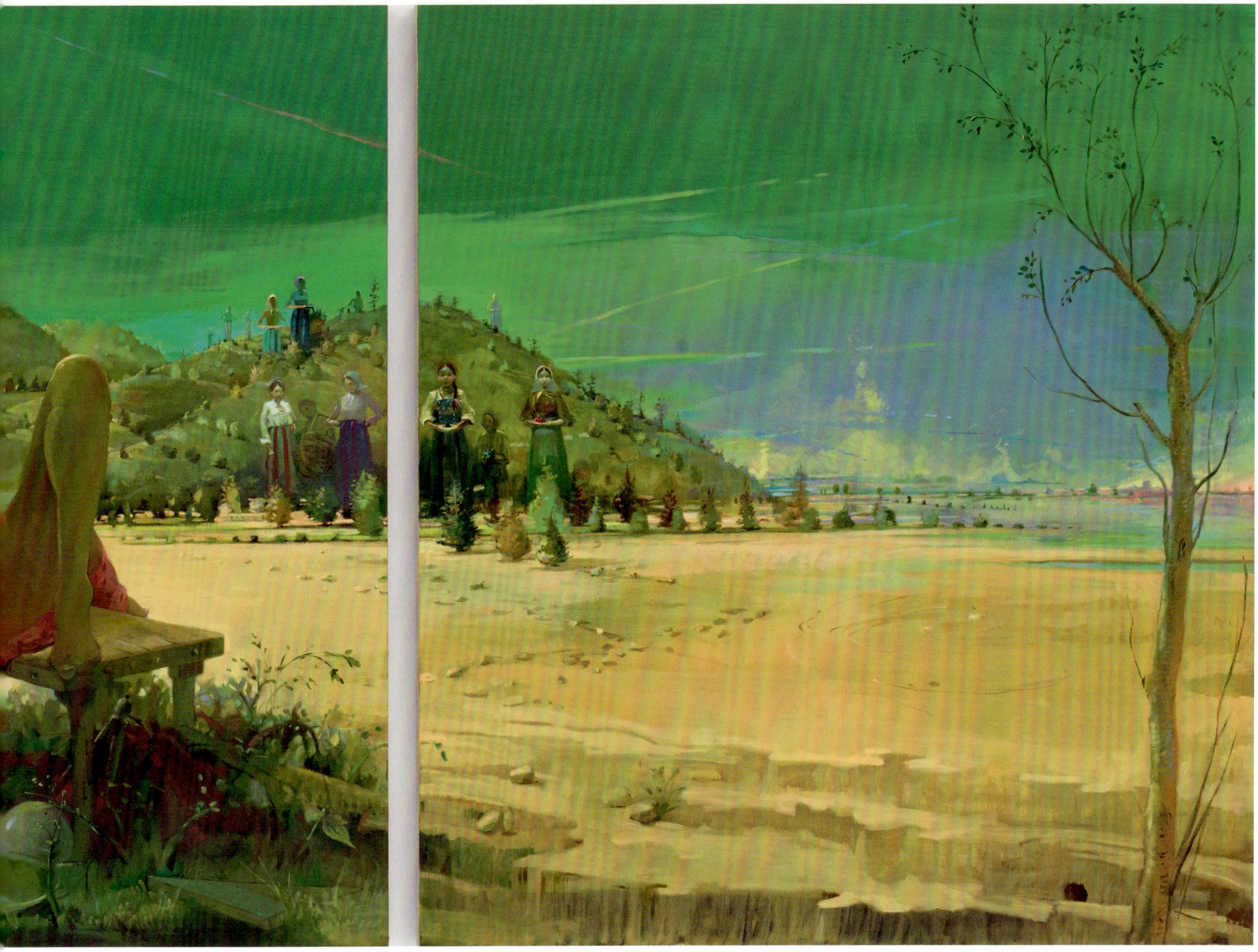

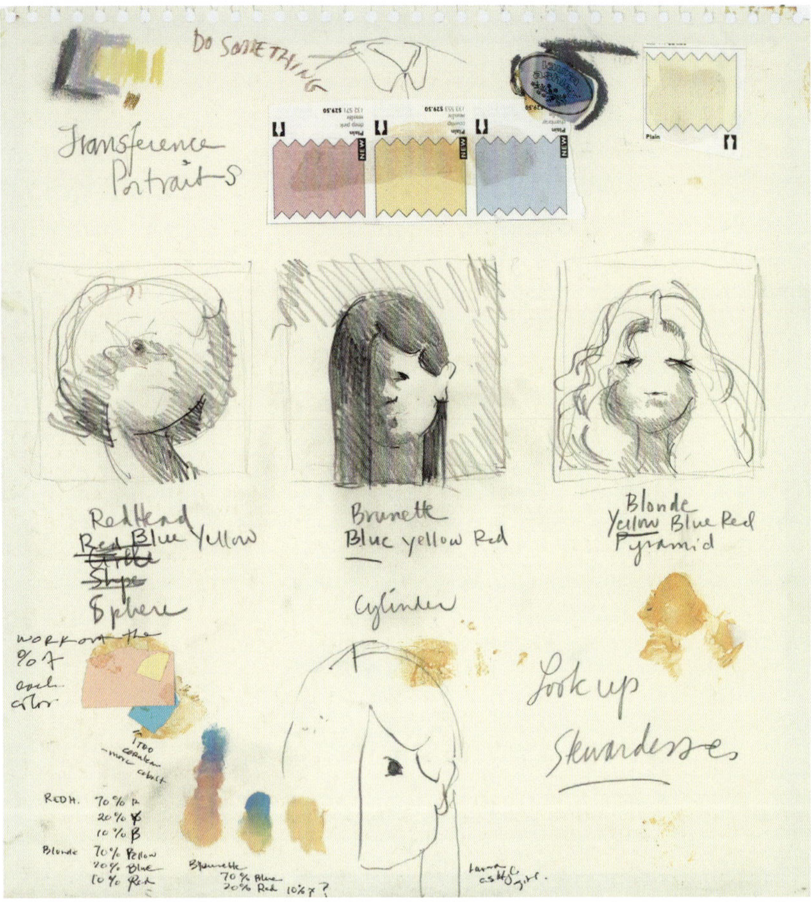

SKETCHES FOR BLONDE BRUNETTE AND REDHEAD, 1994
OIL ON LINEN
31 X 28 CM

opposite and next pages, BLONDE BRUNETTE AND REDHEAD, 1995
OIL ON LINEN
TRIPTYCH
91 X 274 CM

one hand and, on the other, the equally imaginary time of 'these kids today', indulging their sweet tooth and who knows what else as they lie there consuming. But there is also the transhistorical time of the land, its geological and ecological formation, and of human biology, the corporeality that has always been the origin of everyone – the painting's background and foreground.

The painting-within-the-painting of *In the Studio* absents *Triptych*'s faceless, indeed almost bodiless, foreground figure; instead, the painter (who does not resemble Yuskavage, it should be noted) standing in front of it becomes the figure to the painting's ground, takes the place of the missing girl on the bench. And yet the painter, too, with her old-fashioned palette, all green like the painting behind it, gives a glimpse of crotch – unshaven, unlike the one in *Triptych*. Maybe she's also an older version of the lolling lollypop sucker, having grown up a bit in the intervening eleven years – but she's still wearing the same sort of white socks. Moreover, the figure of the painter is derived from yet another of Yuskavage's paintings, from the earliest period of the work that she recognizes as truly her own: *The Ones That Don't Want To: Bad Baby* (1991).

*

Time shifts. I have to interrupt my discussion of *In the Studio* – though even on a purely descriptive level, there is still so much to say about it—and go from its retrospect of moments in the development of Yuskavage's oeuvre to what I think counts as its origin story, the moment of truth when the door opened to a future that the artist is still pursuing.

It's a story she's told many times, always a little differently, always similarly. I'll choose the version she gave to the Canadian critic Robert Enright. She's talking about an event that took place in 1990, four years after she'd received her MFA from the Yale University School of Art. It was every young artist's dream come true: her first one-person show in a good New York Gallery:

I had been making paintings that were extremely categorizable, paintings that were really boring, what a woman artist who went to Yale might make. Certain scales, certain colour. I had a show because I was being rewarded for playing the part. I walked in the exhibition and I thought I was going to die. I couldn't believe how much that work did not have anything to do with me, and I had made it. I had bought a dress and shoes, I did the makeup and the hair, and I hated the work and wanted to leave. I said, "I'm going to die if I paint this way; I literally think it's going to kill me".[8]

What was the nature of this dread that overcame the artist at the opening of her exhibition? It was the feeling that this work was not hers, she couldn't identify with

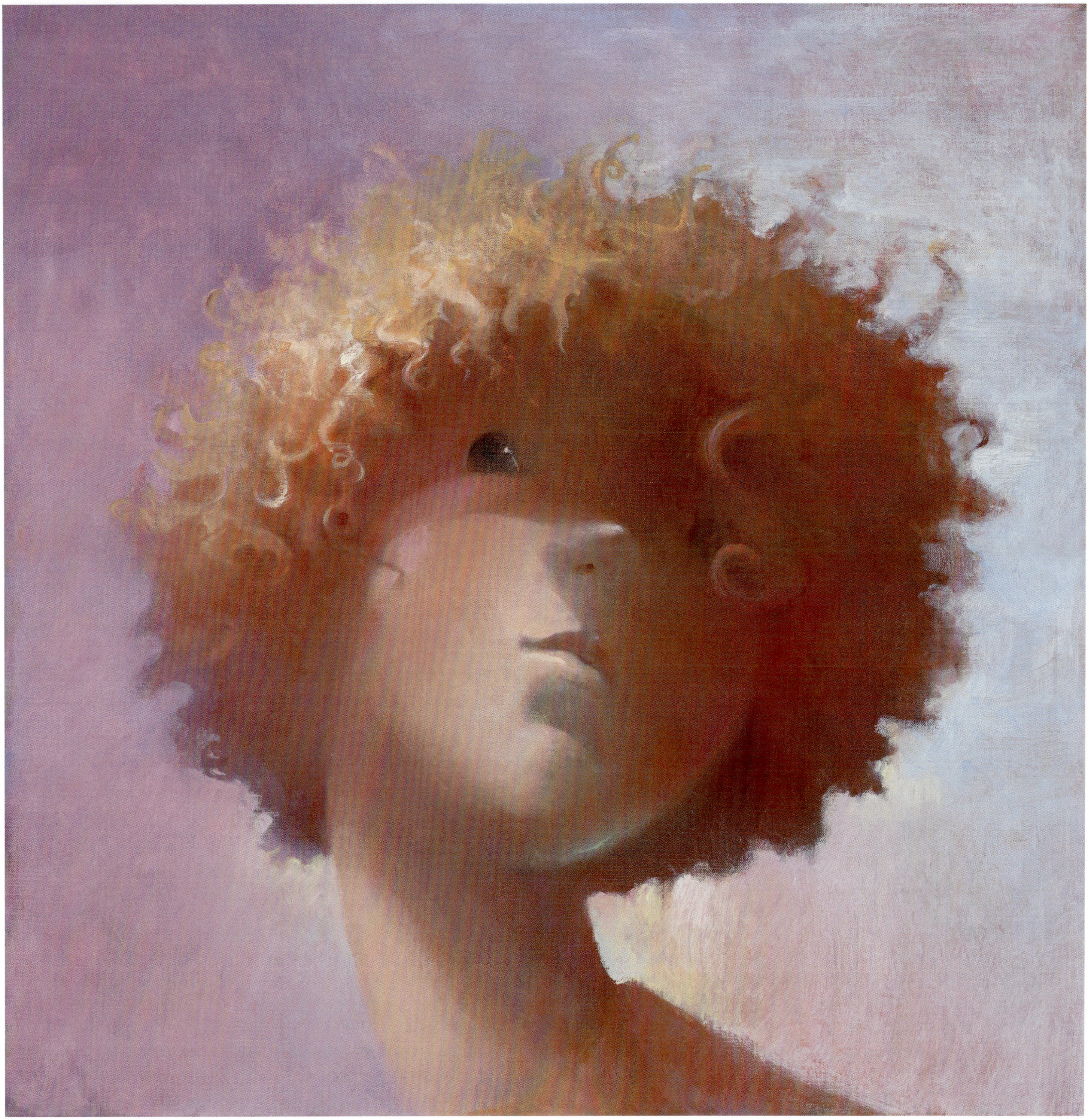

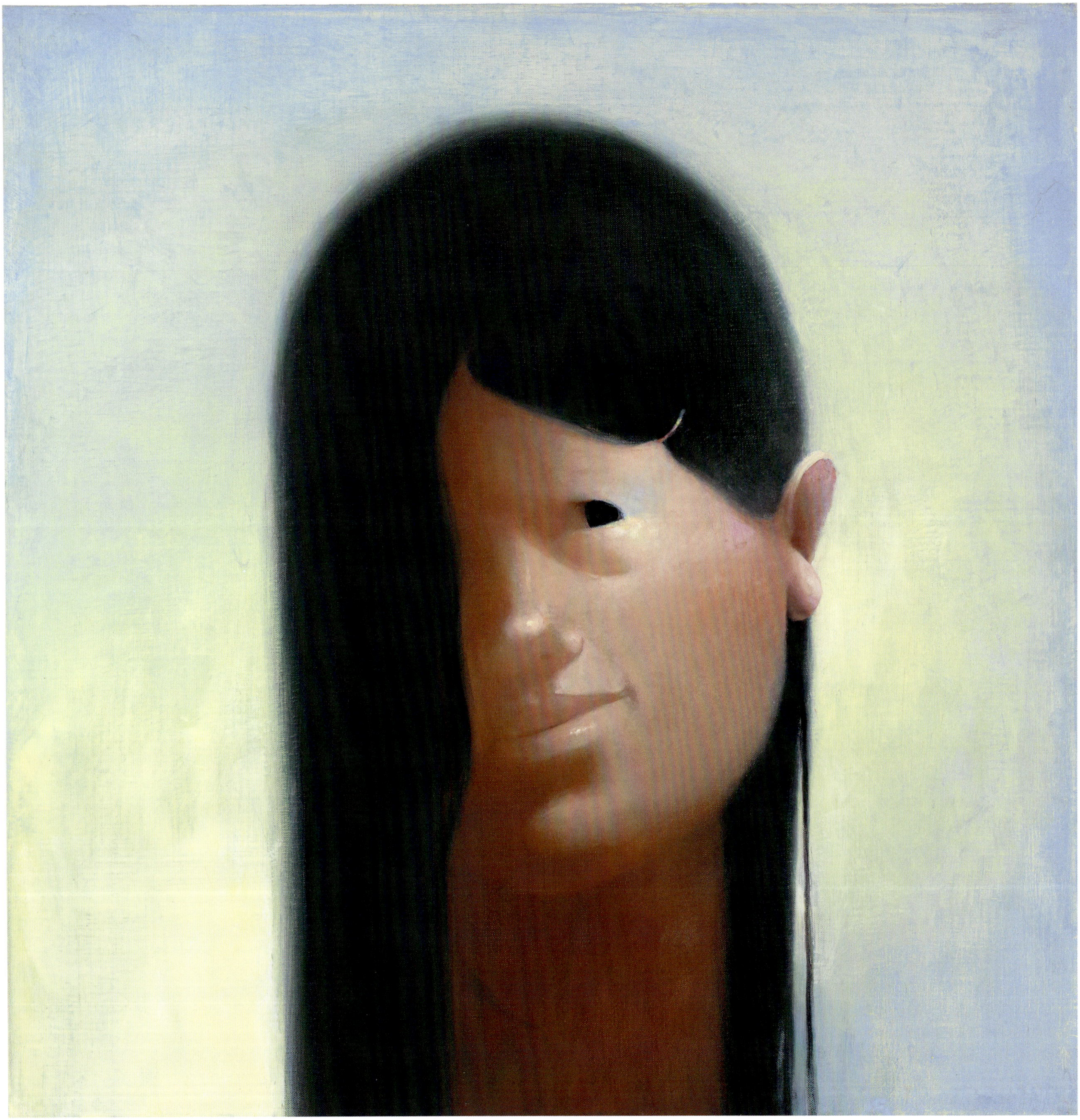

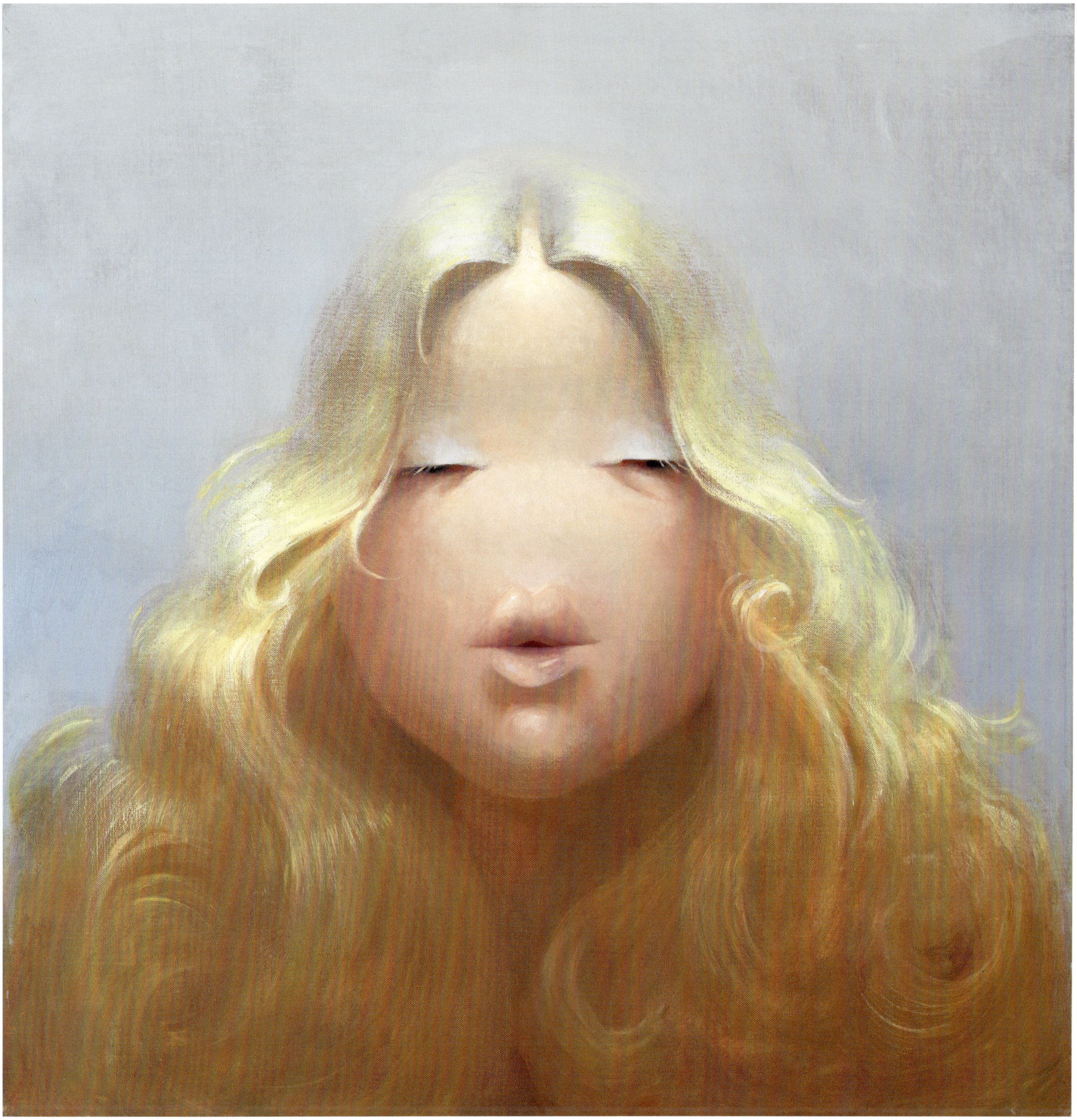

TRULY YOURS, 1990
OIL ON LINEN OVER PANEL
51 X 45 CM

it, that it was something she had done to evade herself (whoever that might turn out to be) and whatever it was that that person, that authentic self, was meant to do. And it had to do with a sense that she was obeying the dictates of a taste that she did not share or respect. She had not yet consciously learned – as she told another interviewer – that 'good taste is in itself bad taste', but instinctively she knew it.[9]

She stopped painting, for what turned out to be about a year. It became a time of 'just thinking, reading, watching movies, and looking at art', she explained to another interviewer, the poet Mónica de la Torre. It was Yuskavage's husband, fellow painter Matvey Levenstein, who told her she could switch personalities with her paintings – become a little more demure, like her paintings had been and let the paintings become more in-your-face, more confrontational, as she tended to be in social situations. I don't believe she ever succeeded in becoming any more decorous in person – and de la Torre, in the interview, suggests the same – but the metamorphosis of the art really happened: 'My work did change overnight… Matvey was listening to me moaning and groaning about how I hated my paintings because I was always painting with my pinky up in the air. I was trying too hard to be somebody I wasn't… So what this switching-places exercise taught me was that there was already a character at play in my work.'[10] The realization was that the style expressed by the otherwise invisible character of the maker is *also* one of the protagonists of the painting, and she had been playing a role that ill-suited her. Her new work would be everything the 'pinky up in the air' paintings she'd been making before were not: blunt, unfiltered.

Sure. But like all origin stories, the one Yuskavage tells has an element of mythology to it. I remember seeing those pre-Yuskavage Yuskavage paintings, and when I hear her tell of an overnight change, of a sudden passage from dreariness into light, I have to wonder: was it really like that? Something changed, and dramatically, to be sure – but the bigger change might have been in the artist's mind's eye. Look at reproductions of Yuskavage's paintings from 1990, the last of the old, supposedly 'really boring' paintings she'd been making after leaving Yale but which were still 'the last hiccup of being a grad student; they were about pleasing the authorities.'[11] And then look at her paintings from 1991, the first of the paintings after her supposedly radical change, which are the 'Bad Baby' series of which *The Ones That Don't Want To: Bad Baby* is the very first. It's easy to make that comparison because on the timeline of the artist's highly informative website they are, of course, right next to each other. (I'll even give you the web address: It's https://yuskavage.com/artworks/?category=&date=1990

What I think you'll see is that the difference between 1990 paintings such as *Mine, Dear Pup*, or *Truly Yours* on the one hand and those begun in 1991 – just four: two completed that year, *The Ones That Don't Want To: Bad Baby*, and *The Ones That Don't Want To: Bad Baby III*, as well as two works completed the following year, *The Ones That Can't: Tea*, and *The Ones That Don't Want To: Black Baby* – is significant, but less dramatic than Yuskavage's story would suggest.

What the 1990 and the 1991 paintings share is a similar figure-ground relationship. Each painting features a single central figure within a nebulous monochromatic surround. And let me emphasize that word *within*: the figures do not stand clear against a distinctly separate backdrop; they are enmisted by an enveloping atmosphere. They are emergent rather than entirely free-standing entities. Or rather – here's the first distinction between the two groups of paintings: while logically, we can't definitively claim that any of the figures are self-evidently surfacing from rather than receding into the surrounding space, it's easy to feel that the 1991 figures might be emerging because they are more or less facing outward while the 1990 ones would seem to be receding because they are facing into the painting, away from the world of the viewer – they are inward-turning.

That's one change. I should specify, however, that the figures in the 1990 paintings can be characterized as elusive,

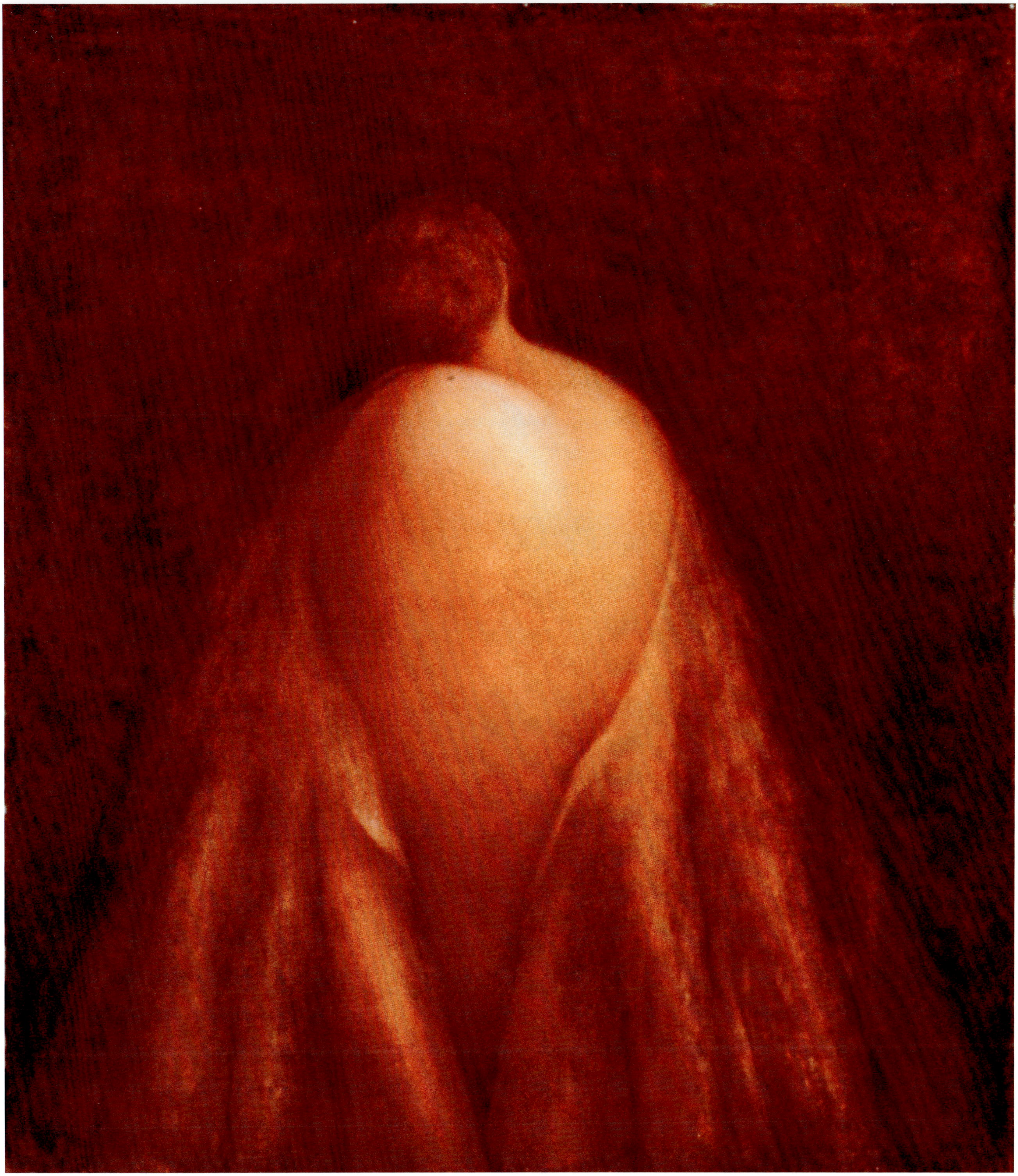

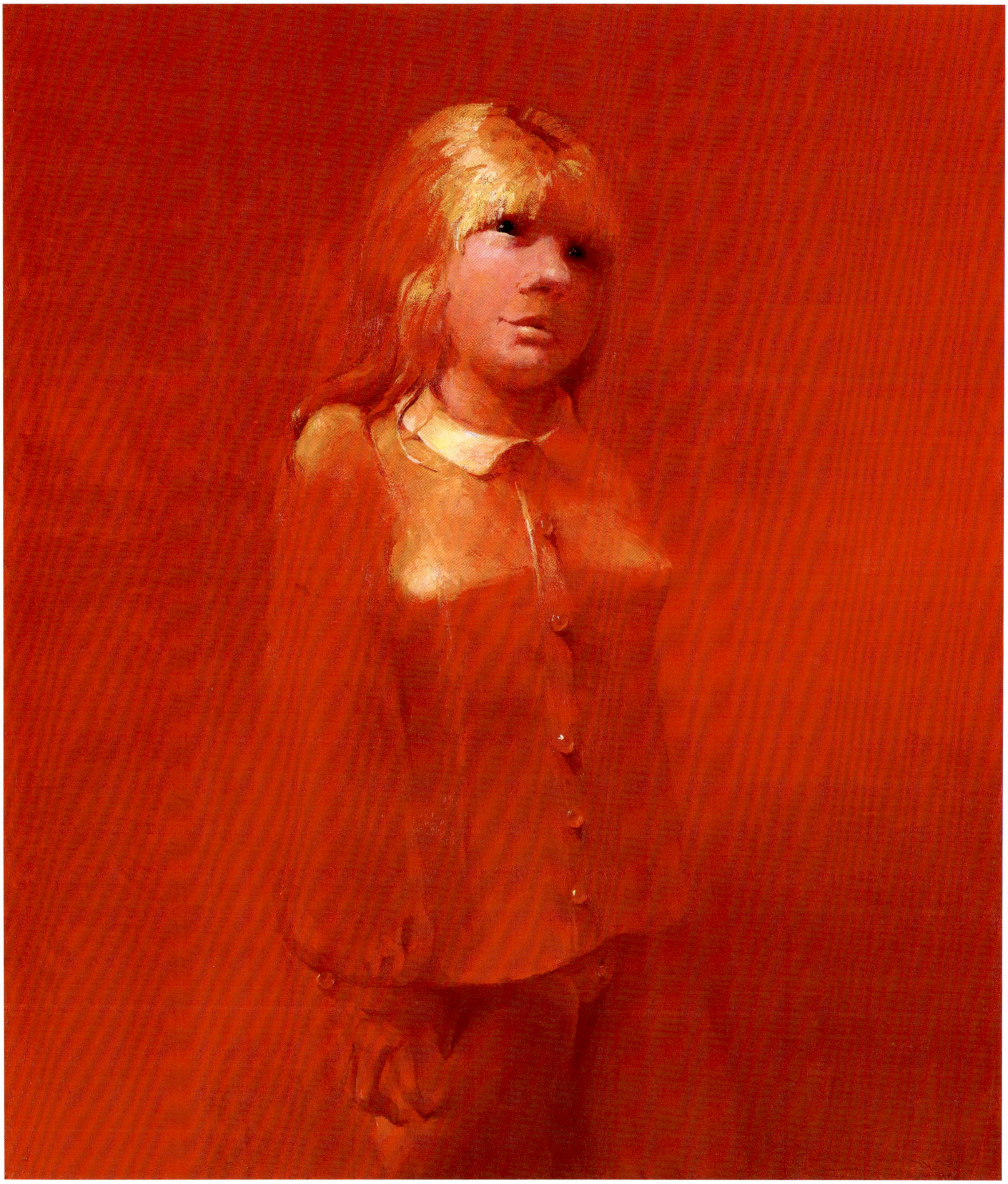

THE ONES THAT DON'T WANT TO: BUTTONS (BAD BABY III),
1991
OIL ON LINEN
87 X 76 CM

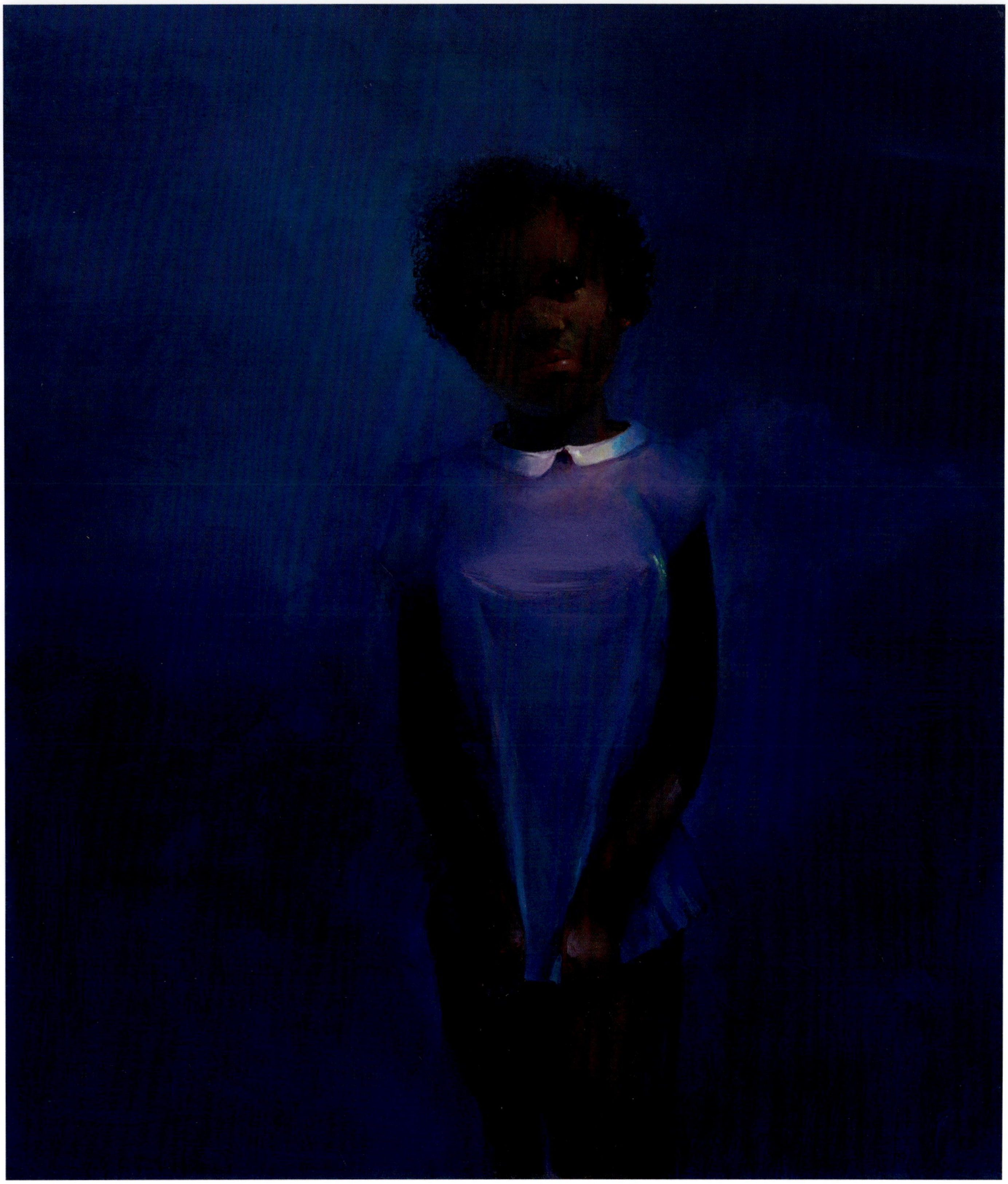

THE ONES THAT DON'T WANT TO: BLACK BABY,
1991–92
OIL ON LINEN
87 X 76 CM

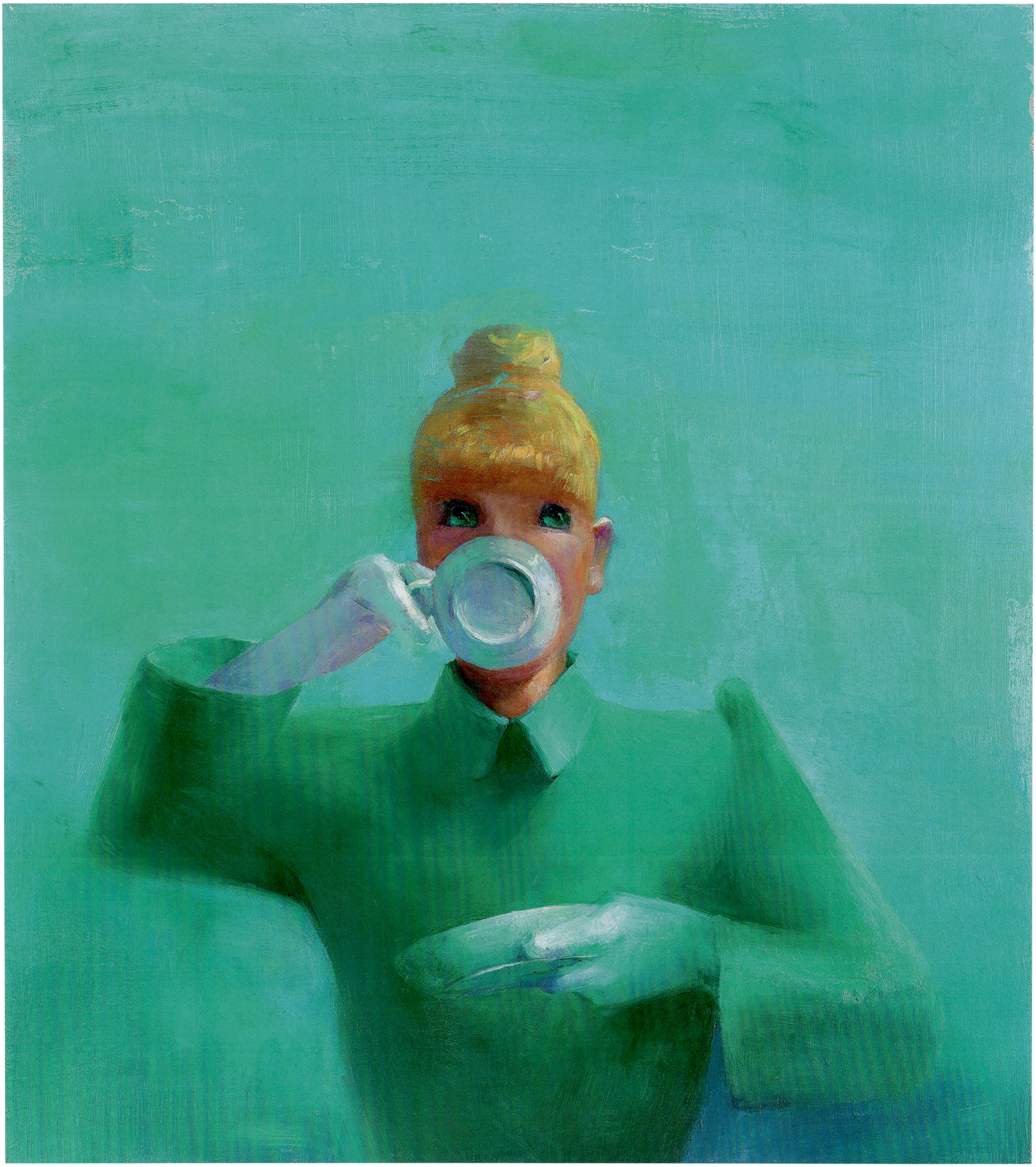

THE ONES THAT CAN'T: TEA,
1991–92
OIL ON LINEN
66 X 61 CM

possibly evasive, certainly reticent, while those in the 1991 paintings, as characters, are hardly assertive or confrontational. When I saw them back in 1993, these young women seemed to 'exude a shameful consciousness of being looked at, of vulnerability before a sentimentalizing gaze that is also a sexualizing one'.[12] In other words, they were not actively showing themselves, but simply acquiescing to the fact of being seen. They 'don't want to' – like Herman Melville's Bartleby, they would 'prefer not to' – but rather than indulging in the scrivener's quiescent noncompliance they are finding in themselves the strength to submit. The question is, perhaps, whether that act of submission is stronger, allows for more possibility, than the act of withdrawal, as it seems to be represented in the 1990 paintings. And in a certain sense, that question is not inherently answerable – not by reason, anyway. Only through experience. And experience reveals that the potential inherent in the bad babies turned out to be practically limitless, we have no experience to tell us what might have been the outcome if Yuskavage had stuck to the aesthetic of withdrawal implied by her paintings up to 1990. Somehow, I find it less plausible that she ever could have been a mediocre painter; I suspect she'd have found a different route to artistic fulfillment because she is an unstoppable force whether coming or going.

But wait. Besides this allegorical facing or turning away of their figures, there's another difference between the paintings of 1990 and those of 1991, and it's an even more striking one: the very different approach to colour. In 1990 – as in her paintings before then – it is earthen and subdued. Am I wrong to feel a connection between the muted hues of Yuskavage's tonally subtle near-monochromy and the dusty blues and bricklike ochres so beloved of William Bailey, the figurative painter who was a longtime force in the Yale painting department (and whose *New York Times* obituary in 2020 cited Yuskavage, as well as her Yale classmate John Currin, among 'the artists influenced by him and his way of seeing')?[13] The influence lay, perhaps, in being shown one way not to be a painter. Still, if his obituarist is right in saying that 'Bailey's female figures, some clothed in a simple shift or robe and others partly or entirely nude, are disconcertingly impassive, implacable and unreadable, fleshly presences breathing an otherworldly air' – and it sounds right to me – then Yuskavage might still have been taking hints from him in 1991, five years after she left the Yale campus.[14]

It was Bailey's chromatic understatement that had to go. That's the real revolt embodied by Yuskavage's paintings – against a classical sense of colour. Even though both *Truly Yours* and *The Ones That Don't Want To: Bad Baby* are close to monochromatic, the hot magenta of the work of 1991 comes from a completely different aesthetic world from the cordovan of its immediate antecedent. This vibrant new kind of colour has a different feeling that is also a different meaning. And the artist was able, right away, immediately, to articulate what that meaning-feeling was: 'I want to expose a specific state of mind that I have experienced as female: the flight from reality through wallowing in one's fantasies and suffocating in the sticky, candy-flavoured sentiment that springs up around this state of mind. It's an extreme case of vertigo – the fear, not of falling, but of the knowledge that you want to fall. I was born as a painter when I woke and found myself drenched in this saccharin-goo.'[15] The affect is in the descriptives: sticky, candy-flavoured, saccharin, goo. It involves the viscous, the excessive, the poisonously enticing. It seems to represent a feeling that a woman experiences in herself but it also represents the effect her presence might have on someone else, possibly but not necessarily male.

*

Before and after the shift that took place in 1991, Yuskavage's paintings exclusively depicted single figures – female, with just a couple of rare exceptions – in undefined settings. In 1995, she essayed several versions of a composition centred on a blonde nude, sometimes (as in *Fleshpot*) depicted with the near-featureless face of a blow-up sex doll, whose background features a pair of small, rather indistinct oval portraits on the wall behind the figure. Those recessive portraits might be reminiscences of Yuskavage's pre-1991 style, but they are also tentative steps towards an increase (by proxy, you might say) in the paintings' population while also functioning as more specific décor than the settings had included

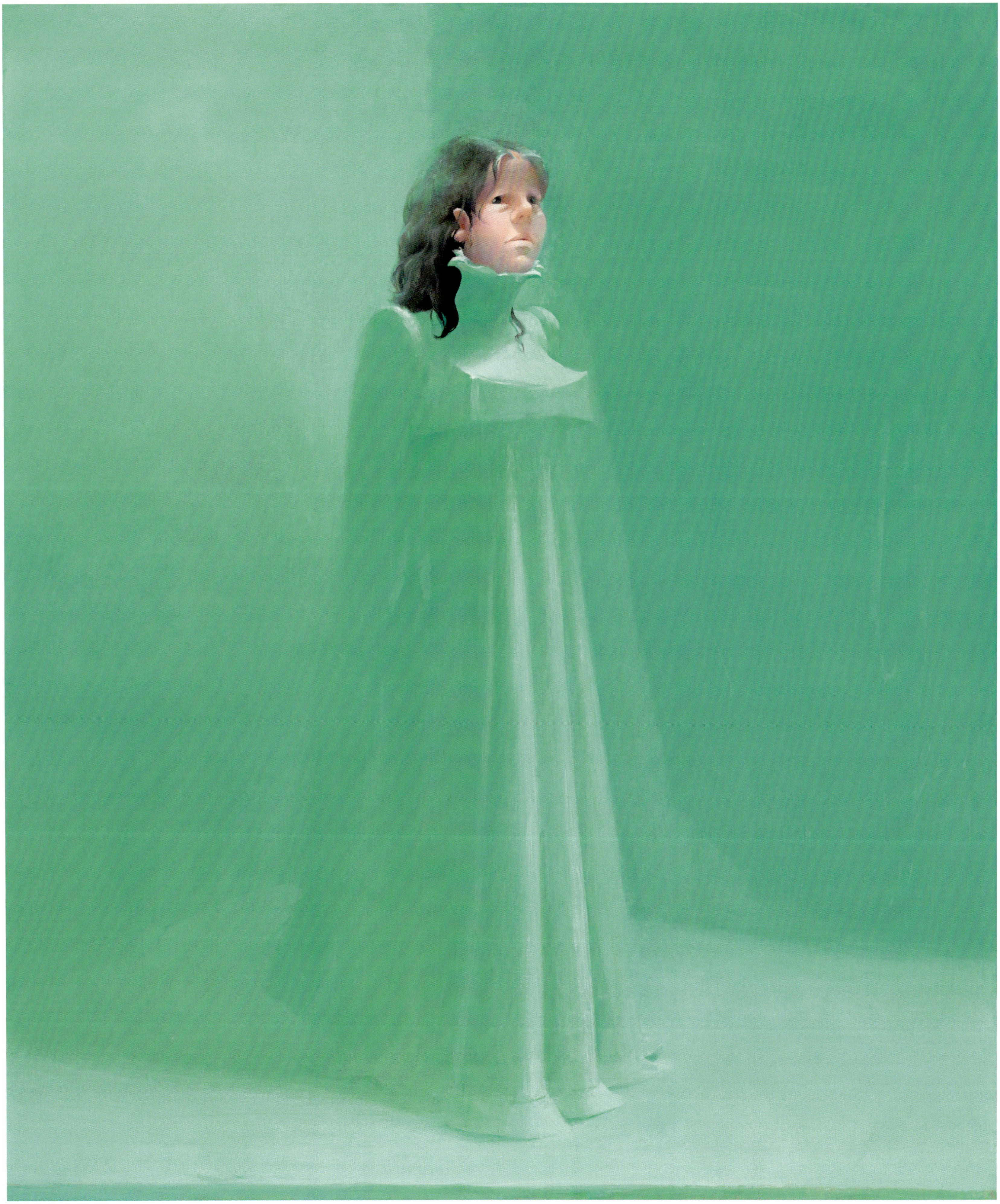

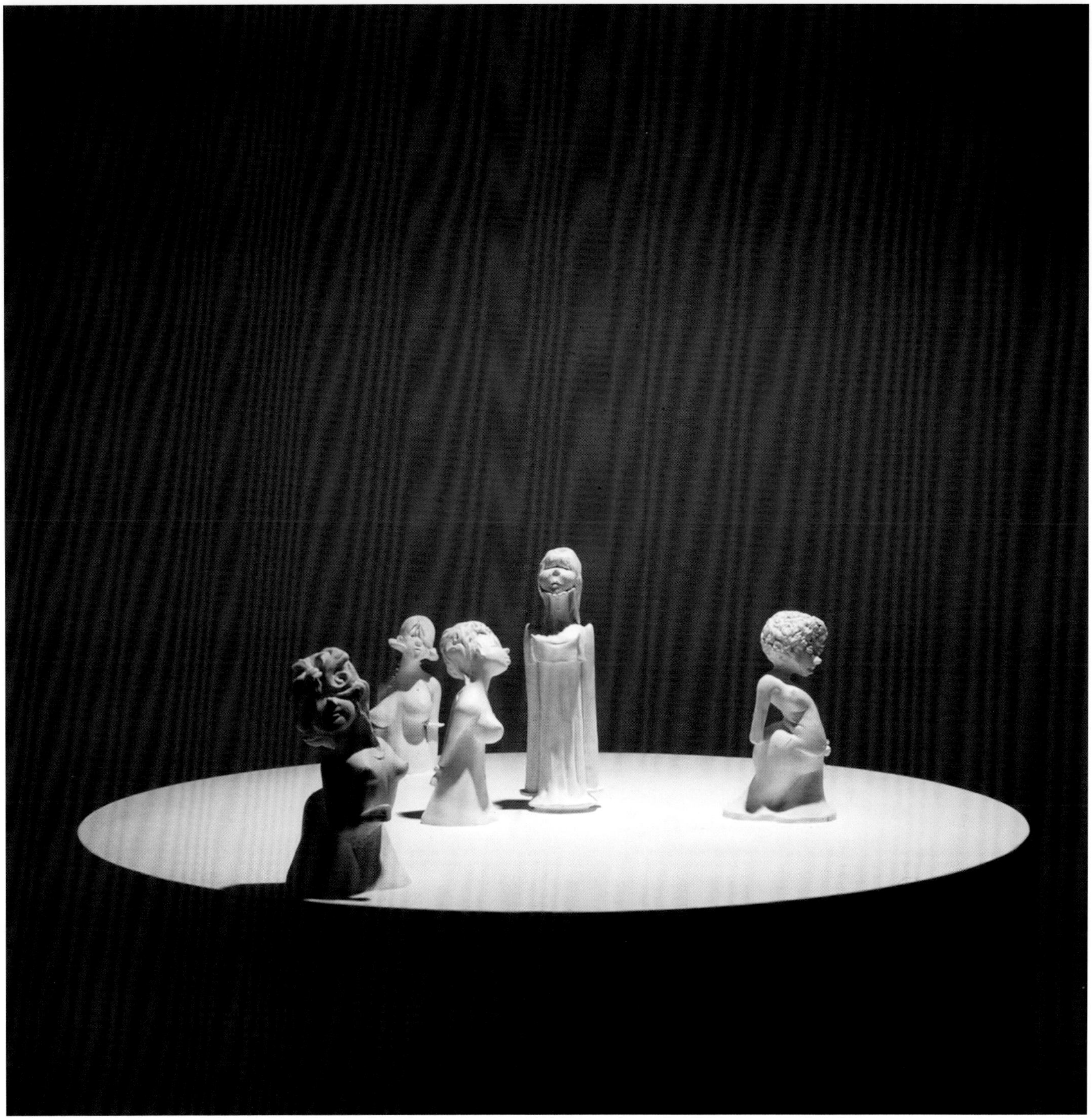

from left,
ASSPICKING, 1996
CAST HYDROCAL WITH
ARTIFICIAL PEARLS AND
ARTIFICIAL FLOWERS
24 X 10 X 13 CM

FOODEATING, 1996
CAST HYDROCAL WITH
ARTIFICIAL PEARLS AND
ARTIFICIAL FLOWERS
26 X 11 X 14 CM

HEADSHRINKING, 1996
CAST HYDROCAL WITH
ARTIFICIAL PEARLS AND
ARTIFICIAL FLOWERS
13 X 11 X 9 CM

SOCIALCLIMBING, 1996
CAST HYDROCAL WITH
ARTIFICIAL PEARLS AND
ARTIFICIAL FLOWERS
24 X 10 X 11 CM

MOTHERFUCKING BAD HABITS, 1996
CAST HYDROCAL WITH
ARTIFICIAL PEARLS AND
ARTIFICIAL FLOWERS
23 X 12 X 9 CM

opposite,
TRANSFERENCE PORTRAIT OF MY SHRINK IN HER STARCHED NIGHTGOWN WITH MY FACE AND HER HAIR, 1995
OIL ON LINEN
213 X 183 CM

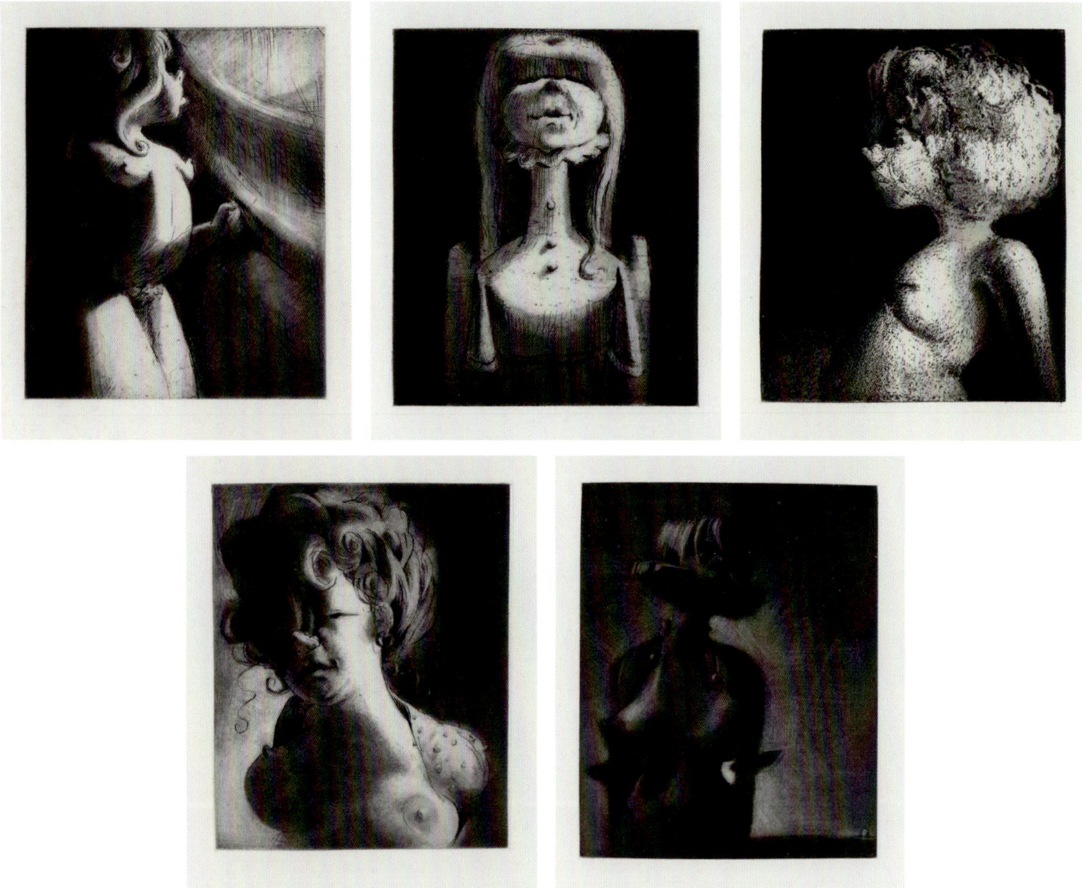

right,
BAD HABITS, 1996–98
INTAGLIO AND MEZZOTINT ON PAPER
45 X 33 CM

opposite,
BAD HABITS, 1996
OIL ON LINEN
213 X 183 CM

up until then. It was the next year, 1996, that Yuskavage first began making paintings with multiple figures, and in retrospect, this was as momentous a shift as the one that had taken place five years earlier.

In the artist's paintings up to 1995 – as I observed in an article two years later – the subject was 'the one-to-one encounter between the painting and its viewer' so that, 'through the figure, the painting allegorizes itself'. As emblematized by their single figures, the paint-ings look at you as you look at them.[16] This was a formal relationship uncontained by the frame – one that is, in Michael Fried's terms, theatrical. One can say of it what Robert Morris said of the Minimalist work that Fried decried as literalist and theatrical: 'The object is just one of the terms' in an aesthetic relationship that becomes 'more reflexive because one's awareness of oneself existing in the same space as the work is stronger than in previous work, with its many internal relationships'.[17] As Fried later reflected, this art 'theatricalized the body, put it endlessly on stage, made it uncanny or opaque to itself … and so on. There is, I might have said, some thing vaguely monstrous about the body in literalism' – remarks that in retrospect seem more apropos of the new figurative painting that Yuskavage was proposing than of anything Carl Andre or Donald Judd ever showed.[18]

But starting in 1996, Yuskavage began to multiply the internal relationships in her paintings, and thereby to put less accent on the reflexivity of the one-to-one confrontation between artwork and viewer. Placing multiple figures in her scenes meant positioning them with respect to each other and therefore called for more specificity and articulation of, precisely, the *place* in which they were set. It also inevitably evokes the possibility of psychological and narrative relationships among them (though these were left elusive and implicit rather than being spelled out). Thus in *Bad Habits*, 1996, we see three figures clearly disposed in space: the one on the right, nude, in the foreground; the one on the left, seminude, in the middle ground; and the central one, clothed, furthest away – which means, in turn, that we read the setting, although it remains absolutely undetailed, as a place, in fact a room, rather than as a nebulous and essentially abstract surround. We are also faced with the question: *is* the background figure meant to be seen as human, or might it be a sculpture, a sort of idol? The painting forces this question upon us without providing an answer. That the three figures do not look at each other – and that in fact the only one of the three whose eyes we become aware of is the distant one who might after all be just a piece of architectural statuary – only makes things more ambiguous.

Bad Habits also raises another insoluble issue, this one irreducible to an either/or. That background statue-woman, like a herm, appears to be armless; the arms of the woman on the right, who is intersected by the

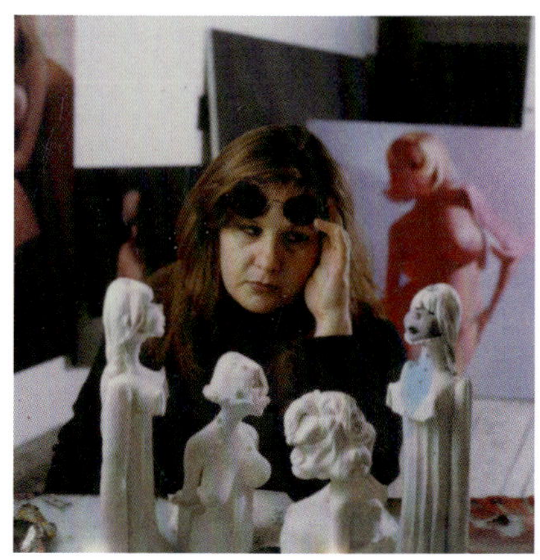

THE ARTIST WITH THE BAD HABITS IN HER NEW YORK STUDIO, 1999

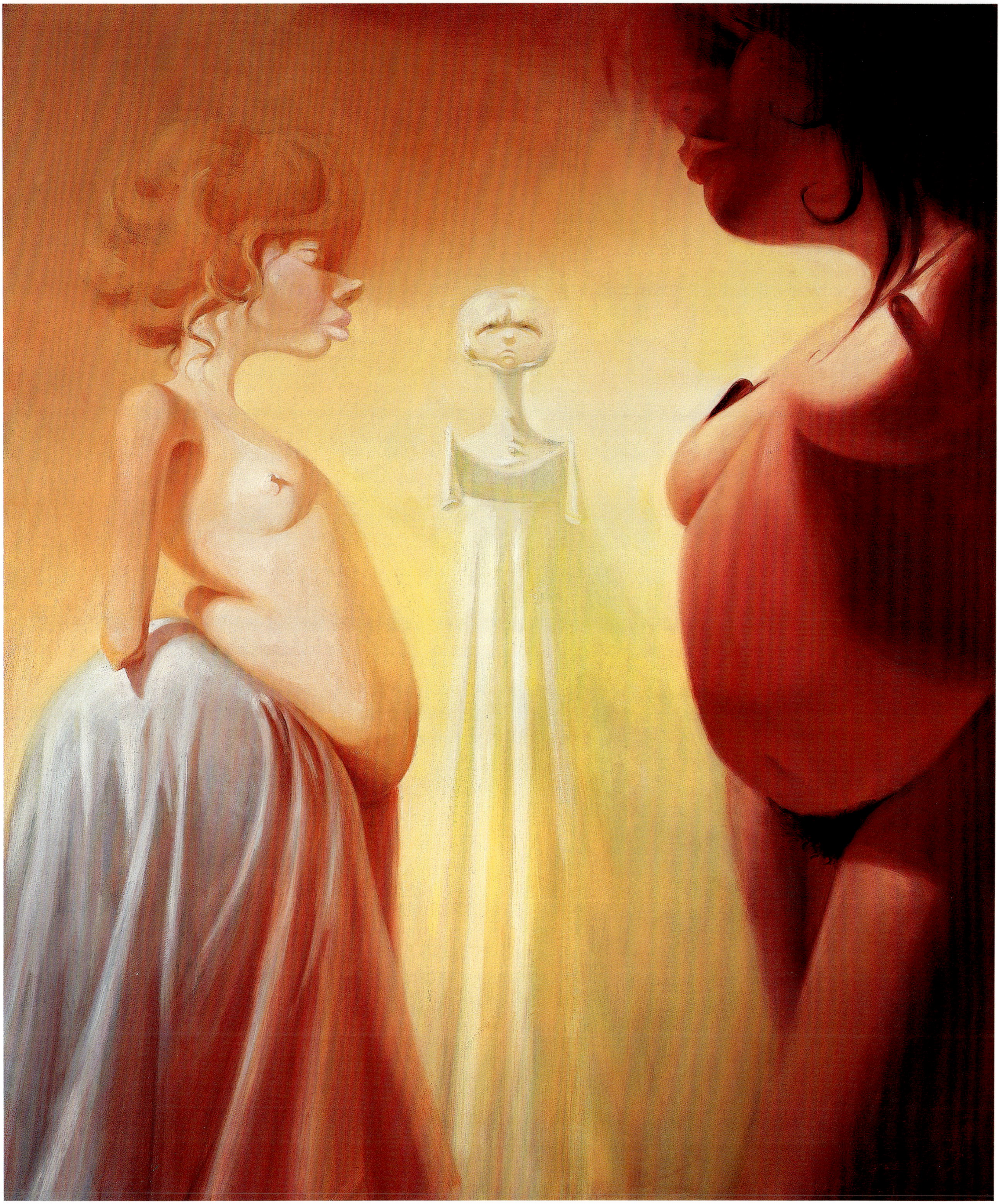

opposite,
NORTHVIEW, 2000
OIL ON LINEN
125 X 140 CM

edge of the rectangle, are unseen, and one would normally assume their unseen presence, but in this context one has to wonder if we are meant to think she too is armless. And then there's the woman on the left, whose right arm we do see. It might be bent at the elbow in such a way that the forearm is hidden, or it might be that she lacks a forearm. (And then what about the wholly unseen left arm?) This painting renders a disquieting vision of dismemberment without establishing that this is what is actually depicted. The viewer has to accept responsibility for what he or she reads into it – and you have to read *something* into it. This is different from the self-consciousness about the gaze evoked by the earlier single-figure paintings; it is a self-consciousness about the act of understanding, rather than about looking as such.

Soon enough, Yuskavage would place her characters – a word that, with its implication of narrative, would come to seem more appropriate than the implicitly formalist and nonnarrative 'figures' – in more fully realized, even almost naturalistic settings. Yet she would never become anything like what one could call a realist. Consider another triangular gathering, *Northview* (2000). Again, we encounter three women in a room, placed in three spatial planes – but the room is now more than merely an extrapolation of the space between figures, it has descriptive specificity, so that one can imagine it without its inhabitants: the upholstered couch, bookcase, wallpaper, heavy drape with its sash pulling it open to reveal a window onto the sky… I think of all those 1940s gothic movies, starting with Alfred Hitchcock's *Rebecca* (1940), in which a woman isolated in a luxurious country house is subjected to some kind of persecution or confinement. Yuskavage ditches the shadowy black-and-white that so effectively lent such films their foreboding atmosphere; instead, the picture is bathed in such a deliciously rosy light that one can well imagine why these three young women would abandon themselves to lounging in daydreams here. And yet their apparent unconsciousness of each other harbours its own kind of spookiness – as if each one were only a phantom to the other two.

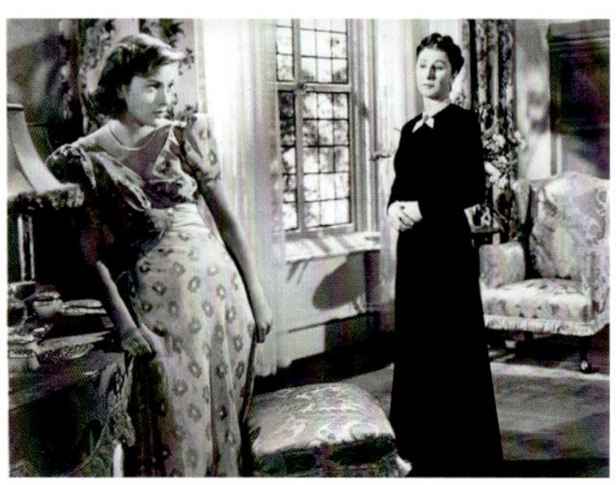

ALFRED HITCHCOCK
REBECCA, 1940
FILM
130 MIN.

Eventually Yuskavage's solipsistic personages would come into some kind of relationship with one another: *Harpo* (2002) and *Grooming* (2003), for instance,

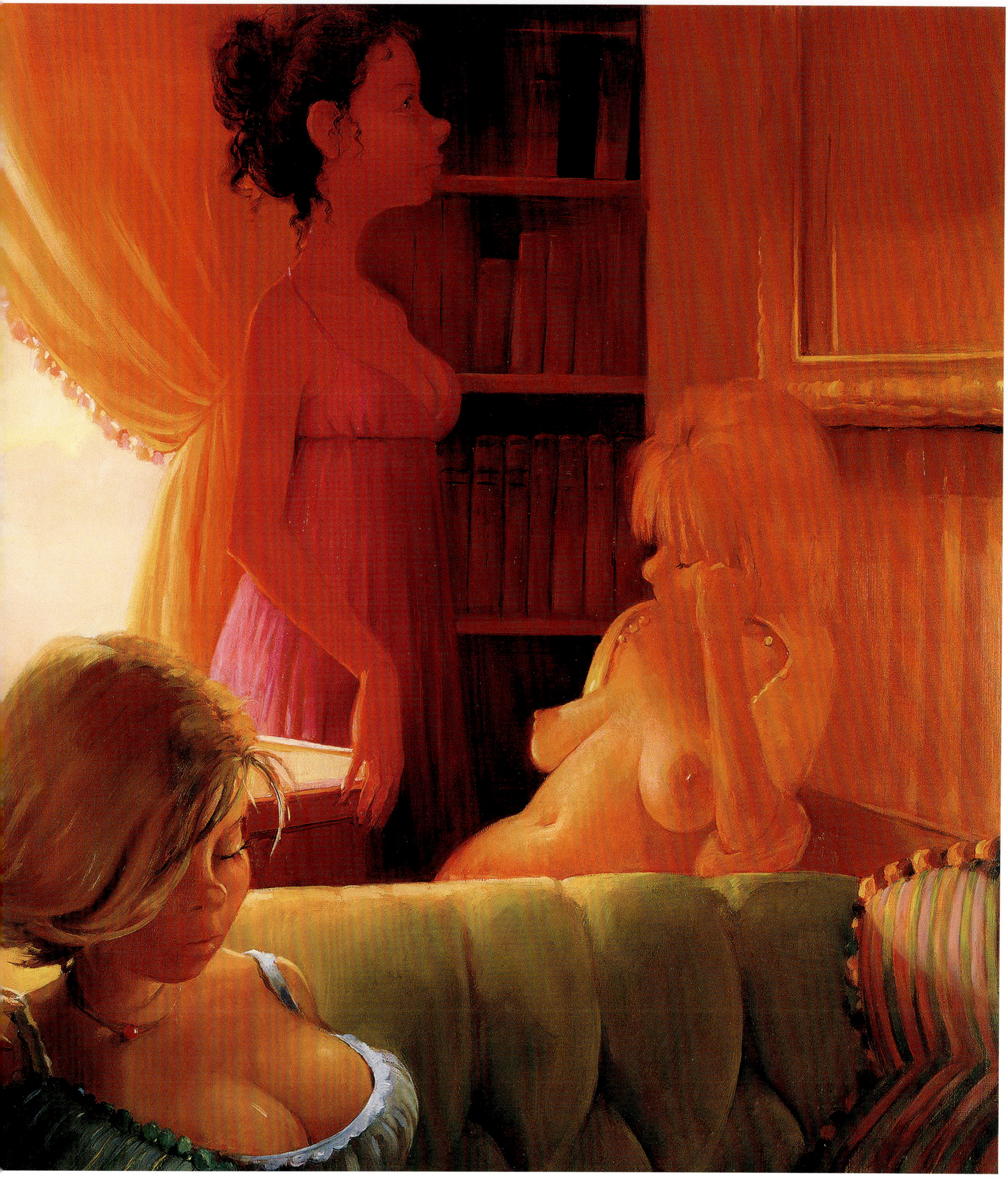

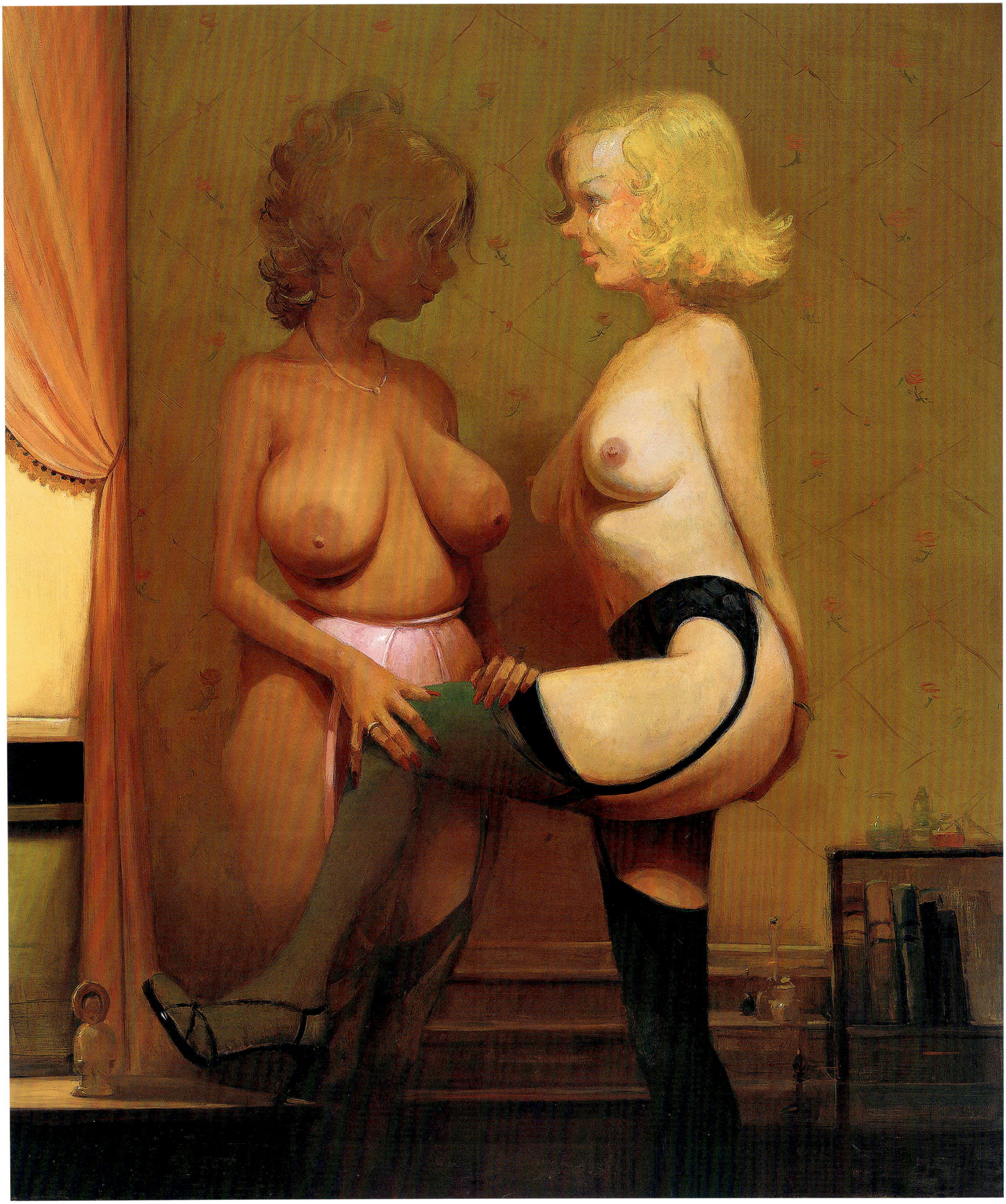

left,
MRS. AND MR. GOLDEN,
2018
OIL ON LINEN
71 X 60 CM

opposite,
HARPO, 2002
OIL ON LINEN
178 X 152 CM

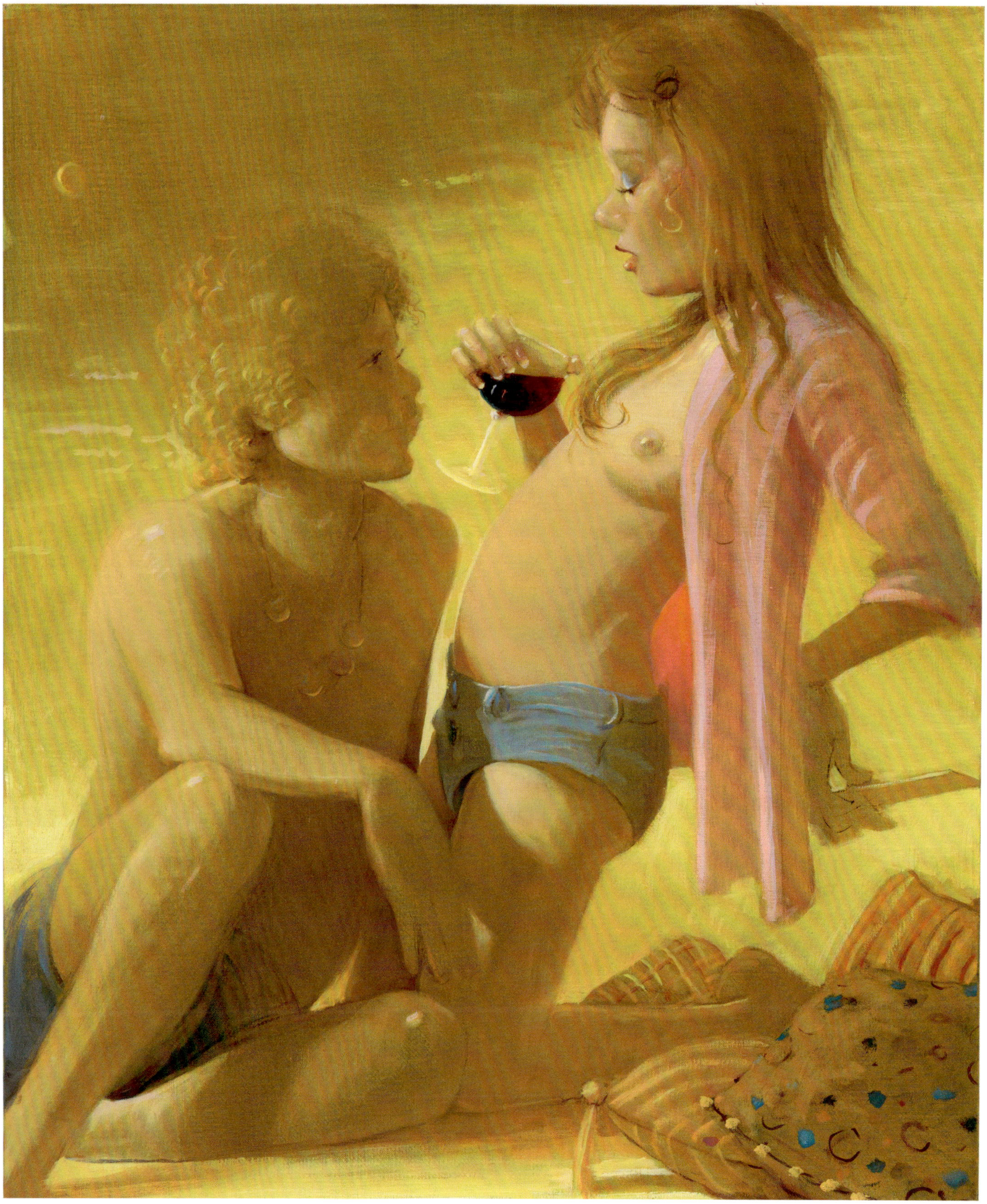

SINGLE WHITE FEMALE,
2018
OIL ON LINEN
123 X 111 CM

are early examples. And the single figure has remained a mainstay of her oeuvre. She is an artist more inclined to add resources to her vocabulary, to keep expanding it, than to exchange one thing for another by eliminating previous solutions. Figures, poses, compositional strategies keep returning in new guises, always morphing. The impossibly spread-eagled girl in the foreground of *Fireplace* (2010), for instance, recalls the sex dolls of some of the 1995 paintings, though she's no longer quite as unnatural in aspect. Her feline face is eerie enough.

Even where Yuskavage returns, as she periodically does, to her basic strategy of the early 1990s – the depiction of a solitary young woman in a more or less undefined space, facing the viewer – the painting's meaning is different: not as much about a direct formal antithesis between artwork and viewer. The headband-sporting hippie chick coyly folding her arms across her fulsome breasts against a Romantically cloudy sky in the programmatically titled *Single White Female* (2018), like the old-fashioned girlie magazine model on whom she might be modelled, is evidently quite conscious of being looked at and seems to enjoy it. She appears to have nothing of the shameful self-awareness of the 'bad babies' of the early 1990s, as is perhaps implied by the title, with its evocation of a singles ad. Her slightly oblique gaze is not that of someone who is being picked out by a gaze that must in turn recognize itself as inherently aggressive.

And yet the work retains the reflexivity of blatant 'art about art', now embodied in the (unusual for Yuskavage) device of allowing an appearance of *non finito*, incompleteness, towards the bottom of the rectangle. At least since the Renaissance, it has been axiomatic that:

There is something curiously intimate, or even invasive about seeing an unfinished work. Every visible brushstroke, line of under-drawing, or smudge of a fingerprint allows us to feel as if we are being let into an artist's secret world... The artist is exposed and rendered vulnerable. Yet somehow they become more relatable, more fallible – more human.[19]

Of course, in *Single White Female* this self-revelation is fictive – knowingly seductive, not unlike the coquettishly averted gaze of its subject. But fictive doesn't mean false. Over three decades, the artist's awareness of the intertwinement of cunning artifice and shamelessly visceral appeal has become more shaded and nuanced. 'I'm interested in formal language and emotional content,' as Yuskavage told de la Torre, 'formalism and feelings have a perfect marriage, if you can handle it.'[20]

*

Yuskavage has evolved her art slowly, deliberately, step by step – and that slow deliberation encompasses, as I've argued, even the supposedly radical leap she made between 1990 and 1991. Change upon change, what has remained constant is that her art has been formally and conceptually self-aware, and she has always insisted on this. In speaking about her art, she has consistently presented herself as a formalist. 'Painters have always had to believe in formal language', she insists, continuing:

It just didn't used to be called into question as much as it is now. It is a belief that pictures can be formally coded and tell a story, and that viewers will understand that code even if they are not painters themselves. In contemporary art the language of painting is like a dialect of ancient

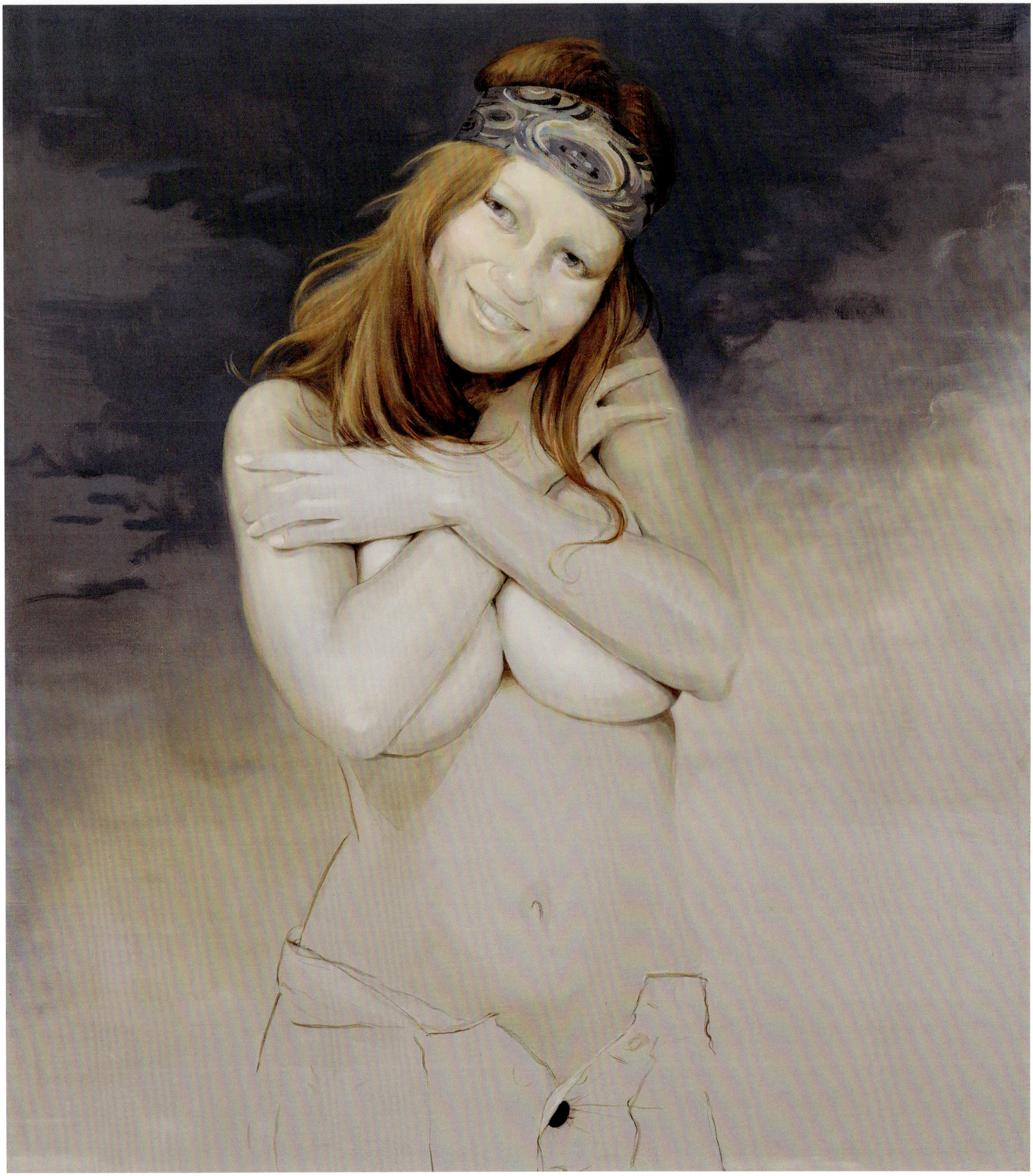

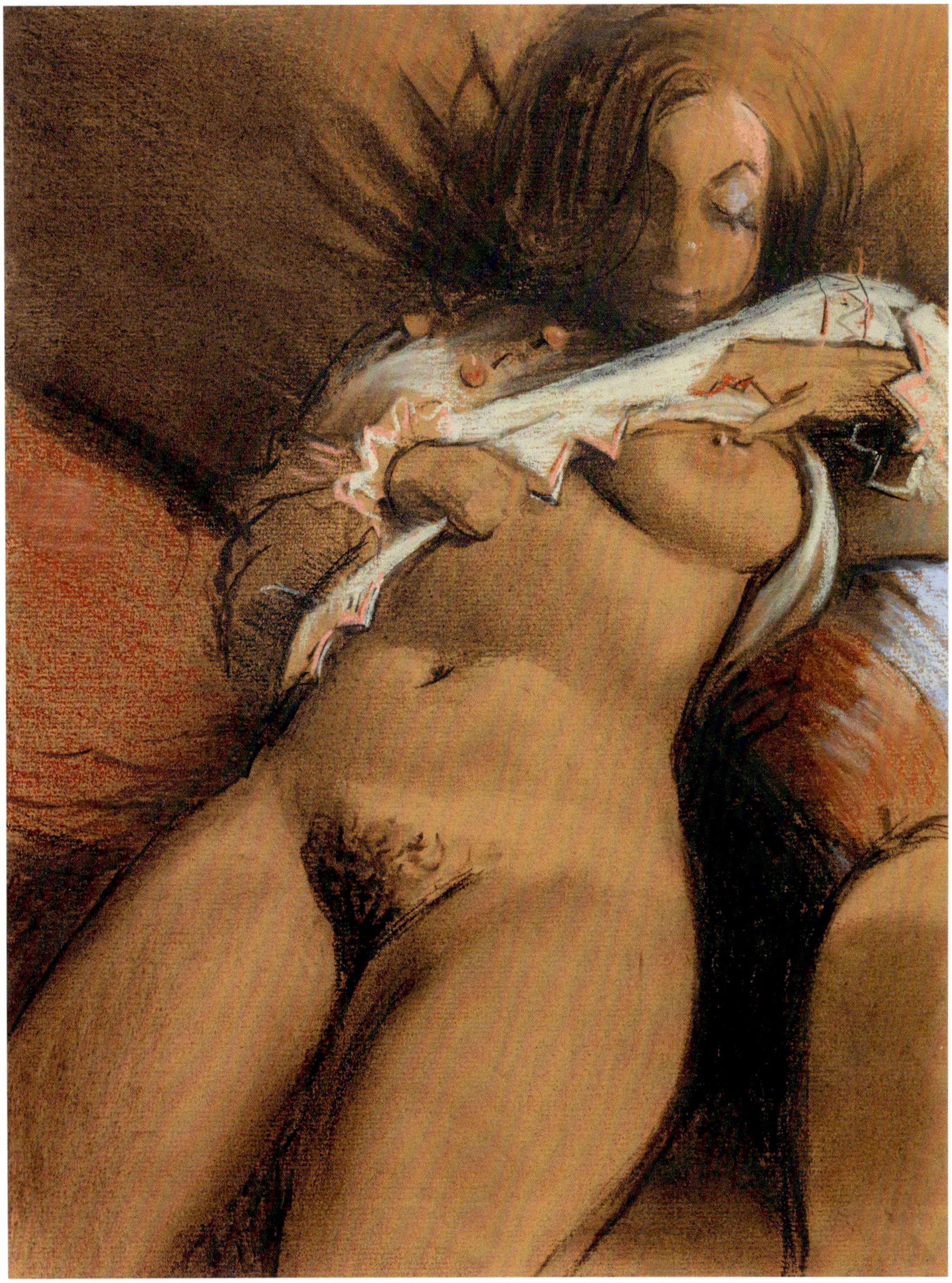

left,
NUDE #4 (SICK CLOWN),
1998
CHARCOAL WITH PASTEL
HEIGHTENING ON PAPER
32 X 25 CM

opposite,
NIPPLE, 1999
OIL ON CANVAS BOARD
24 X 18 CM

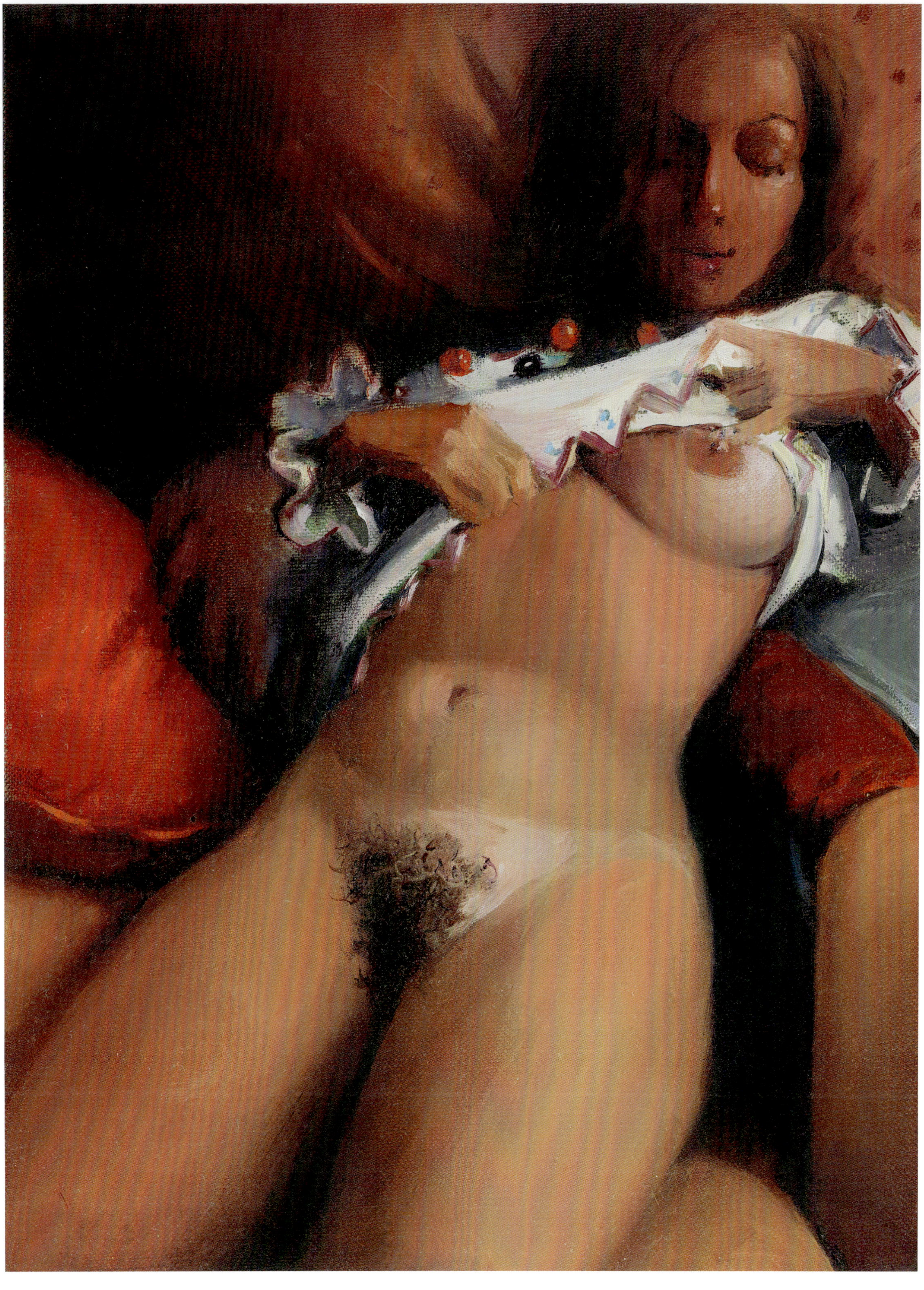

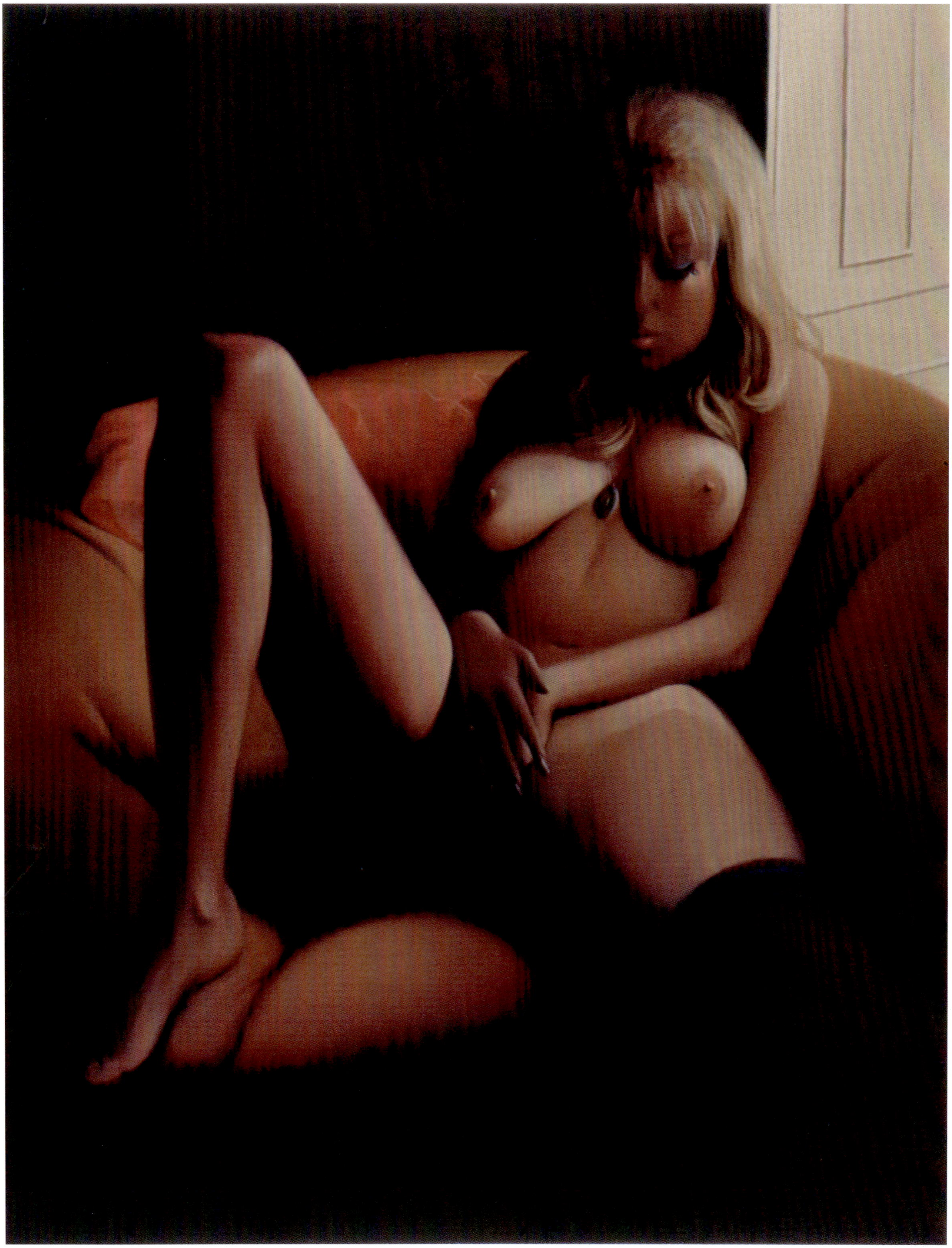

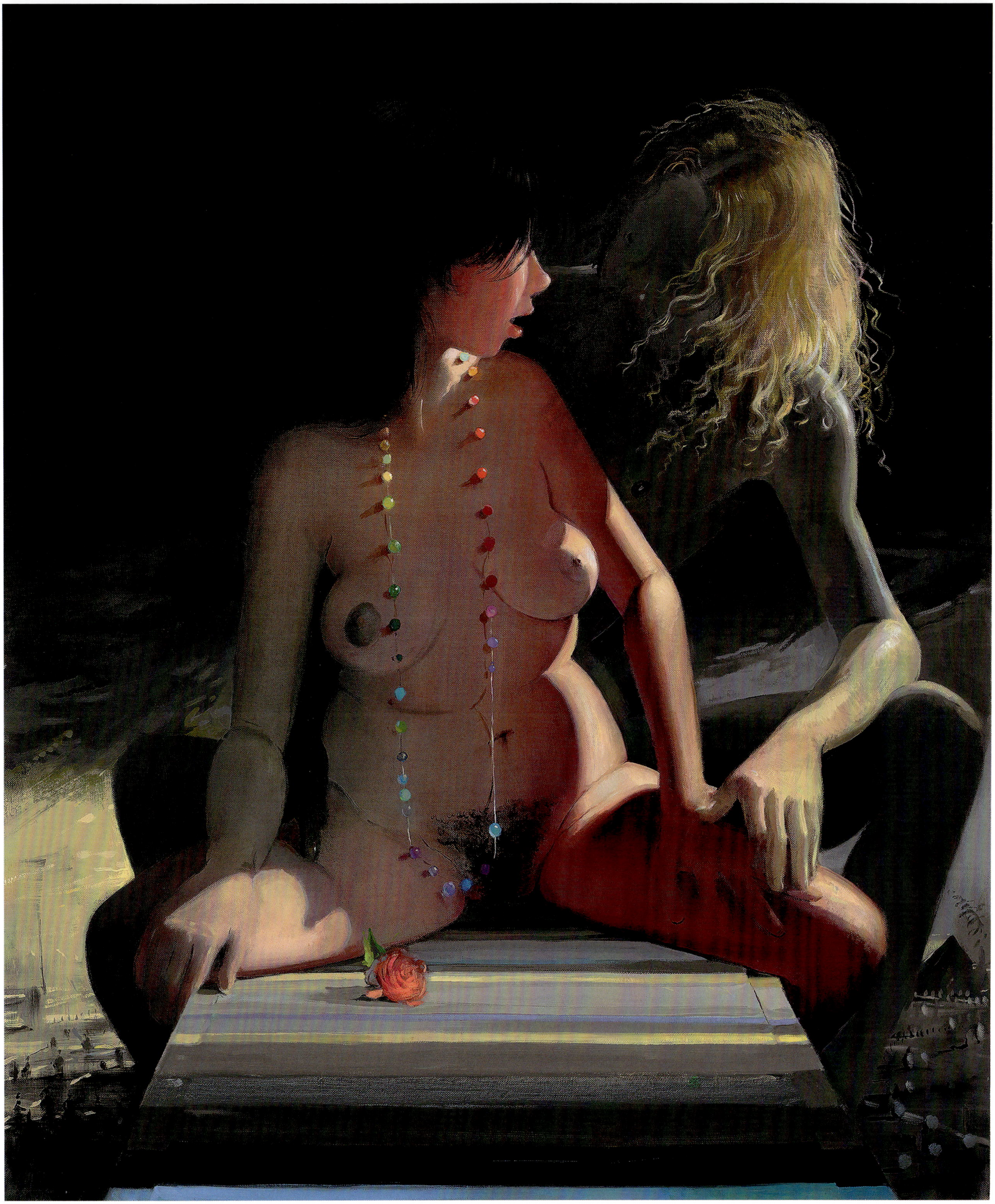

opposite,
INTERIOR: BIG BLONDE WITH BEADED JACKET, 1997
OIL ON LINEN
213 X 183 CM

previous pages, from left,
TRUE BLONDE, 1999
OIL ON LINEN
178 X 142 CM

MARDI GRAS HONEYMOON, 2015
OIL ON LINEN
127 X 108 CM

Greek – most people just don't understand it. Furthermore I don't know how many people are willing to relax and let the meaning of the painting unfold, but I like to think they will feel the power of the form, almost unconsciously, whether they want to or not.[21]

Yuskavage's subject matter is inseparable from this idea of the irrationally effective power of form – and of colour. Consider her recurrent use of masturbation, or in any case sexual self-touching, as a motif: *Big Blonde Jerking Off* (1995); *Interior: Big Blonde with Beaded Jacket* (1997); *Sick Clown* (1999); *True Blonde* (1999) – not to mention many smaller paintings. When Robert Enright questioned her about what seems to be her work's deliberately prurient appeal to the straight male gaze, noting that much of her imagery 'might have come out of a standard skin mag', her response was to insist on ambivalence and contradiction: 'Maybe the best way to approach my work is to recognize what it makes you think about and then think of the opposite. Maybe they can exist at the same time.' Her objection to Enright's 'fair enough' observation is that the gaze of the other does not eliminate inner life and agency, does not exclude that nonetheless we may be 'looking in on something that is purely intimate. And' – besides – 'it's not about any of those things. It's really about the act of painting itself. All my paintings, whether they're about abuse, about one chick climbing another chick, or about masturbation, always seem to me to be about painting' – an activity that is intensely tactile and affect-laden, above all for the person who does it, no matter how incommensurable the pleasure of the viewer might be with that of the maker.[22]

I should probably add here, given my emphasis so far on paintings of self-contained individuals, or of groups that share a space but who all seem to be entirely self-absorbed, that a whole additional essay might be written about the many remarkable paintings Yuskavage has made in which pairs of figures, sometimes but not necessarily 'couples', at first both women, subsequently a woman and a man, touch or embrace. I've already mentioned *Harpo* and *Grooming*; their successors include *Kingdom* (2005); *Piggyback* (2006); *Drag* (2007); *Afternoon Feeding* (2011); *Mardi Gras Honeymoon* (2015); *Wine and Cheese* (2017); *Ludlow Street* (2017)… all together amounting to a symphony of visual tactility, an endless exploration of painting as an orchestration of touches and of touch, perhaps – any kind of touch – as in itself already the beginning of painting.

With all this in mind, it may be time for me to go back to my starting point, the studio paintings Yuskavage made, mostly in 2022, for the exhibition in Paris in 2023. Let's look at a different one this time: *Big Flesh Studio* (2022), which might be the most complex composition Yuskavage has yet made. I'm almost tempted to say, though it may be blasphemy to say this in regard to any contemporary work, that it is her *La Meñinas*, insofar

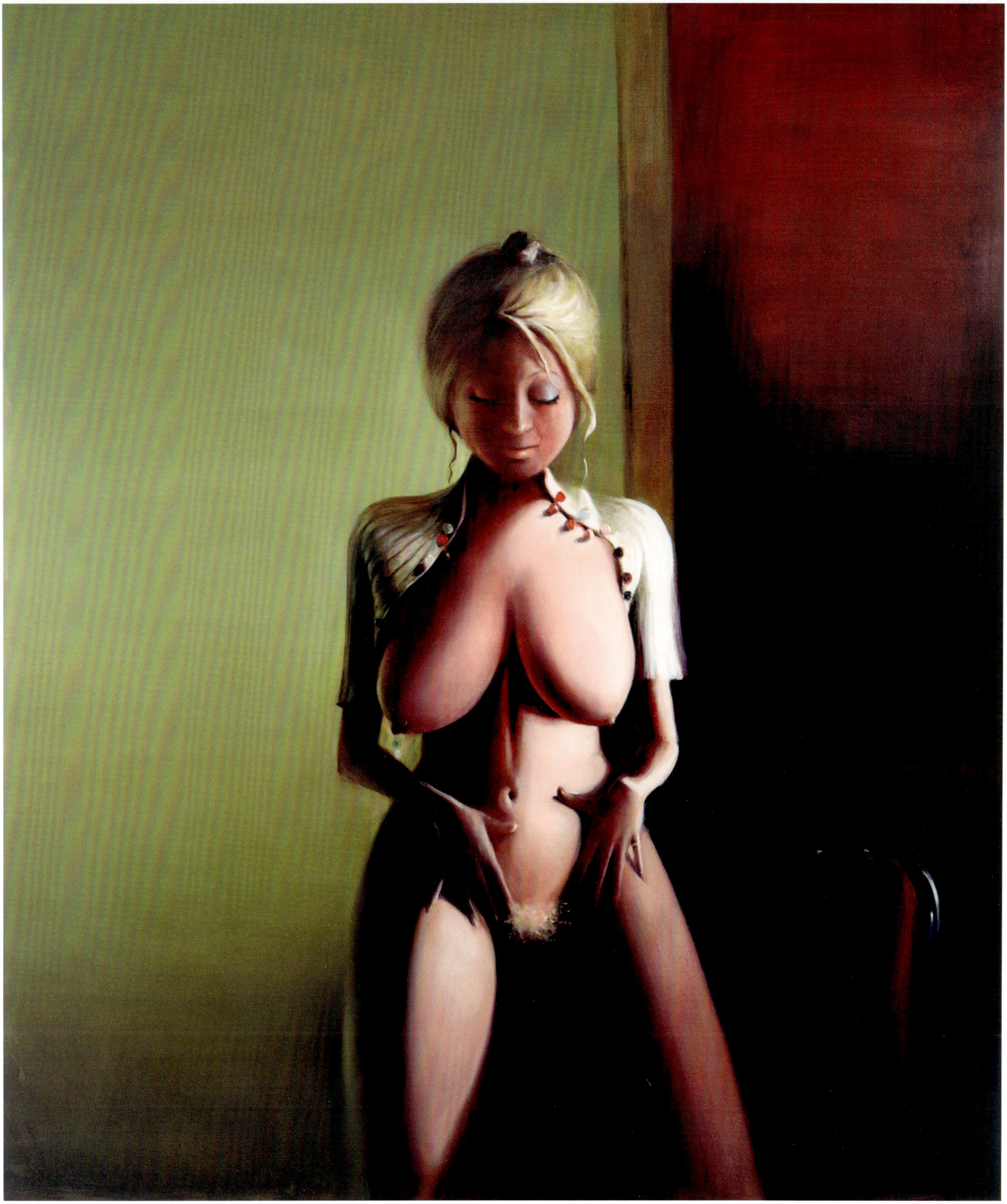

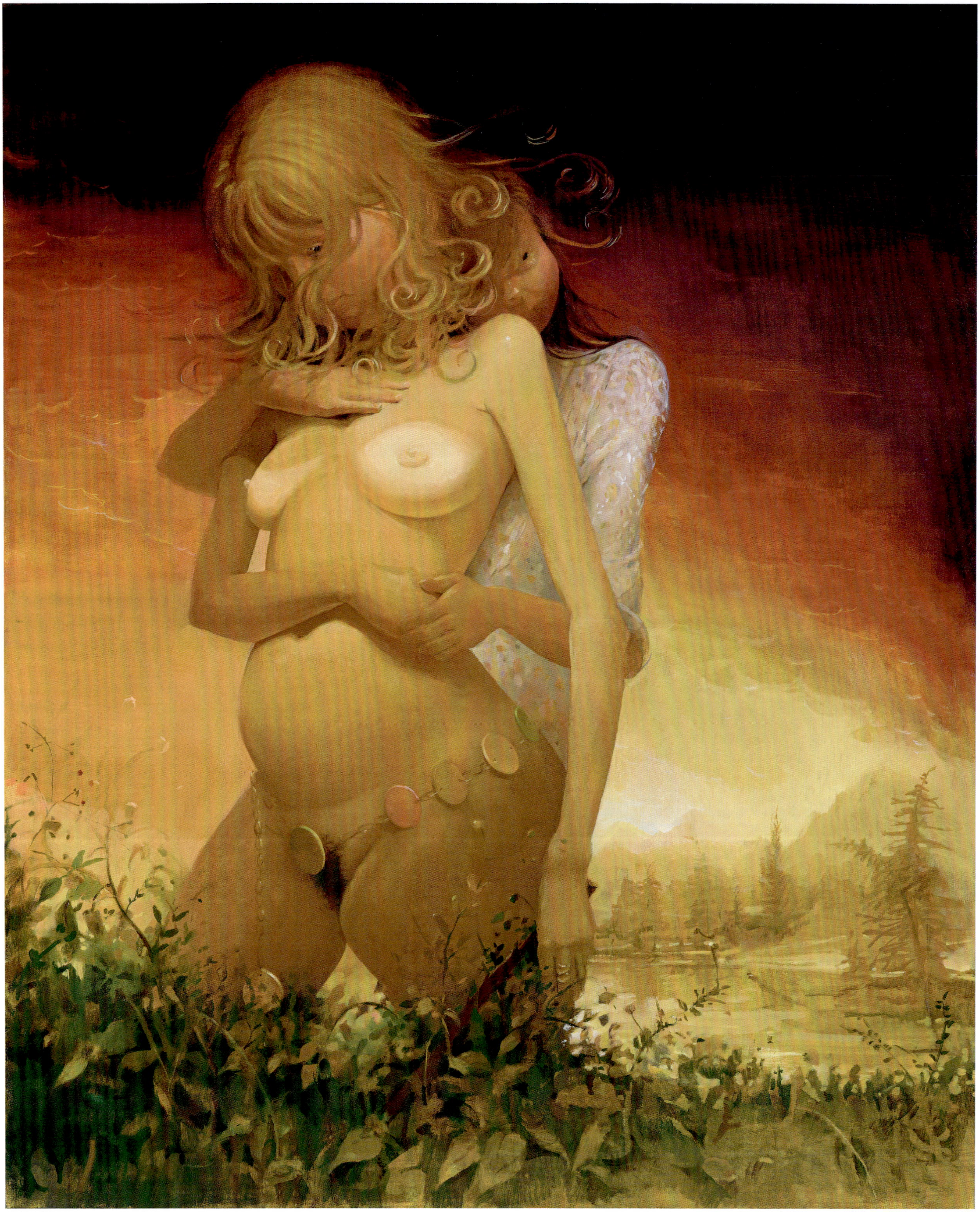

right,
PIGGYBACK RIDE,
2009
CHARCOAL AND PASTEL
ON PAPER
123 X 107 CM

opposite,
PIGGYBACK RIDE, 2009
OIL ON LINEN
152 X 127 CM

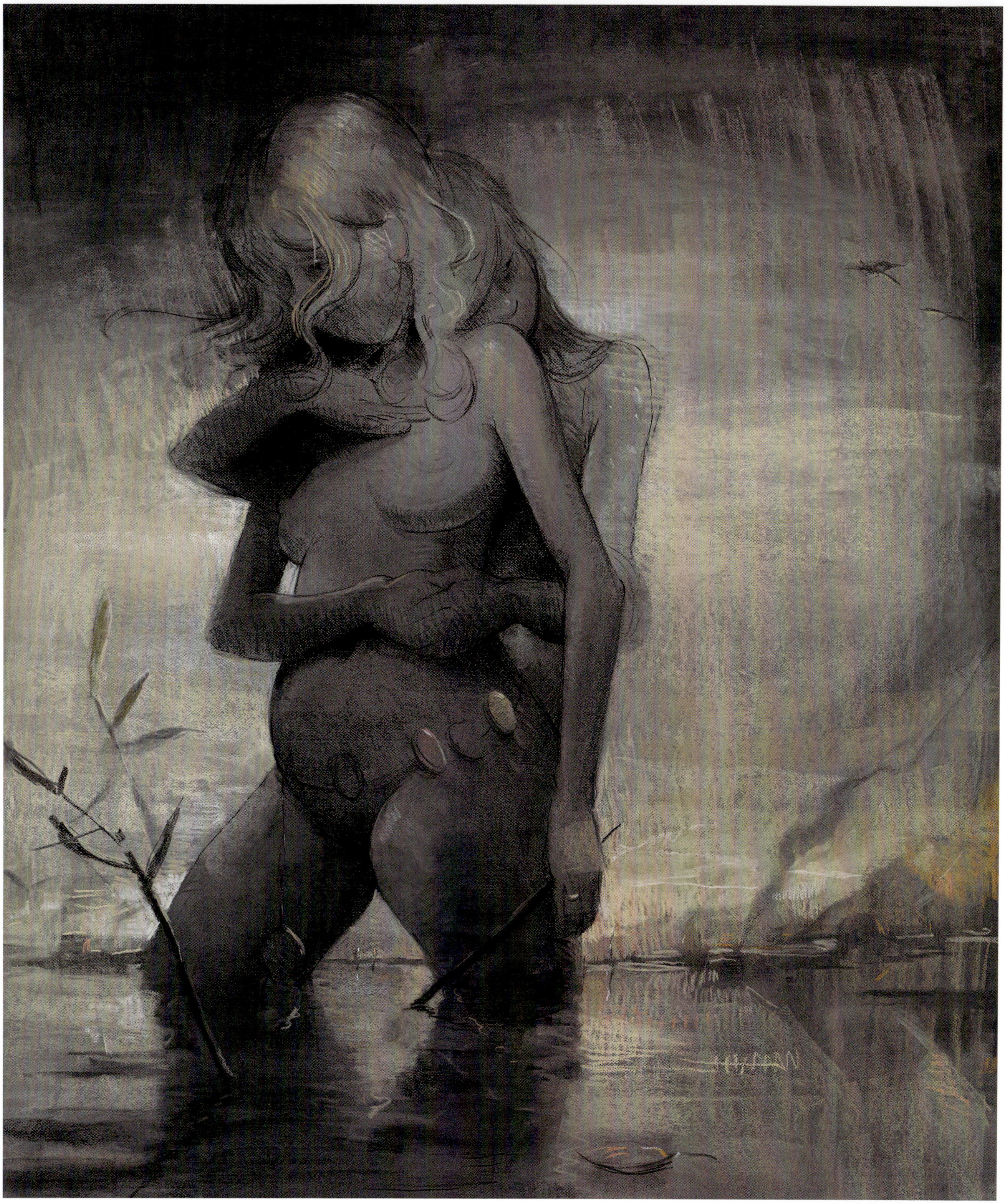

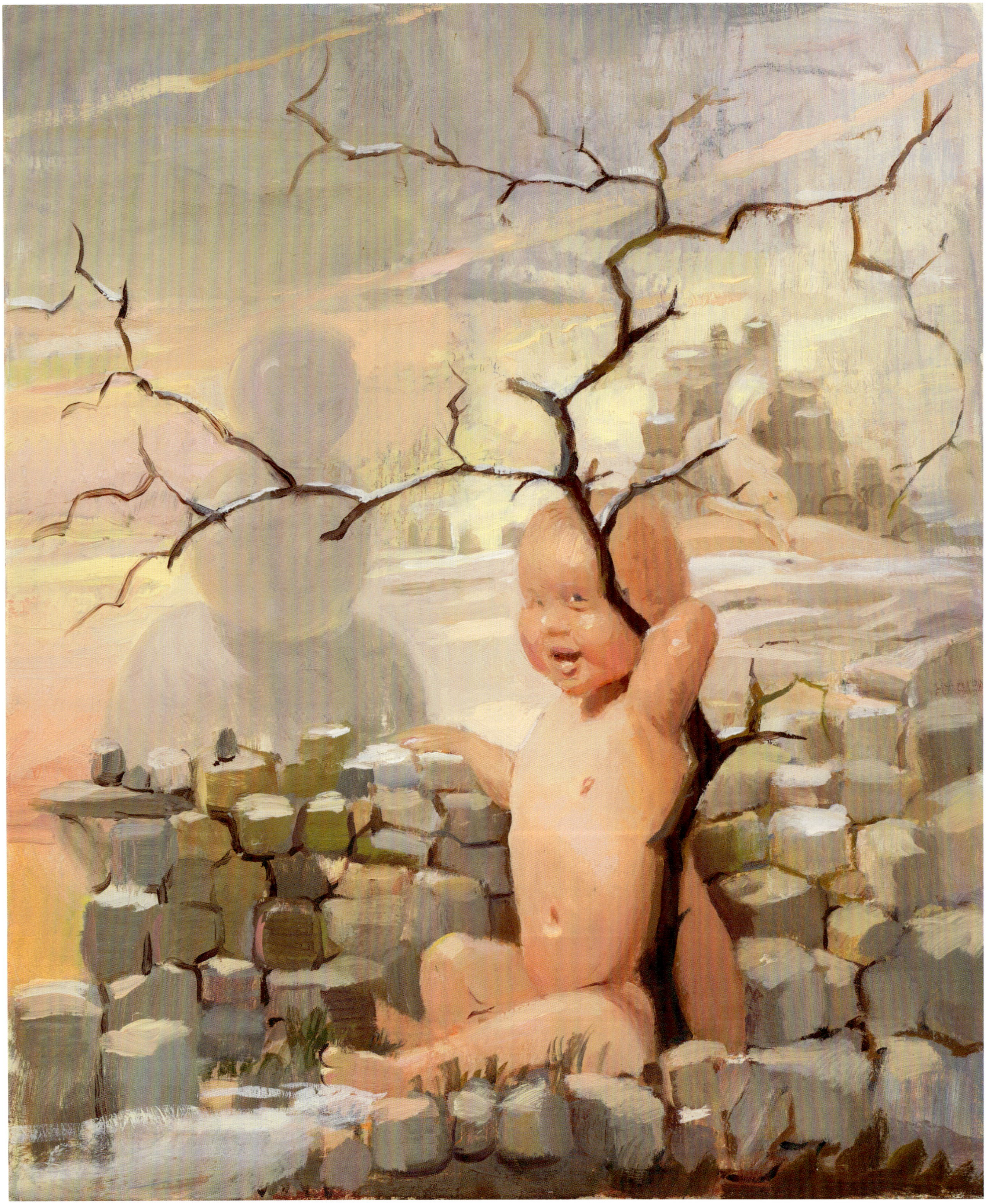

right,
DRAG, 2007
OIL ON LINEN
213 X 152 CM

opposite,
SNOWMAN, 2007
OIL ON LINEN
33 X 28 CM

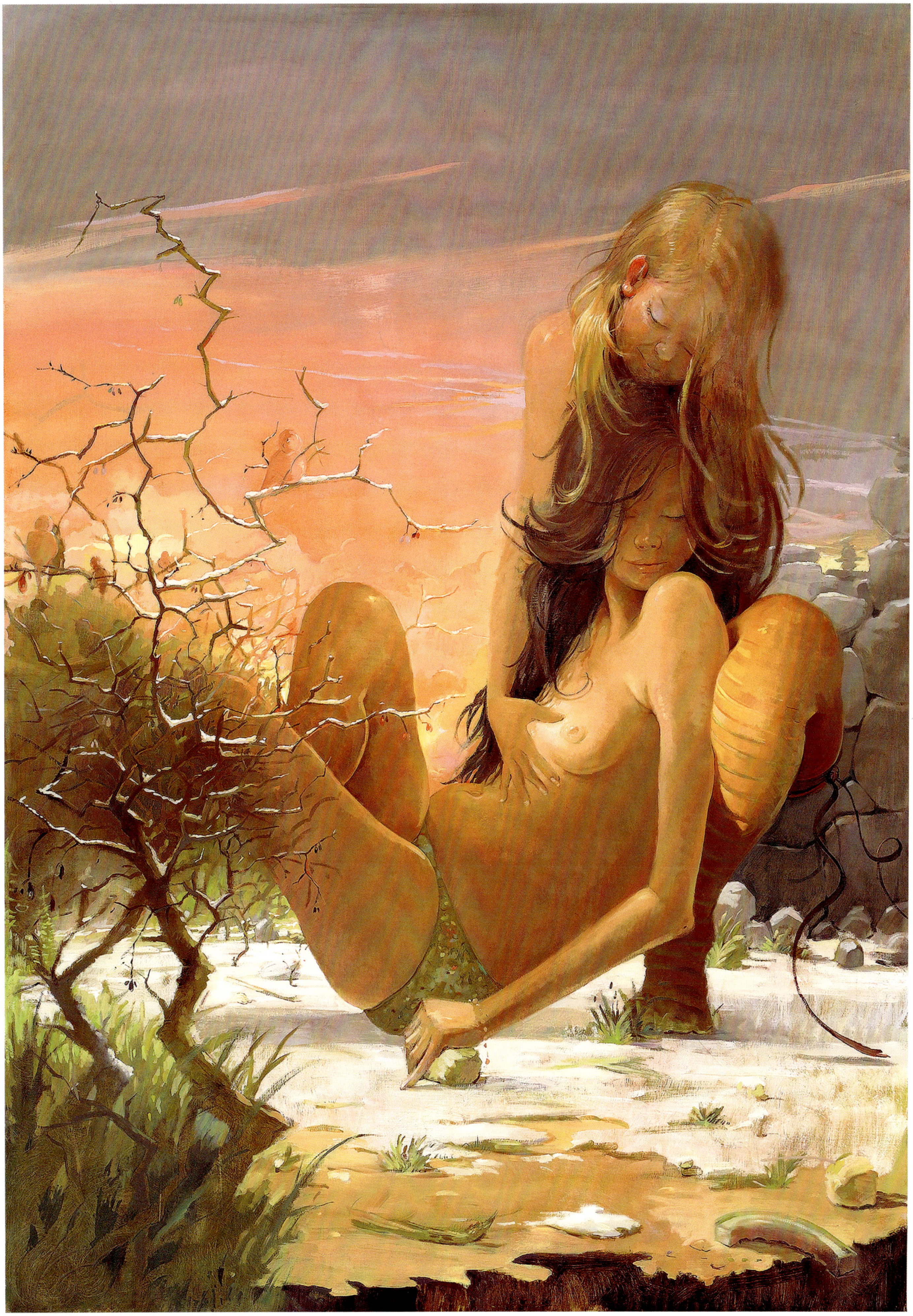

KINGDOM, 2005
OIL ON LINEN
147 X 117 CM

as it is, like the great Velázquez painting, what Michel Foucault famously described as 'a whole complex network of uncertainties, exchanges, and feints'.[23] (Velázquez's masterpiece is not exactly a studio painting in the modern, that is, Courbet-Matisse sense, but as an auto-reflection on the painter at work, it is their forerunner.)

Let me try to trace schematically the compositional structure of *Big Flesh Studio*. It starts in the right foreground, where a pair of women, one naked, the other nearly so, sprawl voluptuously across a small carpet and a furry pouf, along with a pot of flowers and a low cylindrical table surrounded by some indistinguishable globular baubles, one of which rests atop the table. Apparently these women are there to be painted; one feels that they are more like a still-life arrangement than a pair of studio nudes. Both face left, without there being anything in particular they are looking at, but the viewer's gaze is drawn that way to observe, a bit further back in the painting's middle ground, some studio furniture: a step ladder, rolling table, and so on. One among these items of furniture abruptly breaks the overall tonality of the scene (reddish with notes of yellow): a blue chair facing back towards the right. Just past the chair stands a woman painter whom we see from behind. She is so softly conjured up as an embodiment of the painting's rose-coloured atmosphere that she might easily have been lost to view had it not been for her placement behind the chromatically contrasting chair. She faces two paintings: the yellow medium-sized one on which she appears to be at work shows a figure similar to the one on the left panel of the 2010–11 *Triptych*, but flipped from left to right. This painting seems to be leaning – bad studio practice! – against a larger reddish-toned one behind it, which happens to be a modified rendition of Yuskavage's own *Night Classes at the Department of Painting Drawing and Sculpture* (2018–20).

That's to say that *Big Flesh Studio* is a studio picture that has another studio picture nested within it. And they resemble each other. Like *Big Flesh Studio*, *Night Classes* includes three figures, with a still life in the foreground. Just behind the potted flowers and figurine we see a nude young man wearing eyeglasses and smoking a pipe – one feels that the clothes he's not wearing must be tweeds! – caressing a woman clad in the usual striped socks and a towel wrapped around her head; his hand stretches towards her with such tenderness, but in this context, I keep looking for a paintbrush in his hand: I can imagine him fondly painting her into being, a figure brushed onto the canvas of his mind. A little further back, and paying no more attention to the amorous couple than they do to her, a nude model whose hair is adorned with blossoms takes a kneeling pose, as if some artist were busy painting her thus, though none is to be seen; apparently posing – making oneself available for picturing – can also be a solitary pursuit, another one of those activities that can be, as Yuskavage said of masturbation, 'purely intimate'. Besides, one's pure intimacy can be quite crowded with other people no one else can see. The figures of the

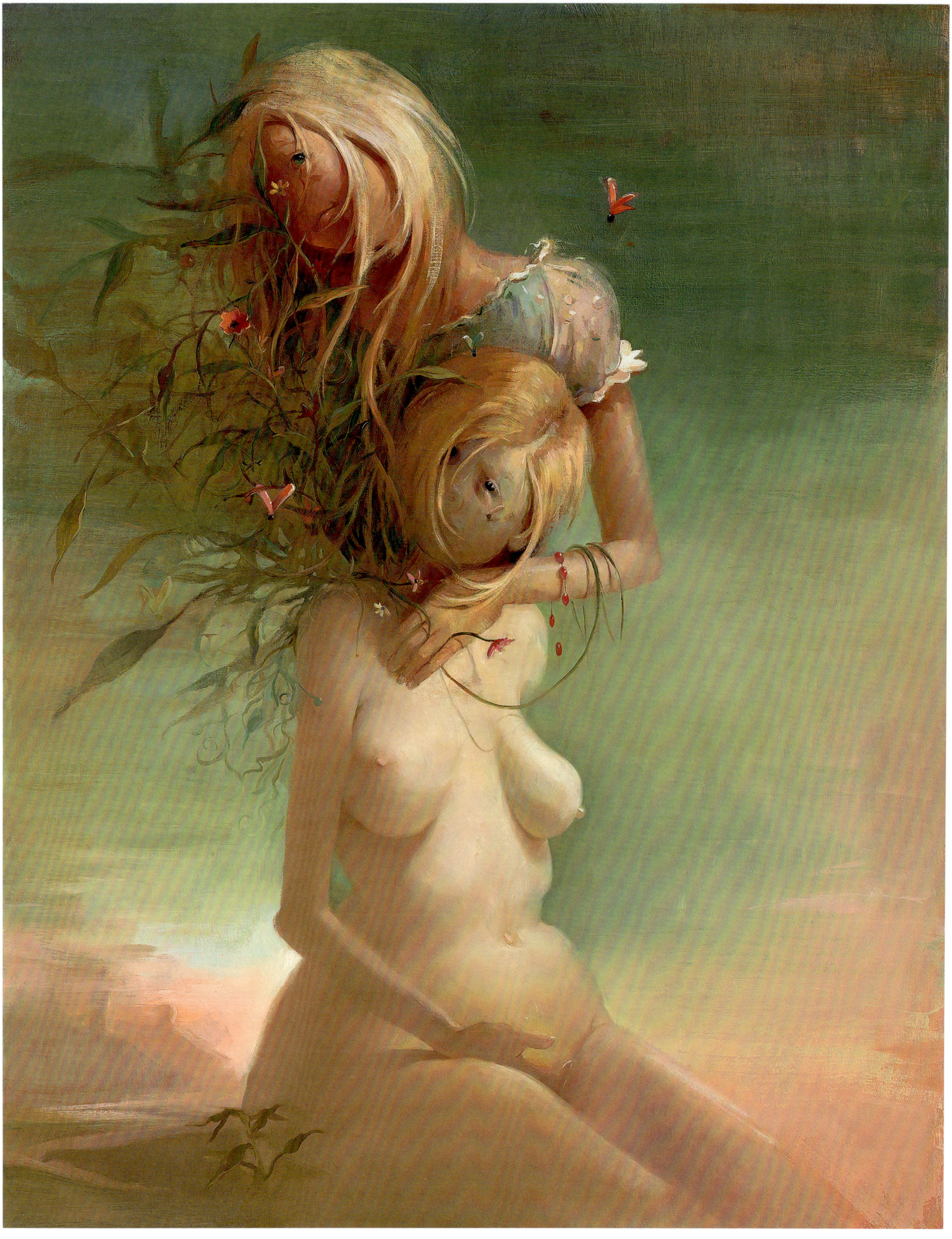

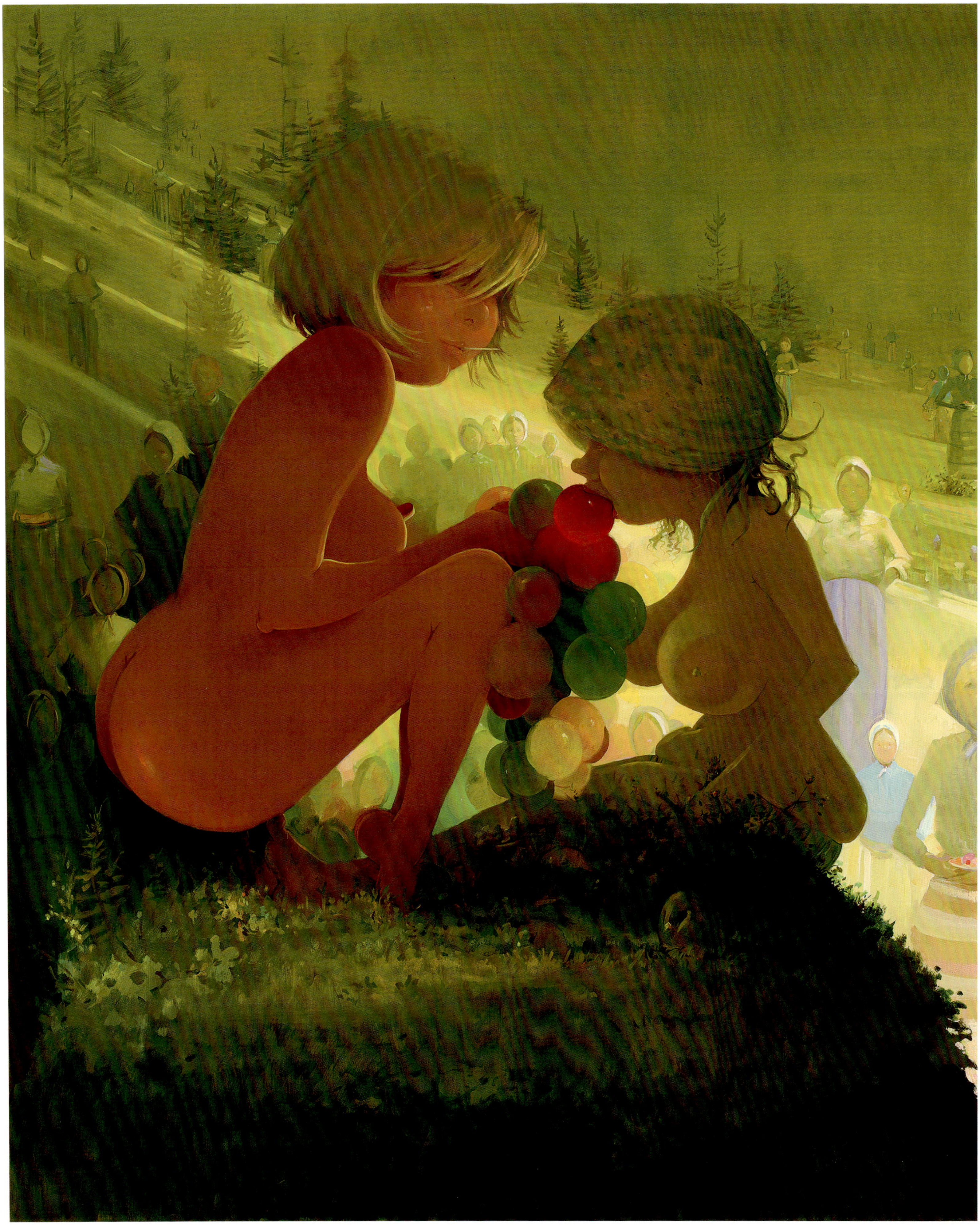

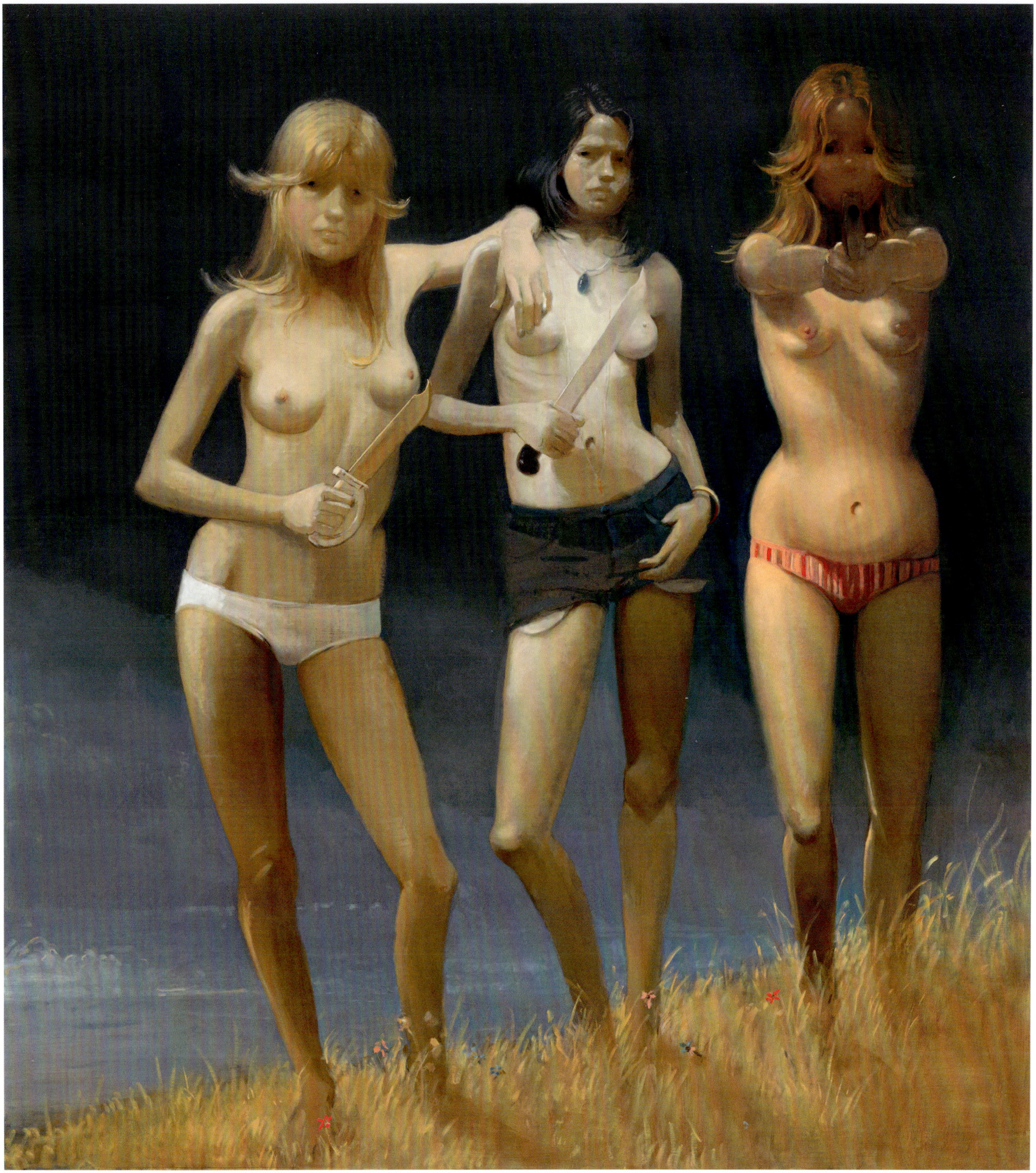

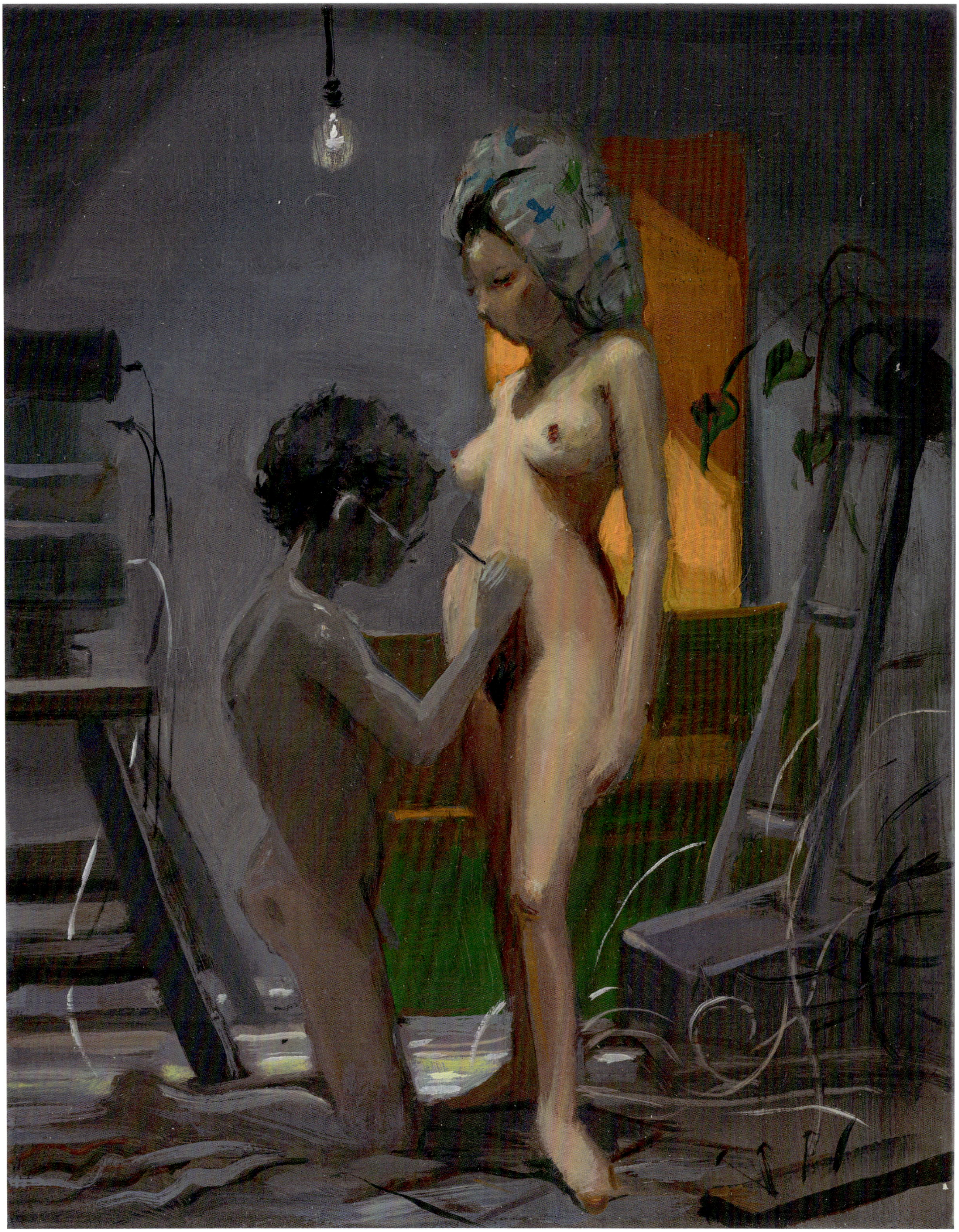

opposite,
LITTLE DEPARTMENT OF PAINTING DRAWING AND SCULPTURE, 2019
OIL ON LINEN
25 X 21 CM

previous pages, from left,
AFTERNOON FEEDING, 2011
OIL ON LINEN
218 X 180 CM

SCISSOR SISTERS, 2020
OIL ON LINEN
195 X 178 CM

two women in *Night Classes* are both framed by canvases leaning behind them, the one towards the foreground by a blue skyscape, the solitary one further back by a yellow monochrome – as if they were already beginning to merge with the pictorial world of which they are, of course, already of, the world represented by the artworks on the studio's back wall, mostly too small to be seen as anything but coloured rectangles, but also including, most notably, Yuskavage's 1991 painting *The Ones That Don't Want To: Bad Baby*.

It may or may not be true that all of Yuskavage's paintings are, as she told Enright, about painting. He seemed to think she was trying to pull a fast one with that assertion – admittedly, that's easy to say, but she actually walks the walk. And besides, a painting of a painting studio would just have to be a painting about painting, and doubly so when one painted studio contains another. And don't forget that Yuskavage has made *Big Flesh Studio* and its inserted version of *Night Classes at the Department of Painting Drawing and Sculpture* chromatically continuous with one another, as if to say that things can shift smoothly from one to the other. I believe they do. As it reasserts itself in *Big Flesh Studio*, however, *Night Classes* has lost its solitary poser (also the 1991 *Bad Baby*). It's as if the yellow canvas behind the intimately self-involved model had slipped off the canvas to become the separate yellow canvas with its sketched-out nude in front of the fully worked canvas. And if that's so, should one say that the nude model in front of the yellow canvas in *Night Classes* has morphed into the nude depicted on a yellow canvas in *Big Flesh Studio*? It makes sense. But would that mean in turn that the faceless painter contemplating that unfinished work is… the bad baby, come to life and now grown up, having recognized her true vocation?

Maybe that's going too far. But what's incontrovertible is that *Big Flesh Studio* is a painting of paintings, and a painting of the painter's work as embodied, not in the physical act of touching a brush to canvas, but of looking, of facing the painting itself (and not, for example, its public). In that sense, the painting contradicts or at least complicates its title. Yuskavage has spent a lifetime making as compelling a case as one could possibly imagine in favour of Willem de Kooning's so-often reiterated statement, 'Flesh was the reason why oil painting was invented'. And yet the same de Kooning knew very well that the mathematical constructions of perspective did not meet their limits in the painter's sensuality, but on the contrary, because 'Painting was more intellectual than that', and that it was through logic rather than desire that the Renaissance painter became, for his picture, 'the idea, the center, and the vanishing point himself – and all at the same time'.[24]

Big Flesh Studio tells us that, even more than de Kooning – and yes, more like Velázquez, though I still fear the gods of painting may strike me dead for mentioning him in regard to any other painter – Yuskavage is above all

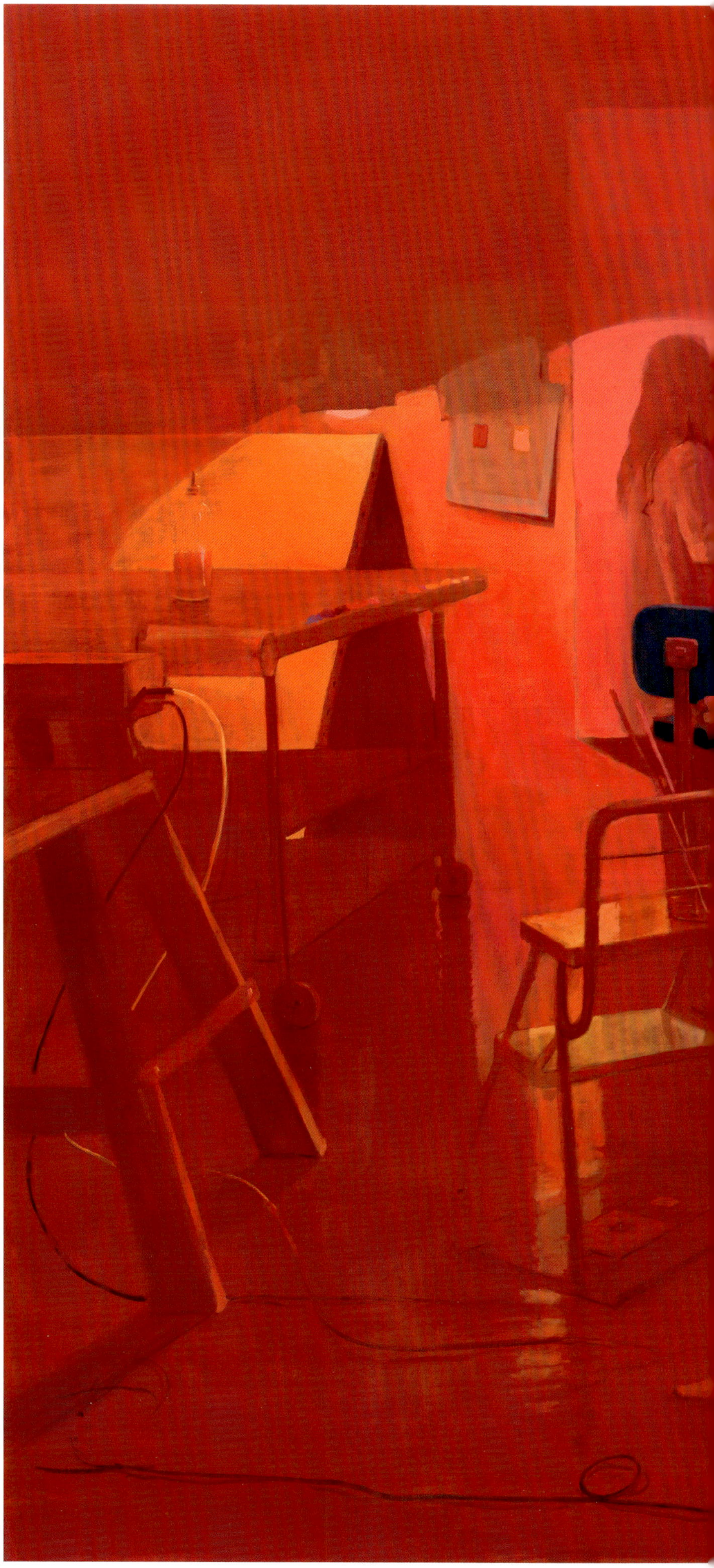

BIG FLESH STUDIO,
2022
OIL ON LINEN
218 X 305 CM

an intellectual painter. In paintings such as this one, with its multiple levels of nested representations, she has constructed, 'a whole complex network of uncertainties, exchanges, and feints', a canny mechanism through which to reflect on the meaning and substance of her pictorial art, and then reflect on the reflection. But notice: the uncertainties are all on the part of the viewer, for it is clear that all the ambiguities contained in the painting have been carefully calculated. The artist is in total control of her enigmatic creation.

*

Yuskavage came into her own as an artist by conceiving of her paintings as a challenge to the viewer. The works emblematized themselves as images of a painful vulnerability, but because they presented that image fearlessly, one could not avoid feeling somehow implicated by them. They were self-consciously provoking the beholder's self-consciousness. As Yuskavage herself said of them:

The images are representations of what the paintings would look like if they were to become human. They did not enjoy being impotent spectacles – they couldn't walk away or defend themselves from the glare or ogle of the viewer. But I could load these characters up with the ability to make the looking feel bad for everyone involved. The exchange would go like this: OK, go ahead and look all you want, but it's going to be unpleasant for both of us. The figure was

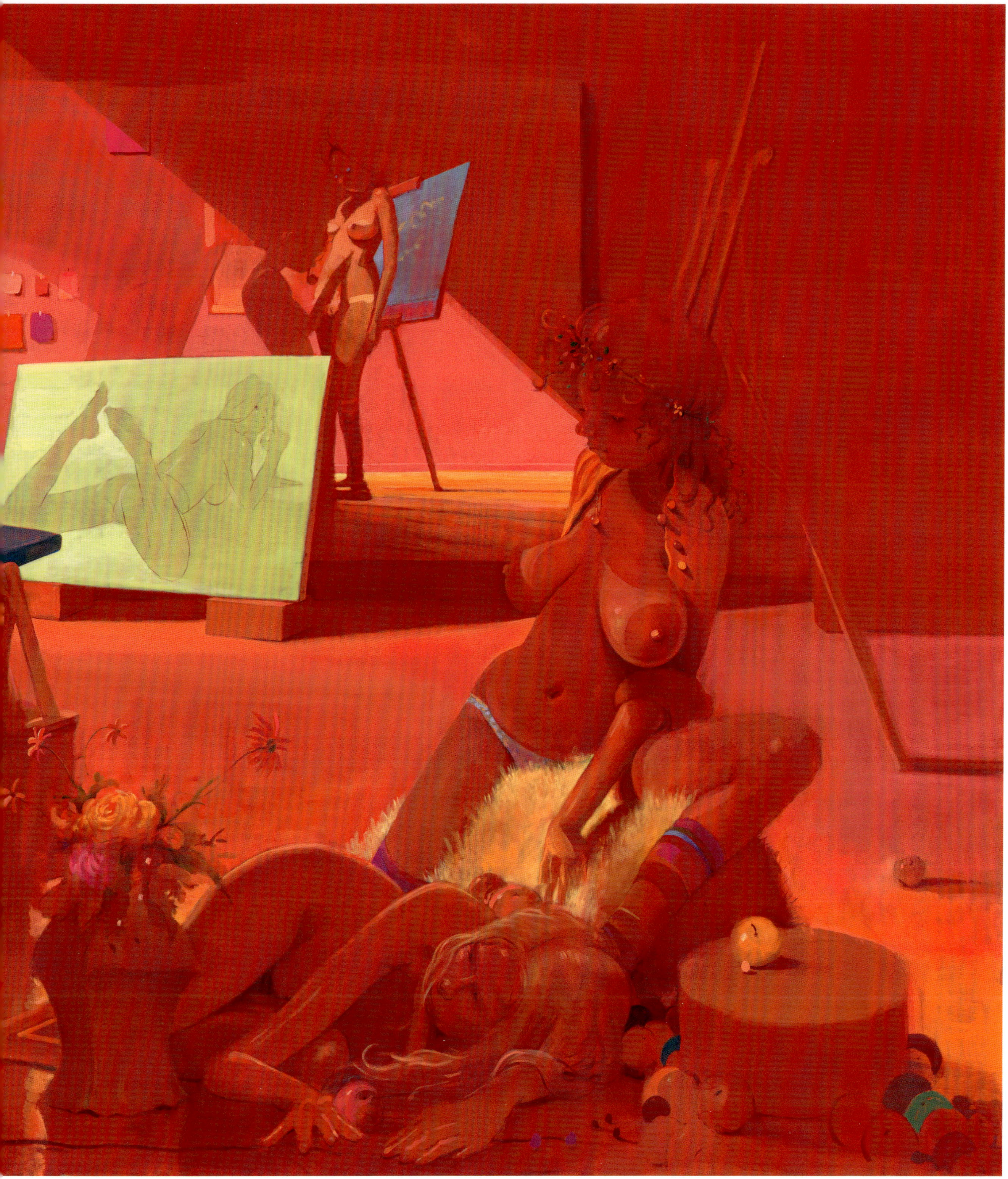

PAINTER, 2024
OIL ON LINEN
31 X 28 CM

in a sfumato field, and though its edges were dematerializing, the eyeballs were always hard and fixed on the viewer. These paintings were angry to boot. And fun to make. They really confused a lot of people.[25]

Since then, her works have become much more nuanced in their exploration of self-consciousness, much more indirect. The paintings don't confront the viewer, don't fix him or her in the compromised position of voyeur, but construct a large, self-referential imaginative space that only secondarily or in part seems addressed to us.

I mentioned at the beginning my early feeling that writing about Yuskavage's art could become an exercise in auto-psychoanalysis. I think I've mostly managed to avoid that, and yet I can't help feeling that, as Yuskavage's art has developed, the persona of the artist herself has been embodied as an unseen voice, somewhere behind my back, as if I were on the couch, recurrently asking the questions, 'And how did you feel about that?' 'What do you think that means?' 'How do you see the problem?' 'Is there something else?' Maybe the paintings are, after all, analyzing me. In any case, like any good psychologist, Yuskavage has developed a method for handling the rawest and most intimate feelings in a disinterested and analytical way – for touching on the truths of the flesh with the energy of the mind.

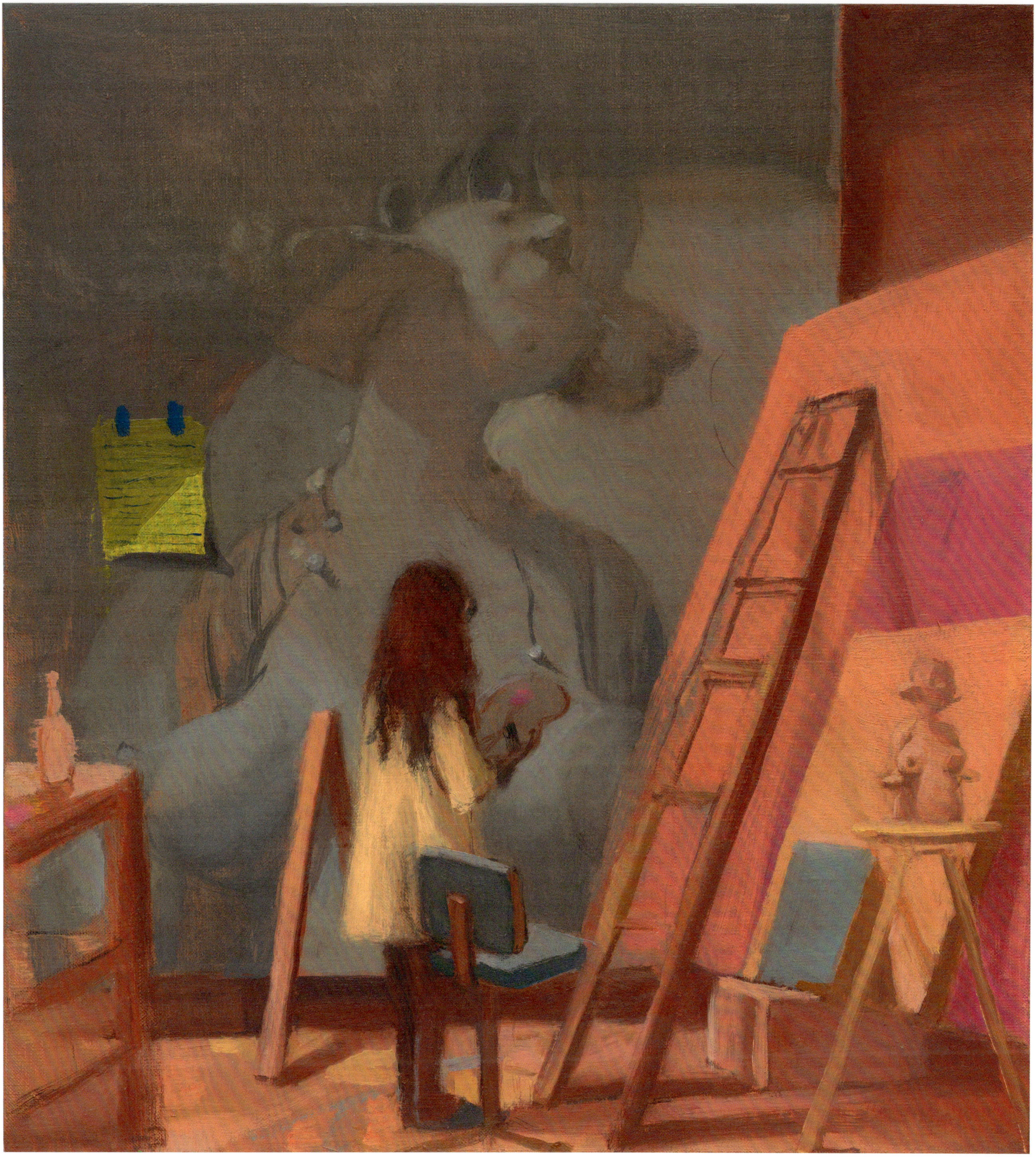

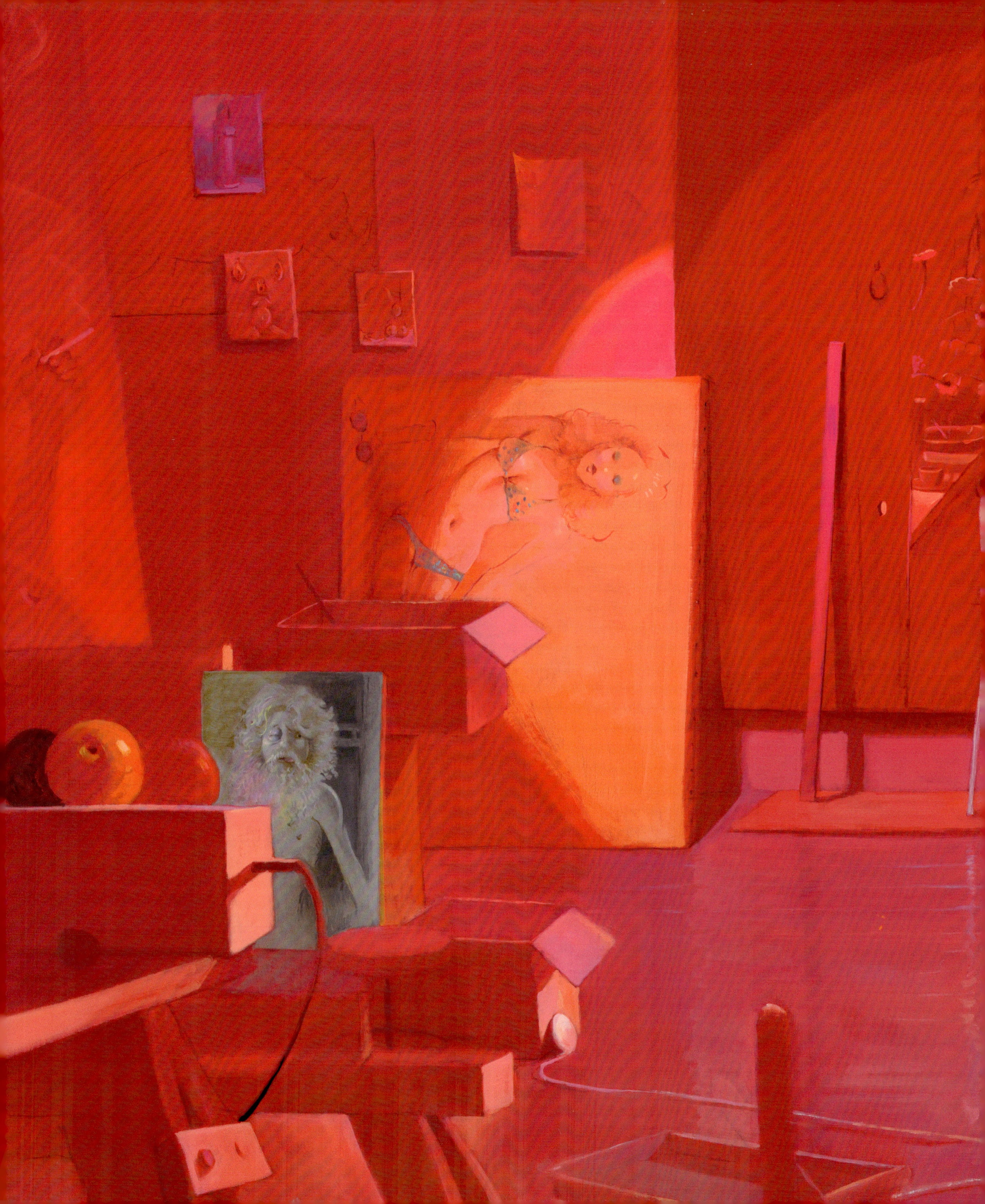

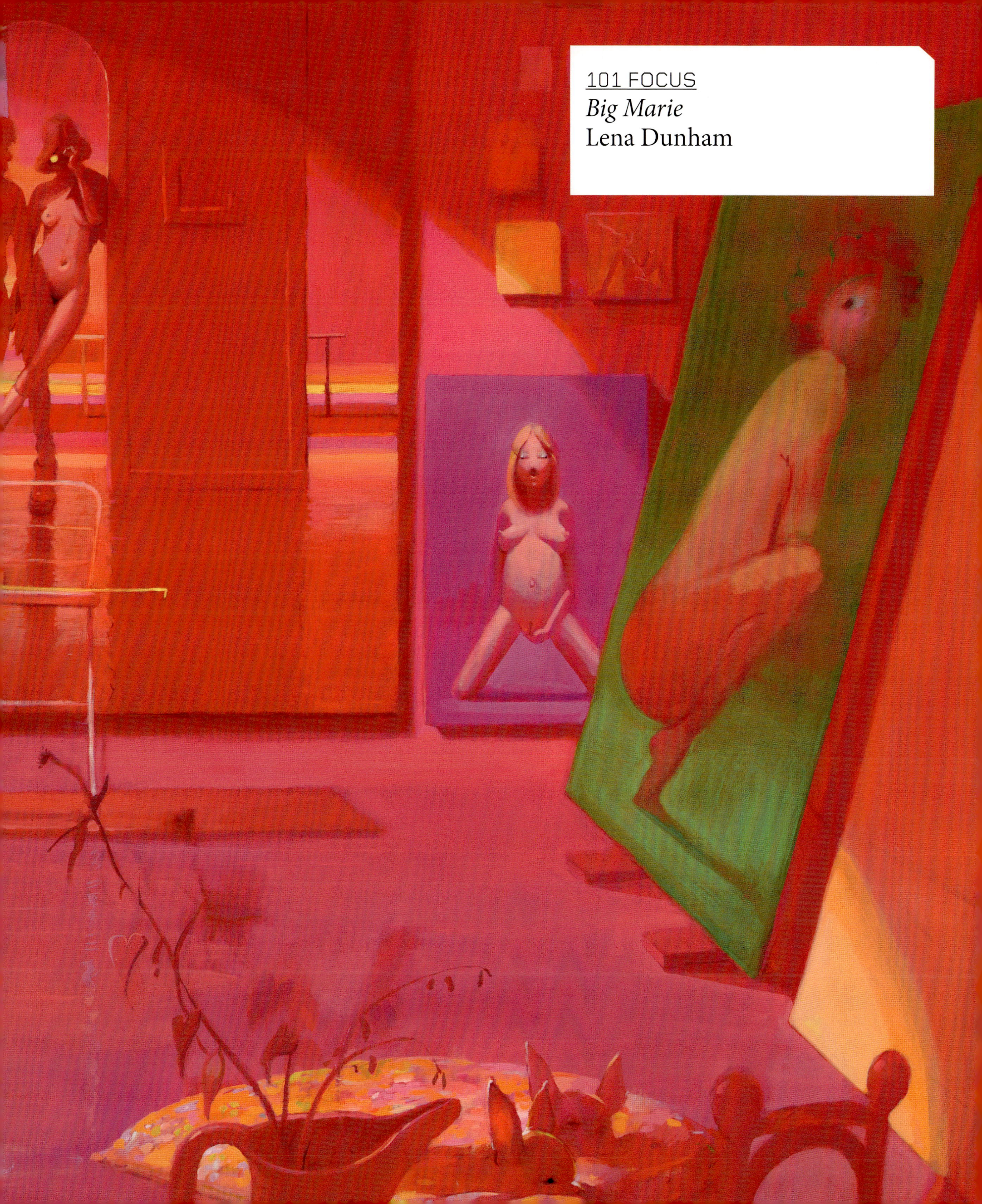

101 FOCUS

Big Marie

Lena Dunham

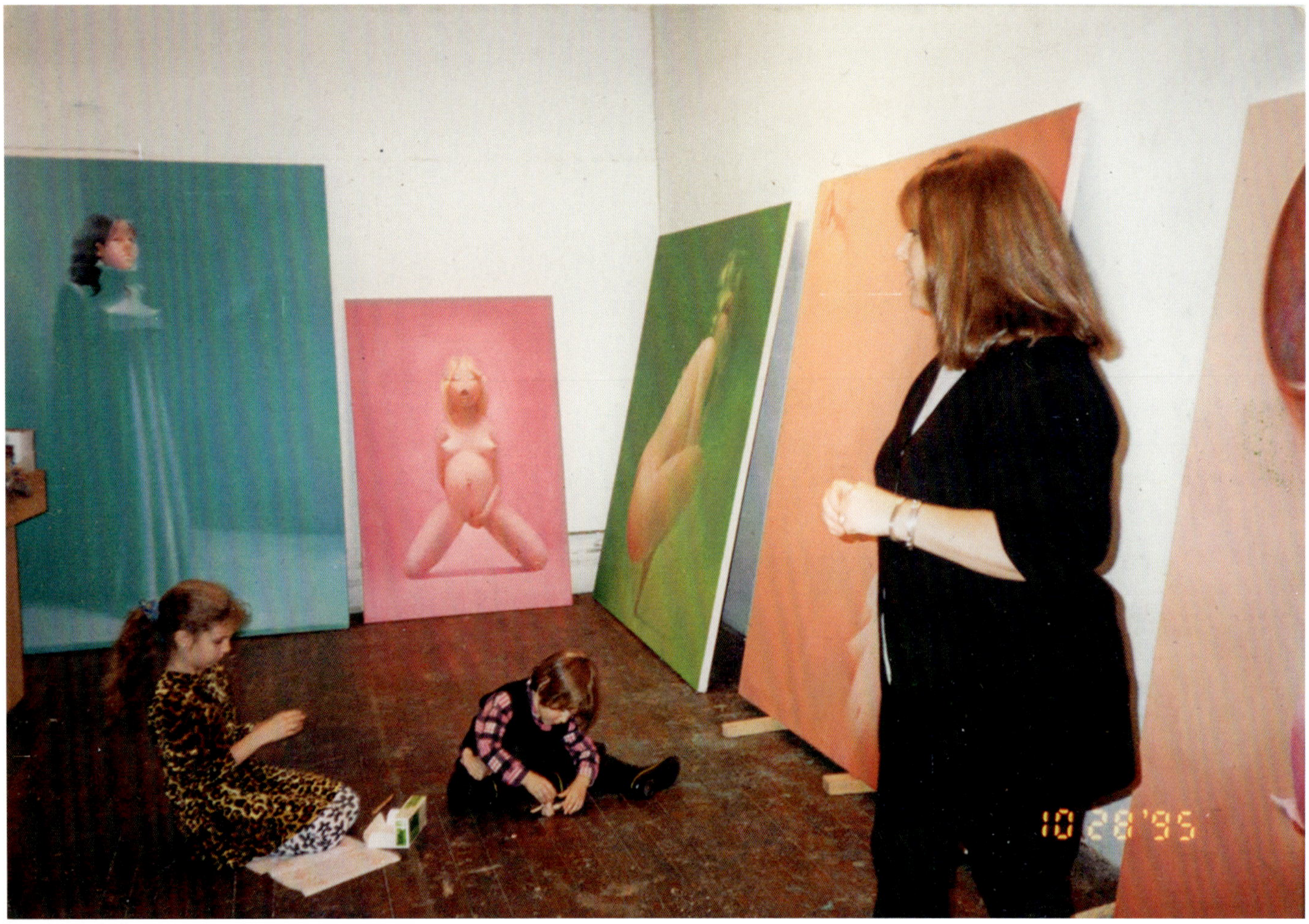

left,
LENA AND CYRUS DUNHAM
VISITING THE ARTIST'S STUDIO,
NEW YORK, 1994

opposite,
BIG BLONDE JERKING OFF,
1995
OIL ON LINEN
152 X 102 CM

previous pages,
PINK STUDIO (RENDEZVOUS)
(DETAIL), 2021
OIL ON LINEN
196 X 178

The studio was a child's dream: pastel canvases on every wall, centring characters who had the beauty of Disney princesses and the bodacious power of super-heroines. On the table were small clay busts that, to the uninitiated, looked like action figures lined up in a comic book store. Lisa seemed able to assemble these models for the paintings they would become with the speed of a child rolling a ball of Play-Doh. I looked around, sure I'd found myself in heaven. It was very different from the first artist's studio I'd visited, but it was certainly the one that spoke the most to my fantasy life. Lisa handed me a bucket of white clay and showed me the general gestures needed to sculpt one of her women – generous globs for breasts and booty, smaller pieces to create their angular features. Mine wound up looking like a melted goblin, but I didn't stop trying when I got home.

My obsession with Lisa's work stayed strong – hers were the only shows I went to willingly, unlike the countless openings I was dragged to against my will. I had no intellectual argument for why I loved them – it was purely gut level, a sense that her women lived in the world the way that I wanted to: alone or in small, complex groupings, against washes of feverish colour, wearing dresses that lived at the intersection of Little House on the Prairie and the gauzy garments discarded in the soft-core porn that played late at night on Cinemax.

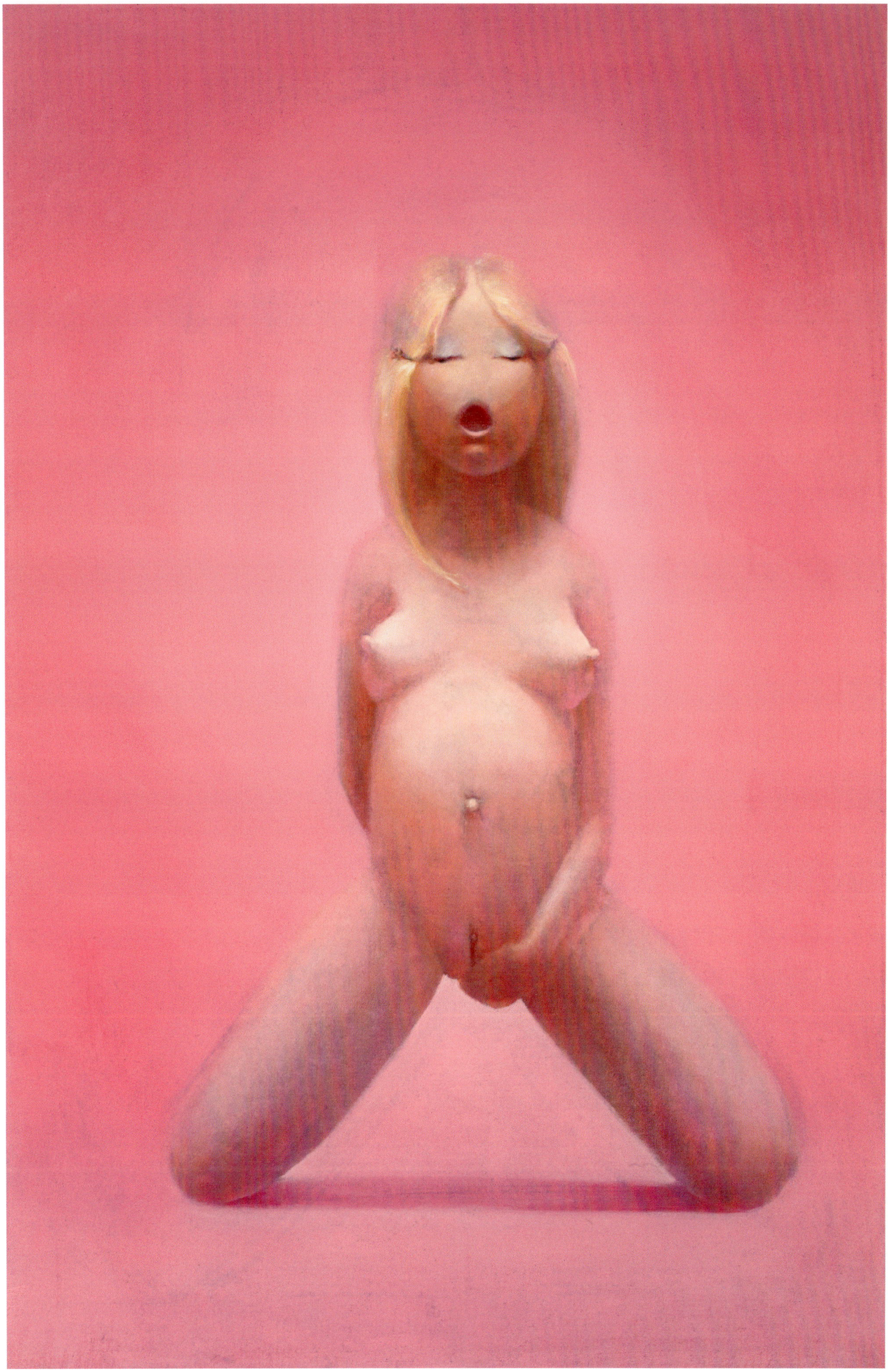

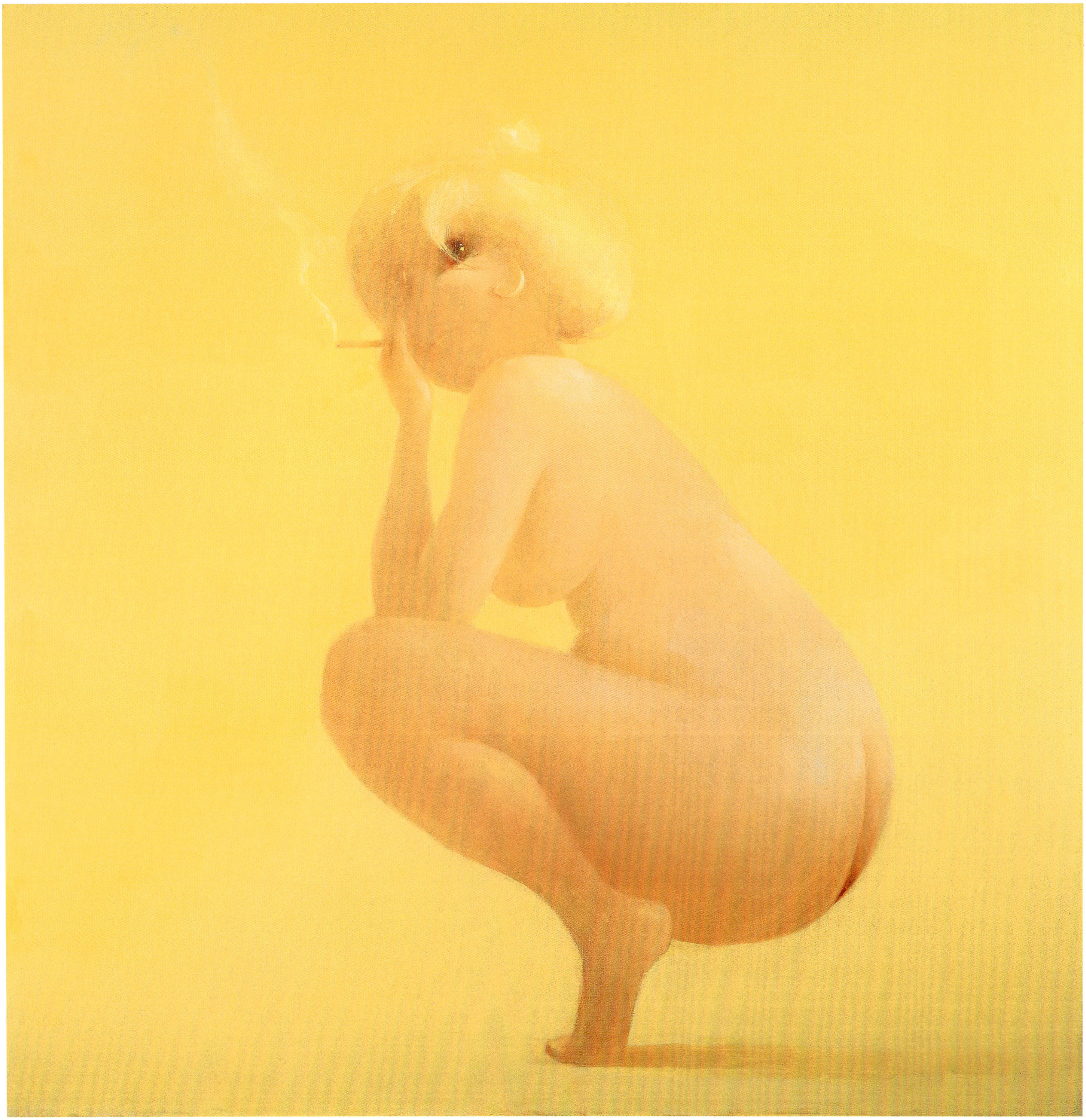

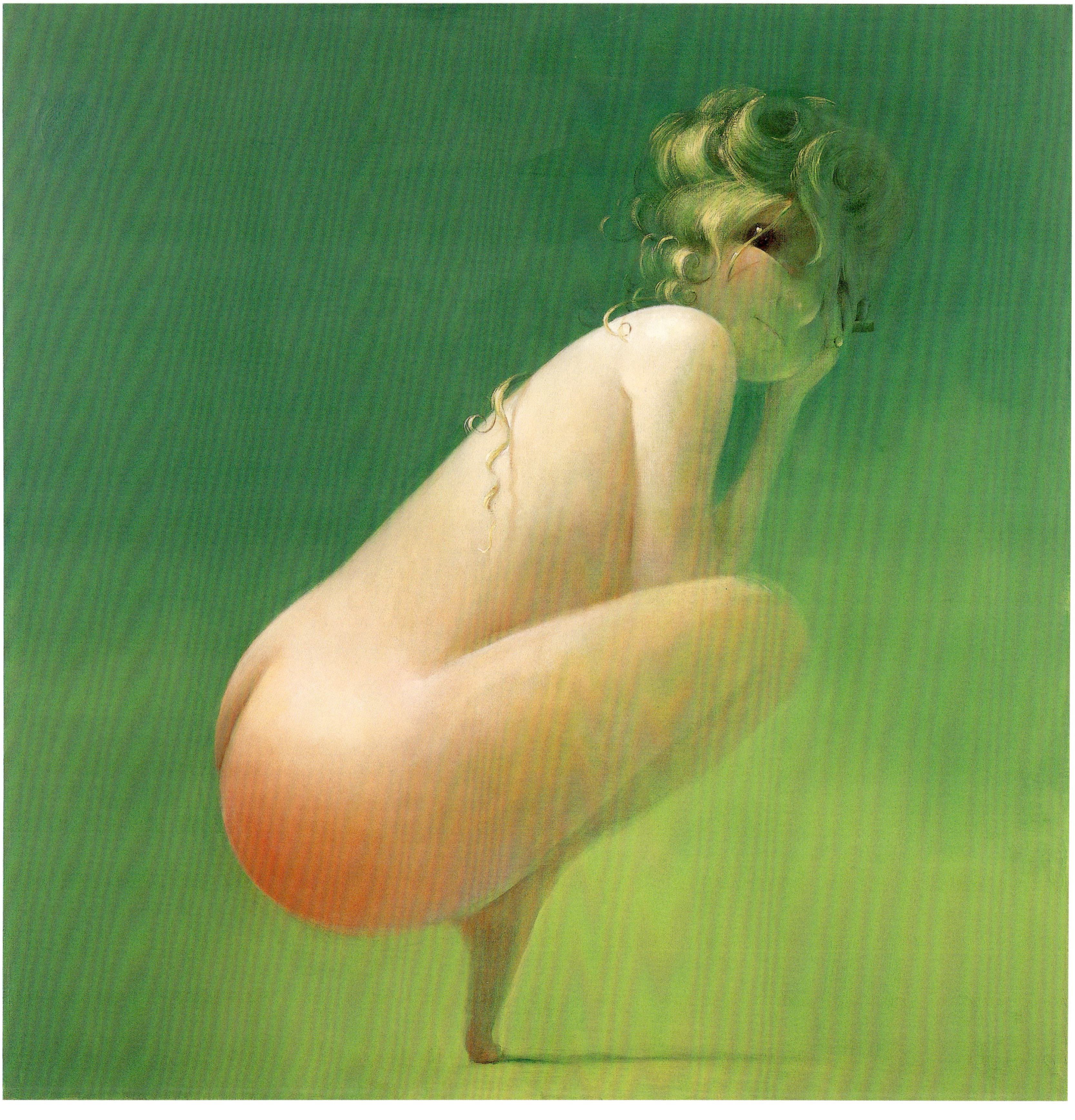

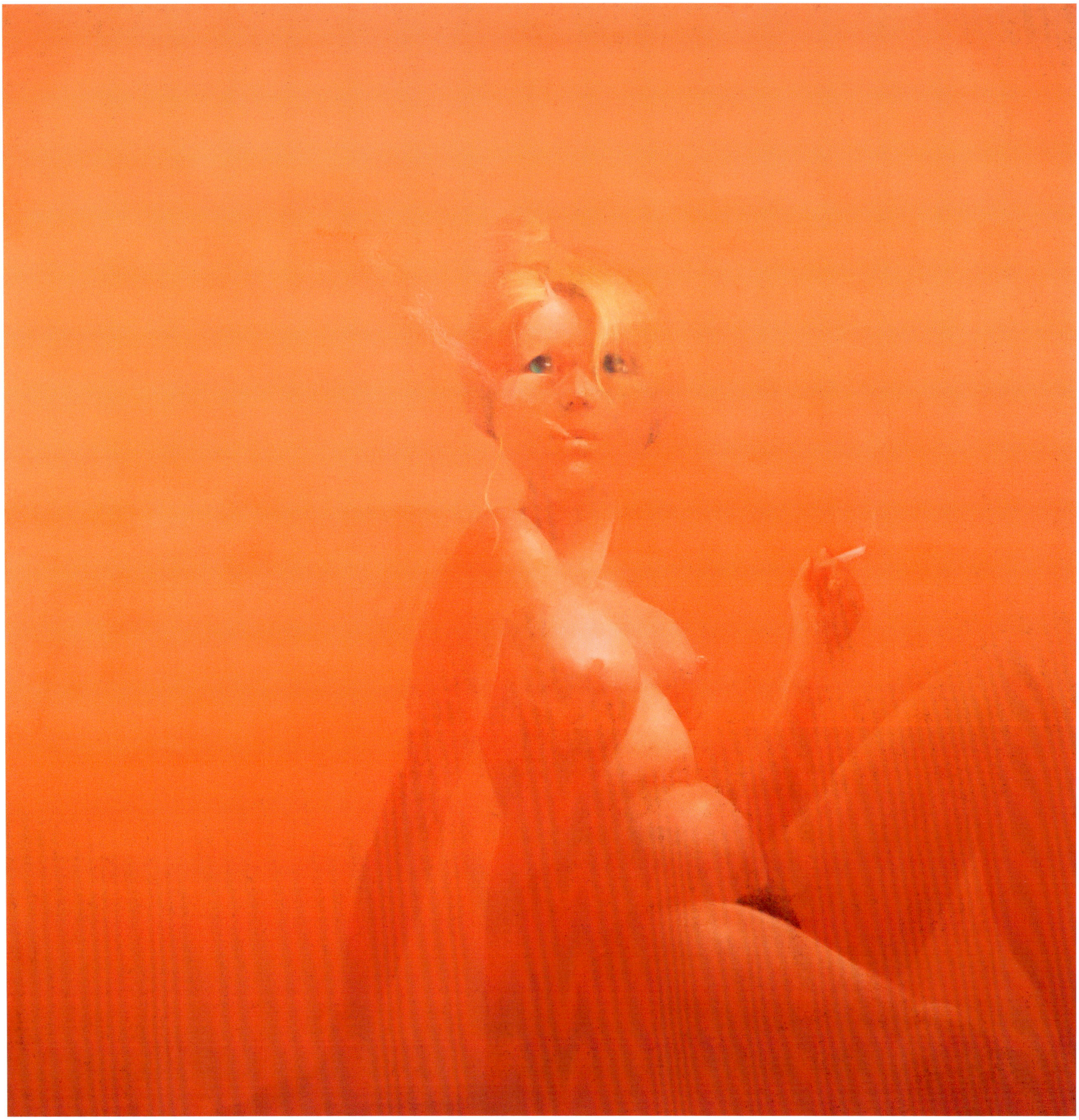

left,
BIG BLONDE SMOKING,
1994
OIL ON LINEN
183 X 183 CM

previous pages, from left,
BIG BLONDE SQUATTING,
1994
OIL ON LINEN
183 X 183 CM

BIG BLONDE WITH HAIRDO,
1994
OIL ON LINEN
183 X 183 CM

It wasn't until my twenties, when my own body became a topic of public interest, that I understood the formative truth of what Lisa's work had meant to me. Long before the term 'body positivity' entered the chat, there were Lisa's women: the proudly nude assembly in Little Hippies (2013), coyly covering their vaginas while their breasts swell like over-ripe fruit. The rounded stomach of the wind-swept conqueror in Outskirts (2011). The pro-pussy slut with a slit in Fireplace (2009). The fat-assed queen making her bed just to get into it again in Changing (2005). Angel (2004), who presides over a mystical table, bearing the kind of body usually forced into a bad Lane Bryant sweater.

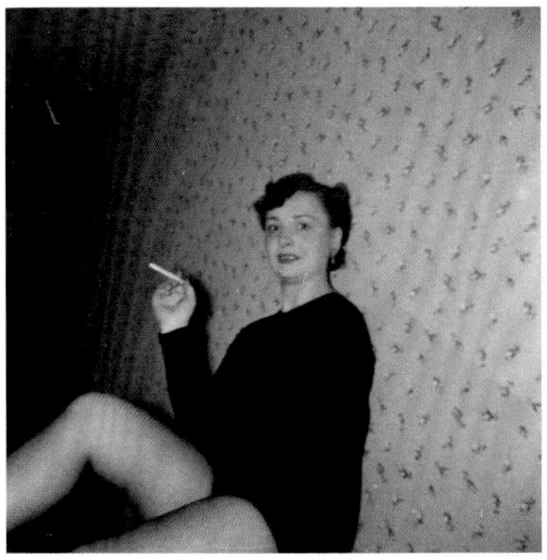

MARIE YUKSKAVAGE, PHILADELPHIA, 1953

And, of course Big Marie (1993), who stands against a verdant green in a romper, her legs (which would be called 'thicc' in modern parlance) as strong as oaks, resting precariously on pointed toes, like a sensual hippo doing a plié in a cartoon. Marie has thick bangs, obtuse eyes, lips that look ready to join the rest of Lisa's characters in some kind of sexual mischief. She wears little white gloves like an archivist, the better to finger you with. Her nipples cannot be contained, in sharp contrast to her child-like Peter Pan collar. She is everything I love about Lisa's works – childlike wonder at the contours of the female form coupled with an R. Crumb passion for the angles we are told are wrong, a Dutch master's facility for light and shadow (the Girl with the Pearl Ass) meeting the unfinished edges of a madman on amphetamines.

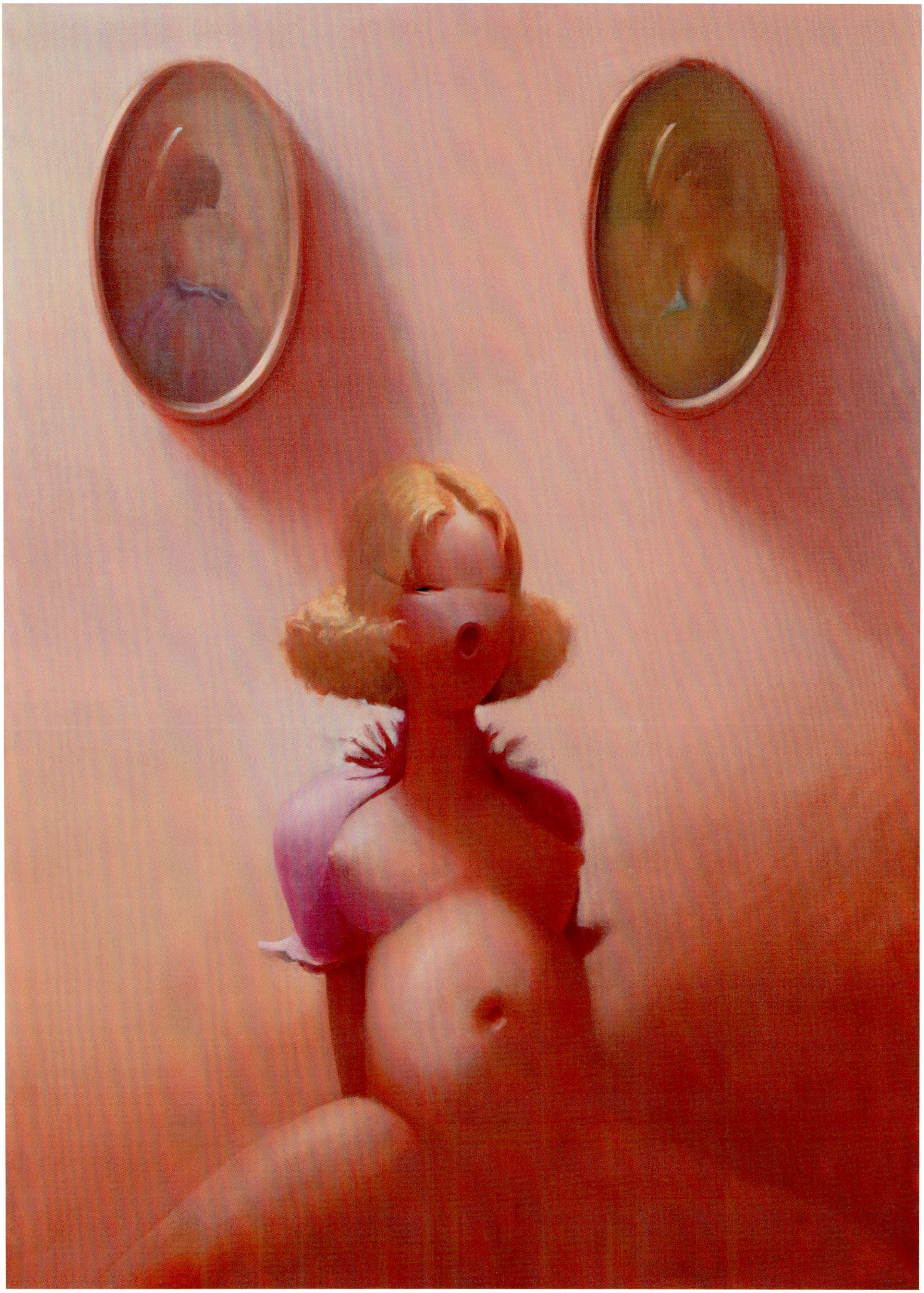

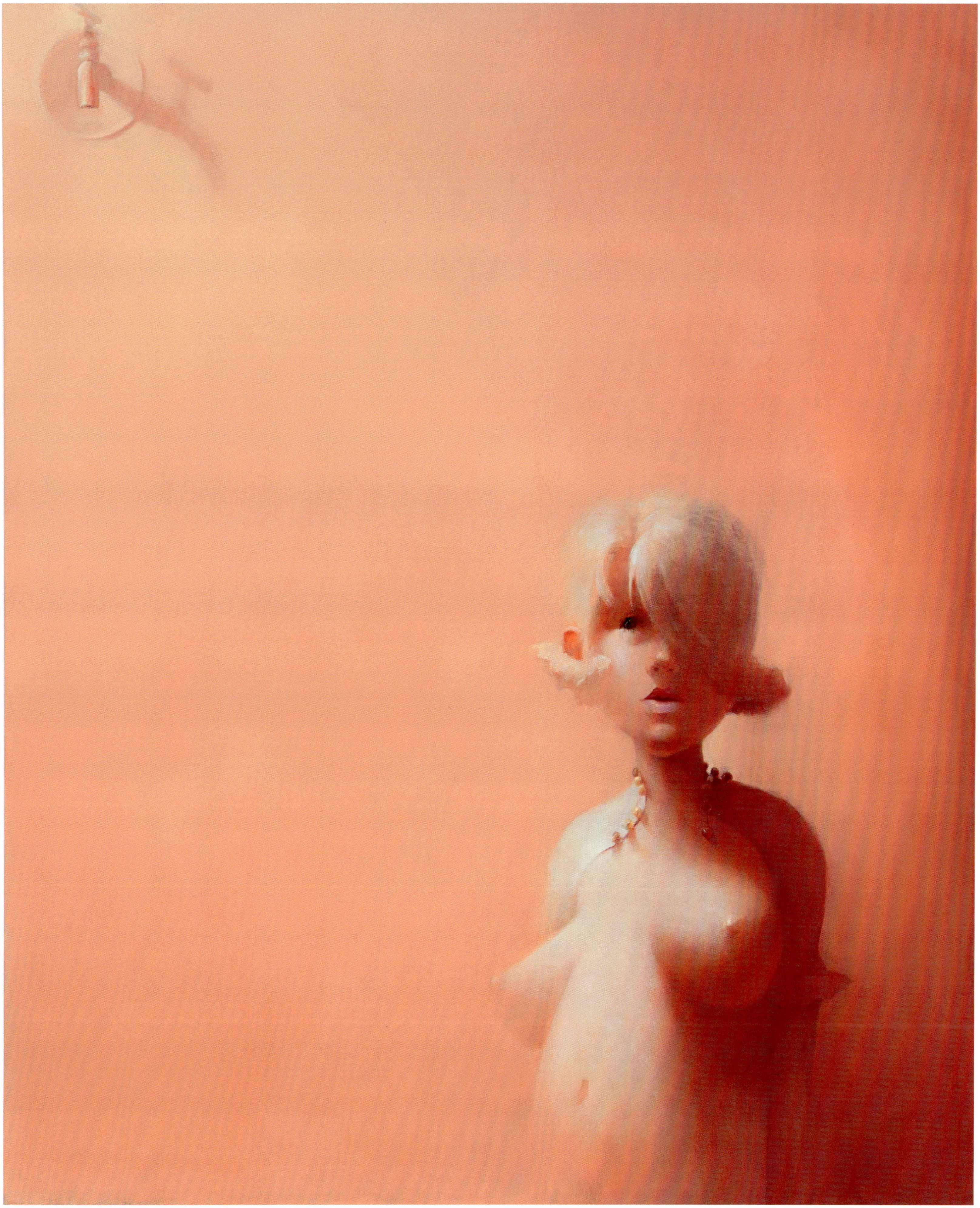

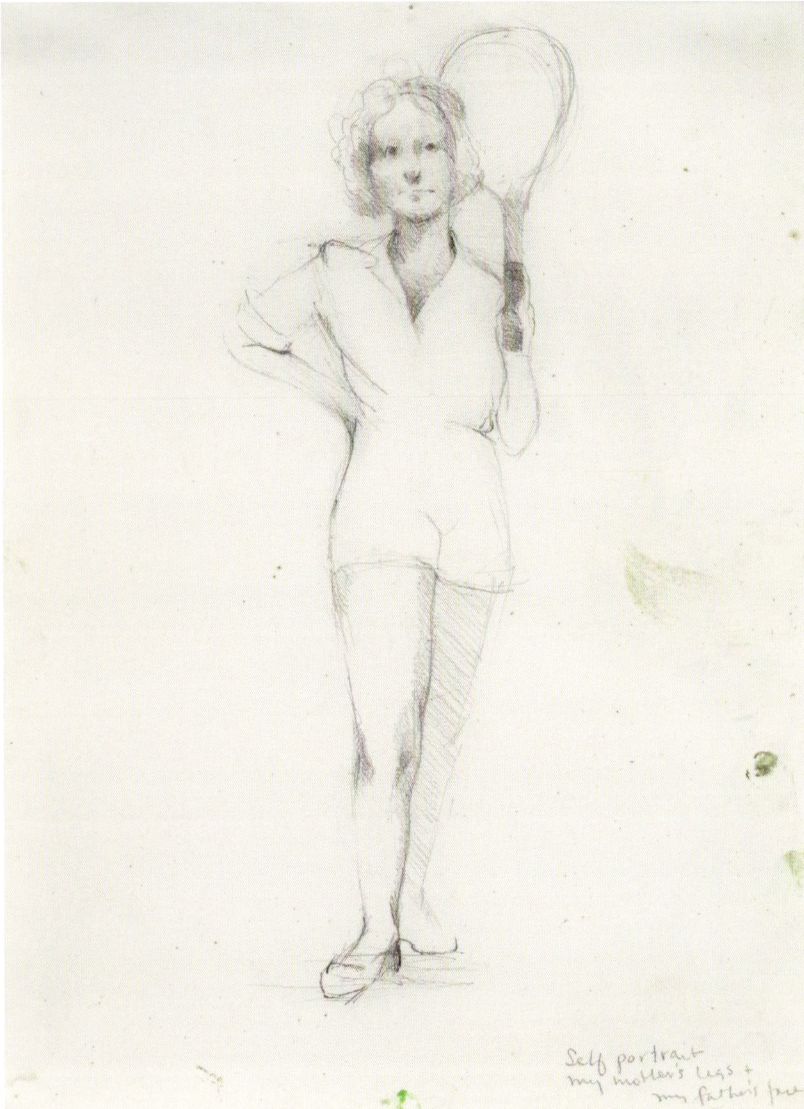

left,
SELF PORTRAIT: MY MOTHER'S LEGS AND MY FATHER'S FACE, 2015
GRAPHITE ON PAPER
31 X 23 CM

opposite,
BIG MARIE, 1993
OIL ON LINEN
162 X 127 CM

previous pages, from left,
FLESHPOT, 1995
OIL ON LINEN
172 X 127 CM

FAUCET, 1995
OIL ON LINEN
183 X 153 CM

It would be too simplistic to say that these paintings are body-positive (after all, the bodies on display are seductive by any measure, even if they are in possession of some surprising angles) and 'sex positive' would also be too trite to apply. The women in the centre of these frames seem much more sex-neutral or sex-apathetic, displaying themselves with the laissez faire attitude of a college kid lolling on a quad, or a McDonald's employee taking your order. To understand their transformative effects, one would have to survey the history of classical painting, consider these bodies against the anaemic ones we are asked to celebrate on lesser canvases and be reminded of just how fraught a topic the vagina has been in the last hundred years of film. Only then will the image of one of Lisa's women, all precarious curves and knobby ankles, spreading her crotch to a view she's too sleepy to look in the eye, matter to you as much as it matters to me.

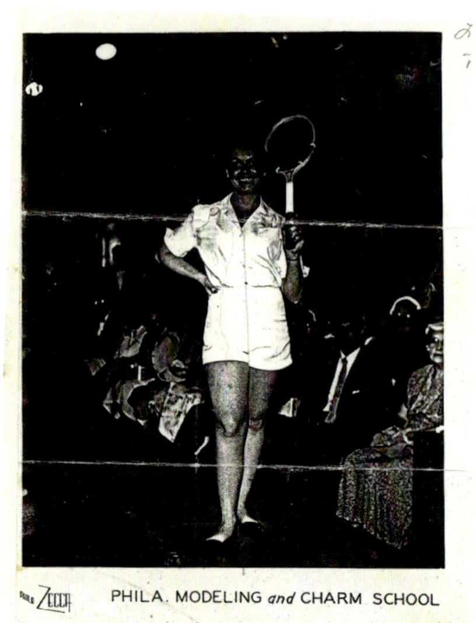

MARIE YUSKAVAGE
PHILADELPHIA MODELING
AND CHARM SCHOOL, 1954

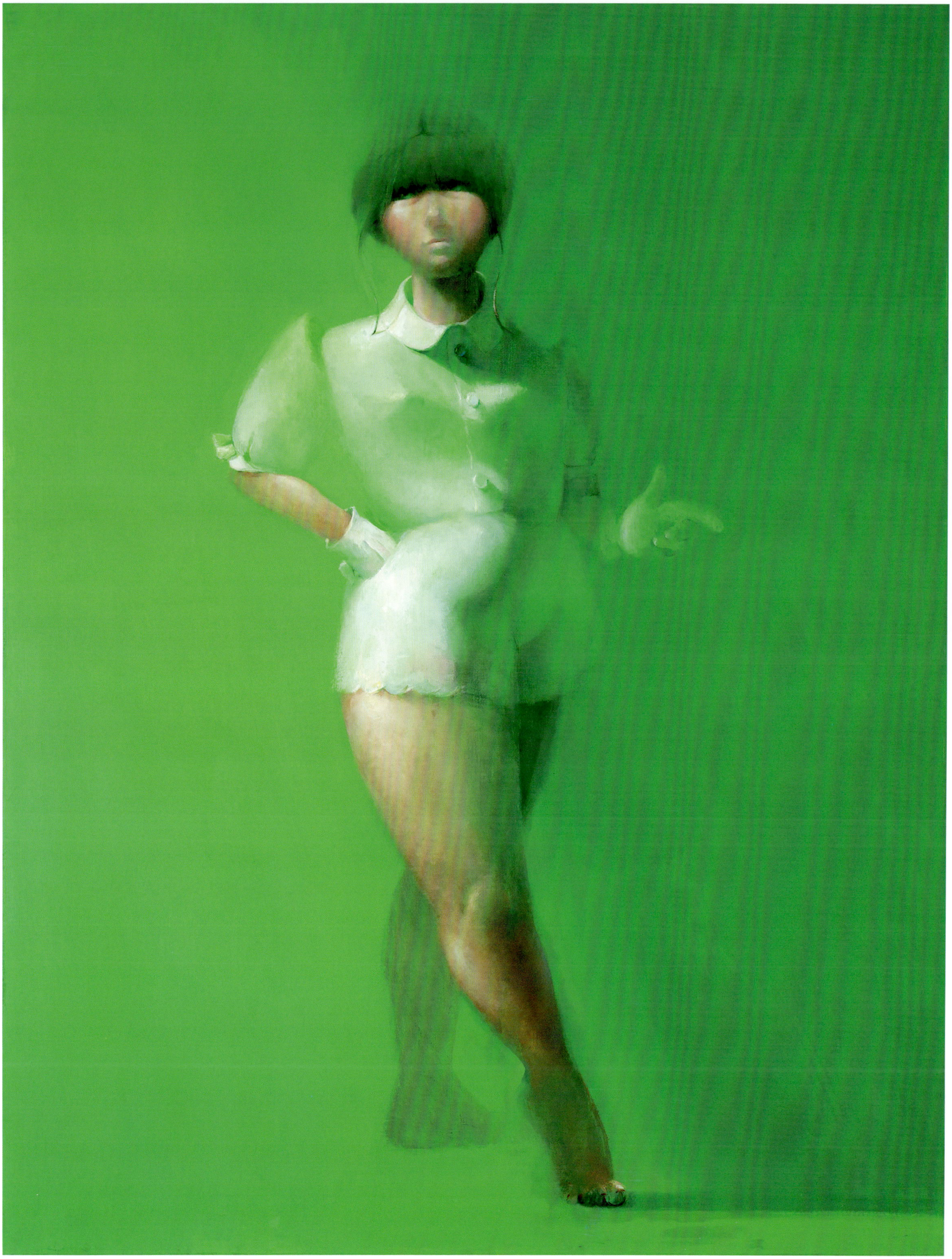

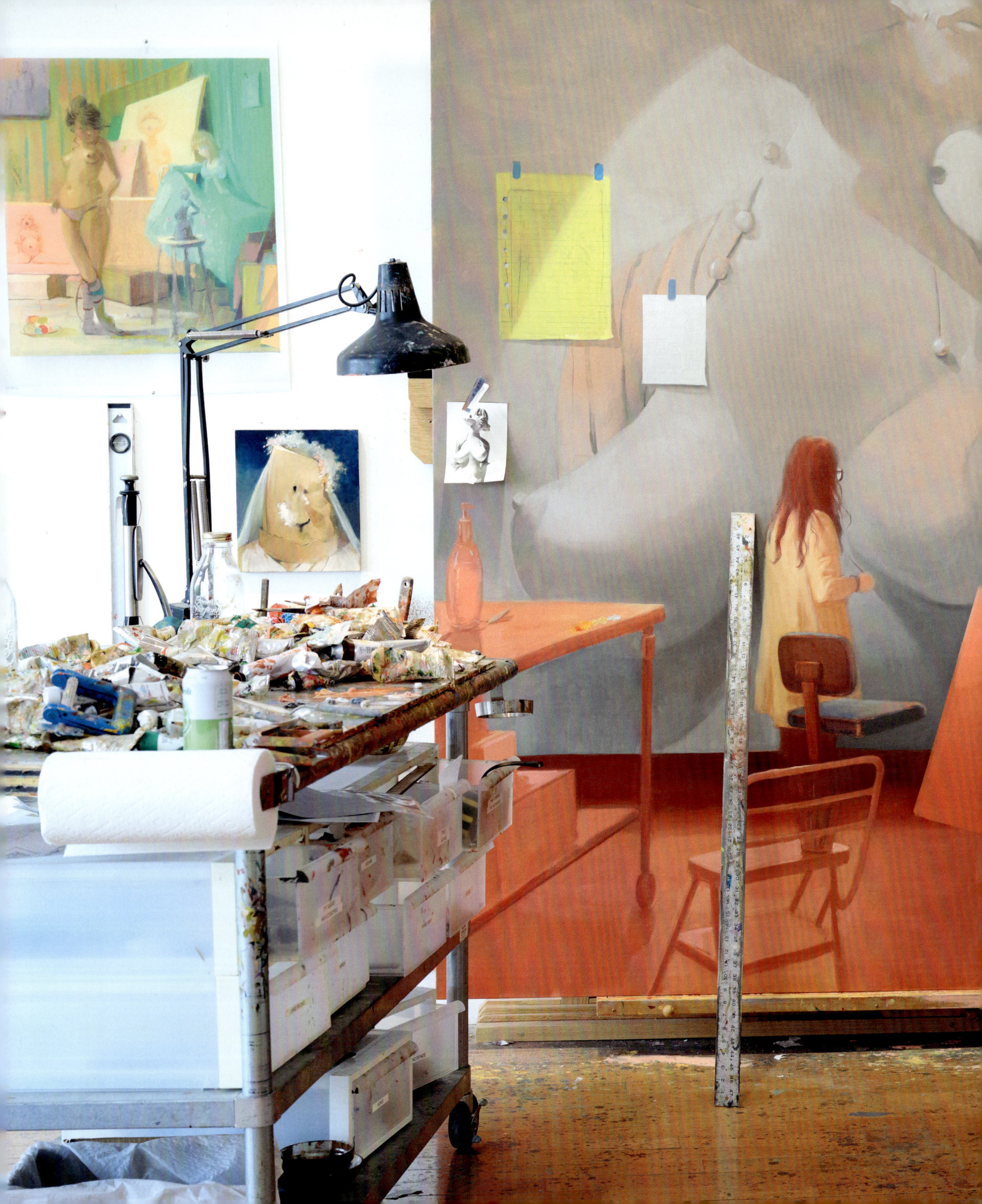

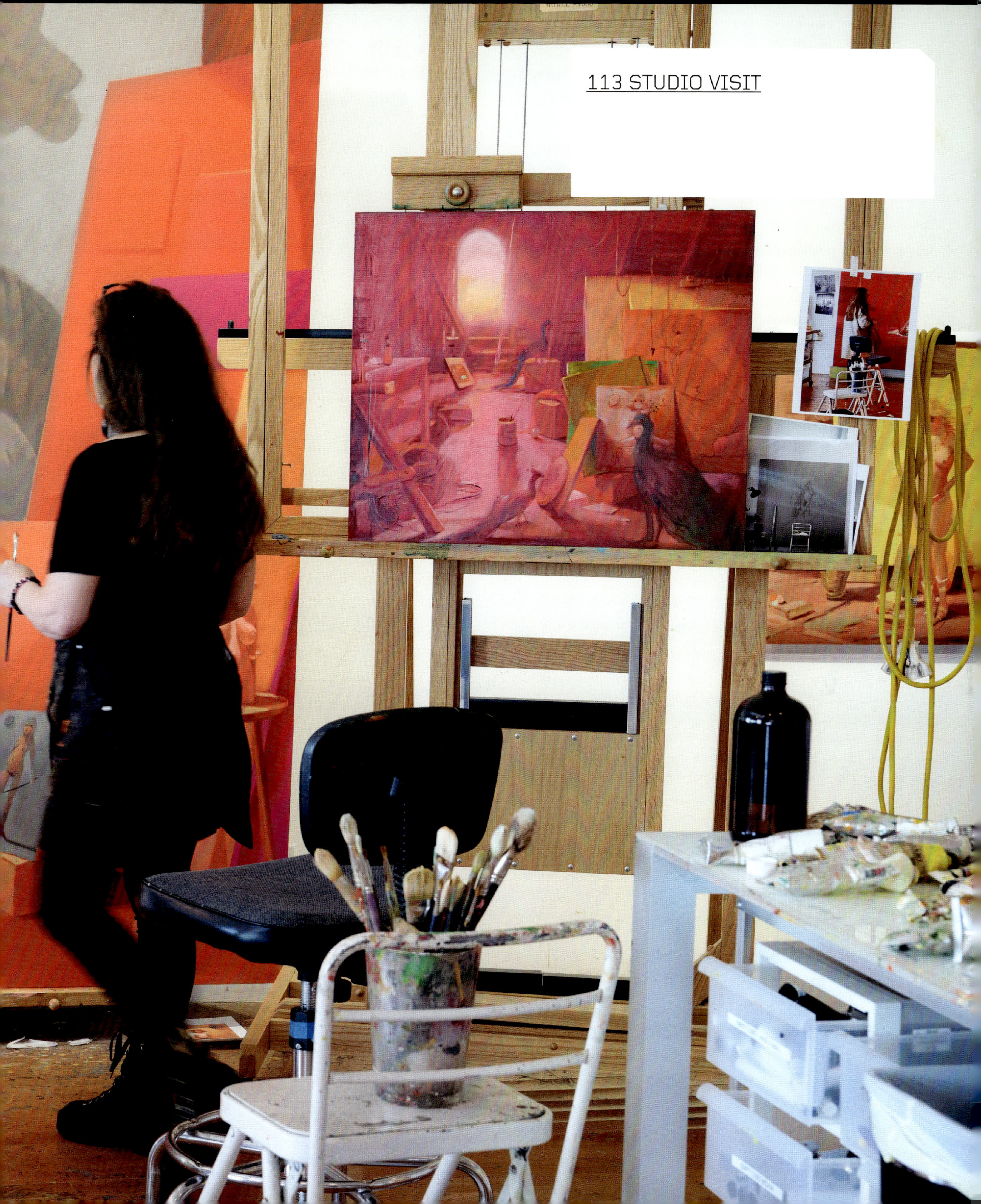

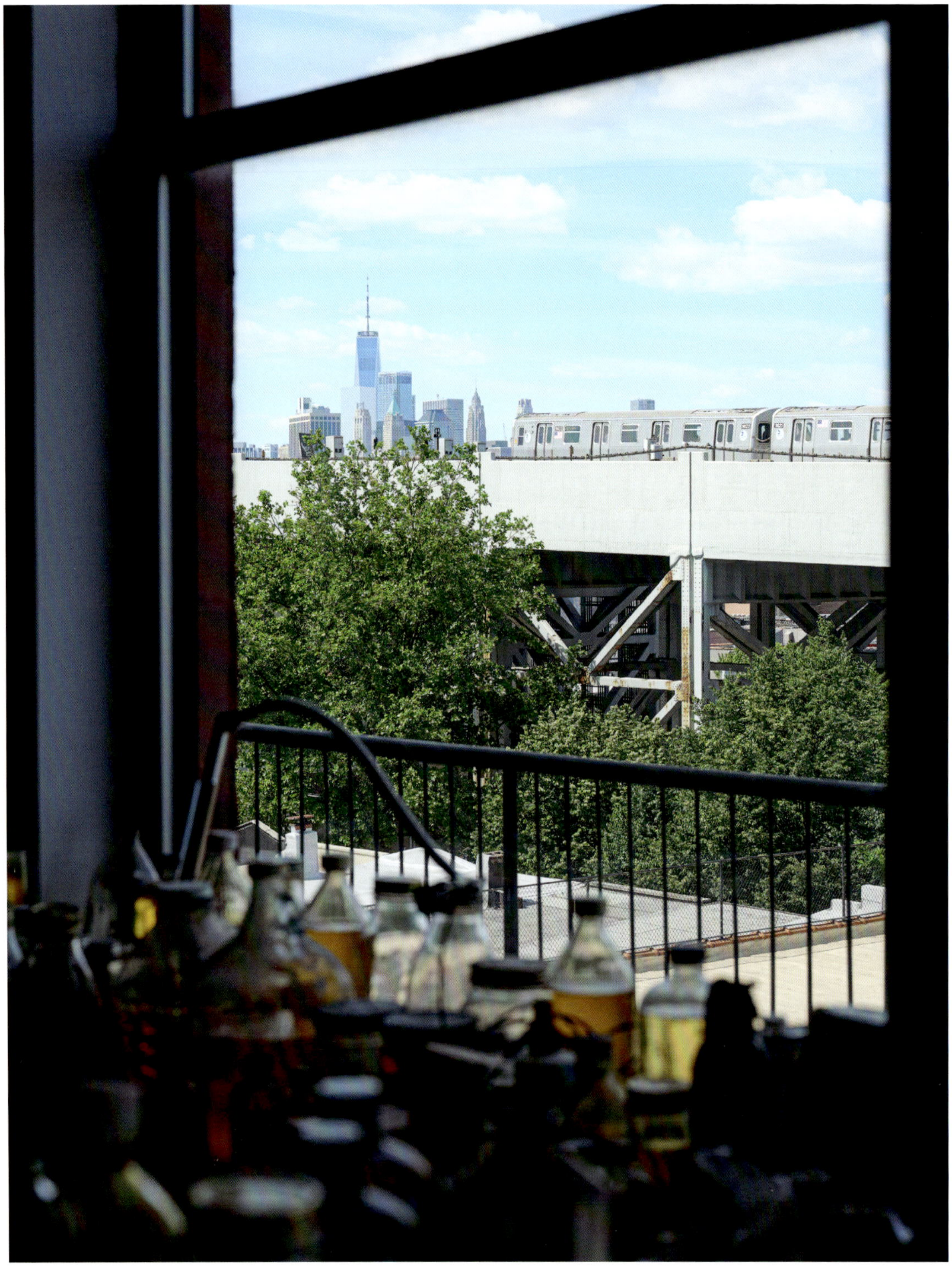

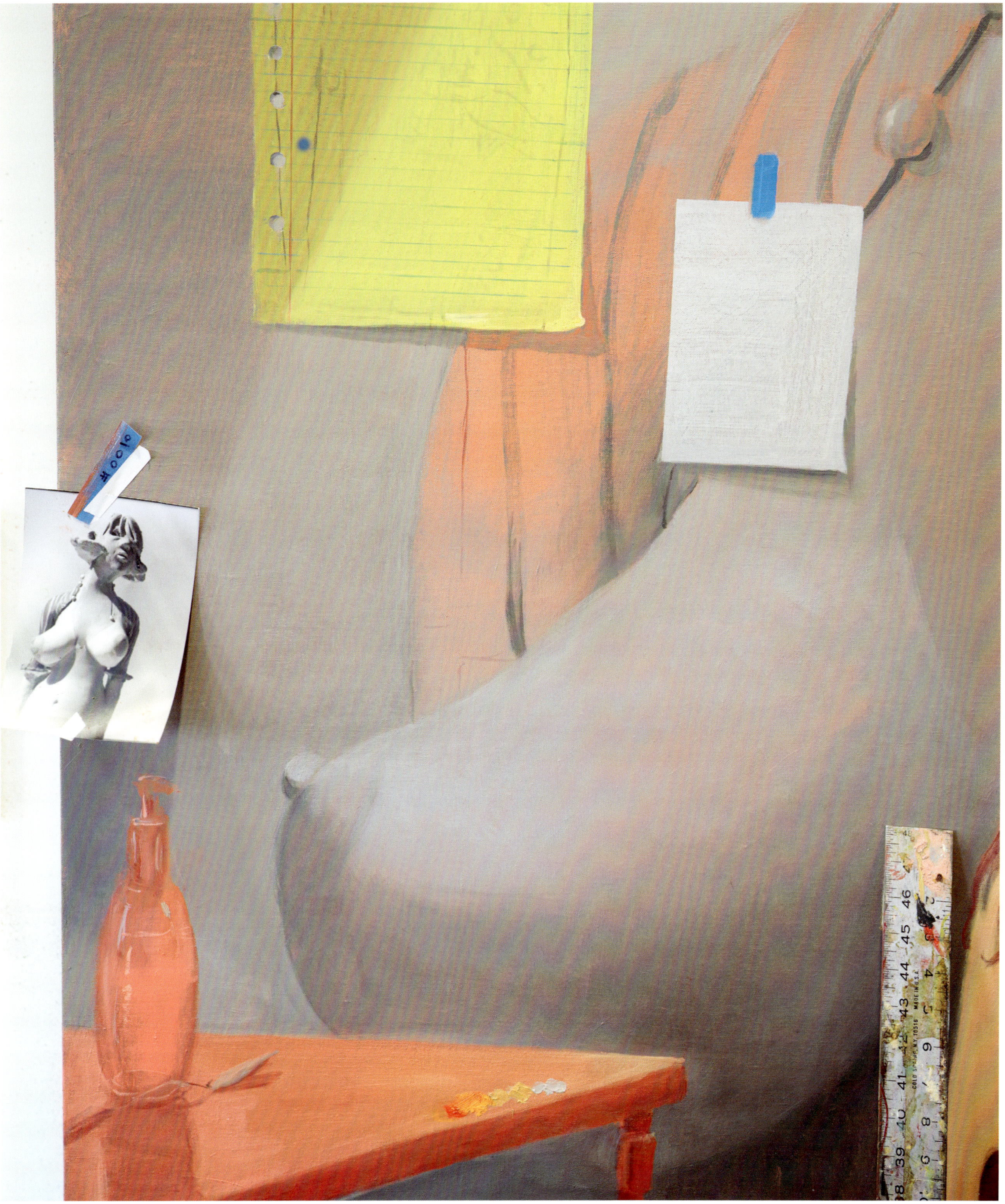

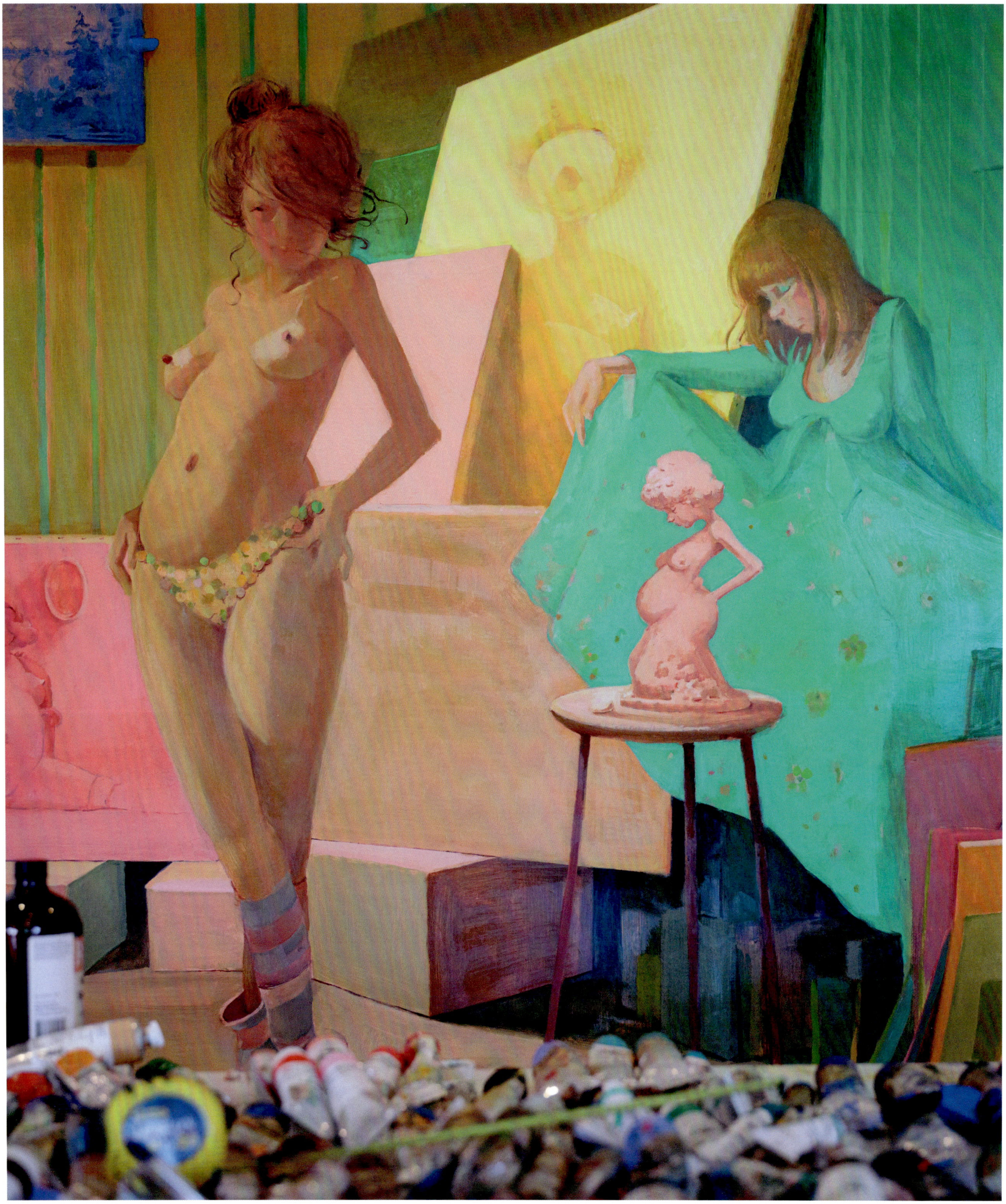

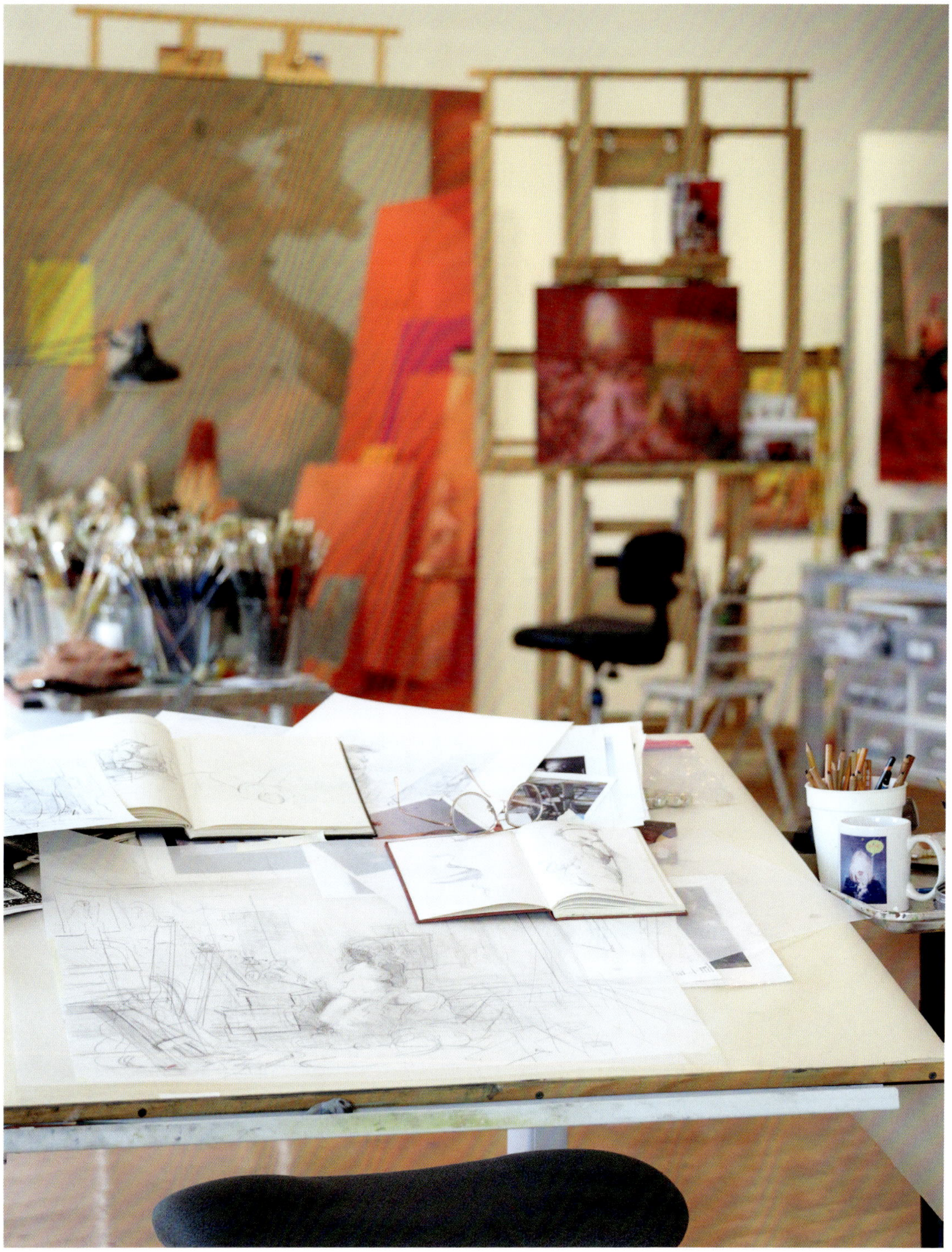

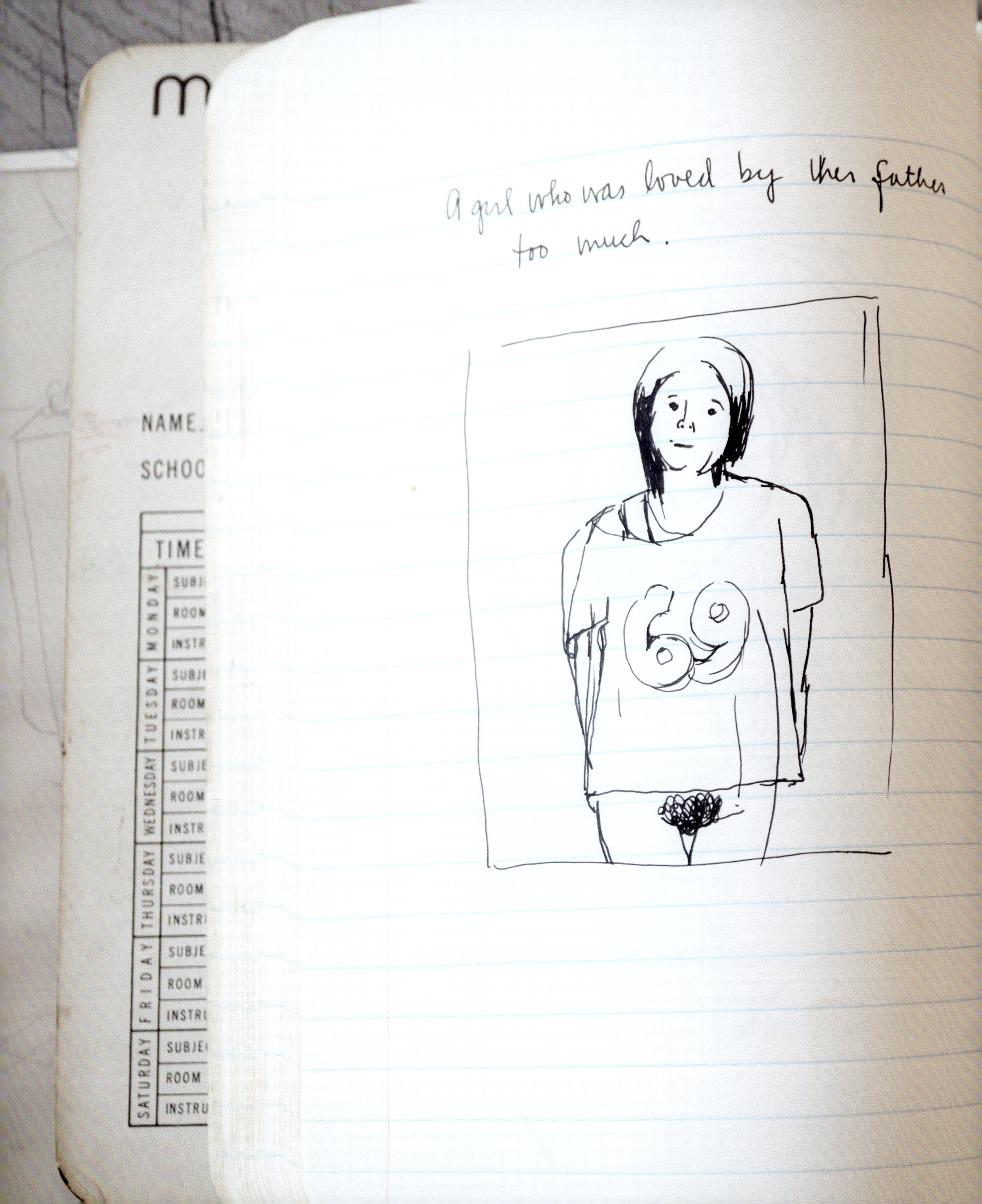
A girl who was loved by her father too much.
69

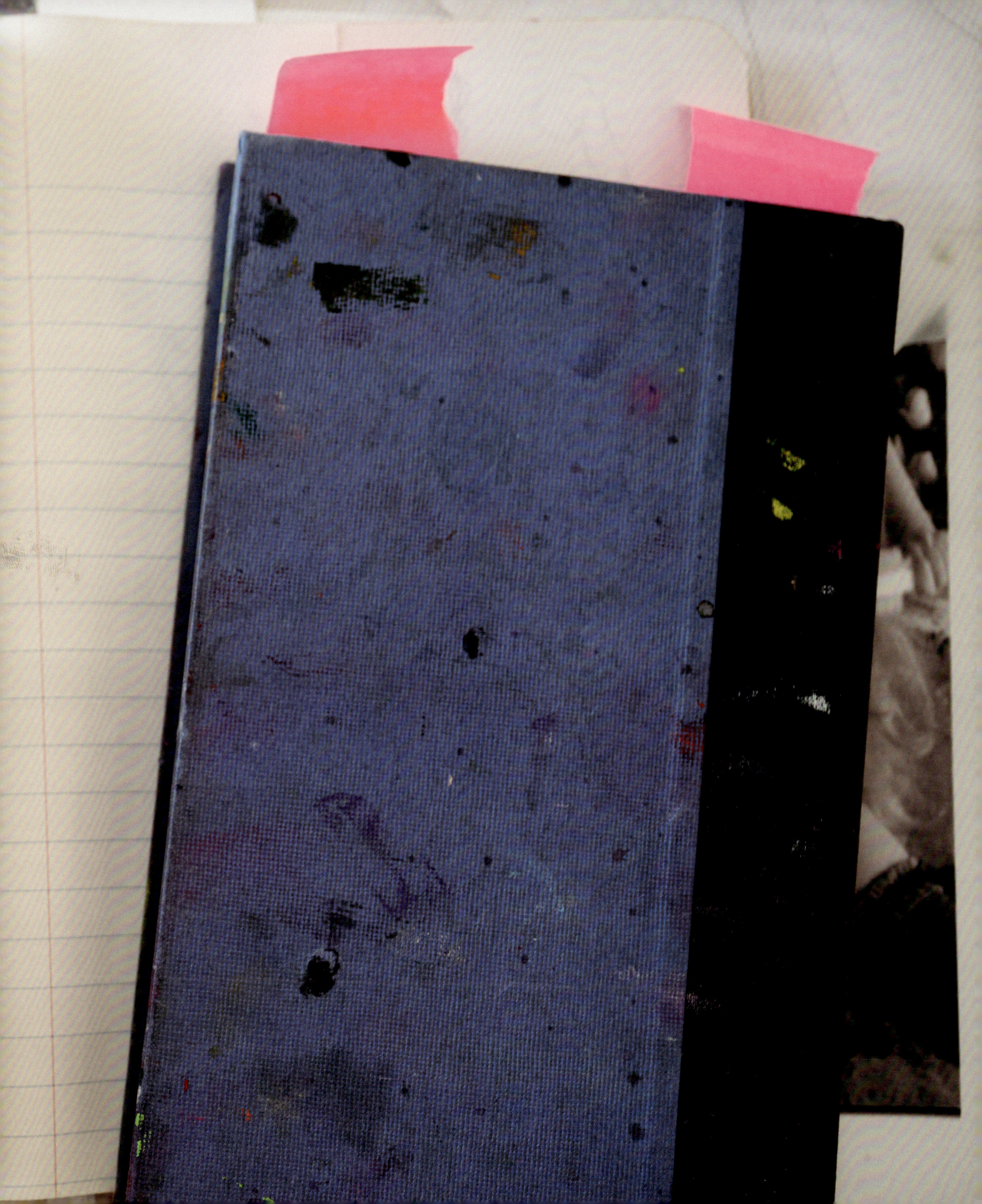

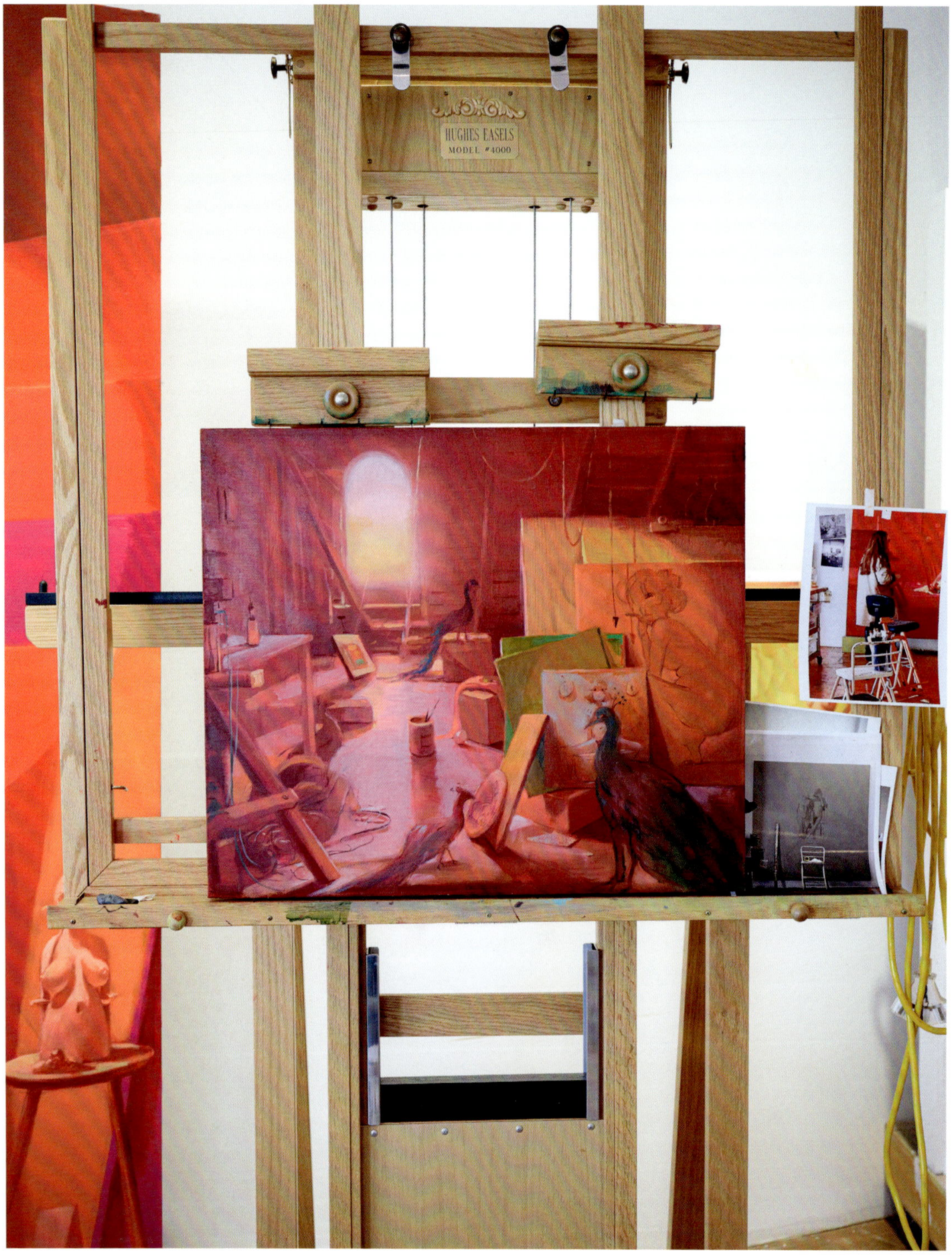
HUGHES EASELS
MODEL #4000

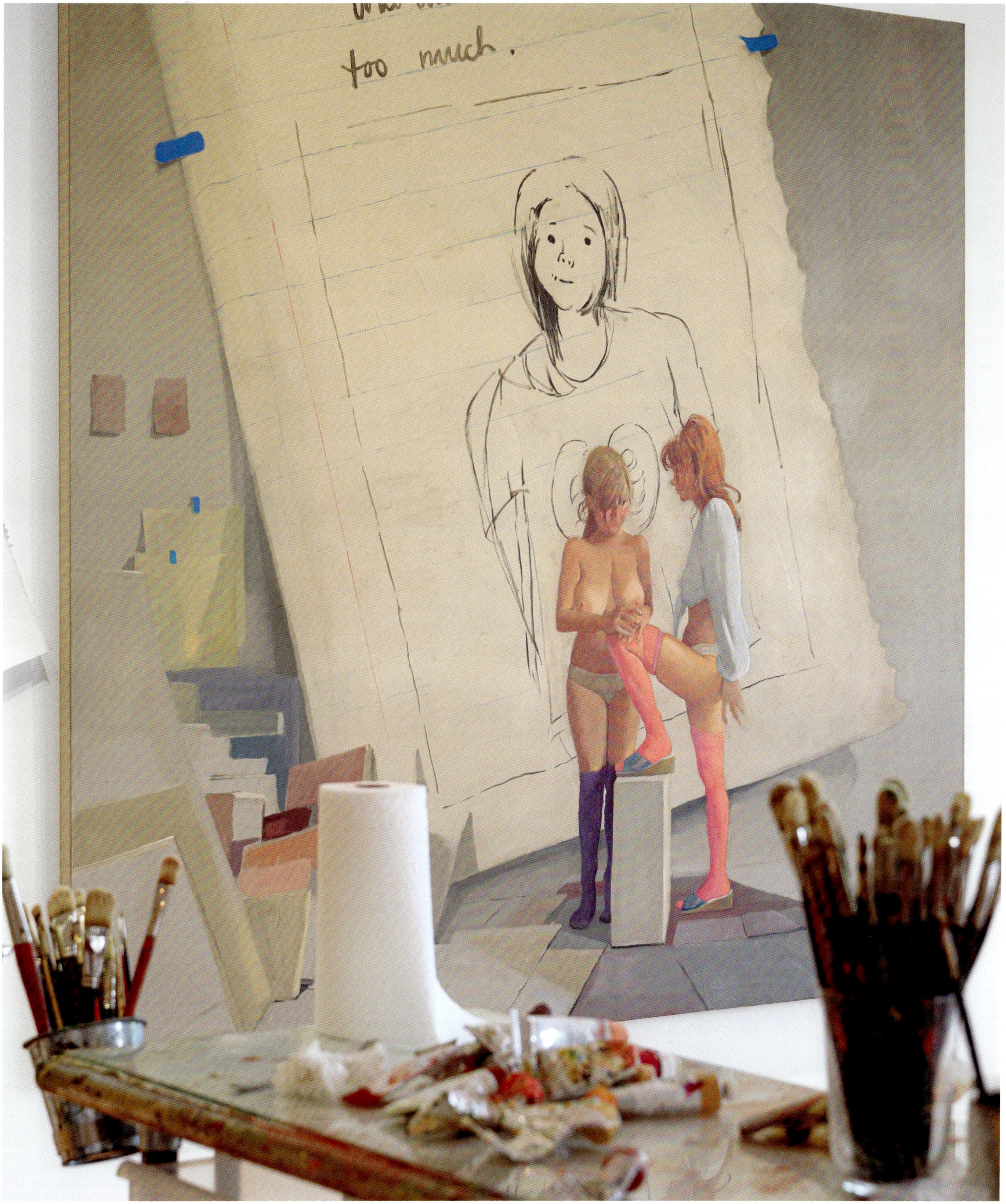
too much.

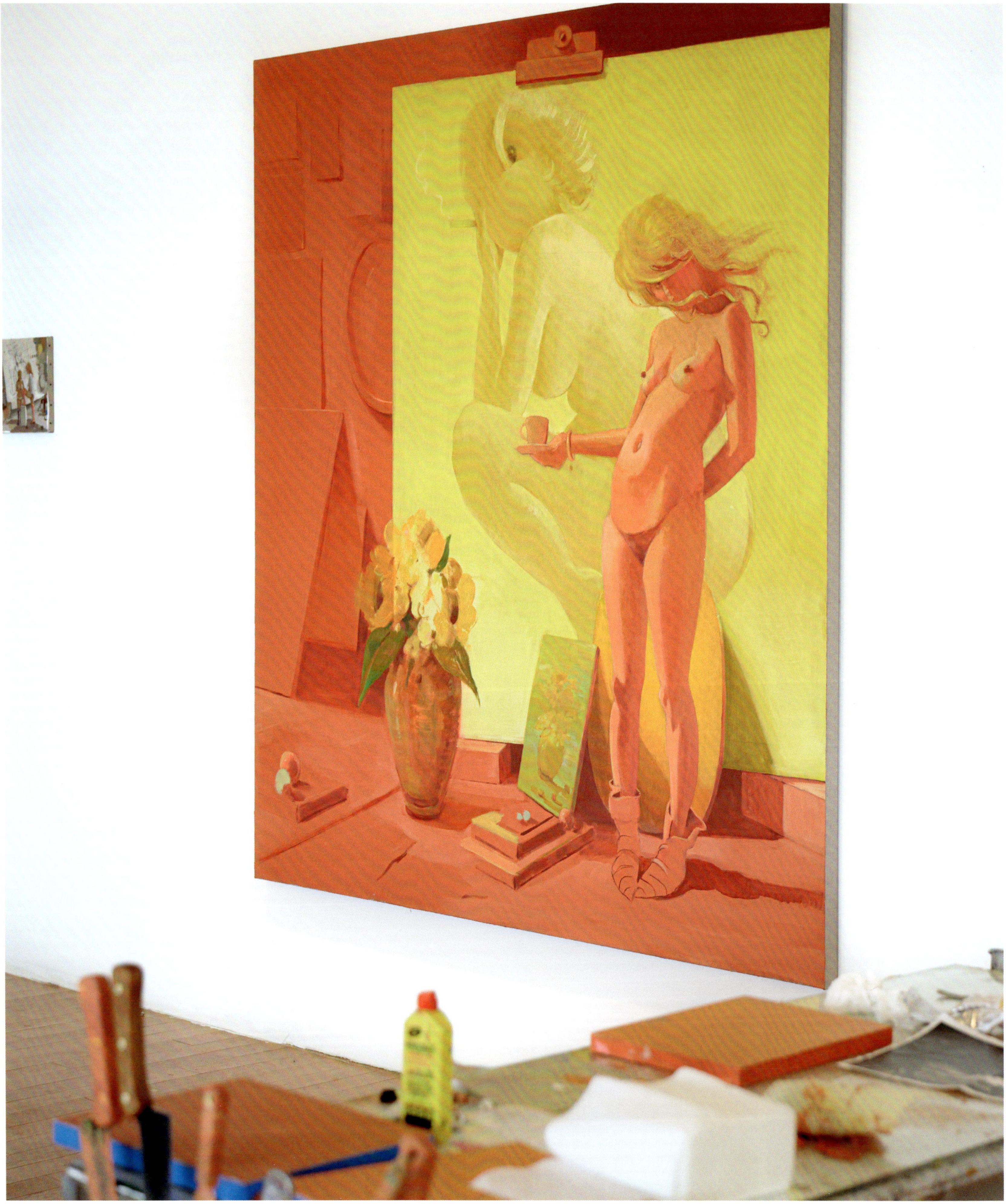

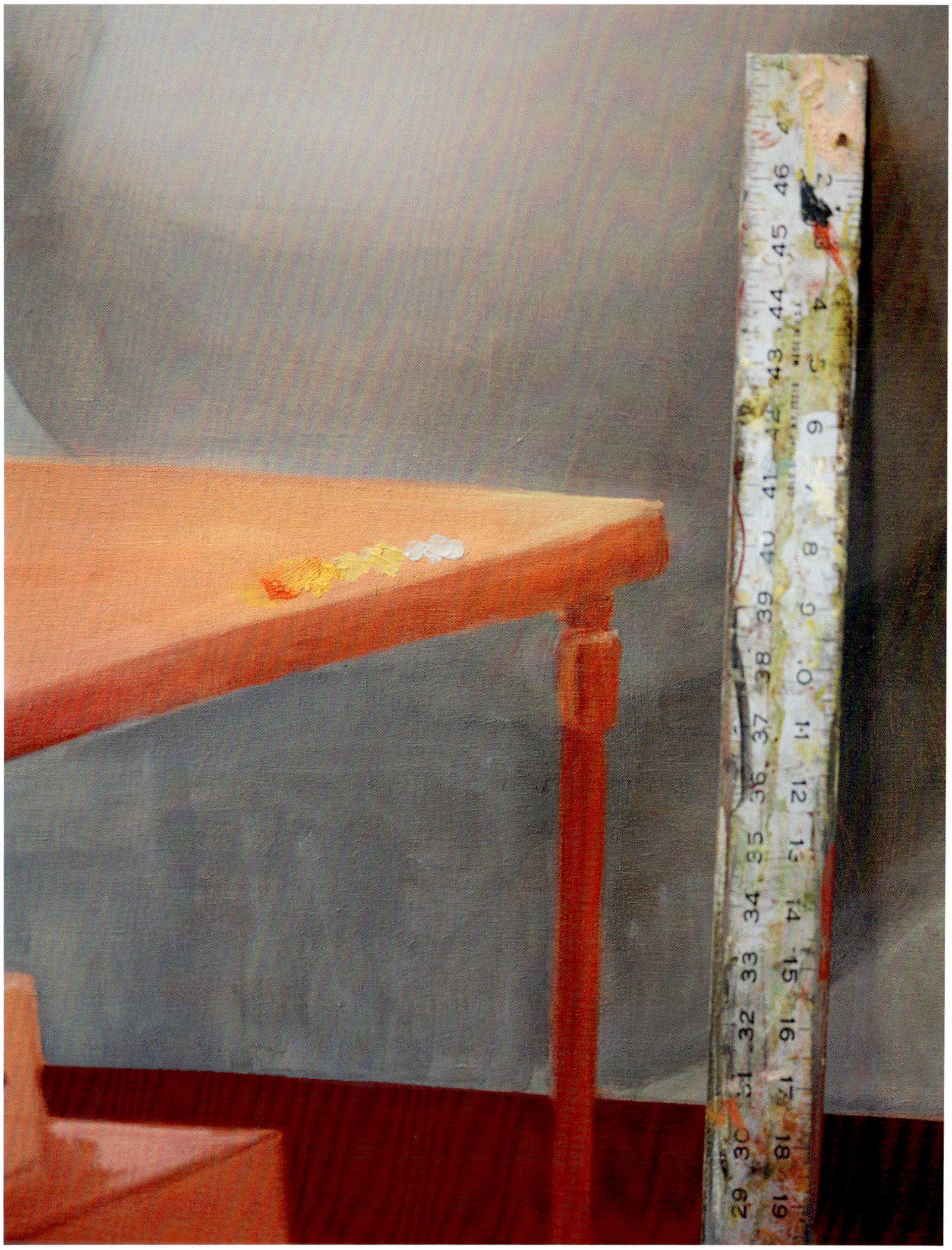

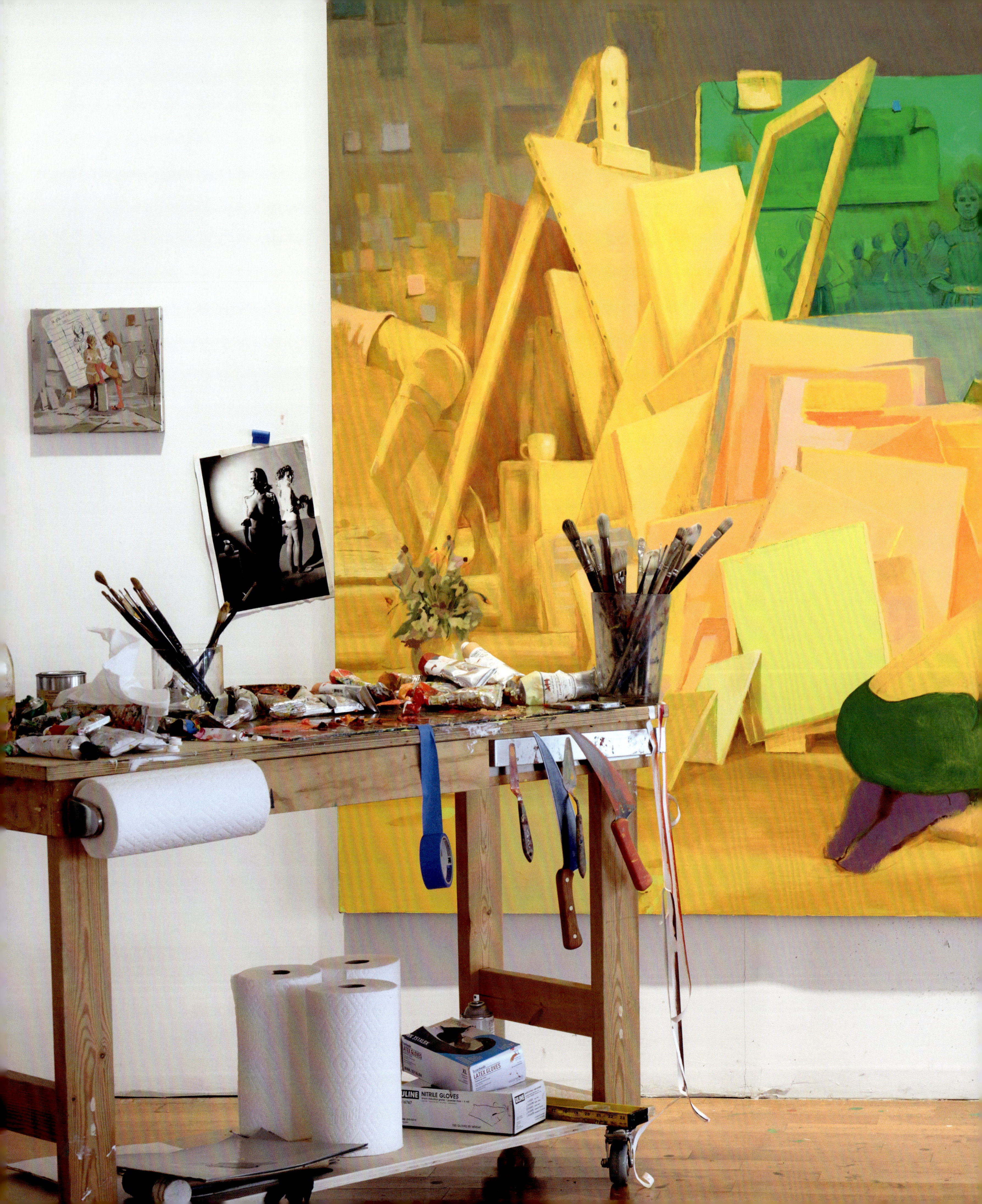
LATEX GLOVES
ULINE NITRILE GLOVES

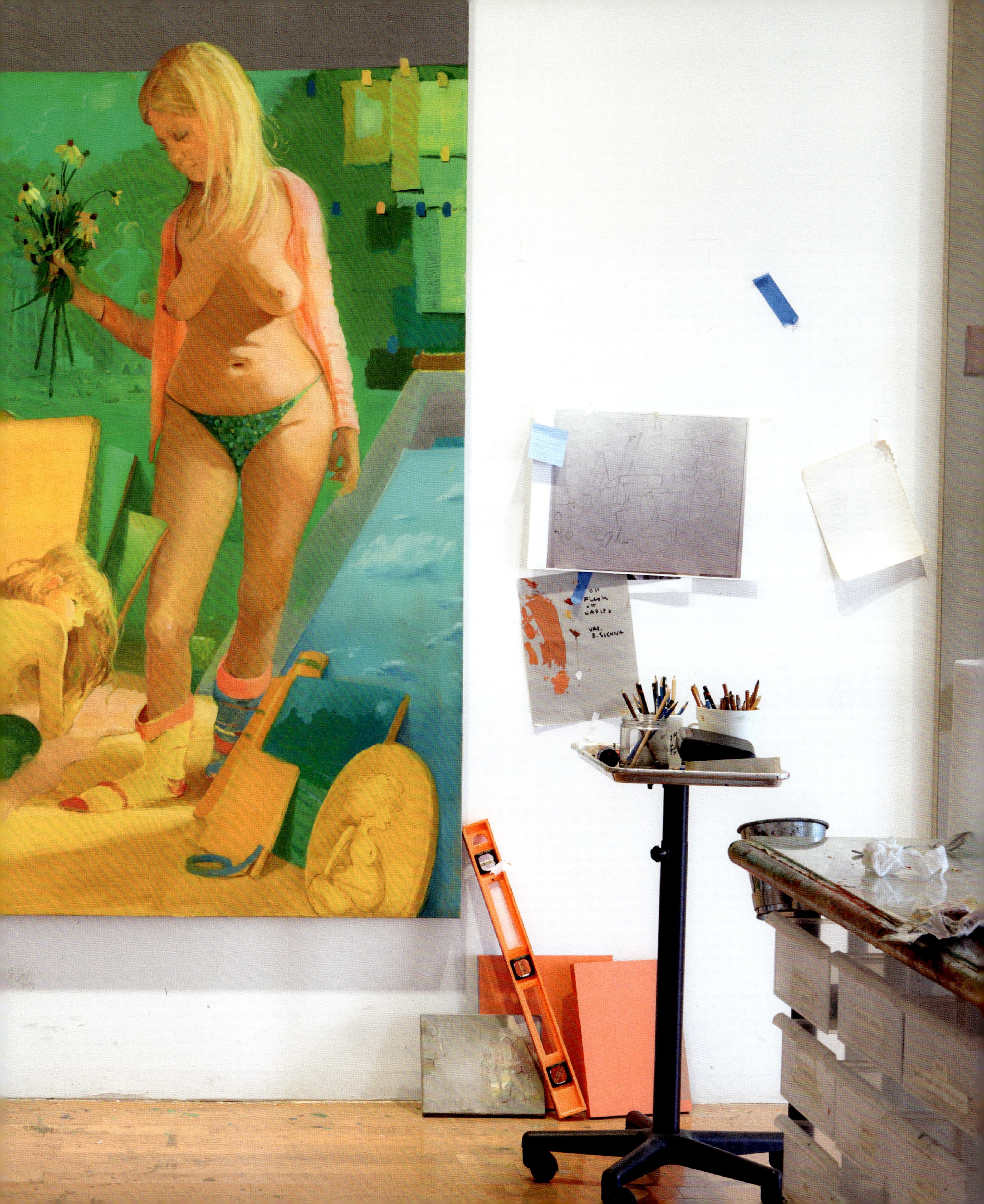
OH
Flesh
OH
NAPLES
VAR.
B. SIENNA

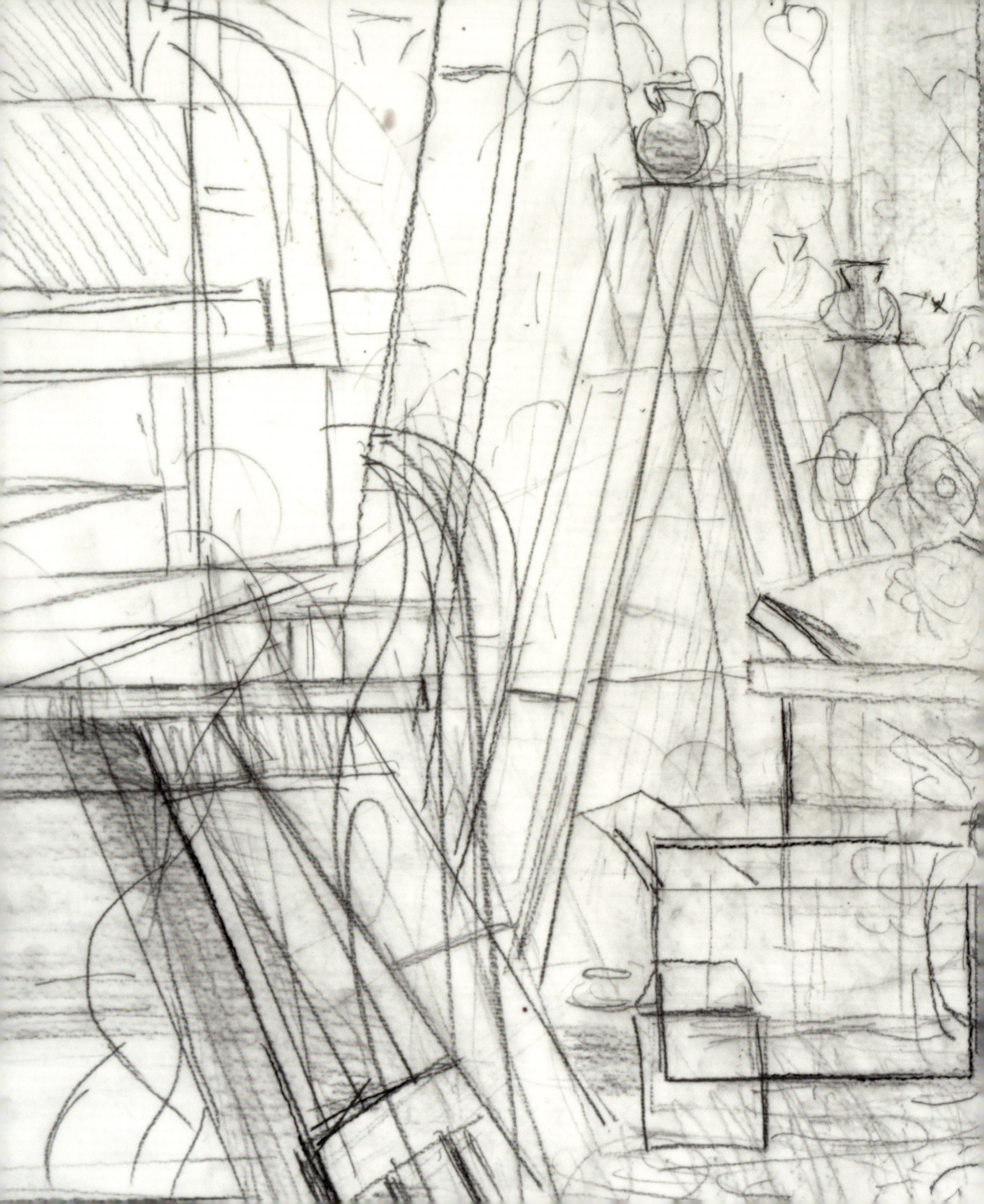

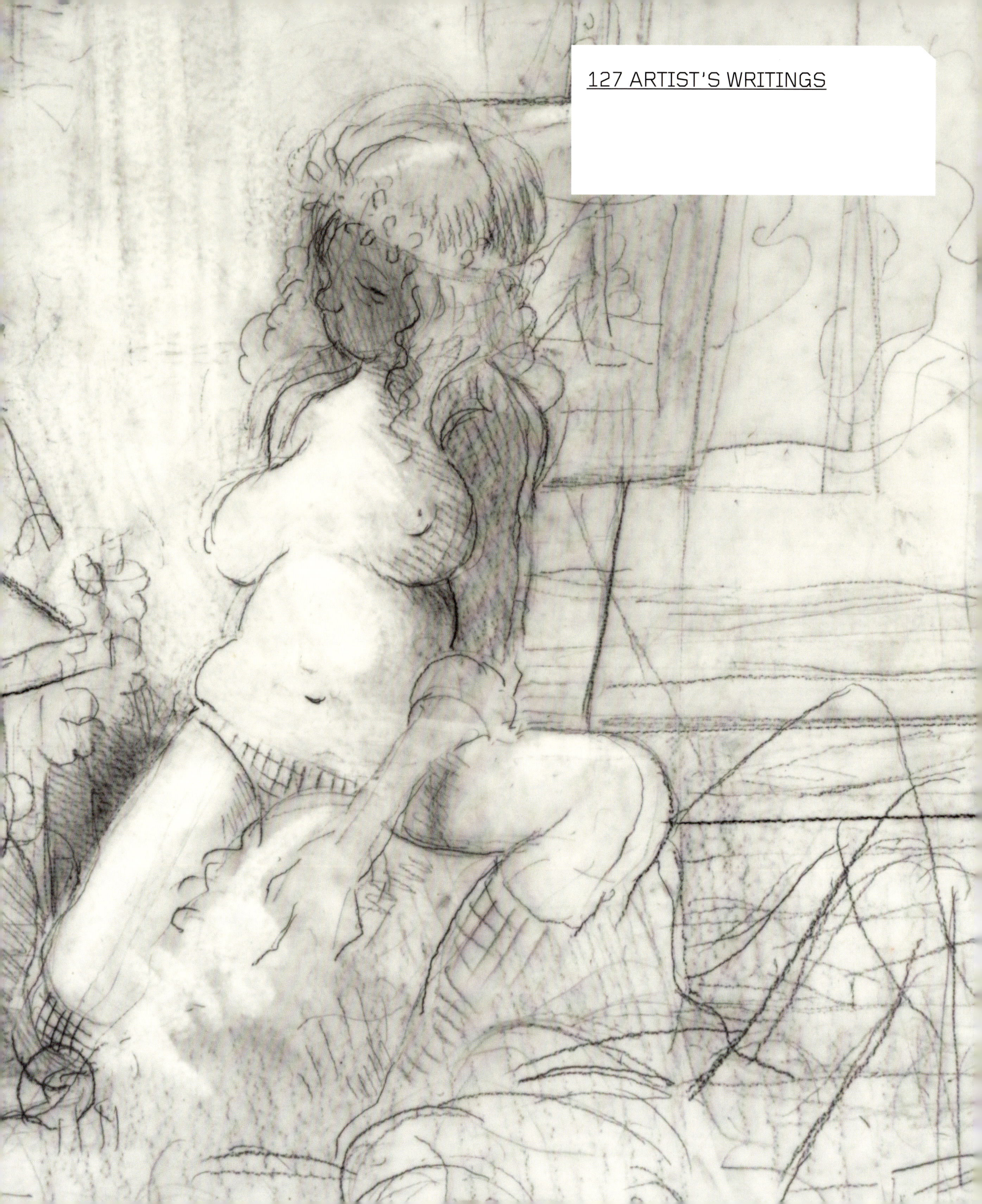

previous pages,
STUDIO STUDY, 2020
GRAPHITE ON VELLUM
56 X 64 CM

opposite,
DRAG, 2007
CHARCOAL, GRAPHITE AND PASTEL ON PAPER
21 X 15 CM

next pages, from left,
SKETCHBOOK PAGE, C. 2013
GRAPHITE ON PAPER
25 X 20 CM

SKETCHBOOK PAGE, C.2008
GRAPHITE ON PAPER
25 X 20 CM

The Role of Uncertainty in the Life of an Artist: Commencement Address to Tyler School of Art, May 17, 2000

I never expected to be here today, but it certainly is an honor. The fact that Dean [Rochelle] Toner and the faculty trust me to pull this off gives me hope. Your Commencement has thrown me into my own strange rite of passage. Ever since I agreed to give this address, I have been assessing almost every day of my life and all my choices since I started Tyler twenty years ago. I was hoping to find something that I could say that would be helpful. To prepare, I read about fifty other commencement addresses—they were all so optimistic that I got depressed. You see, they knew that they were speaking to an audience that was certain to earn a living from their shiny new diplomas. You, on the other hand, have no such certainty. So, this brings me to the topic of my speech today—the role of uncertainty in the life of an artist.

Here's the crux of it:

First, I will give you the good news. Since, in your chosen profession, success, even when you do attain it, is so fickle (as times change and tastes inevitably change along with it) you might as well play by your own rules. But how?

I have always relied upon what I call my center, also known as instinct. As an artist, it is the single best way to judge anything. Just think about what artists actually do—deciding all day what shape should be, what color, and then hope it will take on meaning. How can you ever know that you are right? But it is your work and when you are the only living expert on a subject, who could know better? Especially if you are interested in making work that doesn't resemble everything else. On this topic, I will rely on an inspirational lyric from the—I-can't-believe-I-am-actually-quoting-him-in-this-commencement-address—incomparable Mr. Billy Joel: "Your mistakes are the only thing you can ever really call your own." So, does this mean I'm saying that great artists get known for screwing things up? Well, yes. And to quote Dave Hickey: "From Eduard Manet to Cindy Sherman, the practice of art has invariably been the product of 'wrong thinking' made right … It's a dangerous game, but it's the only one in town." The artistry is in making it seem not just right but necessary.

And now the bad news: your BFA and MFA don't make you an artist. While other students out there somewhere today receiving their MDs will automatically become doctors, your only professional authenticity will come from how you will approach your life and your work every single day for the rest of your life. Though there are days I wish it were true, smelling like paint doesn't make you an artist either. Something I learned in an English class at Tyler, called, "The Modern Novel," where we read among other things, Virginia Woolf's *To the Lighthouse*, and were asked to find the real artist in the story, is that the artist wasn't necessarily the person who wrote, painted or sculpted, but rather, the character who lived gracefully in openness and uncertainty. There will be time when you will face grave self-doubt—when everything you choose in your life and your work will seem to be in direct contradiction to the advice of others. And on the topic of taking advice, I am departing from the generally dispensed wisdom of all those other "optimistic" Commencement speakers who all seemed to say, "Don't listen to advice," and say that you should listen to advice, but the real trick is whose advice and how much of it? The answers will lie within your instincts. This means that a great part of your responsibilities will be to work hard on knowing yourself, finding out, without apologies, who you are. So, if you haven't done it yet, find your center. If you already have good instincts, hone them. This is your greatest treasure to uncover: it will be everything to you—your ruby slippers. Your center will tell you more truth about yourself than any shrinks or fortune-tellers, and at the absolute least, which shrinks and which fortune-tellers.

In closing, what you have elected to do by following the calling to be artists—and this may be a Romantic idea—is to embrace, function and even thrive in uncertainty.

If this sounds exciting, you're in luck.

Thank you.

THE ARTIST'S TEMPLE UNIVERSITY | TYLER SCHOOL OF ART STUDENT I.D. CARD, 1984

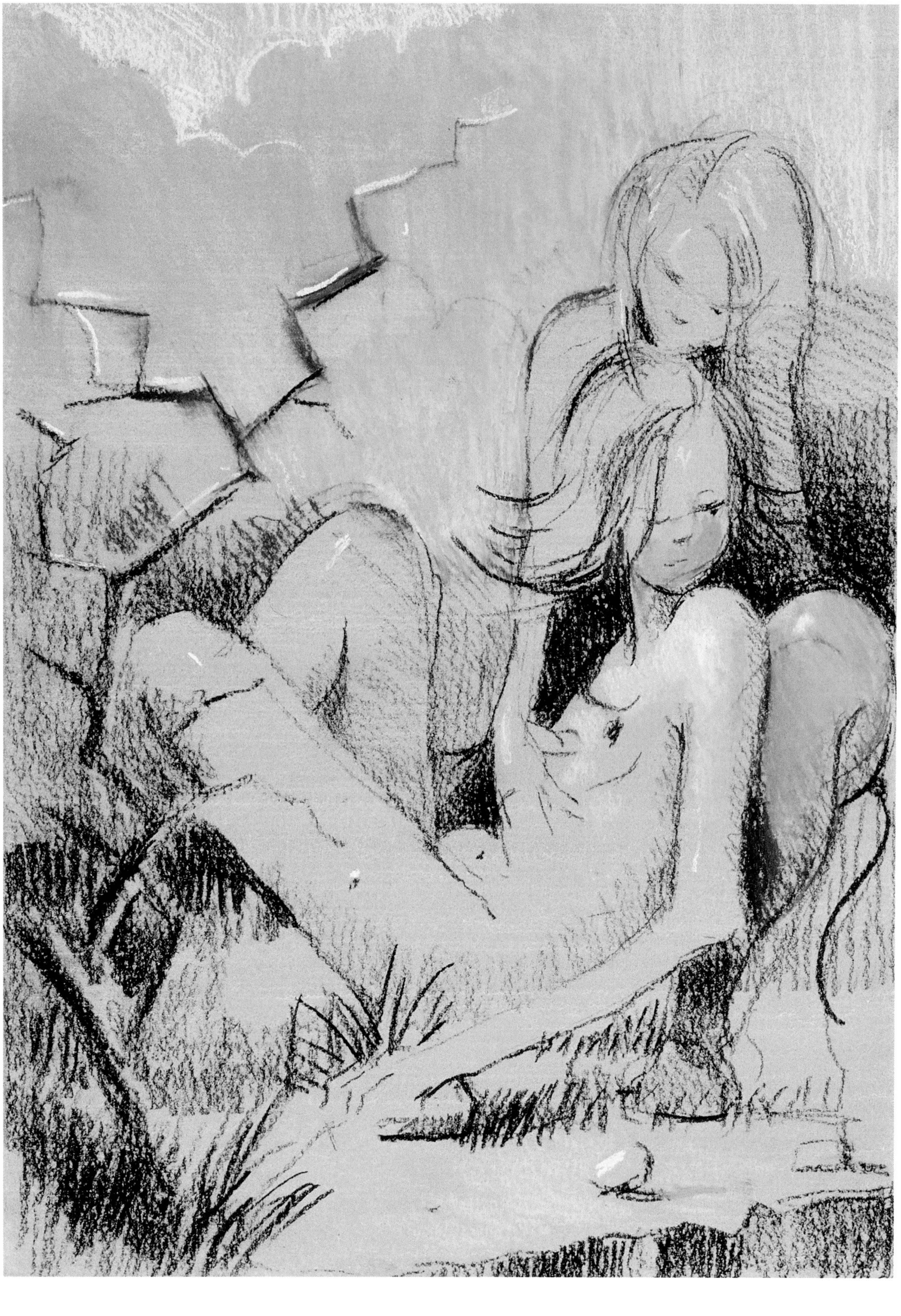

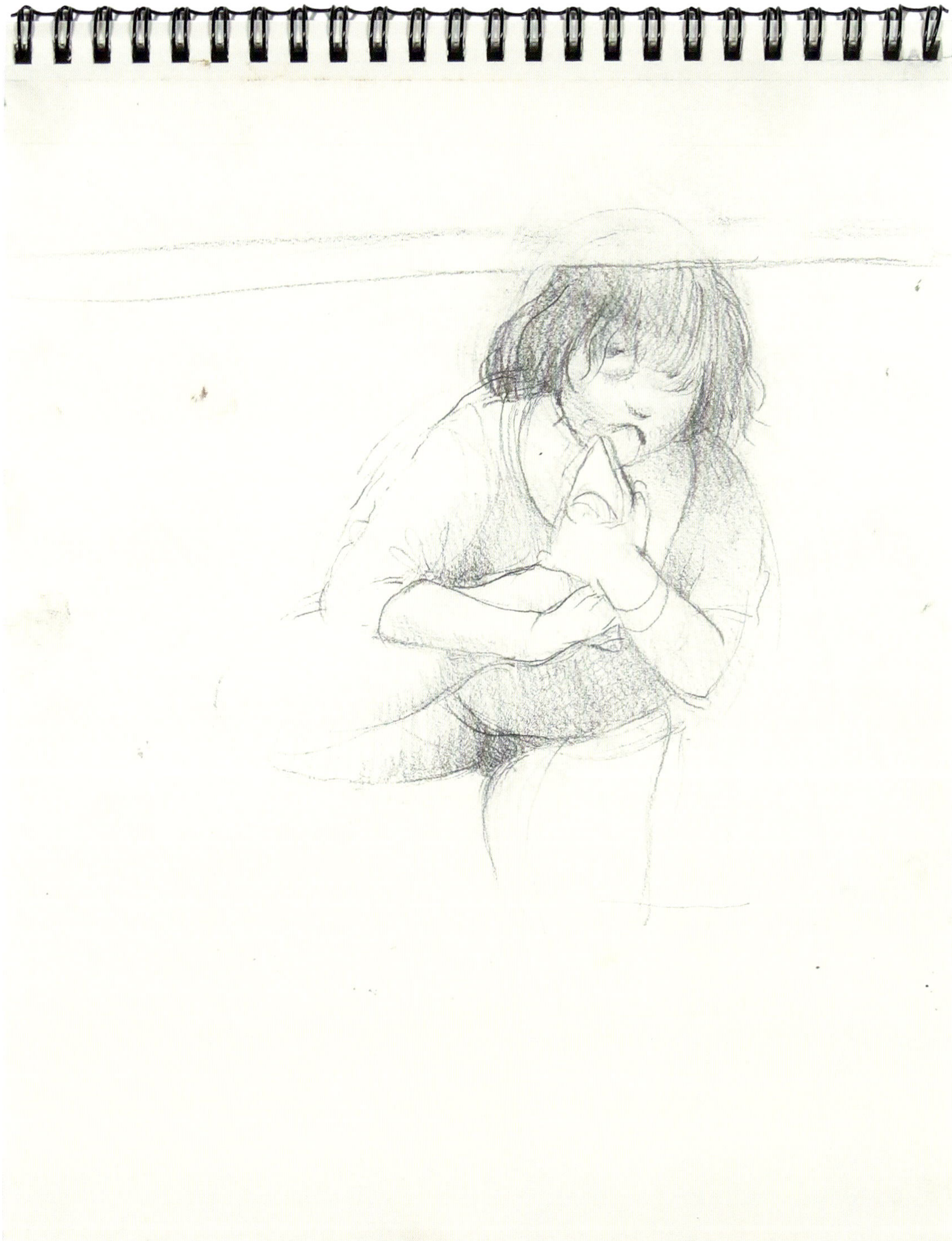

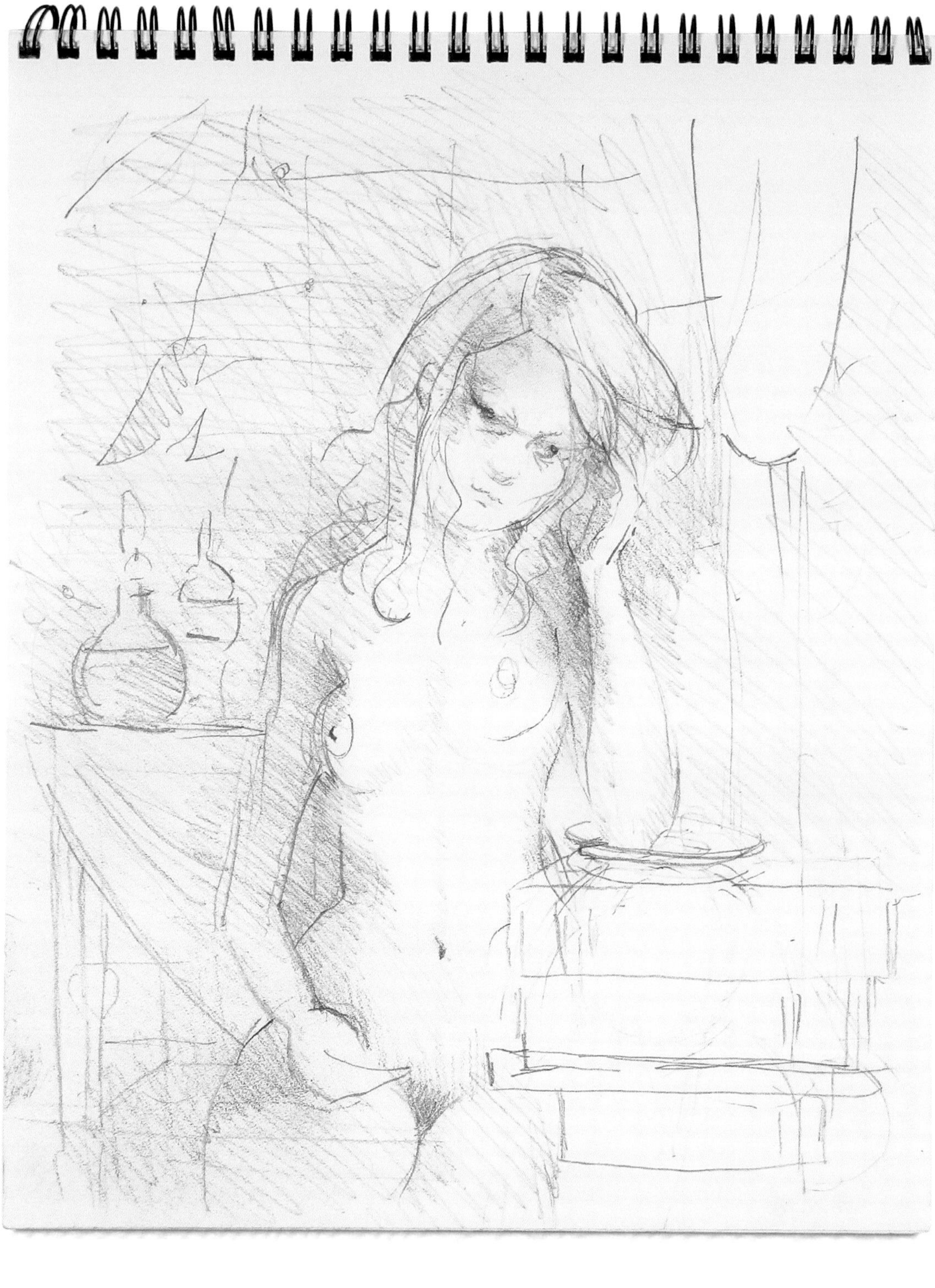

NUDE #1, 1998
PASTEL ON PAPER
29 X 23 CM

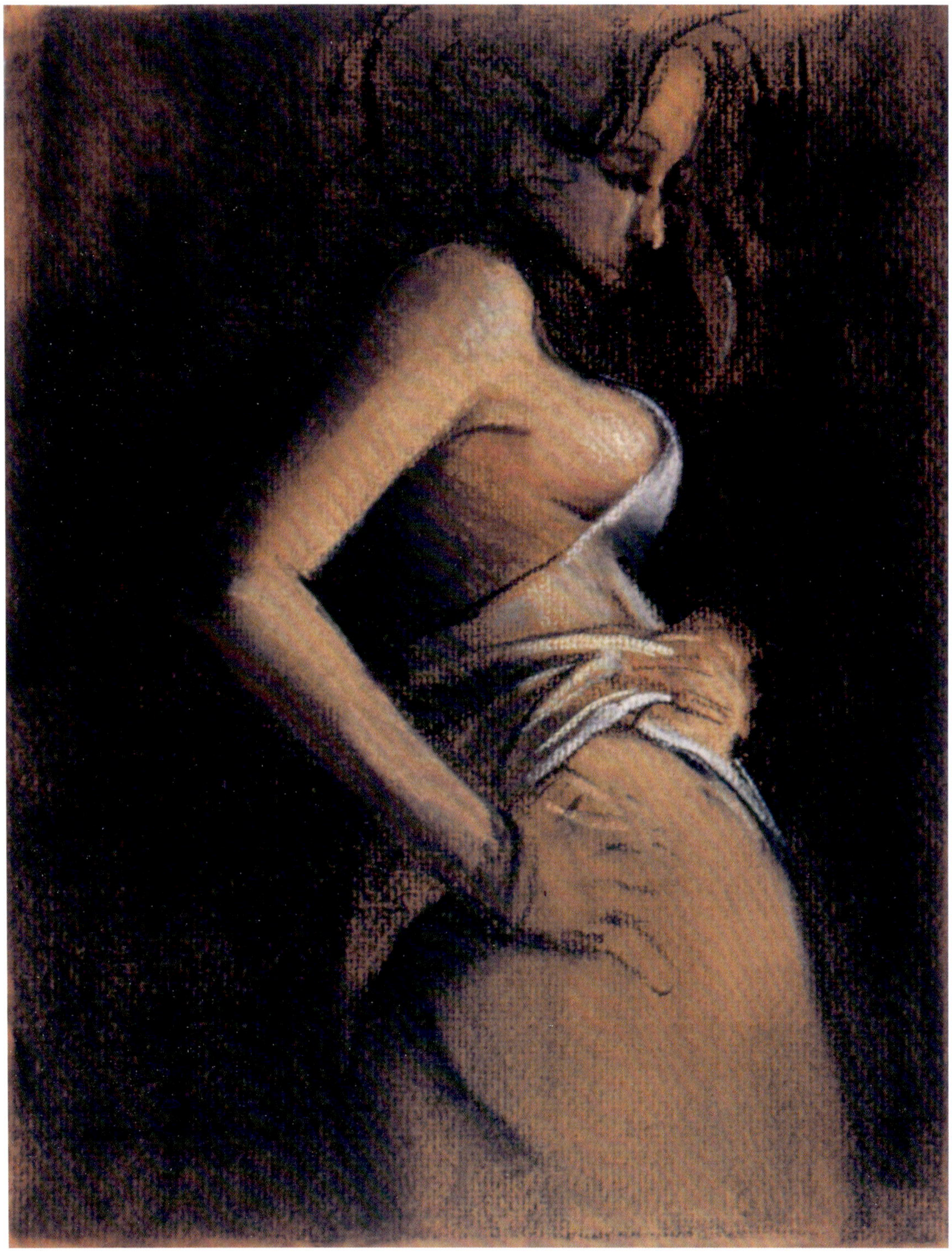

NUDE #2, 1998
PASTEL ON TONED PAPER
29 X 23 CM

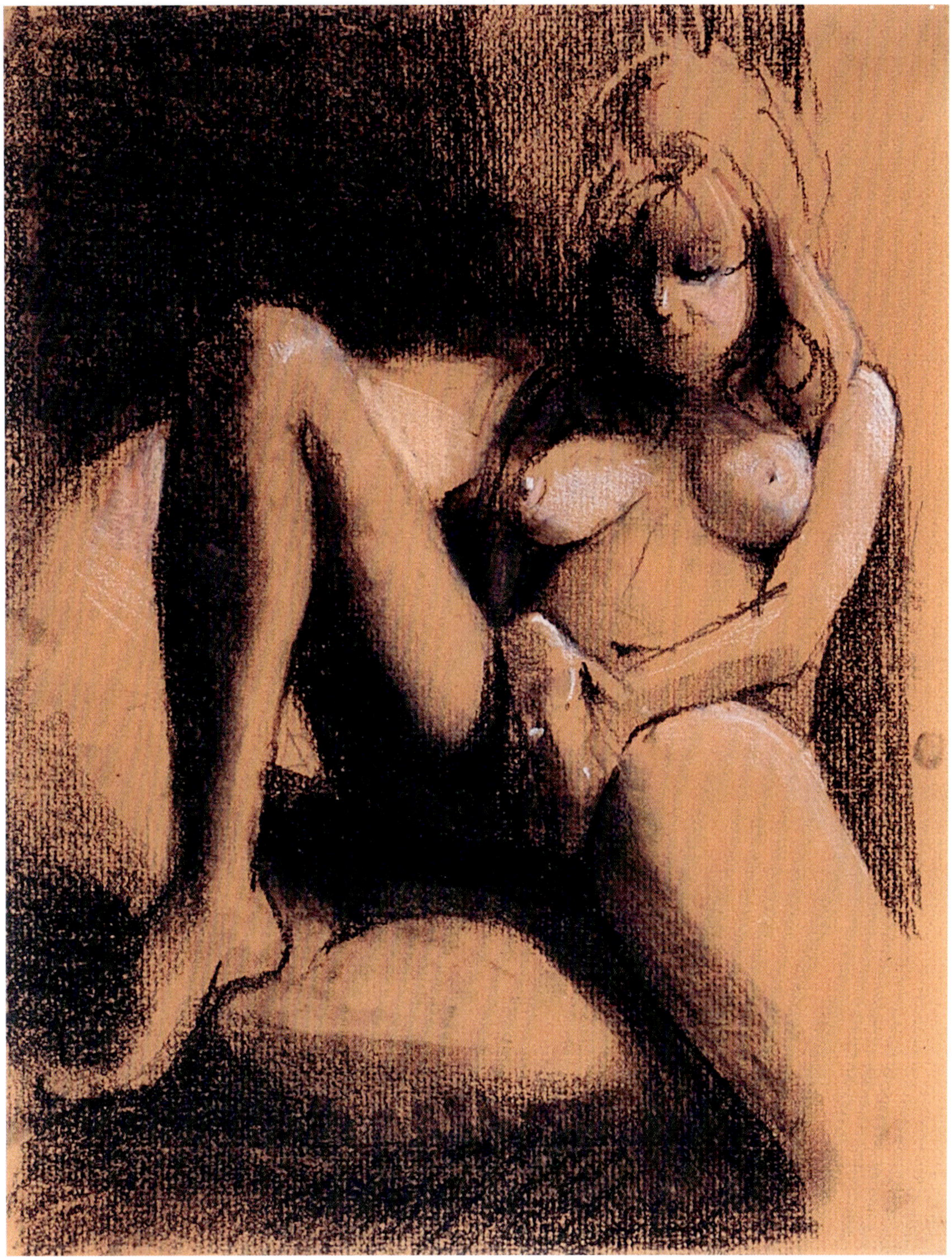

ENDLESS STUDIO, 2024
OIL ON LINEN
TRIPTYCH
OVERALL: 31 X 79 CM
PANEL 1: 31 X 25 CM
PANEL 2: 31 X 25 CM
PANEL 3: 31 X 28 CM

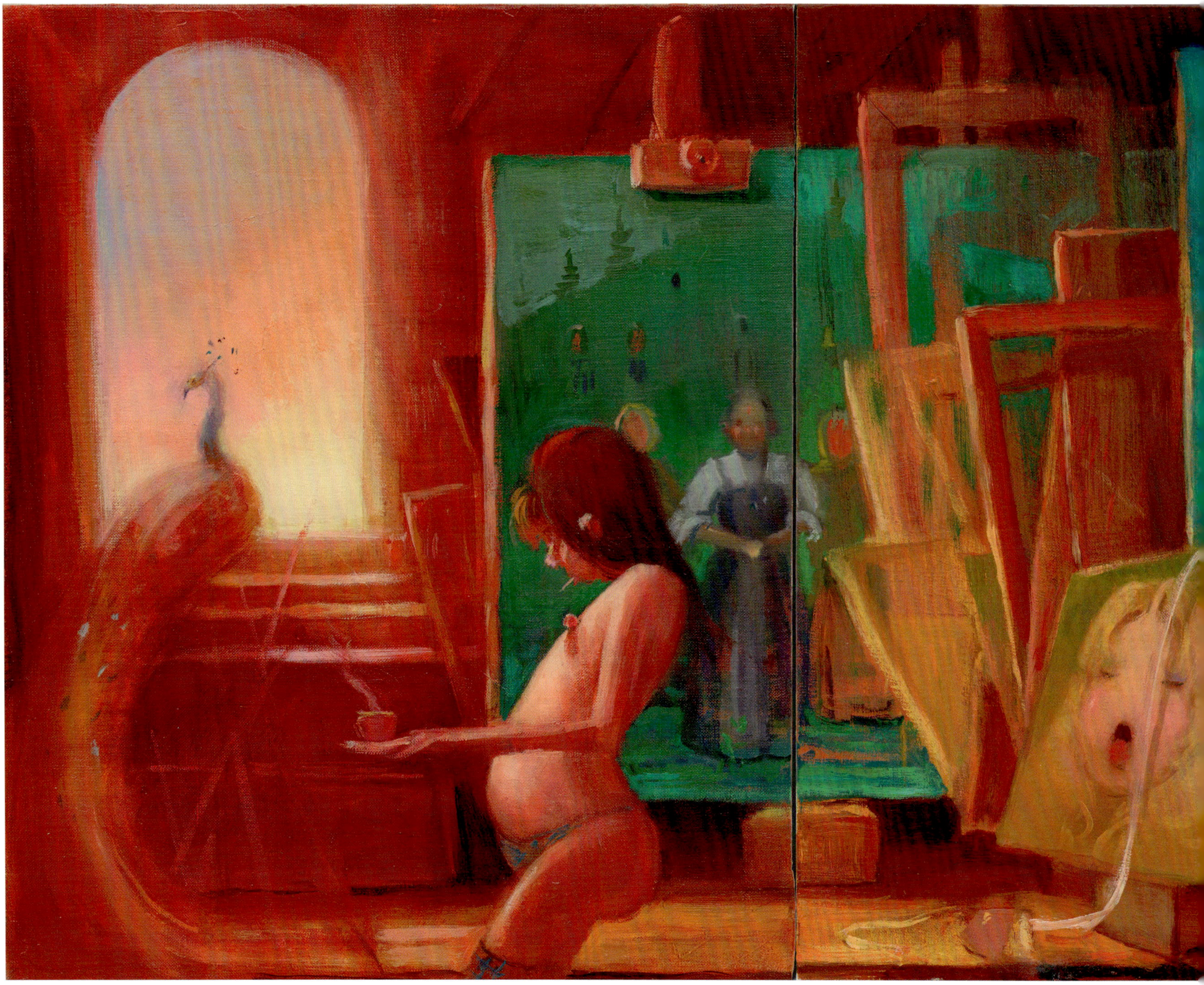

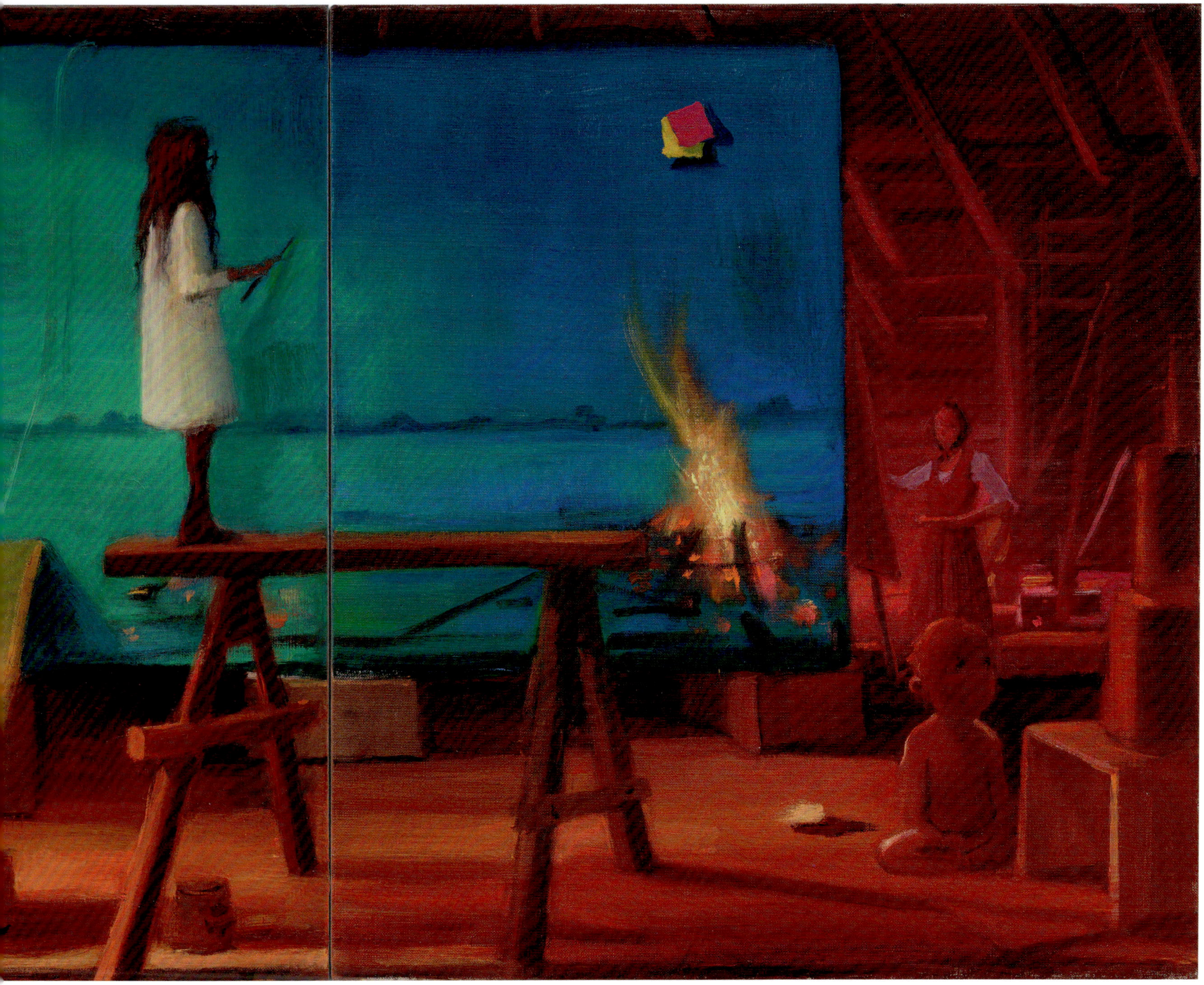

SKETCHBOOK PAGES, 1990
INK ON PAPER
14 X 41 CM

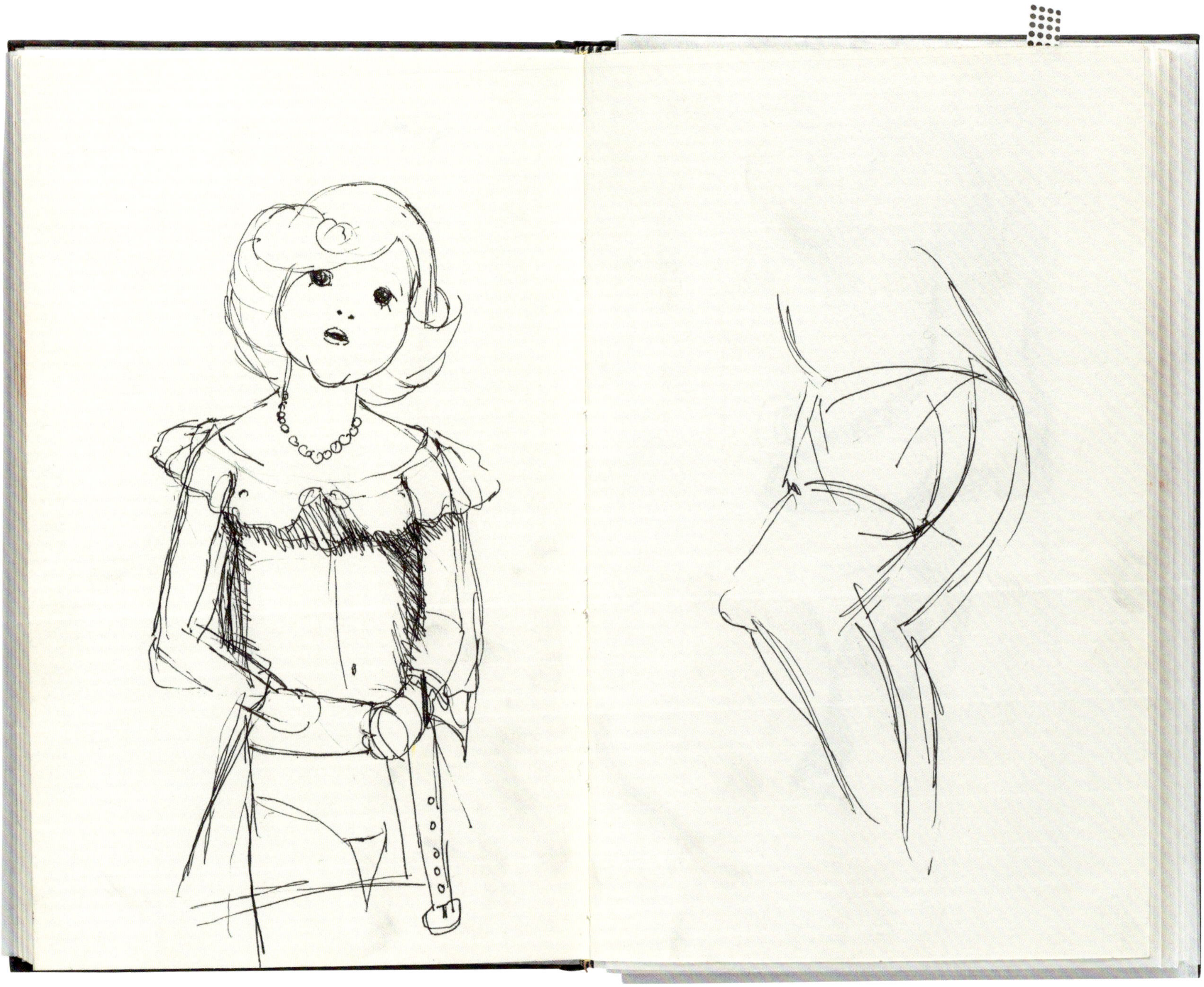

SKETCHBOOK PAGES, 1991
GRAPHITE ON PAPER
22 X 27 CM

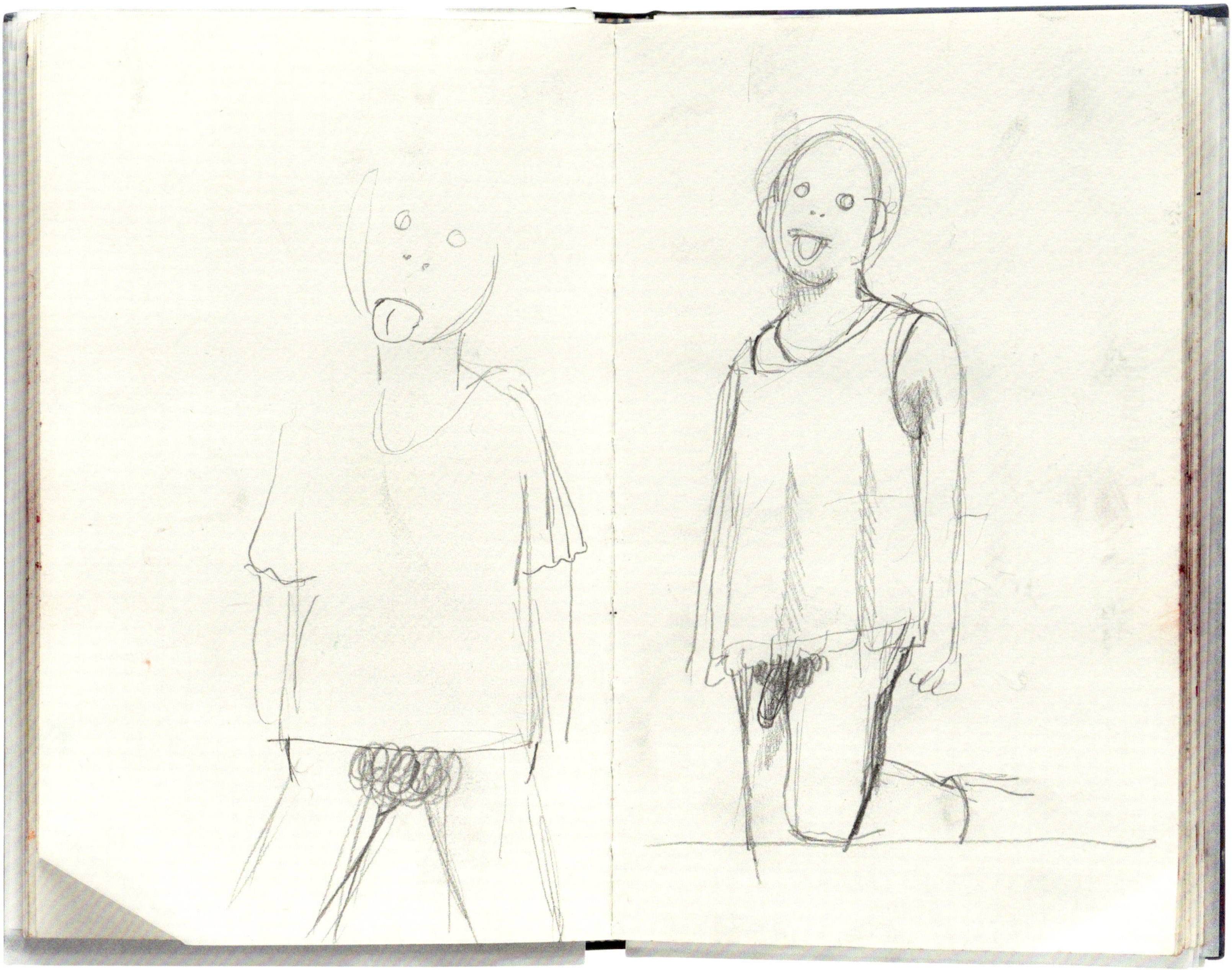

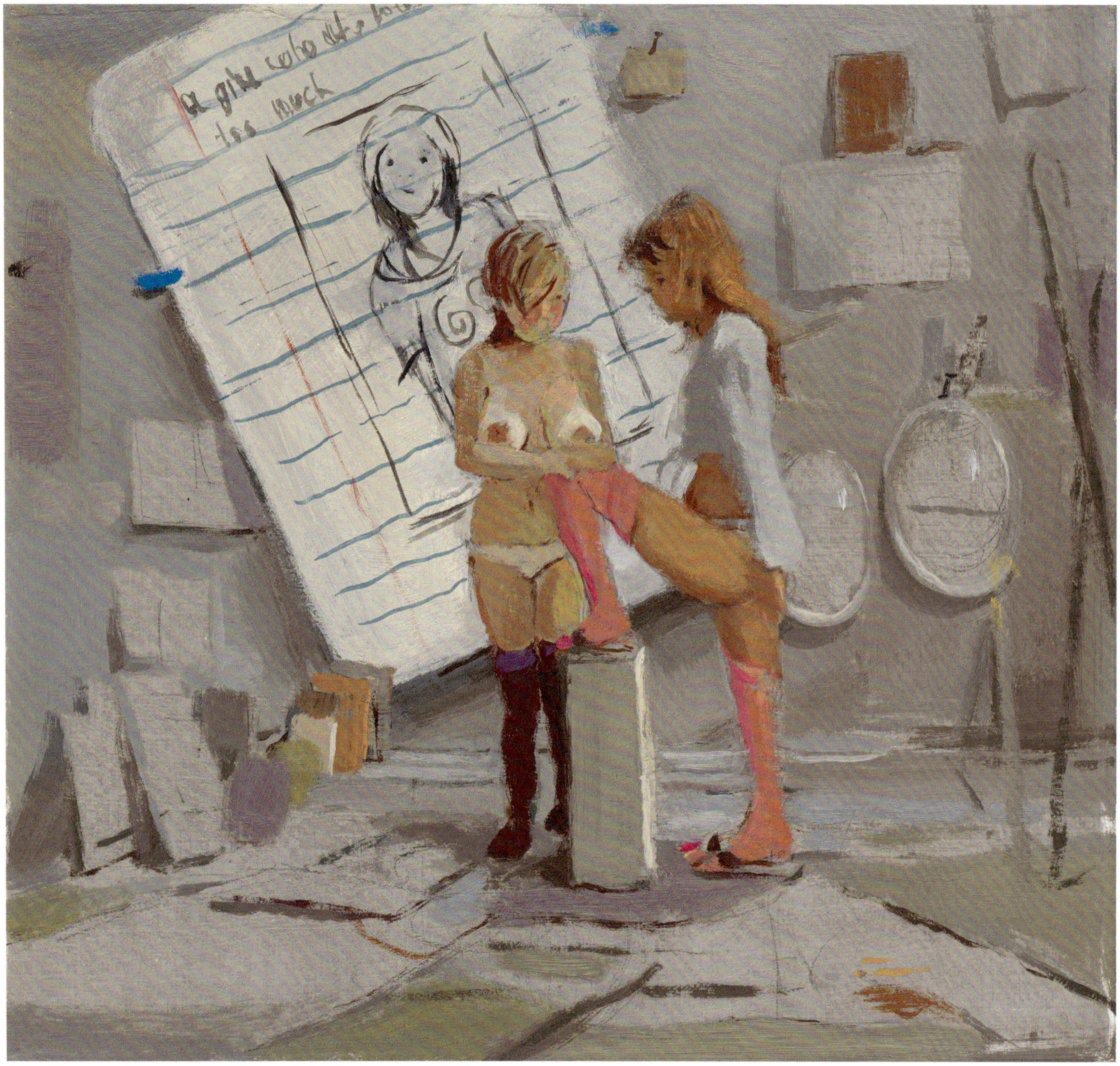

left,
NOTEBOOK (LOVED TOO MUCH),
2024
OIL ON LINEN
26 X 25 CM

opposite,
NOTEBOOK (LOVED), 2024
OIL ON LINEN
193 X 203 CM

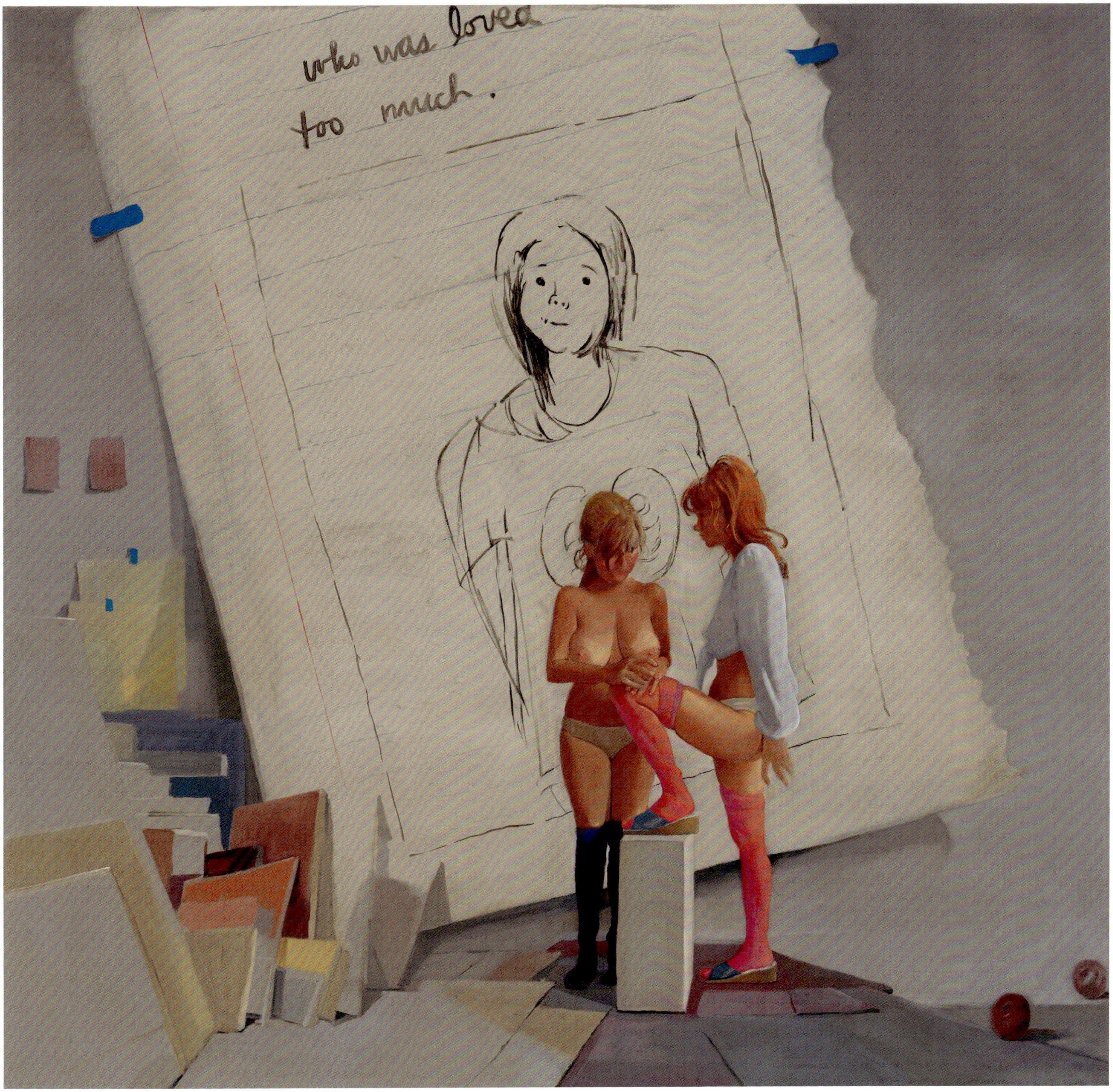
who was loved
too much.

NOTES

opposite,
SPECTRAL, 2016
OIL ON LINEN
203 X 203 CM

next pages, from left,
NO MAN'S LAND, 2012
OIL ON LINEN
196 X 183 CM

WILDERNESS, 2009
OIL ON LINEN
196 X 305 CM

INSTALLATION VIEW AT ASPEN ART MUSEUM, 2020

SURVEY: PAGES 50–99

1 Barry Schwabsky, 'Lisa Yuskavage, Elizabeth Koury Gallery', *Artforum* (April 1993): 98–99, online at https://www.artforum.com/events/lisa-yuskavage-7-214854/.

2 Jarrett Earnest, 'In the Studio: Lisa Yuskavage', *Art in America* (30 September 2015), https://www.artnews.com/art-in-america/features/in-the-studio-lisa-yuskavage-63113/.

3 'Lisa Yuskavage: Interview by Sabine Heller', *Purple* (Spring–Summer 2012), https://purple.fr/magazine/ss-2012-issue-17/lisa-yuskavage.

4 Paul Laster, 'Lisa Yuskavage previews her latest paintings', *Time Out New York*, https://www.timeout.com/newyork/art/lisa-yuskavage-previews-her-latest-paintings.

5 Levy, op. ibid.

6 Stéphane Mallarmé, 'Remémoration des amis belges/Remembrance of Belgian Friends', *The Poems in Verse*, translated by Peter Manson (Oxford, Ohio: Miami University Press, 2012), pp. 124–25, translation modified.

7 Frances Richard, 'Lisa Yuskavage, David Zwirner Gallery/Zwirner&Worth', *Artforum* (January 2007), online at https://www.artforum.com/events/lisa-yuskavage-201010/.

8 Robert Enright, 'The Overwhelmer: An Interview with Lisa Yuskavage', *Border Crossings* (August 2007), https://bordercrossingsmag.com/article/the-overwhelmer-an-interview-with-lisa-yuskavage.

9 'Lisa Yuskavage: Interview by Sabine Heller', *Purple* (Spring–Summer 2012), https://purple.fr/magazine/ss-2012-issue-17/lisa-yuskavage.

10 Mónica de la Torre, 'Lisa Yuskavage', *Bomb Magazine* (Fall 2011), https://bombmagazine.org/articles/lisa-yuskavage/.

11 ibid.

12 Schwabsky, 'Lisa Yuskavage: Elizabeth Koury Gallery'.

13 William Grimes, 'William Bailey, Modernist Figurative Painter, Dies at 89', *The New York Times* (18 April 2020), https://www.nytimes.com/2020/04/18/arts/william-bailey-dead.html.

14 ibid.

15 Lisa Yuskavage, 'The Question of Gender in Art', *Tema Celeste* (Autumn 1992), pp. 70–71, https://www.yuskavage.com/wp-content/uploads/2015/09/9462.pdf.

16 Barry Schwabsky, 'Picturehood is Powerful', *Art in America* (December 1997), pp. 83, 85, online at https://yuskavage.com/wp-content/uploads/2015/09/9378.pdf

17 Robert Morris, quoted by Michael Fried, *Art and Objecthood: Essays and Reviews* (Chicago: University of Chicago Press, 1998), p. 153.

18 Fried, p. 43.

19 Lydia Figes, 'Unfinished: why are we drawn to imperfection?', *Art UK* (22 August 2019), https://artuk.org/discover/stories/unfinished-why-are-we-drawn-to-imperfection.

20 De la Torre, ibid.

21 Earnest, ibid.

22 Enright, ibid.

23 Michel Foucault, *The Order of Things: An Archeology of the Human Sciences* (New York: Vintage Books, 1994), p. 4.

24 Willem de Kooning, 'The Renaissance and Order', https://www.dekooning.org/documentation/words/the-renaissance-and-order.

25 De la Torre, ibid.

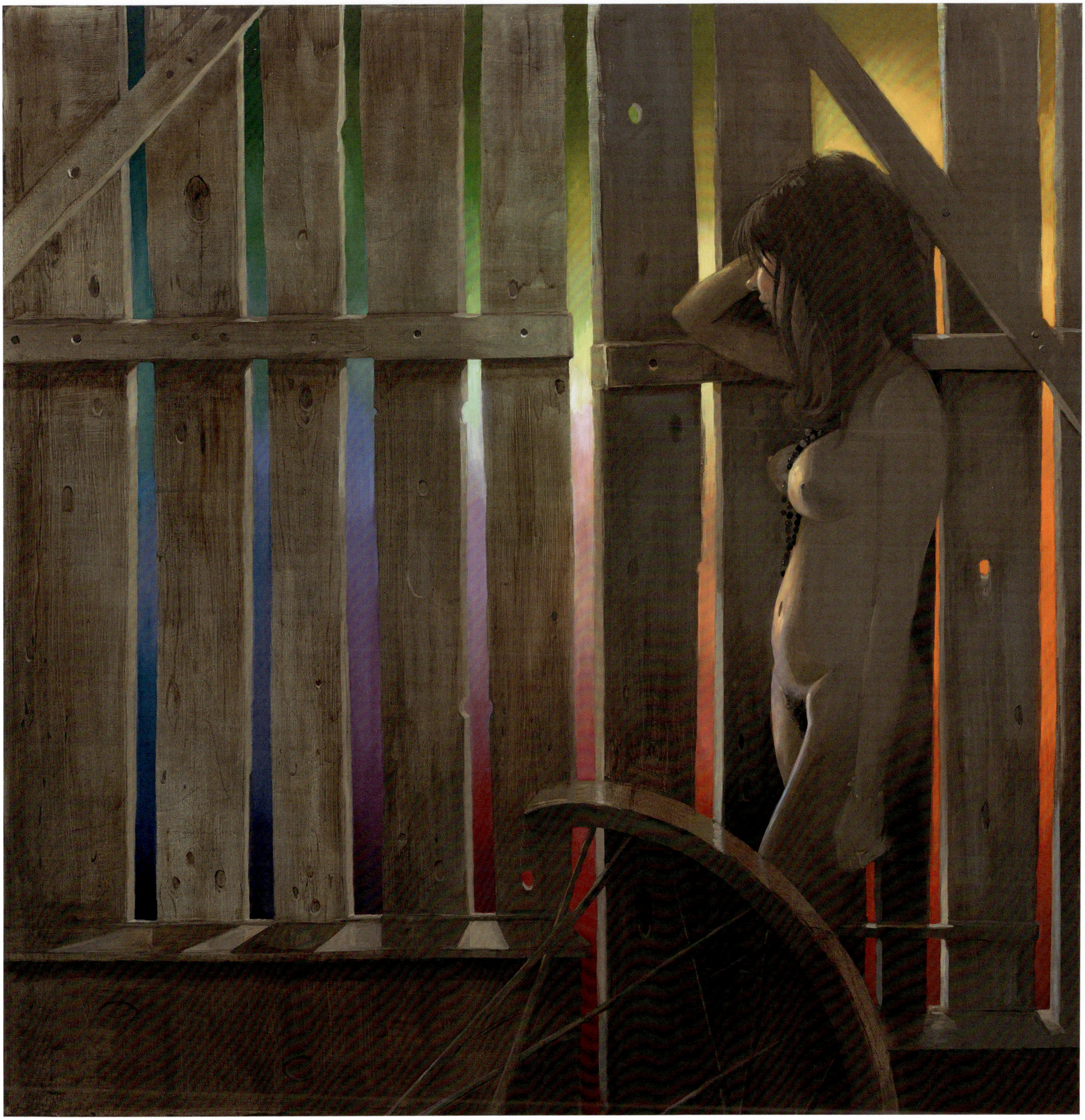

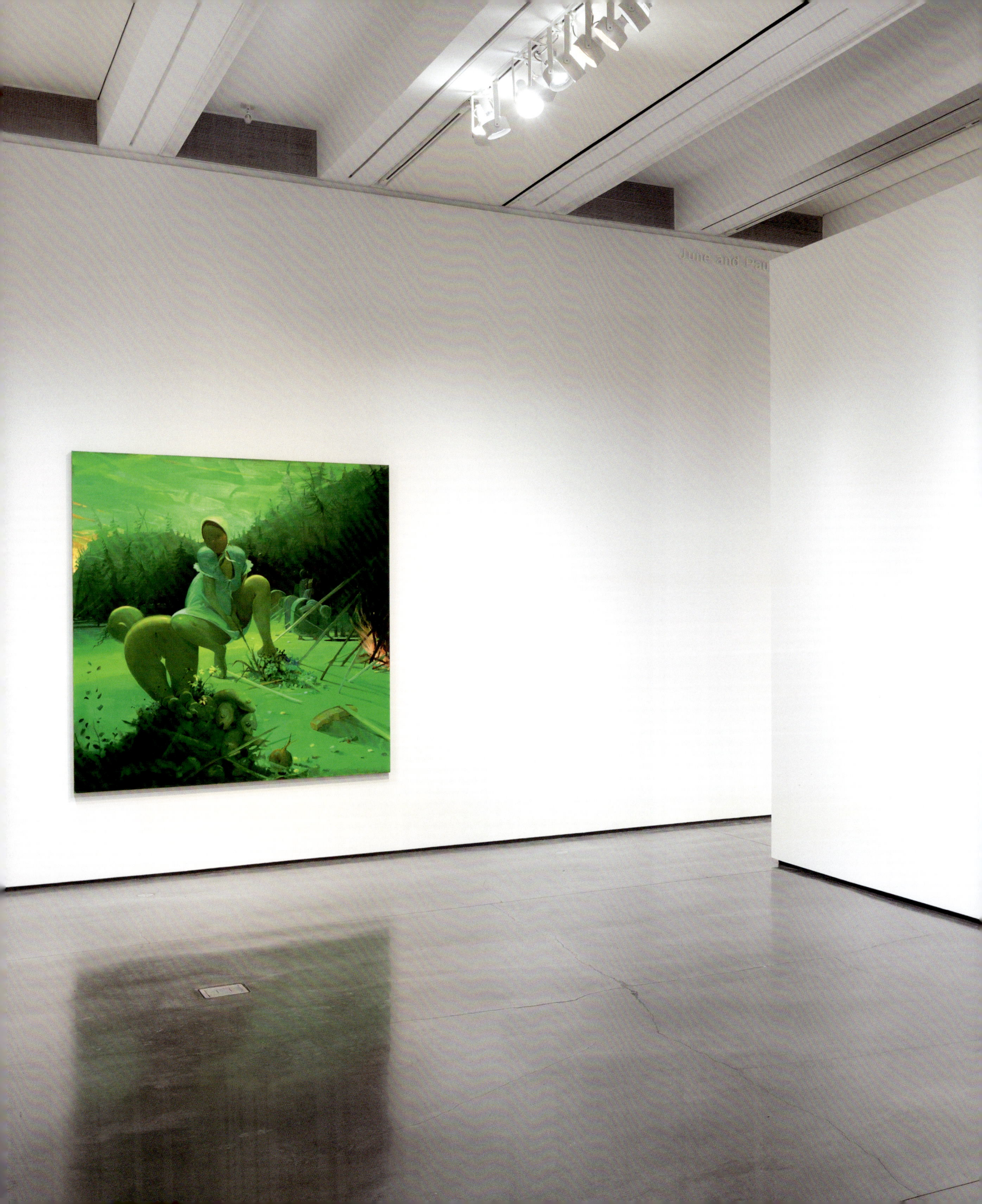

143 CHRONOLOGY

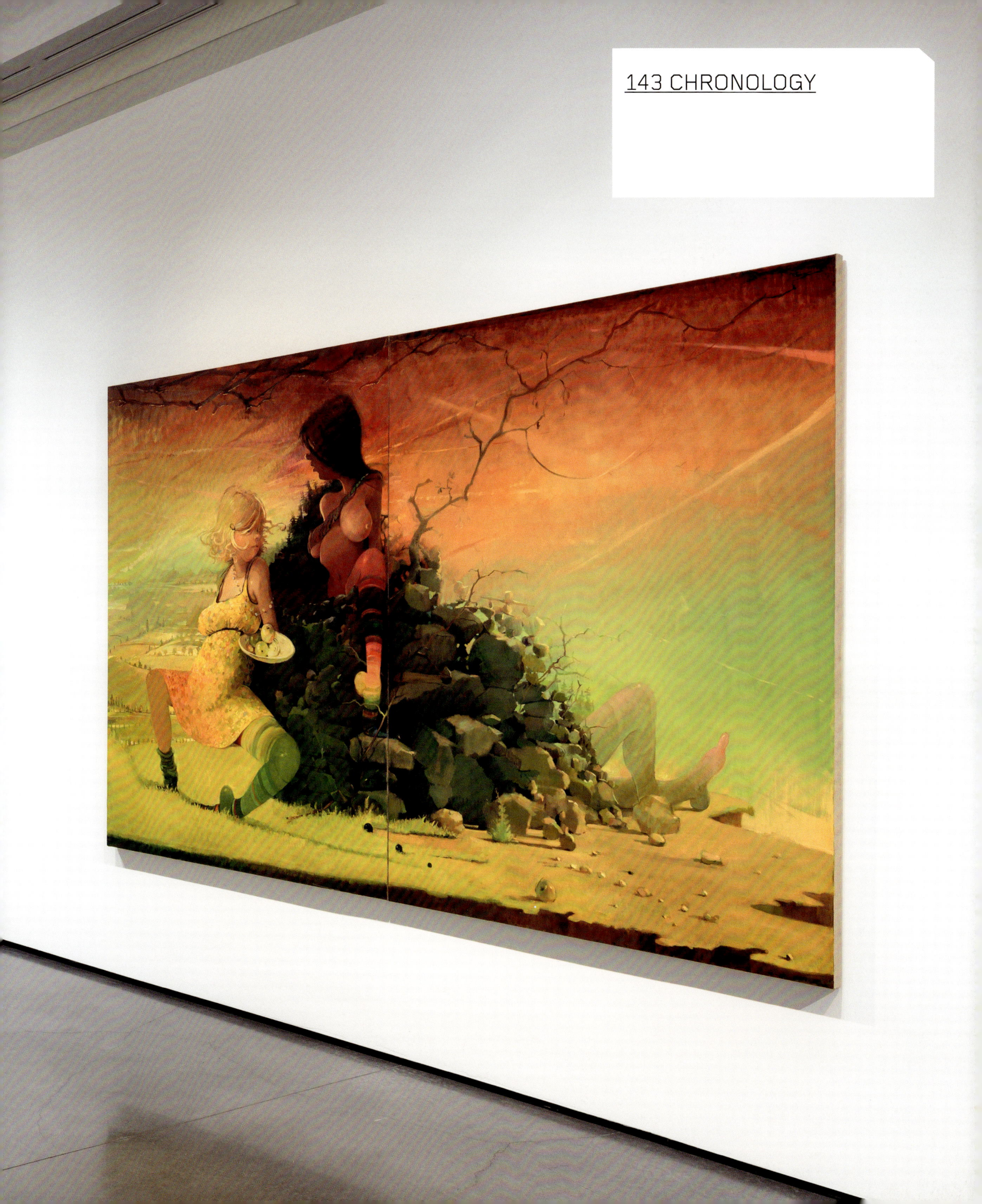

CHRONOLOGY: Lisa Yuskavage, born 1962 in Philadelphia. Lives and works in New York.

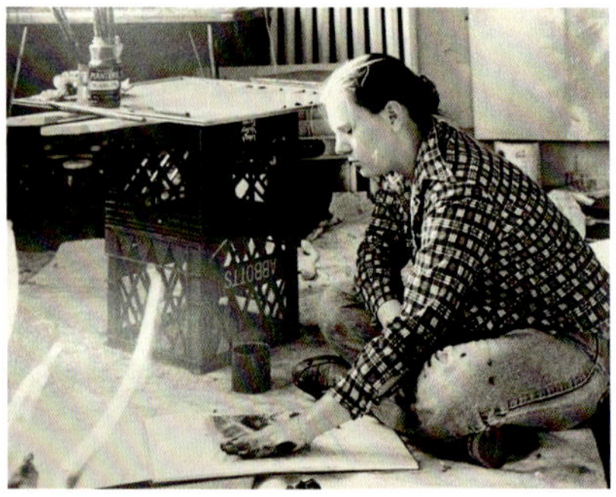

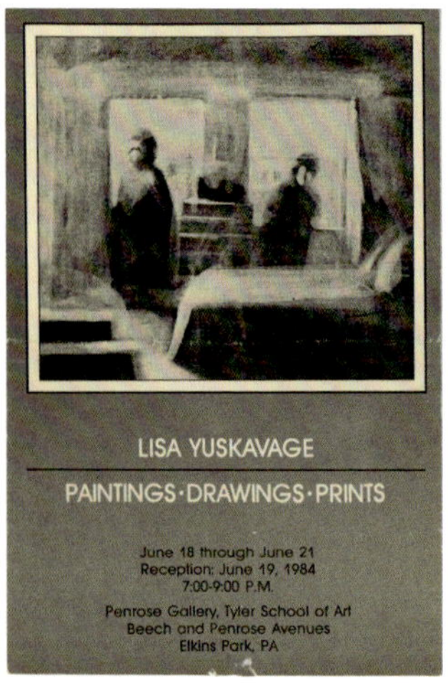

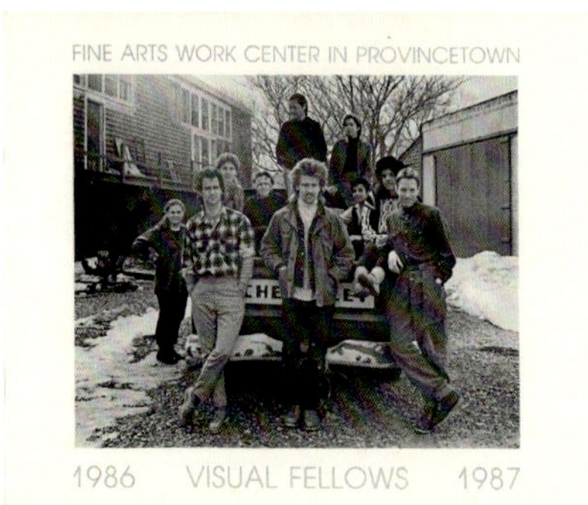

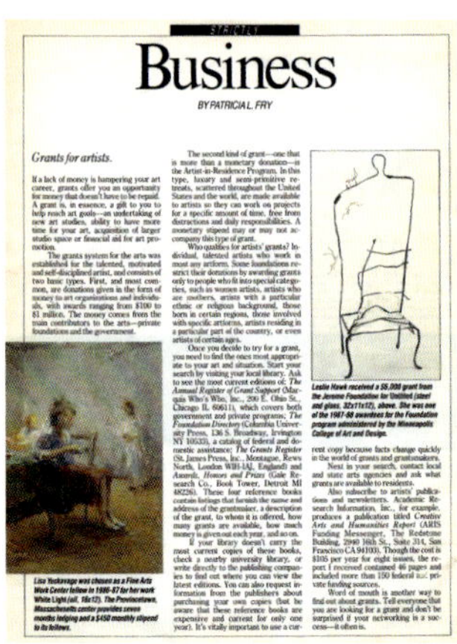
Business

SELECTED EXHIBITIONS AND PROJECTS 1982–92

1982
Attends Temple Abroad, Tyler School of Art, Rome

1984
'Lisa Yuskavage: Paintings, Drawings, and Prints',
PENROSE GALLERY, TYLER SCHOOL OF ART, Philadelphia (solo)

Obtains a BFA, Tyler School of Art, Temple University, Philadelphia

1986
'Lisa Yuskavage: MFA Thesis',
YALE SCHOOL OF ART, New Haven, Connecticut (solo)

'New Talent',
ALPHA GALLERY, Boston (group)

Obtains an MFA, Yale School of Art, New Haven, Connecticut

1987
'New Work, New Talent',
NEW HAVEN, HARCUS GALLERY, Boston (group)

1988
'Lisa Yuskavage: Paintings',
MAURICE M. PINE FREE PUBLIC LIBRARY, Fairlawn, New Jersey (solo)

'Emerging Artists',
WWAC GALLERY, Westport, Connecticut (group)

'Twenty Artists Choose Twenty Artists',
PROVINCETOWN ART MUSEUM, Massachusetts (group)

1989
'Juried Show '89',
NEW JERSEY CENTER FOR THE VISUAL ARTS, Summit

'Selections by Fine Arts Work Center Fellowship Recipients',
TWINING ALCOVE GALLERY, New York (group)

1990
'Lisa Yuskavage',
PAMELA AUCHINCLOSS GALLERY, New York (solo)

1991
'Fine Arts Work Benefit Show',
TWINING GALLERY, New York (group)

1992
'A Paper Trail',
BERLAND/HALL GALLERY, New York (group)

'The Anti-Masculine',
KIM LIGHT GALLERY, Los Angeles (group)

'FIAR International. Art Under 30',
PALAZZO DELLA PERMANENTE, Milan, toured to GALLERIA DEL CHIOSTRO, Rome; L'ESPACE PIERRE CARDIN, Paris; ACCADEMIA ITALIANA DELLA ARTI, London; NATIONAL ACADEMY OF DESIGN, New York; WIGHT ART GALLERY, UNIVERSITY OF CALIFORNIA, Los Angeles (group)

'Little Men/Little Women',
WHITE COLUMNS, New York (group)

SELECTED ARTICLES AND INTERVIEWS 1982–92

1986
Campbell, Julie Freeman, 'Fellows: 1986–1987', Provincetown Arts, Fall

1988
Watkins, Eileen, 'Gladstone Exhibition Showcases "Realism" with Interesting Results in Various Forms', The Star Ledger, January 24

Fry, Patricia L, 'Strictly Business: Grants for Artists', The Artist's Magazine, September

1992
Yuskavage, Lisa, 'The Question of Gender in Art', Tema Celeste, no. 37-38, Autumn

SELECTED EXHIBITIONS AND PROJECTS
1992–95

SELECTED ARTICLES AND INTERVIEWS
1992–95

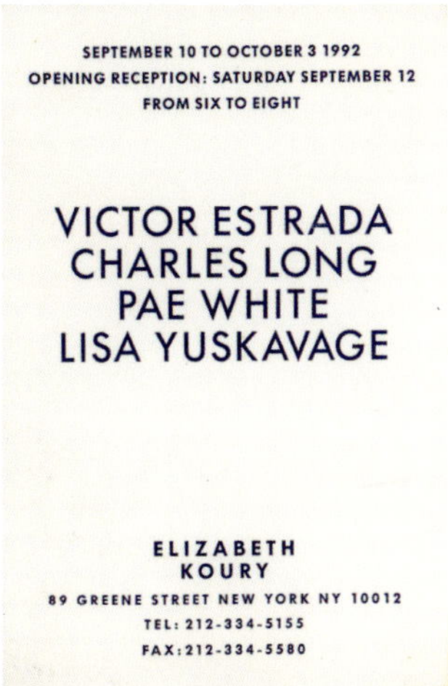

1992 (cont.)

'Victor Estrada, Charles Long, Pae White, Lisa Yuskavage',
ELIZABETH KOURY, New York (group)

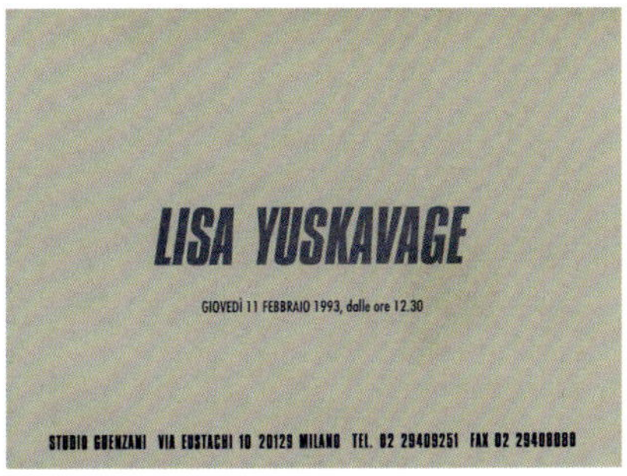

1993

'Lisa Yuskavage',
ELIZABETH KOURY, New York (solo)

'Lisa Yuskavage',
STUDIO GUENZANI, Milan (solo)

'The Figure as Fiction: The Figure in Visual Art and Literature',
CONTEMPORARY ARTS CENTER, Cincinnati (group)

'Medium Messages',
WOOSTER GARDENS, New York (group)

'The Return of the Cadavre Exquis',
THE DRAWING CENTER, New York, toured to CORCORAN GALLERY OF ART, Washington, D.C.; SANTA MONICA MUSEUM OF ART, California; FORUM FOR CONTEMPORARY ART, St. Louis; THE AMERICAN CENTER, Paris (group)

'Tabu: Women, Painting, Subversion',
FOUR WALLS, Brooklyn (group)

'Yale Collects Yale',
YALE UNIVERSITY ART GALLERY, New Haven, Connecticut (group)

1993

Lloyd, Ann Wilson, 'Where Are They Now?', Provincetown Arts, Spring

Schwabsky, Barry, 'Review: Lisa Yuskavage, Elizabeth Koury', Artforum, April

Hirsch, Faye, 'Review: Lisa Yuskavage at Elizabeth Koury', Art in America, June

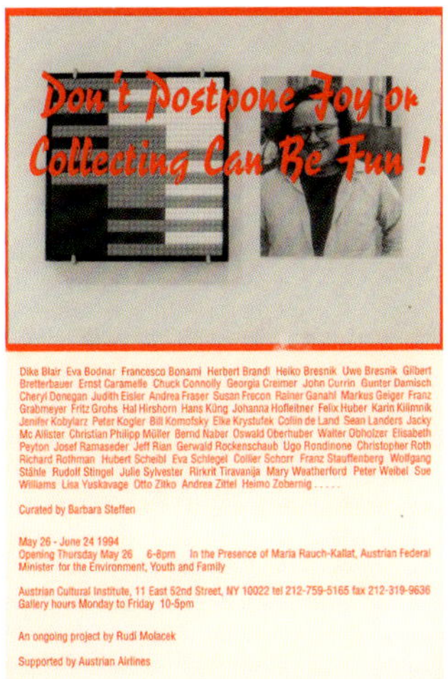

1994

'Lisa Yuskavage',
CHRISTOPHER GRIMES GALLERY, Santa Monica, California (solo)

'Lisa Yuskavage',
LUHRING AUGUSTINE, New York (solo)

'Watercolors',
ELIZABETH KOURY, New York (solo)

'Desire',
DIFFA VISIONAIRE/CHARLES COWLES GALLERY, New York (group)

'Don't Postpone Joy or Collecting Can Be Fun',
NEUE GALERIE AM LANDESMUSEUM JOANNEUM, Graz, toured to AUSTRIAN CULTURAL INSTITUTE, New York (group)

'I, Myself & Me',
THE INTERART CENTER, New York (group)

'NY-NL-XX',
GEMEENTEMUSEUM HELMOND, The Netherlands

'Out West and Back East: New Work from Los Angeles and New York',
SANTA MONICA MUSEUM OF ART, California (group)

'Up the Establishment',
SONNABEND GALLERY, New York (group)

1994

Knight, Christopher, 'Review: A Bicoastal Flashback', Los Angeles Times, 18 February

Cotter, Holland, 'Art in Review: The Joys of Childhood Re-examined', The New York Times, 25 March

Schwabsky, Barry, 'The Sublime, the Beautiful, the Gender of Painting: Confessions of a Male Gaze', New Art Examiner, April

Smith, Roberta, 'Art in Review: Up the Establishment, Sonnabend Gallery', The New York Times, 3 June

Kandel, Susan, 'Review: Visions of Seduction, Repulsion', Los Angeles Times, 9 June

Saltz, Jerry, 'A Year in the Life: Tropic of Painting', Art in America, October

Relyea, Lane, 'Review: Lisa Yuskavage, Christopher Grimes Gallery', Artforum, November

1995

'Diverse Group/One Direction',
APEXART, New York (group)

'Gang Warfare',
THE MAC, Dallas (group)

'Not Not (Who's There?): Part III',
E.S. VANDAM, New York (group)

1995

'Cadavre Exquis Revisited', Manhattan File, May

Yuskavage, Lisa, 'Interview: Chuck Close by Lisa Yuskavage', BOMB Magazine, Summer

Connors, Thomas, 'Review: Youth Culture Killed My Dog (but I don't really mind)', New Art Examiner, September

Damianovic, Maia, 'The Fantastic in Art', Tema Celeste, no. 55, Winter

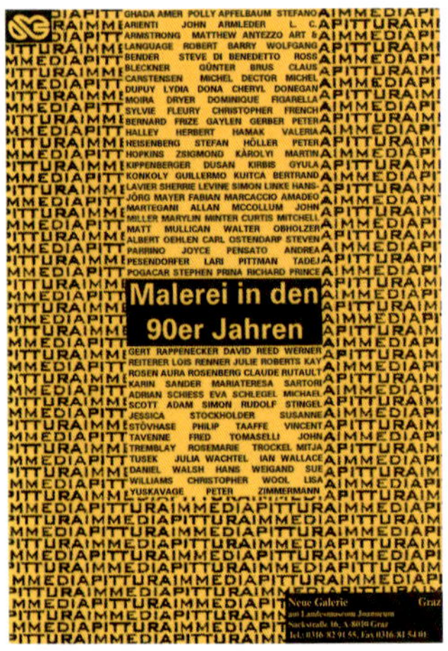

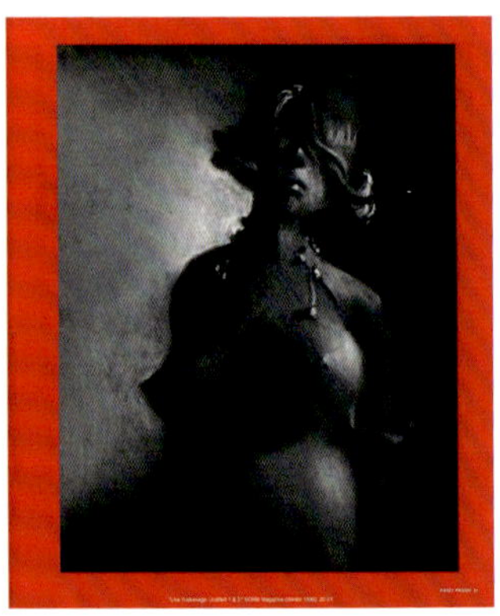

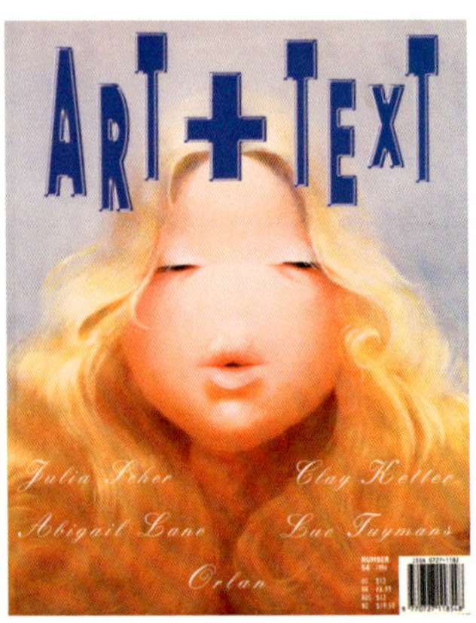

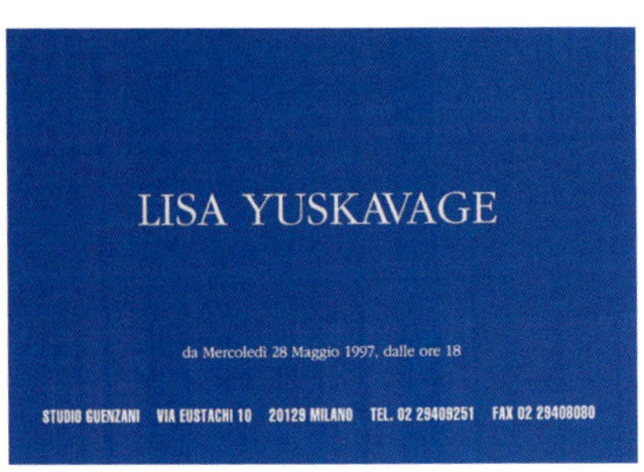

SELECTED EXHIBITIONS AND PROJECTS
1995–97

1995 (cont.)
'Pittura/Immedia: Malerei in den 90e Jahren',
NEUE GALERIE AM LANDESMUSEUM JOANNEUM AND KÜNSTLERHAUS, Graz, toured to MŰCSARNOK, Budapest (group)

'Youth Culture Killed My Dog (but I don't really mind)',
CONTEMPORARY ARTS COUNCIL, Chicago (group)

1996
'Lisa Yuskavage',
BOESKY & CALLERY, New York (solo)

'Lisa Yuskavage',
CHRISTOPHER GRIMES GALLERY, Santa Monica, California (solo)

'Adicere Animos',
CESENA-CESENATICO, Bologna (group)

'Norfolk '96',
YALE UNIVERSITY SUMMER SCHOOL OF MUSIC AND ART, Norfolk, Connecticut (group)

'Rome Selection: 30 Years of Tyler School of Art Temple/Rome Program',
TYLER SCHOOL OF ART, TEMPLE UNIVERSITY, Philadelphia (group)

'What I did on my summer vacation',
WHITE COLUMNS, New York (group)

1997
'Lisa Yuskavage',
STUDIO GUENZANI, Milan (solo)

'Pictures, Patents, Monkeys, and More…On Collecting',
WESTERN ART GALLERY, WESTERN WASHINGTON UNIVERSITY, Bellingham, toured to JOHN MICHAEL KOHLER ARTS CENTER, Sheboygan, Wisconsin; AKRON ART MUSEUM, Ohio; SOUTH BEND REGIONAL MUSEUM, Indiana; INSTITUTE OF CONTEMPORARY ART, UNIVERSITY OF PENNSYLVANIA, Philadelphia; PITTSBURGH CENTER FOR THE ARTS (group)

'My Little Pretty: Images of Girls by Contemporary Women Artists',
MUSEUM OF CONTEMPORARY ART CHICAGO (group)

'Slad',
APEXART, New York (group)

'Women's Work: Examining the Feminine in Contemporary Painting',
SOUTHEASTERN CENTER FOR CONTEMPORARY ART, Winston-Salem, North Carolina (group)

SELECTED ARTICLES AND INTERVIEWS
1995–97

1996
Kandel, Susan, 'Review: Yuskavage's Works Embark on a Psycho Sexual Adventure', Los Angeles Times, 15 January

Cooper, Jacqueline, 'Review: Lisa Yuskavage at Christopher Grimes', New Art Examiner, March

Joyce, Julie, 'Review: Lisa Yuskavage at Christopher Grimes', Art No.s, March–April

Zellen, Jody, 'Review: Lisa Yuskavage, Christopher Grimes Gallery', Art Press, April

Brooks, Rosetta, 'Lisa Yuskavage: Some Girls Do', Art+Text, May

Plagens, Peter, 'Lady Painters? Smile When You Say That', Newsweek, 30 September

Arning, Bill, 'Review: Lisa Yuskavage, Boesky & Callery', The Village Voice, 29 October

Saltz, Jerry, 'Review: Lisa Yuskavage at Boesky & Callery', Time Out New York, 31 October–7 November

Dalton, Jennifer, 'Review: Lisa Yuskavage at Boesky & Callery', Review, 1 November

Smith, Roberta, 'Palettes Full of Ideas About What Painting Should Be: Lisa Yuskavage at Boesky & Callery', The New York Times, 1 November

Boccella, Kathy, 'A Juniata Park Native Hits It Big On The Art Scene', The Philadelphia Inquirer, 6 November

'Portfolio: Lisa Yuskavage', BOMB Magazine, Winter

1997
Clifford, Katie, 'Review: Lisa Yuskavage at Boesky & Callery', Art Papers, January–February

Hill, Shawn, 'Sex and Sensibility', Bay Windows, 16 January

Condon, Elisabeth, 'Review: Lisa Yuskavage, Boesky & Callery', New Art Examiner, February

Vine, Richard, 'Review: Lisa Yuskavage at Boesky & Callery', Art in America, February

Pokorny, Sydney, 'Review: Lisa Yuskavage, Boesky & Callery', Artforum, February

Ritchie, Matthew, 'Lisa Yuskavage at Boesky & Callery', Flash Art, no. 193, March–April

Wye, Pamela, 'Desiring Machines and Exquisite Corpulence: Lisa Yuskavage's Girlies', Sulfur, Spring

Pollack, Barbara, 'Interview with Lisa Yuskavage', TeenMom, 24 April

Schwabsky, Barry, 'Picturehood is Powerful', Art in America, December

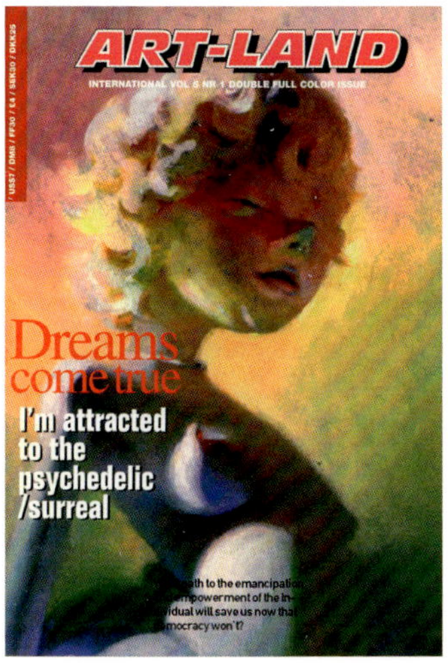

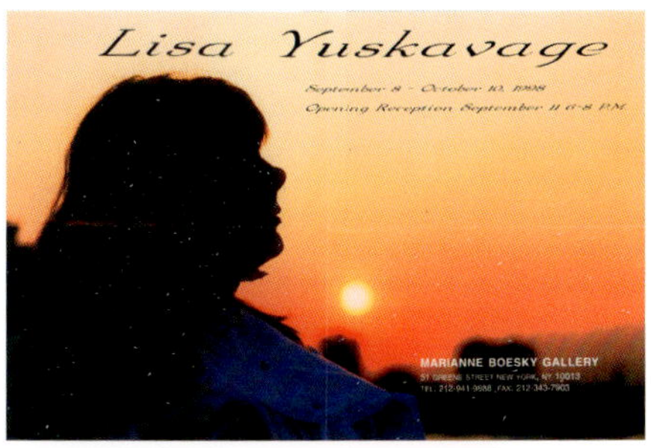

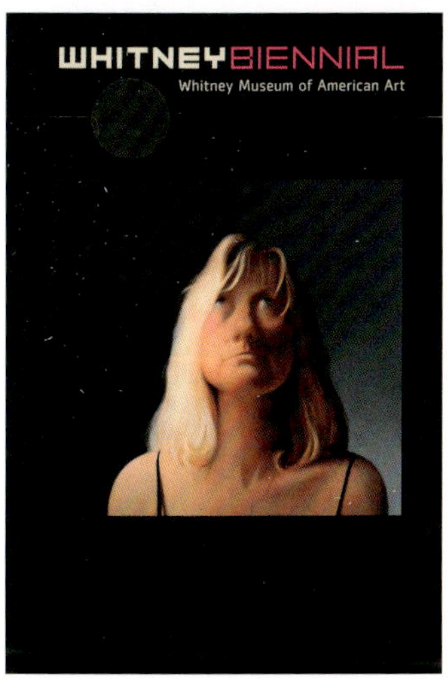

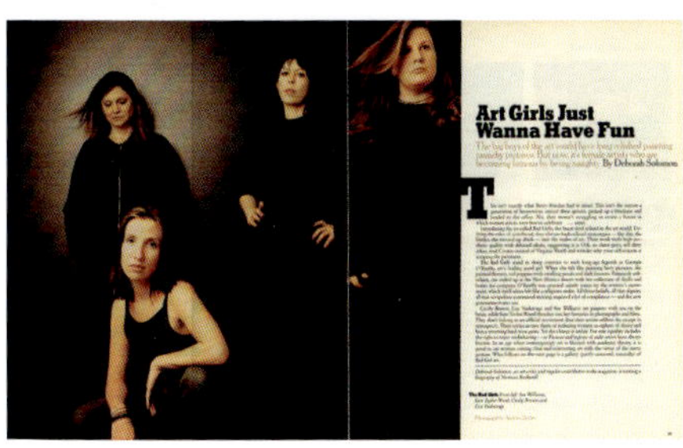

SELECTED EXHIBITIONS AND PROJECTS
1998–2000

1998
'Lisa Yuskavage',
MARIANNE BOESKY GALLERY, New York (solo)

'A Portrait of Our Times: An Introduction to the Logan Collection',
SAN FRANCISCO MUSEUM OF MODERN ART (group)

'Pop Surrealism',
ALDRICH CONTEMPORARY ART MUSEUM, Ridgefield, Connecticut (group)

'Presumed Innocence',
ANDERSON GALLERY, VIRGINIA COMMONWEALTH UNIVERSITY, Richmond, toured to CONTEMPORARY ARTS CENTER, Cincinnati (group)

'Then and Now and Later',
YALE UNIVERSITY ART GALLERY, New Haven, Connecticut (group)

'Young Americans 2',
SAATCHI GALLERY, London (group)

1999
'Lisa Yuskavage',
GREENGRASSI, London (solo)

6th ISTANBUL BIENNIAL (group)

'Etcetera',
SPACEX GALLERY, Los Angeles (group)

'Invitational Exhibition of Painting and Sculpture',
AMERICAN ACADEMY OF ARTS AND LETTERS, New York (group)

'Looking at Ourselves: Works by Women Artists from the Logan Collection',
SAN FRANCISCO MUSEUM OF MODERN ART (group)

'Negotiating Small Truths',
BLANTON MUSEUM OF ART, UNIVERSITY OF TEXAS AT AUSTIN (group)

'The Nude in Contemporary Art',
ALDRICH CONTEMPORARY ART MUSEUM, Ridgefield, Connecticut (group)

'Spellbound',
KARYN LOVEGROVE GALLERY, Los Angeles (group)

'The Time of Our Lives',
NEW MUSEUM OF CONTEMPORARY ART, New York (group)

2000
'Lisa Yuskavage',
INSTITUTE OF CONTEMPORARY ART, UNIVERSITY OF PENNSYLVANIA, Philadelphia (solo)

'00',
BARBARA GLADSTONE GALLERY, New York (group)

2000 WHITNEY BIENNIAL OF AMERICAN ART, New York (group)

46th CORCORAN BIENNIAL OF CONTEMPORARY PAINTING, Washington, D.C. (group)

SELECTED ARTICLES AND INTERVIEWS
1998–2000

1998
Whitehead, Jayson, 'The Paintings of Lisa Yuskavage', Gadfly, April

Hayt, Elizabeth, 'Evoking the Fitful Passage to Womanhood', The New York Times, 10 May

Burns, Anna, 'Children and Sexuality in the Visual Arts', Contemporary, Summer

Bevan, Roger, 'Saatchi Shows More Young Americans', Art+Auction, September–October

Schjeldahl, Peter, 'Purple Nipple: Lisa Yuskavage, Marianne Boesky Gallery', The Village Voice, 29 September

Cotter, Holland, 'Art in Review: Lisa Yuskavage, Marianne Boesky Gallery', The New York Times, 2 October

Manami, Fujimori, 'Lisa Yuskavage', Bijutsu Techo, November

Siegel, Katy, 'Review: Lisa Yuskavage, Marianne Boesky Gallery', Artforum, November

Jones, Ronald, 'The Best of 1998: Lisa Yuskavage at Marianne Boesky Gallery', Artforum, December

1999
Dobrzynski, Judith H, 'A Painter and Her Art Trade Places', The New York Times, 28 January

Licht, Matthew, 'Titty as a Picture!', Juggs, March

Decker, Andrew, 'Art's Next Wave', Cigar Aficionado, March–April

Dietrich, Dorothea, 'Working Proof', Art on Paper, March–April

Russo, Giuseppe, 'Z la formica, la mongolfiera, il senso del mondo e l'arte contemporane', Tema Celeste, no. 73, March–April

Schwendener, Martha, 'Review: Lisa Yuskavage, Marianne Boesky Gallery', Flash Art, no. 211, March–April

'Lisa Yuskavage', Tank, April

Knight, Christopher, 'Brush Strokes of Genius', Robb Report, June

Arning, Bill, 'The Nude in Contemporary Art: Body Politics', Time Out New York, 8–15 July

Cohen, Michael, 'Pittura a New York', Flash Art Italia, no. 18, October–November

'Lisa Yuskavage', Bust, Fall

'Lisa Yuskavage [artist portfolio]', Columbia: A Journal of Literature and Art, Winter

2000
Solomon, Deborah, 'Art Girls Just Wanna Have Fun', T: The New York Times Style Magazine, 30 January

Schjeldahl, Peter, 'The Art World: Pragmatic Hedonism', The New Yorker, 3 April

Saltz, Jerry, 'My Sixth Sense', The Village Voice, 4 April

Siegel, Katy, 'Blonde Ambition: The Art of Lisa Yuskavage', Artforum, May

Moreno, Gean, 'High Noon in Desire County', Art Papers, May–June

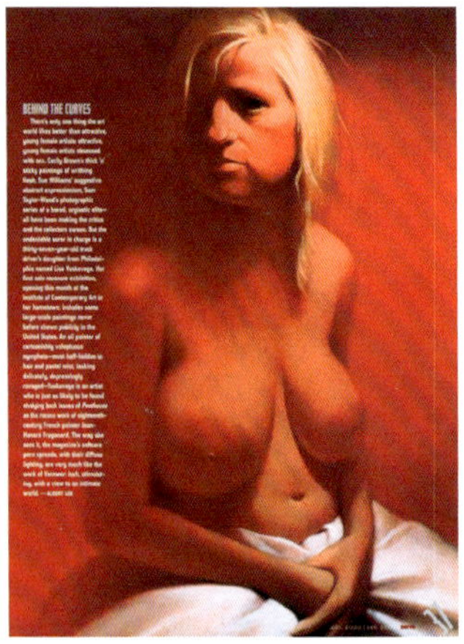

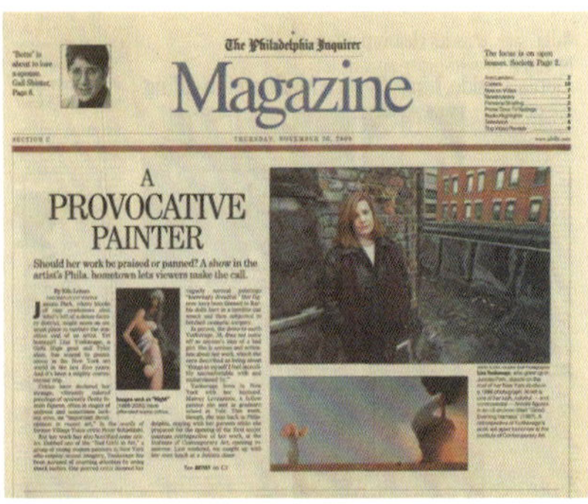

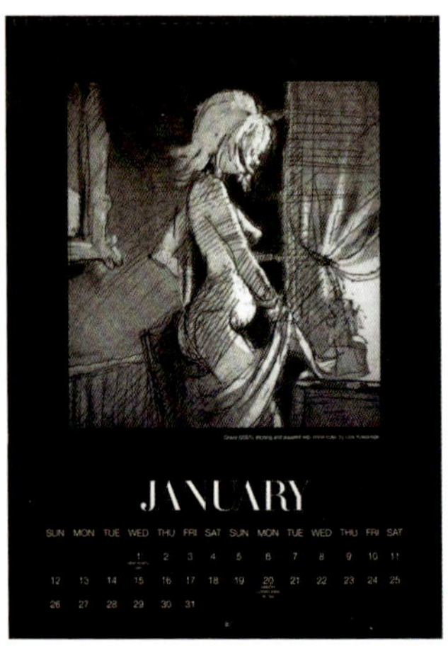

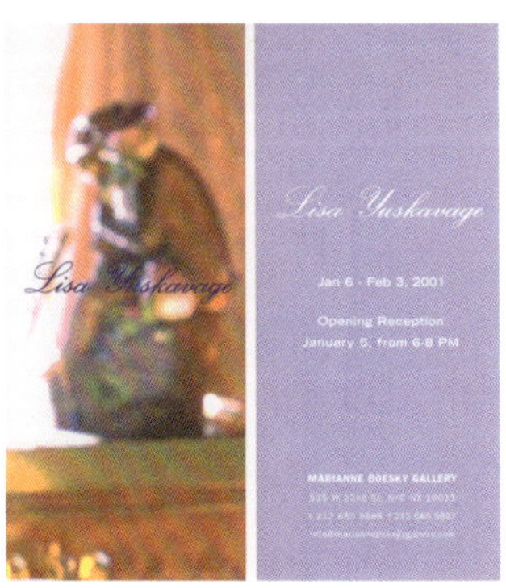

SELECTED EXHIBITIONS AND PROJECTS
2000–02

2000 (cont.)
'A Plurality of Truths',
SCHICK ART GALLERY, SKIDMORE COLLEGE, Saratoga Springs, New York (group)

'The Figure: Another Side of Modernism',
NEWHOUSE CENTER FOR CONTEMPORARY ART, SNUG HARBOR CULTURAL CENTER, New York (group)

'Go Figure',
NORFOLK PUBLIC LIBRARY, Connecticut (group)

'Greater New York',
P.S.1 CONTEMPORARY ART CENTER, Long Island City, New York (group)

'Persona(l): Selections from the Robert J. Shiffler Collection',
GRUNWALD GALLERY OF ART, INDIANA UNIVERSITY, Bloomington (group)

'Salon',
DELFINA PROJECT SPACE, London (group)

'Works on Paper 2000',
AMERICAN AMBASSADOR'S RESIDENCE, Bratislava (group)

Receives Founder's Day Certificate of Honor, Tyler School of the Arts, Philadelphia

2001
'Lisa Yuskavage',
CENTRE D'ART CONTEMPORAIN, Geneva (solo)

'Lisa Yuskavage',
MARIANNE BOESKY GALLERY, New York (solo)

'Lisa Yuskavage: Watercolors 2001',
STUDIO GUENZANI, Milan (solo)
2001 (cont.)

'Arte Contemporáneo Internacional',
MUSEO DE ARTE MODERNO, Mexico City (group)

'Contemporary Collectors XVI',
MUSEUM OF CONTEMPORARY ART SAN DIEGO, La Jolla, California (group)

'Lateral Thinking: Art of the 1990s',
MUSEUM OF CONTEMPORARY ART, San Diego, La Jolla, California (group)

2002
'Lisa Yuskavage',
GREENGRASSI, London (solo)

'Lisa Yuskavage',
GREENGRASSI AT THE GALLERIES SHOW, ROYAL ACADEMY OF ARTS, London (solo)

SELECTED ARTICLES AND INTERVIEWS
2000–02

2000 (cont.)
Smith, Roberta, 'Critic's Notebook: Portrait of the Artist as a Young Woman', The New York Times, 5 July

Seidel, Miriam, 'Art Attack', Philadelphia Magazine, September

Lotozo, Eils, 'A Provocative Painter', The Philadelphia Inquirer, 30 November

Goodman, Wendy, 'The Art of Living', New York Magazine, 6 November

Melada, Geoffrey W., 'Blonde Ambition', Philadelphia Magazine, December

Seidler, Rosa, 'Shock of The Nude', Elle, December

Fallon, Roberta, 'The Body Shop', Philadelphia Weekly, 6 December

Fabbri, Anne R, 'Not 'Easelly Forgotten: Three Thought-Provoking Exhibitions Open at ICA', Philadelphia Daily News, 8 December

Sozanski, Edward J, 'A Provocative Take on Female Sexuality', The Philadelphia Inquirer, 10 December

Denker, Carol, 'Artist's Work Has Taken Her Far, but Is Planted in Her Juniata Roots', The North Star, 13 December

Fowler, Maria, 'A Walk on the Wild Side at the ICA', King of Prussia Courier, 27 December

Lee, Albert, 'Behind the Curves', Nerve, December–January

2001
Smiley, Jane, 'Just Like a Woman', Harper's Bazaar, January

Smith, Roberta, 'Art in Review: A Painter Who Loads the Gun and Lets the Viewer Fire It', The New York Times, 12 January

Viveros-Fauné, Christian, 'Review: Lisa Yuskavage, Institute of Contemporary Art/Marianne Boesky Gallery', New York Press, 17–23 January

Gardner, James, 'Lisa Yuskavage', New York Post, 15 January

Fabianich, Eric, 'Lisa Yuskavage', NY Arts Magazine, February

Gilmore, Jonathan, 'Lisa Yuskavage, Marianne Boesky Gallery', Tema Celeste, no. 84, March–April

Newhall, Edith, 'Lisa Yuskavage', ARTnews, April

Schwabsky, Barry, 'Lisa Yuskavage at Institute of Contemporary Art/Marianne Boesky Gallery', Artforum, April

Lovelace, Carey, 'Lisa Yuskavage: Fleshed Out', Art in America, July

Siegel, Katy, 'Passages: Balthus Remembered; Katy Siegel talks with Lucian Freud, Lisa Yuskavage, David Salle, and John Currin', Artforum, Summer

Clifford, Christen, 'Lisa Yuskavage', Black & White Magazine, December

2002
Tuttle, Richard, 'Artists Curate: Cosmic Relief', Artforum, February
Girst, Thomas, 'Zurück zur Figur', Süddeutsche Zeitung, 12 April

Koroxenidis, Alexandra, 'Through the Eyes of Women', Kathimerini Newspaper/Herald Tribune, 29 July

Holmes, Pernilla, 'The Royal Treatment', Art+Auction, October

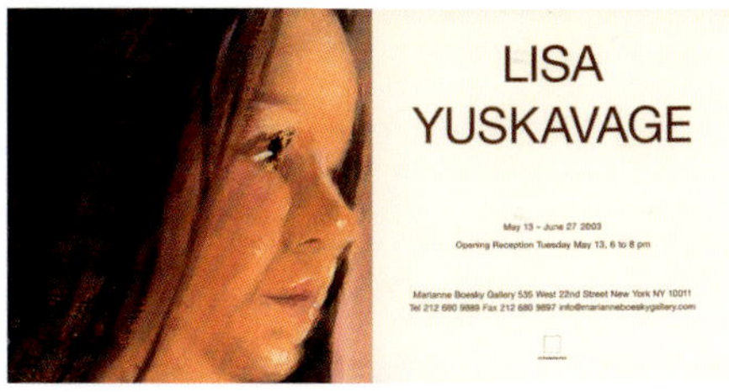

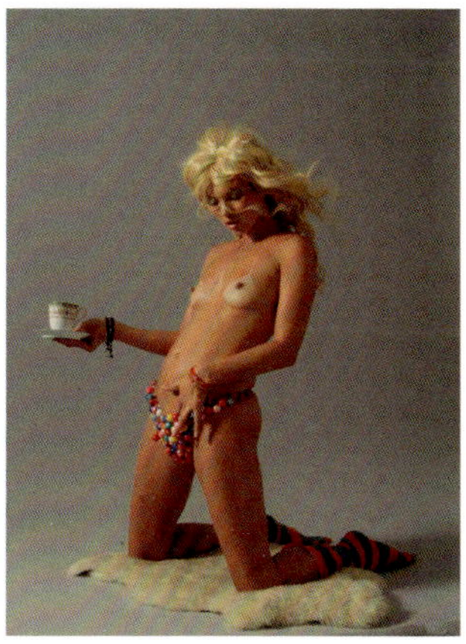

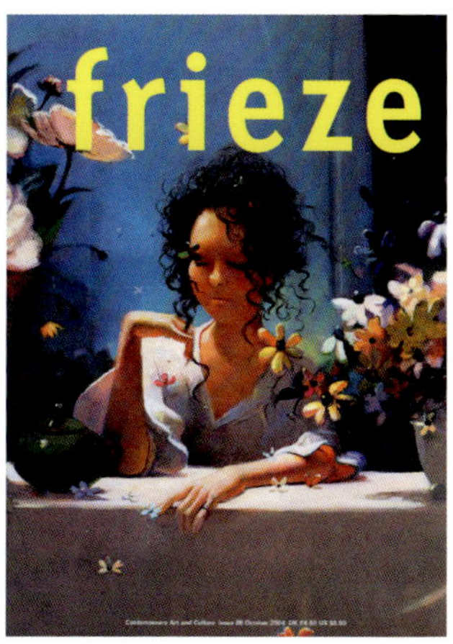

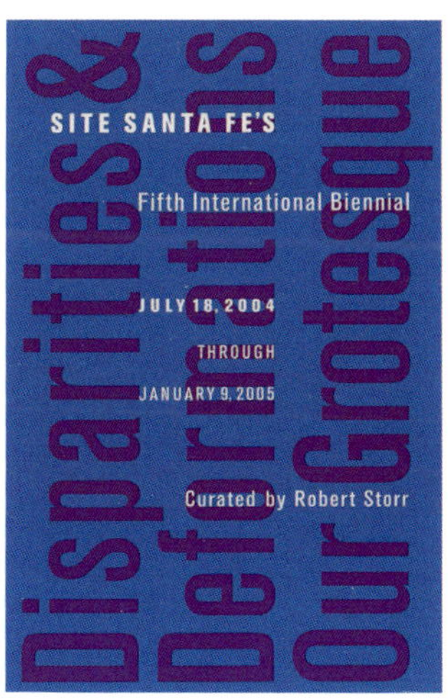

SELECTED EXHIBITIONS AND PROJECTS
2002–05

SELECTED ARTICLES AND INTERVIEWS
2002–05

2002 (cont.)

177th ANNUAL NATIONAL ACADEMY OF DESIGN EXHIBITION,
New York (group)

'Fusion Cuisine',
DESTE FOUNDATION, Athens (group)

'New Prints 2002/Summer',
INTERNATIONAL PRINT CENTER, New York (group)

'Visual Jury 2002 Exhibition',
FINE ARTS WORK CENTER, Provincetown, Massachusetts (group)

2003

'Lisa Yuskavage',
MARIANNE BOESKY GALLERY, New York (solo)

'De Kooning to Today: Highlights from the Permanent Collection',
WHITNEY MUSEUM OF AMERICAN ART, New York (group)

'Reverie: Works from the Collection of Douglas S. Cramer',
THE SPEED ART MUSEUM, Louisville, Kentucky (group)

'Skowhegan Faculty Exhibition',
INSTITUTE OF CONTEMPORARY ART, MAINE COLLEGE OF ART, Portland (group)

'Stephen Greene: Painter and Teacher,
ADDISON GALLERY OF AMERICAN ART, PHILLIPS ACADEMY, Andover, Massachusetts (group)

'Supernova: Art of the 1990s from the Logan Collection,
SAN FRANCISCO MUSEUM OF MODERN ART (group)

'Woman on Woman,
WHITEBOX ART CENTER, New York (group)

2003

Clem, Chivas, 'Review: Lisa Yuskavage, Marianne Boesky Gallery', Time Out New York, 12–19 June

Johnson, Ken, 'Art in Review: Lisa Yuskavage, Marianne Boesky Gallery', The New York Times, 20 June

Horyn, Cathy, 'Critic's Notebook: Fashion and Art Embrace, if not Passionately', The New York Times, 5 August

Yuskavage, Lisa, 'The Kate Moss Portfolio', W Magazine, September

Avgikos, Jan, 'Review: Lisa Yuskavage, Marianne Boesky Gallery', Artforum, September

Boucher, Brian, 'Lisa Yuskavage at Marianne Boesky Gallery', Flash Art, no. 232, October

Yuskavage, Lisa, 'To Philip Guston', The Brooklyn Rail, November

Mitchell, Claire, 'What It Feels Like For A Girl', Nylon, December–January

---

2004

'Lisa Yuskavage',
GREENGRASSI, London (solo)

'The Charged Image: From the Collection of Douglas S. Cramer',
JOSELOFF GALLERY, UNIVERSITY OF HARTFORD, Connecticut (group)

'New Prints 2004/Spring',
INTERNATIONAL PRINT CENTER, New York (group)

'The Print Show',
EXIT ART, New York (group)

5th SANTA FE INTERNATIONAL BIENNIAL, New Mexico (group)

2004

Landi, Ann, 'Disturbing Beauty', ARTnews, January

Kastner, Jeffrey, 'Deviation Standard: Jeffrey Kastner on SITE Santa Fe', Artforum, May

O'Reilly, Sally, 'Review: Lisa Yuskavage at greengrassi', Time Out London, 16–23 June

Honigman, Ana Finel, 'The good, the bad and the ugly', Art Review, July–August

Higgie, Jennifer, 'Women on the Verge', Frieze, no. 86, October

Rosenberg, Karen, 'Conversation: Lisa Yuskavage and Tamara Jenkins', New York Magazine, 22 November

---

2005

'Drawn Across the Century: Highlights from the Dillard Collection of Art on Paper',
GALLERY OF CONTEMPORARY ART, UNIVERSITY OF COLORADO SPRINGS (group)

'Laguna's Hidden Treasures: Art from Private Collections',
LAGUNA ART MUSEUM, Laguna Beach, California (group)

'Post and After: Contemporary Art from the Brandeis University Art Collection',
THE ROSE ART MUSEUM, BRANDEIS UNIVERSITY, Waltham, Massachusetts (group)

Receives the Temple University Gallery of Success Award,
Temple University, Philadelphia

2005

Prose, Francine, 'Preemptive Strike: Lisa Yuskavage's very weird women', Modern Painters, March

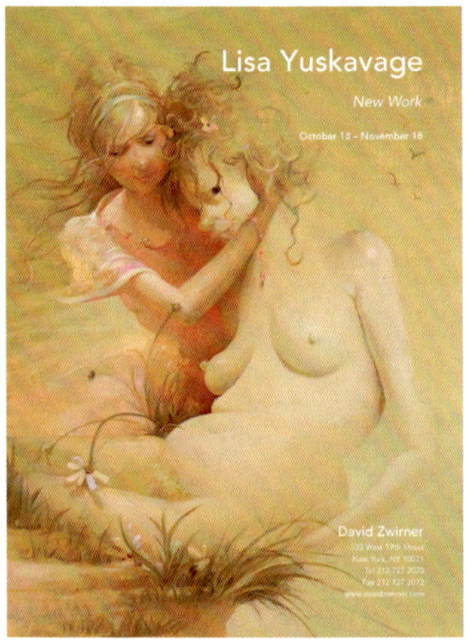

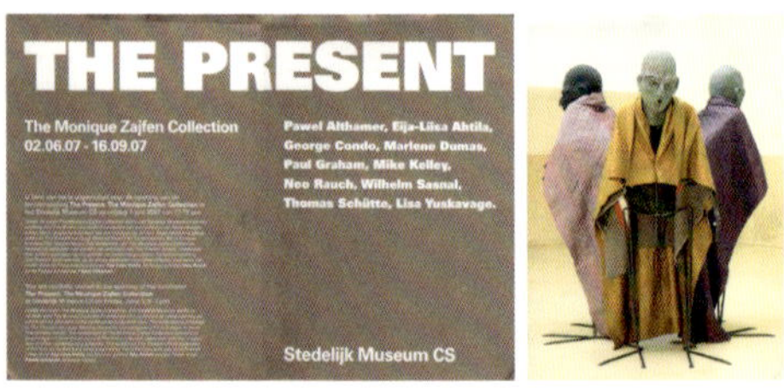

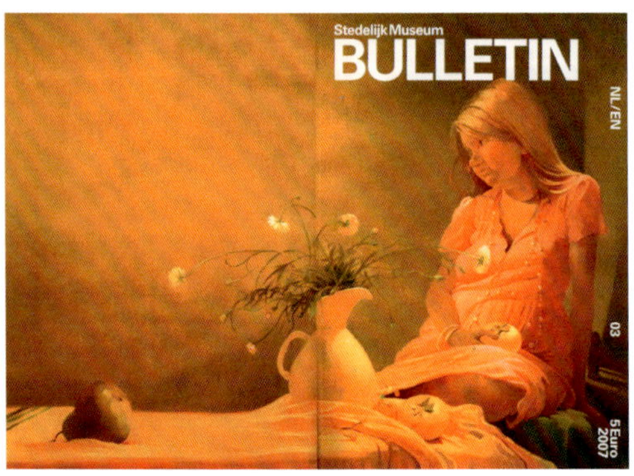

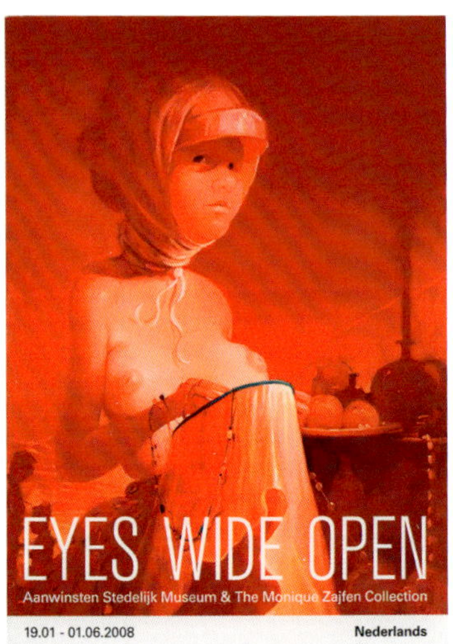

SELECTED EXHIBITIONS AND PROJECTS
2006–08

2006
'Lisa Yuskavage',
MUSEO TAMAYO ARTE CONTEMPORÁNEO, Mexico City (solo)

'Lisa Yuskavage: New Work',
ZWIRNER & WIRTH and DAVID ZWIRNER, New York (solo)

'Painting Codes/I codici della pittura',
GALLERIA COMUNALE D'ARTE CONTEMPORANEA, Monfalcone, Italy (group)

'People: Volti, corpi e segni contemporanei dalla collezione di Ernesto Esposito',
MUSEO D'ARTE CONTEMPORANEA DONNA REGINA, Naples (group)

2007
'Lisa Yuskavage',
GREENGRASSI, London (solo)

'Art in America: Three Hundred Years of Innovation',
NATIONAL ART MUSEUM OF CHINA, Beijing, toured to SHANGHAI MUSEUM AND SHANGHAI MUSEUM OF CONTEMPORARY ART; PUSHKIN MUSEUM OF FINE ARTS, Moscow; GUGGENHEIM MUSEUM Bilbao (group)

'Artist Collaborations: Fifty Years at Universal Limited Art Editions',
THE MUSEUM OF MODERN ART, New York (group)

'Don't Look: Contemporary Drawings from an Alumna's Collection (Martina Yamin, Class of 1958)',
DAVIS MUSEUM AND CULTURAL CENTER, WELLESLEY COLLEGE, Massachusetts (group)

'Multiplex: Directions in Art 1970 to Now',
THE MUSEUM OF MODERN ART, New York (group)

'Paper',
FISHER LANDAU CENTER FOR ART, Long Island City, New York (group)

'The Present: The Monique Zajfen Collection',
STEDELIJK MUSEUM, Amsterdam (group)

2008
'Attention to Detail',
THE FLAG ART FOUNDATION, New York (group)

'Bad Painting/Good Art',
MUSEUM MODERNER KUNST STIFTUNG LUDWIG WIEN, Vienna (group)

'Diana and Actaeon: The Forbidden Glimpse of the Naked Body/Diana und Actaeon: Der verbotene Blick auf die Nacktheit',
MUSEUM KUNSTPALAST, Düsseldorf (group)

'Eyes Wide Open: Acquisitions to the Stedelijk & The Monique Zajfen Collection',
STEDELIJK MUSEUM, Amsterdam (group)

'Female Forms and Facets: Artwork by Women from 1975 to the Present',
CENTRAL CONNECTICUT STATE UNIVERSITY ART GALLERIES, New Britain (group)

'Go for it! Olbricht Collection (a sequel)',
WESERBURG MUSEUM FÜR MODERNE KUNST, Bremen, Germany (group)

'Légende',
DOMAINE DÉPARTEMENTAL DE CHAMARANDE, France (group)

SELECTED ARTICLES AND INTERVIEWS
2006–08

2006
Kunitz, Daniel, 'Take a Bite of Peach: Lisa Yuskavage', Art Review, October

Yuskavage, Lisa, 'When in Rome', Culture & Travel, September–October

Scott, Andrea K, 'Lisa Yuskavage: Flesh for fantasy', Time Out New York, 19–25 October

Belcove, Julie L, 'Lisa's Women', W Magazine, November

Kastner, Jeffrey, 'Art in Review: Lisa Yuskavage, David Zwirner and Zwirner & Wirth', The New York Times, 10 November

2007
Neil, Jonathan T.D, 'Lisa Yuskavage', Art Review, January

Richard, Frances, 'Review: Lisa Yuskavage, David Zwirner/Zwirner & Wirth', Artforum, January

Heartney, Eleanor, 'Review: Lisa Yuskavage at David Zwirner and Zwirner & Wirth', Art in America, February

Schwabsky, Barry, 'Review: Lisa Yuskavage, David Zwirner/Zwirner & Wirth', Map, Spring

Butler, Cornelia and Amelia Jones, 'Lisa Yuskavage: Critiquing Prurient Sexuality … or Disingenuously Peddling a Soft-Core Porn Aesthetic?', The Washington Post, April

Karcher, Eva, 'Jenseits von Hardcore', Monopol, May

Enright, Robert, 'The Overwhelmer: The Art of Lisa Yuskavage', Border Crossings, August

Herbert, Martin, 'Review: Lisa Yuskavage, greengrassi', Time Out London, 17–23 October

2008
Bodin, Claudia, 'Die Meisterin des Obszönen', Art, January

'The Image Only Issue 2', Empty, no. 16

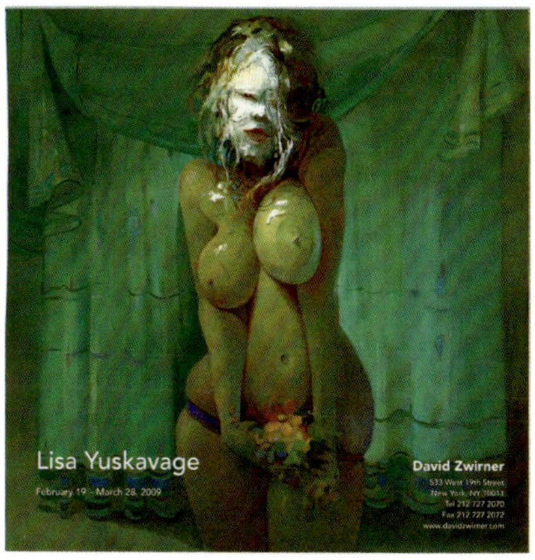

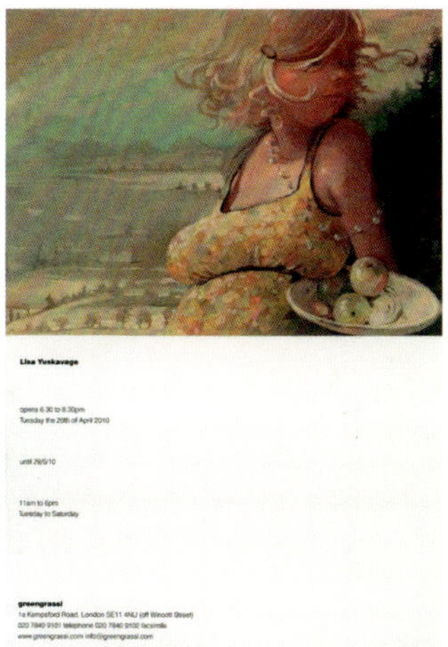

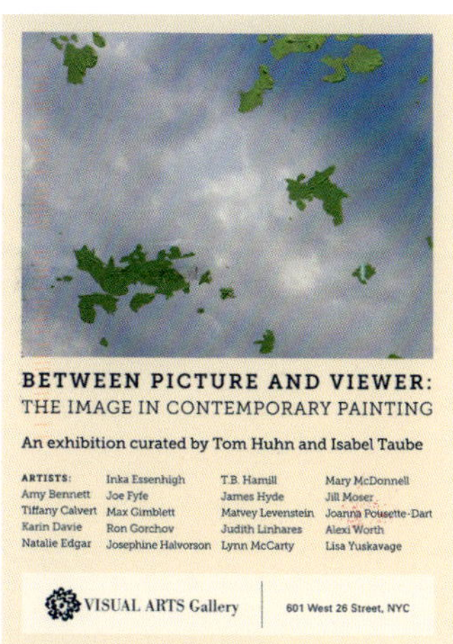

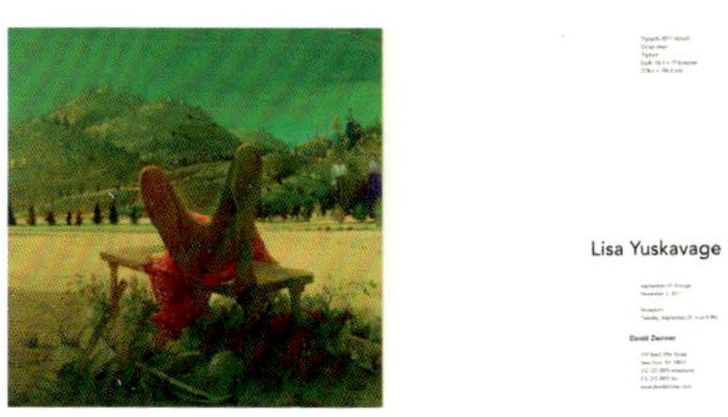

SELECTED EXHIBITIONS AND PROJECTS
2008–11

2008 (cont.)
'Out of Shape: Stylistic Distortions of the Human Form in Art from the Logan Collection',
FRANCES LEHMAN LOEB ART CENTER, VASSAR COLLEGE, Poughkeepsie, New York (group)

'Paint Made Flesh',
THE FRIST CENTER FOR THE VISUAL ARTS, Nashville (group)

'Philadelphia Collects: Works on Paper',
DELAWARE CENTER FOR CONTEMPORARY ARTS, Wilmington (group)

2009
'Lisa Yuskavage',
DAVID ZWIRNER, New York (solo)

'30th Anniversary',
CHRISTOPHER GRIMES GALLERY, Santa Monica, California (group)

'Bad Habits',
ALBRIGHT-KNOX GALLERY, Buffalo, New York (group)

'The Female Gaze: Women Look at Women',
CHEIM & READ, New York (group)

'The Modern Wing',
ART INSTITUTE OF CHICAGO (group)

'Paint Made Flesh',
THE FRIST CENTER FOR THE VISUAL ARTS, Nashville, toured to THE PHILLIPS COLLECTION, Washington, D.C.; MEMORIAL ART GALLERY, UNIVERSITY OF ROCHESTER, New York (group)

'Robert Rauschenberg and His Contemporaries: Recent Prints from Universal Limited Art Editions',
HECKSCHER MUSEUM OF ART, Huntington, New York (group)

2010
'Lisa Yuskavage',
GREENGRASSI, London (solo)

'American Printmaking Now',
NATIONAL ART MUSEUM OF CHINA, Beijing, toured to GUAN SHANYUE ART MUSEUM, Shenzhen; ZHEJIANG ART MUSEUM, Hangzhou; SHANGHAI ART MUSEUM (group)

'Between Picture and Viewer: The Image in Contemporary Painting',
VISUAL ARTS GALLERY, SCHOOL OF VISUAL ARTS, New York (group)

'Face to Face',
MUSEUM OF CONTEMPORARY ART, Denver (group)

'The Library of Babel/In and Out of Place',
ZABLUDOWICZ COLLECTION, London (group)

'Size Does Matter',
THE FLAG ART FOUNDATION, New York (group)

'Until Now: Collecting the New (1960–2010)',
MINNEAPOLIS INSTITUTE OF ARTS, Minnesota (group)

2011
'Lisa Yuskavage',
DAVID ZWIRNER, New York (solo)

'Lisa Yuskavage: Tragic Land',
THE ROYAL HIBERNIAN ACADEMY, Dublin (solo)

SELECTED ARTICLES AND INTERVIEWS
2008–11

2009
Bui, Phong, 'In Conversation: Lisa Yuskavage with Phong Bui', The Brooklyn Rail, March

Carlin, T.J, 'Review: Lisa Yuskavage, David Zwirner', Time Out New York, March

Rosenberg, Karen, 'Art in Review: Lisa Yuskavage, David Zwirner', The New York Times, 6 March

Yuskavage, Lisa, 'Francis Bacon', Vogue, April

Kley, Elisabeth, 'Review: Lisa Yuskavage, David Zwirner', ARTnews, June

Coulter, Gerry, 'Lisa Yuskavage', Ctrl+P Journal of Contemporary Art, no. 15, October

2010
Sinclair, Charlotte, 'Naked truth', British Vogue, May

2011
'Nouveau Magazine Erotique', Extra Extra, no. 2

Murg, Stephanie, 'In the Studio: Lisa Yuskavage', Art+Auction, September

Yuskavage, Lisa, 'Muse: Jesse Murry, 1948–1993', Art in America, October

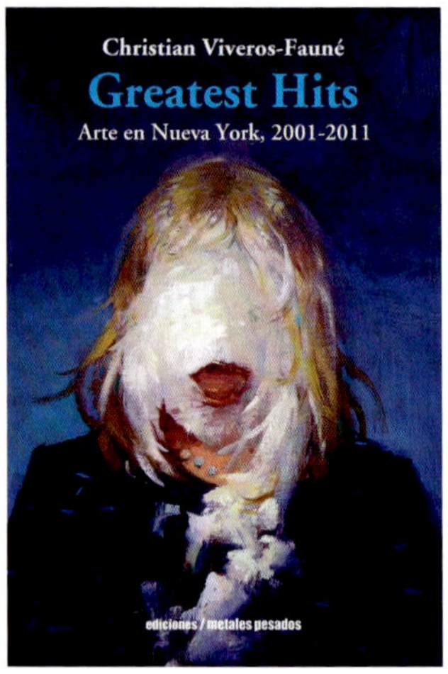

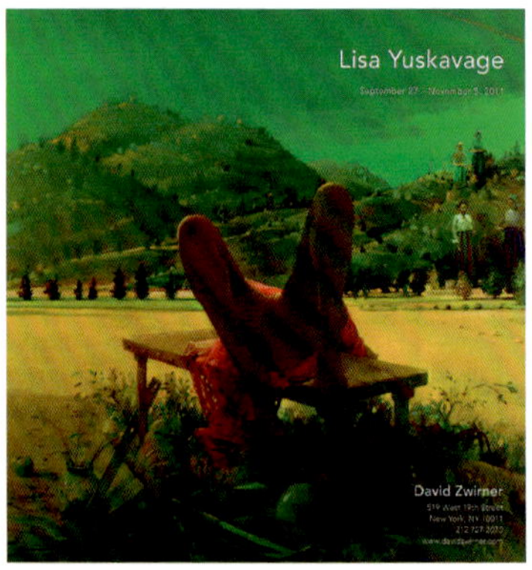

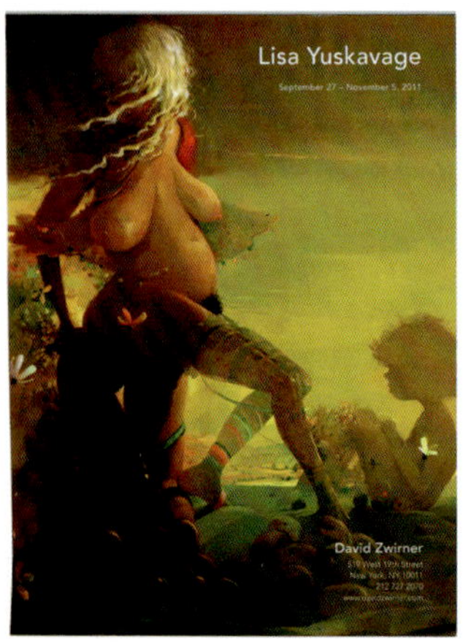

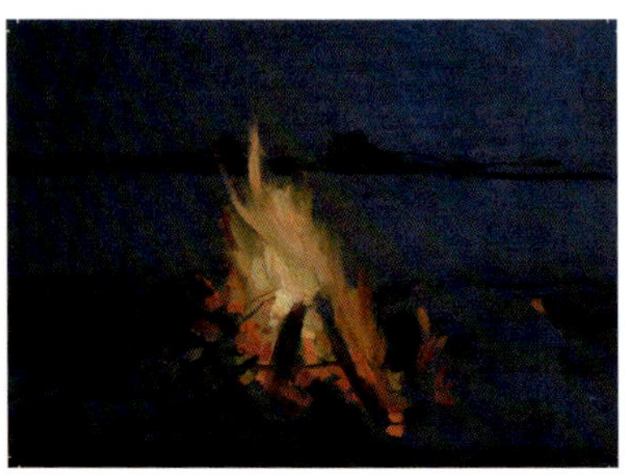

SELECTED EXHIBITIONS AND PROJECTS
2011–13

2011 (cont.)
'80 @ 80',
PU GALLERY OF AMERICAN ART, PHILLIPS ACADEMY, Andover, Massachusetts (group)

'American Exuberance',
RUBELL FAMILY COLLECTION, Miami (group)

'Creating the New Century: Contemporary Art from the Dicke Collection',
THE DAYTON INSTITUTE, Ohio (group)

DUBLIN CONTEMPORARY 2011 (group)

'Full Circle: The Evolution of Fine Art Printmaking at Universal Limited Art Editions',
GARDINER ART GALLERY, OKLAHOMA STATE UNIVERSITY, Stillwater (group)

'Legacy: Selections from Emily Fisher Landau's Gift to the Whitney Museum of American Art',
FISHER LANDAU CENTER FOR ART, Long Island City, New York (group)

'New York Prints of Mind: Prints from the Universal Limited Art Editions',
SCHWEINFURTH MEMORIAL ART CENTER, Auburn, New York, toured to STONE QUARRY HILL ART CENTER, Cazenovia, New York (group)

'Sammler-Leidenschaft',
MUSEUM STIFT ADMONT, Austria (group)

'Secret Societies',
SCHIRN KUNSTHALLE, Frankfurt, toured to MUSÉE D'ART CONTEMPORAIN DE BORDEAUX (group)

'Universal Limited Art Editions',
ABERSON EXHIBITS, Tulsa, toured to HIRAM BUTLER GALLERY, Houston (group)

2012
'Decade: Contemporary Collecting 2002–12',
ALBRIGHT-KNOX ART GALLERY, Buffalo, New York (group)

'Faces',
ONASSIS CULTURAL CENTRE, Athens (group)

'Haunting Narratives: Detours from Philadelphia Realism, 1935 to the Present',
WOODMERE ART MUSEUM, Philadelphia (group)

'New to the Print Collection: Matisse to Bourgeois',
THE MUSEUM OF MODERN ART, New York (group)

'Print/Out',
THE MUSEUM OF MODERN ART, New York (group)

2013
'Lisa Yuskavage',
GREENGRASSI, London (solo)

'Come Together: Surviving Sandy, Year 1',
INDUSTRY CITY, Brooklyn (group)

'The Distaff Side',
THE GRANARY, Sharon, Connecticut (group) (group)

'Expanding the Field of Painting',
INSTITUTE OF CONTEMPORARY ART, Boston

SELECTED ARTICLES AND INTERVIEWS
2011–13

2011 (cont.)
De la Torre, Mónica, 'Interview with Lisa Yuskavage', BOMB Magazine, Fall

Johnson, Ken, 'Art in Review: Lisa Yuskavage, David Zwirner', The New York Times, 7 October

Scott, Andrea K, 'Critic's Notebook: Dangerous Beauty', The New Yorker, 24 October

Lindquist, Greg, 'Review: Lisa Yuskavage, David Zwirner', The Brooklyn Rail, November

Indrisek, Scott, 'Review: Lisa Yuskavage, David Zwirner', Modern Painters, December–January

Viveros-Fauné, Christian, 'The Best Art Shows of 2011: Lisa Yuskavage, David Zwirner', The Village Voice, 28 December

2012
Princenthal, Nancy, 'Review: Lisa Yuskavage at David Zwirner', Art in America, January

Heller, Sabine, 'Purple Interview: Lisa Yuskavage', Purple Fashion Magazine, Spring–Summer

Landi, Ann, 'Double Exposure', ARTnews, May

Kleeblatt, Norman L., 'Looking at Art: Seeing Double', ARTnews, September

2013
Januszczak, Waldemar, 'Crazy for You', The Sunday Times, 5 May

'The Approval Matrix', New York Magazine, 28 October

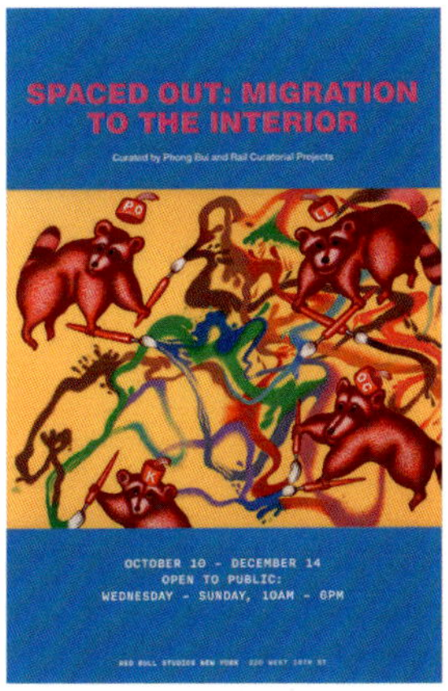

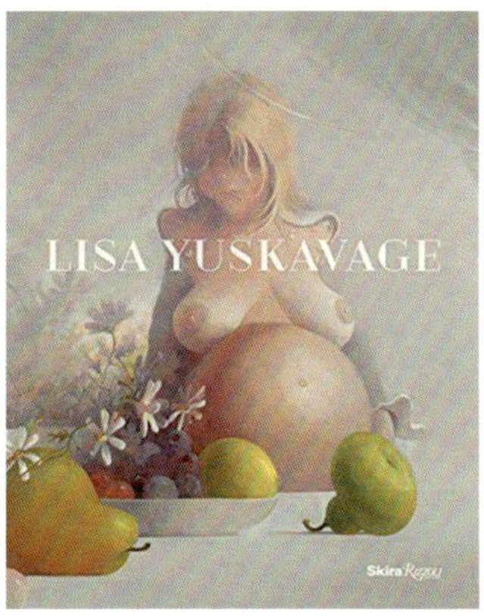

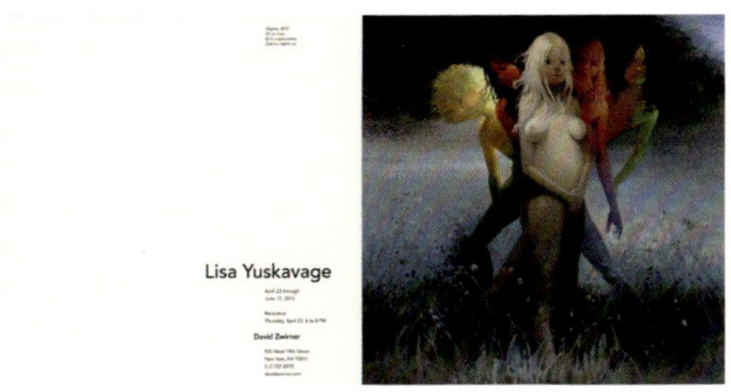

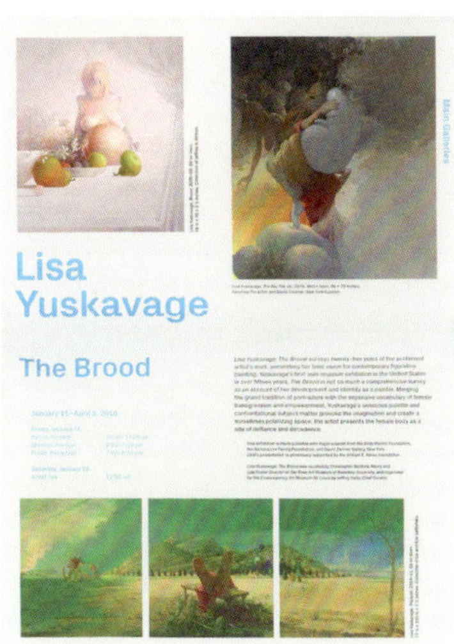

SELECTED ARTICLES AND INTERVIEWS
2014–16

SELECTED ARTICLES AND INTERVIEWS
2014–16

2014
'Disturbing Innocence',
THE FLAG ART FOUNDATION, New York (group)

'Hidden and Revealed: Representations of Women by Women',
ANGLES GALLERY, Los Angeles (group)

'Love Story: The Anne and Wolfgang Titze Collection',
WINTER PALACE AND 21ER HAUS, BELVEDERE, Vienna (group)

'Nude',
GEMEENTEMUSEUM, The Hague (group)

'Queensize: Female Artists from the Olbricht Collection',
ME COLLECTORS ROOM/STIFTUNG OLBRICHT, Berlin (group)

'She: Picturing women at the turn of the 21st Century',
DAVID WINTON BELL GALLERY, BROWN UNIVERSITY, Providence, Rhode Island (group)

'Somos Libres II: Works from the Mario Testino Collection',
PINACOTECA GIOVANNI E MARELLA AGNELLI, Turin (group)

2015
'The Brood',
THE ROSE ART MUSEUM, BRANDEIS UNIVERSITY, Waltham, Massachusetts, toured to CONTEMPORARY ART MUSEUM ST. LOUIS (solo)

'Lisa Yuskavage',
DAVID ZWIRNER, New York (solo)

'The Art of Our Time',
MUSEUM OF CONTEMPORARY ART, Los Angeles (group)

'Collection in Focus',
THE ROSE ART MUSEUM, BRANDEIS UNIVERSITY, Waltham, Massachusetts (group)

'Intimacy in Discourse: Unreasonable Sized Paintings',
MANA CONTEMPORARY AND THE SCHOOL OF VISUAL ARTS, New York (group)

'No Man's Land: Women Artists from the Rubell Family Collection',
RUBELL FAMILY COLLECTION, Miami (group)

'Print Up Ladies',
ISLIP ART MUSEUM, East Islip, New York (group)

'Studio Guenzani Milano 1986–2015: Molto-Tutto',
STUDIO GUENZANI, Milan (group)

'True Monotypes',
INTERNATIONAL PRINT CENTER, New York (group)

'Unrealism',
THE MOORE BUILDING, Miami (group)

2015
Bedford, Christopher, 'Sightlines: Progeny', Art in America, February

Earnest, Jarrett, 'In Conversation: Lisa Yuskavage on Nina Simone and Giovanni Bellini', The Brooklyn Rail, February

Gorashi, Hannah, 'Lisa Yuskavage Joined Grindr to Prep for Her New Show of Rainbow Nudes', i-D, 28 April

Grebremedhin, Thomas, 'Good World to Be In: An Interview with Lisa Yuskavage', The Paris Review, 30 April

Prickett, Sarah Nicole, 'Critics' Pick', Artforum, 1 May

Smith, Roberta, 'Review: Lisa Yuskavage at David Zwirner', The New York Times, 1 May

Schjeldahl, Peter, 'Lisa Yuskavage', New Yorker, 18 May

Jordan, Eliza, 'Men, Incubi, and Succubi Intertwine in Lisa Yuskavage's New Show', Whitewall, 18 May

Steadman, Ryan, 'Both Sides Now: Yuskavage Tackles the Other Sex', The Observer, 29 May

Bui, Phong, 'Lisa Yuskavage', The Brooklyn Rail, 3 June

Solondz, Todd, 'Lisa Yuskavage', Interview, September

Semmel, Joan, 'Joan Semmel on Lisa Yuskavage', Painters on Paintings, 9 September

Smee, Sebastian, 'Porn-inspired Art that Pulses with Intelligence', The Boston Globe, 17 September

Edgers, Geoff, 'A Solo Show for an Acclaimed Artist', The Washington Post, 25 September

Earnest, Jarrett, 'Lisa Yuskavage: In the Studio', Art in America, October

2016
'First Light: A Decade of Collecting at the ICA',
INSTITUTE OF CONTEMPORARY ART, Boston (group)

'Hey You! Who Me?',
32 EDGEWOOD GALLERY, YALE SCHOOL OF ART, New Haven, Connecticut (group)

2016
Beall, Dickson, 'The Brood: Lisa Yuskavage's much talked about exhibit at the Contemporary Art Museum now on view', West End Word, 26 January

Fraiman, Jeff, 'Lisa Yuskavage: The Brood', The Brooklyn Rail, 3 February

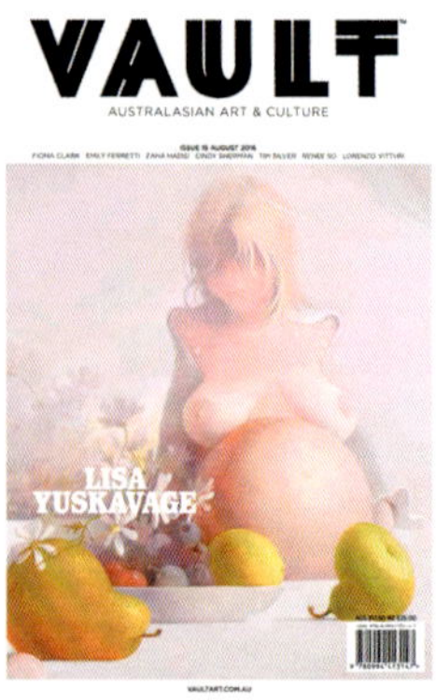

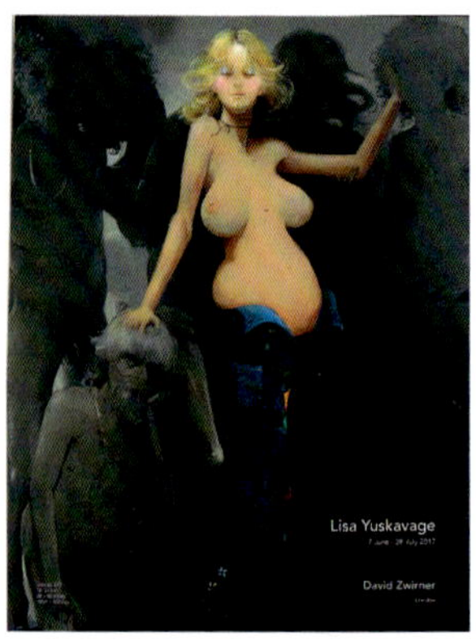

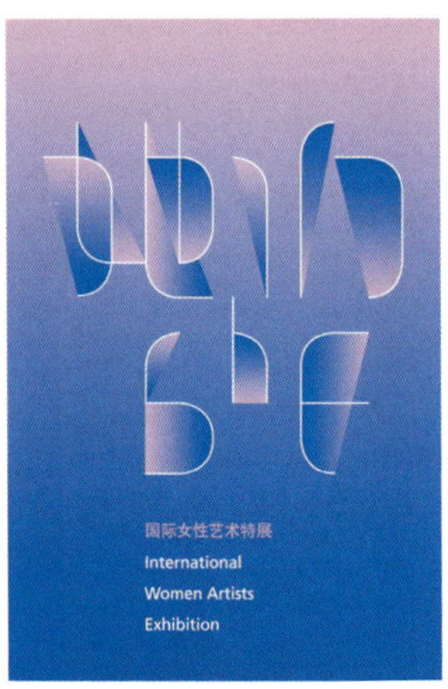

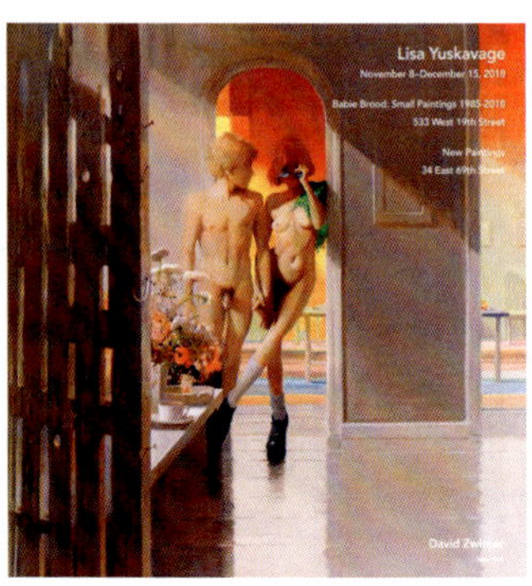

SELECTED EXHIBITIONS AND PROJECTS
2016–20

SELECTED ARTICLES AND INTERVIEWS
2016–20

2016 (cont.)
'More Than Words',
WESTPORT ARTS CENTER, Connecticut (group)

'She: International Women Artists Exhibition',
THE LONG MUSEUM, Shanghai, China (group)

'Transactions',
THE KNOCKDOWN CENTER, Maspeth, New York (group)

2016 (cont.)
Yuskavage, Lisa, 'Dennis Freedman', Interview, March

Yuskavage, Lisa, 'My 10 Favorite Books: Lisa Yuskavage',
T: The New York Times Style Magazine, 22 July

Kale, Neha, 'Lisa Yuskavage: Dancer in the Dark', Vault, August

Rosenblatt, Pam, 'On being bold: the Lisa Yuskavage: The Brood exhibition at Brandeis University's the Rose Art Museum',
Wilderness House Literary Review, 1 November

Haas, Lidija, 'Lisa Yuskavage: The Brood, Paintings 1991–2015',
Bookforum, December–January

2017
'Lisa Yuskavage',
DAVID ZWIRNER, London (solo)

'Hope and Hazard: A Comedy of Eros',
HALL ART FOUNDATION, Reading, Vermont (group)

2017
Frankel, Eddy, 'Lisa Yuskavage', Time Out London, 6 June

Farr, Kristin, 'The Erotic and Angelic: Lisa Yuskavage on View @ David Zwirner, London', Juxtapoz Magazine, 7 June

Allsop, Laura, 'A Conservation with Lisa Yuskavage', Ocula, 7 July

Cole, Rachel T., 'Lisa Yuskavage on Trusting Your Creative Instincts',
The Creative Independent, 15 June

Walsh, Meeka and Robert Enright, 'Lisa Yuskavage: Musings of an Edge-of-Towner', Border Crossings, September

---

2018
'Lisa Yuskavage: Babie Brood, Small Paintings 1985–2018'
and 'New Paintings',
DAVID ZWIRNER, New York (solo)

'David Zwirner: 25 Years',
DAVID ZWIRNER, New York (group)

'The Female Touch',
GEMEENTEMUSEUM, Den Haag, the Netherlands (group)

2018
Spellings, Sarah, 'Two Artists on Breasts, Labels, and Ignoring Critics', The Cut, August 8

Gebremedhin, Thomas, 'Lisa Yuskavage's Art Continues to Defy Characterization', Wall Street Journal, 6 November

Balasz, Takac, '5 Lisa Yuskavage Nudes From Her Upcoming Survey at David Zwirner', Widewalls, 7 November

Cohen, Alina, 'Lisa Yuskavage Doesn't Want to Be a "Good Feminist", Her Paintings Are Better for It', Artsy, 14 November

Michalarou, Efi, 'Art Cities: N. York-Lisa Yuskavage',
Dream Idea Machine, 26 November

Ambrose, David, 'Lisa Yuskavage: Babie Brood: Small Paintings 1985–2018', Whitehot Magazine of Contemporary Art, December

Heartney, Eleanor, 'Lisa Yuskavage: New Paintings & Babie Brood',
The Brooklyn Rail, December

2019
'Artists Need to Create on the Same Scale that Society Has the Capacity to Destroy: Mare Nostrum',
CHIESA DI SANTA MARIA DELLE PENITENTI, Venice (group)

'Das Kollegium',
GRAPHICS FOUNDATION NEO RAUCH, Aschersleben, Germany (group)

'Trouble in Paradise: Rattan Chadha Collection',
KUNSTHAL ROTTERDAM, Rotterdam (group)

Receives the Aspen Award for Art

2019
Time Out New York Contributors, 'The 100 Best Paintings in New York', Time Out New York, 24 January

Binlot, Ann, 'All Art is Voyeuristic: Lisa Yuskavage on the Joy of Provocation', Document, 3 August

Goldston, Bill, 'Lisa Yuskavage with Bill Goldston', The Brooklyn Rail, December–January

---

2020
'Lisa Yuskavage: Wilderness',
ASPEN ART MUSEUM, Colorado, toured to BALTIMORE MUSEUM OF ART (solo)

2020
Felsenthal, Julie, 'A Painter Who Wants Art to Shock', T: The New York Times Style Magazine, 12 February

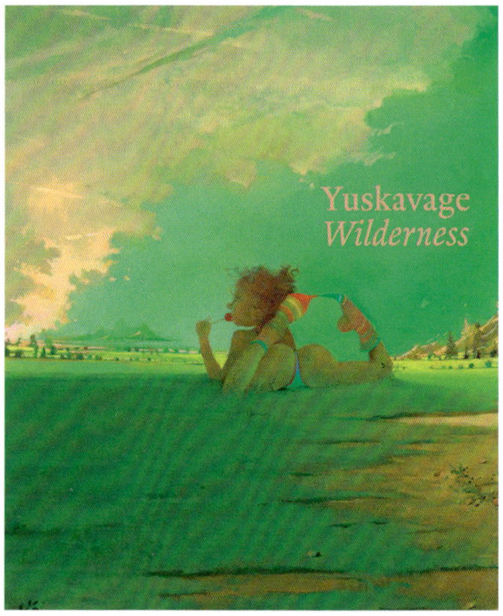

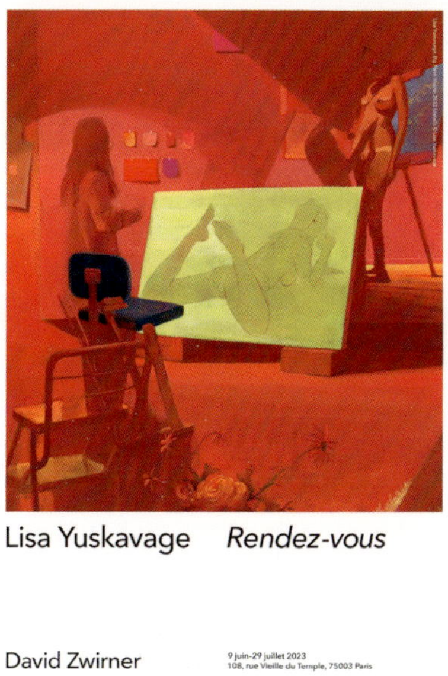

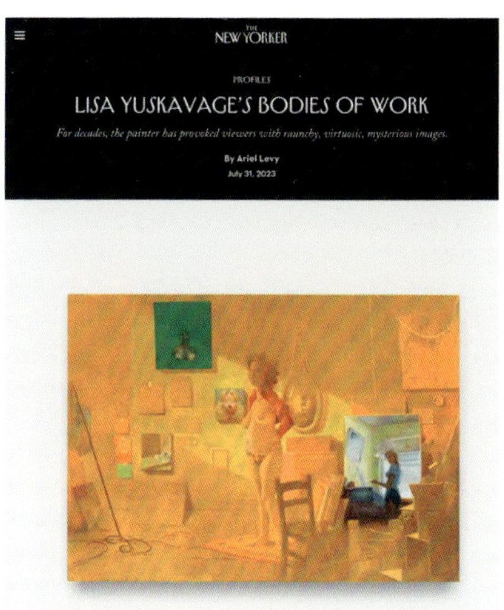

SELECTED EXHIBITIONS AND PROJECTS
2020–25

2020 (cont.)
'The Remaking of Myths and Tales: Selections from the Prints & 'Drawings Collection',
MUSEUM OF FINE ARTS, Houston (group)

2021
'Lisa Yuskavage: New Paintings',
DAVID ZWIRNER, New York (solo)

'Lisa Yuskavage: Wilderness',
BALTIMORE MUSEUM OF ART, Baltimore (solo)

'And I will wear you in my heart of heart',
FLAG ART FOUNDATION, New York (group)

'Knowledge of the Past Is the Key to the Future',
METROPOLITAN MUSEUM OF ART (group)

'New to the Collection',
RHODE ISLAND SCHOOL OF ART AND DESIGN MUSEUM (group)

'The Remaking of Myths and Tales: Selections from the Prints & Drawings Collection',
MUSEUM OF FINE ARTS, Houston (group)

2022
'Artists Inspired by Music: Interscope Reimagined',
LOS ANGELES COUNTY MUSEUM OF ART (group)

'Competere',
BO BARTLETT CENTER, Columbus, Georgia (group)

'Singing in Unison',
SCULLY-TOMASKO FOUNDATION, New York (group)

'What's Going On',
RUBELL MUSEUM, Washington, D.C. (group)

'Women Painting Women',
MODERN ART MUSEUM OF FORT WORTH, Fort Worth, Texas (group)

2023
'Lisa Yuskavage',
DAVID ZWIRNER, Paris (solo)

'50 Paintings',
MILWAUKEE ART MUSEUM (group)

'In New York, Thinking of You - Part I',
FLAG ART FOUNDATION, New York (group)

'Your Gaze: Selections from The Karpidas Collection',
KARPIDAS COLLECTION, Dallas (group)

2024
'In Print: Universal Limited Art Editions',
MUSEUM OF FINE ARTS, Houston (group)

'In the House of the Trembling Eye',
ASPEN ART MUSEUM (group)

2025
'Lisa Yuskavage: Drawings'
THE MORGAN LIBRARY, New York (solo)

DAVID ZWIRNER, Los Angeles (solo)

SELECTED ARTICLES AND INTERVIEWS
2020–25

2020 (cont.)
Travers, Andrew, 'Lisa Yuskavage's Fantastical Landscapes at the Aspen Art Museum', The Aspen Times, 13 February

Mistretta, Augustina, 'Agus on Art: Lisa Yuskavage Reclaims History at the Aspen Art Museum', Aspen Daily News, 28 February

2021
Powers, Bill, 'The Island Issue: Lisa Yuskavage', Purple Magazine, Spring–Summer

Freeman, Nate, 'True Colors: The Search for a Center of Gravity at an Ever-Expanding Armory Week', Vanity Fair, 10 September

Molesky, David, 'In Review: The Armory Show, Future Fair and the NY Art Fair Week', Juxtapoz Magazine, 14 September

Smith, Roberta, 'A New Level of Ambition in Art by 3 Women', The New York Times, 16 September

Kan-Sperling, Olivia, 'The Review's Review: Reproducing Bodies', The Paris Review, 23 September

Rosenfeld, Jason, 'Lisa Yuskavage: New Paintings', The Brooklyn Rail, October

2022
Cunningham, Joseph, 'Yesterday and Today: Art and Design (Part I)', The Magazine Antiques, May–June

'30 YRS part 29: Women and Painting', Purple Magazine, Paris, Fall–Winter

2023
'Lisa Yuskavage, Ron Mueck: Stars des 1990s', La République de l'Art, 12 June

Gluibizzi, Amanda, 'ArtSeen: Lisa Yuskavage: Rendez-vous', The Brooklyn Rail, July–August

Luque-Gad, Ingrid, 'Lisa Yuskavage ou l'histoire de l'art pour les mauvaises filles', Les Inrockuptibles, July

Levy, Ariel, 'Lisa Yuskavage's Bodies of Work', The New Yorker, 31 July

2025
Halperin, Julia, 'She 'defies the archetype of the good feminist', The Financial Times, 15 Feburary

Moss, Adam, 'Lisa Yuskavage Becomes the Protagonist', New York Times Magazine, 24 February

BIBLIOGRAPHY

MONOGRAPHS, BROCHURES AND ARTIST'S BOOKS

Yuskavage, Lisa, Faye Hirsch and Chuck Close, Lisa Yuskavage, Smart Art Press, Santa Monica, California, 1996

Yuskavage, Lisa, Marcia B. Hall, Katy Siegel and Claudia Gould, Lisa Yuskavage, Institute of Contemporary Art, University of Pennsylvania, Philadelphia, 2000

Yuskavage, Lisa, and Tamara Jenkins, Lisa Yuskavage: Small Paintings 1993–2004, Harry N. Abrams, New York, 2004

Yuskavage, Lisa, Tobias Ostrander and Christian Viveros-Fauné, Lisa Yuskavage, Museo Tamayo Arte Contemporáneo, Mexico City 2006

Yuskavage, Lisa, and David Zwirner, Lisa Yuskavage, David Zwirner, New York , 2006

Yuskavage, Lisa, Christopher Bedford, Suzanne Hudson, Catherine Lord, Siddhartha Mukherjee and Katy Siegel, Lisa Yuskavage: The Brood Paintings 1991–2015, Skira Rizzoli, New York, 2015

Yuskavage, Lisa, Jarrett Earnest and Hanna Schouwink, Lisa Yuskavage: Babie Brood/Small Paintings 1985–2018, David Zwirner Books, New York, 2019

Yuskavage, Lisa, Christopher Bedford, Helen Molesworth, Heidi Zuckerman and Mary Weatherford, Lisa Yuskavage: Wilderness, Gregory Miller & Company, New York, 2020

Yuskavage, Lisa, Bo Batlett and Betsy Eby, Competere, Columbus State University, 2022

Yuskavage, Lisa, Jesse Murry, Jarrett Earnest (ed.) and Christian Viveros-Fauné, Rising/Necessary Angels: Jesse Murry & Lisa Yuskavage, University of South Florida Contemporary Art Museum, Tampa, 2022

SELECTED GENERAL PUBLICATIONS AND GROUP EXHIBITION CATALOGUES

Adams, Brooks, and Lisa Liebmann, Young Americans 2: New American Art at the Saatchi Gallery, Saatchi Gallery, London, 1998

Als, Hilton, Helen Molesworth and David Rimanelli, (Nothing but) Flowers, Karma Books, New York, 2021

Ambrose, Jennifer, William H. Gerdts, Nancy Hall-Duncan, and Anne Lanford, The Great American Nude, Bruce Museum of Arts and Science, Greenwich, Connecticut, 2002

Anderson, Maxwell L., Michael G. Auping, Valerie Cassel, Hugh M. Davies, Jane Farver, Andrea Miller-Keller and Lawrence R. Rinder, Whitney Biennial, Whitney Museum of American Art, New York, 2000

Badelt, Sandra, Beat Wismer (eds), Bettina Baumgärtel, Maria Moog-Grünewald, Beat Wismer et al, Diana and Actaeon: The Forbidden Glimpse of the Naked Body, Hatje Cantz, Ostfildern, and Museum Kunstpalast, Düsseldorf, 2009

Badura-Triska, Eva, Susanne Neuburger, Stefan Neuner, Friedrich Petzel et al, Bad Painting/Good Art, DuMont, Cologne and Museum Moderner Kunst Stiftung Ludwig Wien, Vienna, 2008

Baier, Lesley K., and Sasha Newman, Yale Collects Yale, Phoenix, New Haven, Connecticut, 1993

Barak, Ami, Art Under 30: FIAR International Prize, Palazzo della Permanente, Milan, 1991

Barlow, Anne, Xochitl Dorsey, Anne Ellegood, Philip Koplin, Marcia Tucker and Anja Zimmermann, The Time of Our Lives, New Museum of Contemporary Art, New York, 1999

Basualdo, Carlos, Francesco Bonami, Dan Cameron, Okwui Enwezor, Matthew Higgs, Hou Hanru, Susan Kandel, Rosa Martínez, Asa Nacking and Hans Ulrich Obrist, Cream: Contemporary Art and Culture, Phaidon, London, 1998

Bell, Esther Bell, George T. M. Shackelford (eds.), Martha Lucy, Nicole Myers, Lisa Yuskavage and Alison de Lima Greene, Renoir: The Body, The Senses, Clark Art Institute, Williamstown, Massachusetts, 2019

Bloemheuvel, Marente, and Jaap Guldemond (eds.), Twisted. Urban Visionary Landscapes in Contemporary Painting, NAi Publishers, Rotterdam and Van Abbemuseum, Eindhoven, The Netherlands, 2000

Bollen, Christopher, and Alix Browne, Artists, Edition 7L, Paris, 2006

Boris, Staci, My Little Pretty: Images of Girls by Contemporary Women Artists, Museum of Contemporary Art Chicago, 1998

Braun, Emily, Kenneth E. Silver, Kenneth Wayne et al, Modigliani and His Models, Royal Academy of Arts, London, 2006

Bronson, Ellie, Jim Dicke and Jan Driesbach, Creating the New Century: Contemporary Art from the Dicke Collection, Dayton Art Institute, Dayton, Ohio, 2011

Bruciati, Andrea, and Alessandra Galasso (eds), Painting Codes: I codici della pittura, Galleria Comunale d'Arte Contemporanea Monfalcone, Italy, 2006

Bui, Phong, Faith Holland and Vincent Katz, Spaced Out: Migration to the Interior, Red Bull Studios, New York, 2014

Bui, Phong, Intimacy in Discourse: Unreasonable Sized Paintings, Rail Curatorial Projects and SVA Chelsea Gallery, New York, 2015

Buszek, Maria Elena, Pin-up Grrrls: Feminism, Sexuality, Popular Culture, Duke University Press, Durham, North Carolina, 2006

Cameron, Dan, On Beauty, Regina Gallery, Moscow, 1995

Campbell, Thomas P., and Christopher Noey, The Artist Project: What Artists See When They Look At Art, Phaidon, London, 2018

Cawley, Jennifer, Jordan Kantor and Elizabeth Wycoff, Don't Look: Contemporary Drawings from an Alumna's Collection (Martina Yamin, Class of 1958), Davis Museum and Cultural Center, Wellesley College, Massachusetts, 2007

Caws, Mary Ann, Elizabeth Finch, Ingrid Schaffner and Charles Simic, The Return of the Cadavre Exquis, The Drawing Center, New York, 1994

Coetzee, Mark, Not Afraid: Rubell Family Collection, Phaidon, London, 2004

Colombo, Paolo, 6th Istanbul Biennial: The Passion and the Wave, International Istanbul Biennial, 1999

Conklin, Jo-Ann (ed.), and Ian Alden Russell, She: Picturing Women at the Turn of the 21st Century, Brown University, Providence, Rhode Island, 2014

Cooperider, Carrie, Melissa Hiller and Jennifer Poole, The Figure, Another Side of Modernism, Newhouse Center for Contemporary Art, Snug Harbor Cultural Center, New York, 2000

Cozzolino, Robert, and Mariah Keller (ed.), The Female Gaze: Women Artists Making Their World, Pennsylvania Academy of the Fine Arts, Philadelphia, 2012

Cycelin, Eduardo, and Mario Codgnato, People: Volti, corpi e segni contemporanei dalla collezione di Ernesto Esposito, Mondadori Electa, Milan, and Museo Donna Regina, Naples, 2006

Davidson, Susan, Art in America: Three Hundred Years of Innovation, Solomon R. Guggenheim Foundation, New York, and Merrell, London, 2007

DiMeo Carlozzi, Annette, Negotiating Small Truths, Blanton Museum of Art, University of Texas at Austin, 1999

Earnest, Jarrett, Lucas Zwirner (eds.), and Phong Bui, Tell Me Something Good: Artist Interviews From the Brooklyn Rail, David Zwirner Books, New York, 2016

Ebony, David, Jane Harris, Frances Richard, Martha Schwendener, Sarah Valdez and Linda Yablonsky, Curve The Female Nude Now, Universe, New York, 2003

Fischl, Eric (ed.), James Frey and A. M. Homes, Disturbing Innocence, The Flag Art Foundation, New York, 2014

Flam, Jack (ed.), Come Together: Surviving Sandy, Year 1, Skira Rizzoli, New York, 2015

Fogle, Douglas, Olivier Mosset et al, Qu'est-ce que la peinture aujourd'hui?, Beaux Arts/TTM Editions, Paris, 2008

Frey, James, and Shaquille O'Neal, Size Does Matter, The Flag Art Foundation, New York, 2010

Friese, Peter, Go for it! Olbricht Collection (a sequel), Weserburg Museum für moderne Kunst, Bremen, 2009

Galitz, Kathryn Calley, Thomas P. Campbell, et al, The Metropolitan Museum of Art: Masterpiece Paintings, Skira Rizzoli, New York, 2016

Garrels, Gary, A Portrait of Our Times: An Introduction to the Logan Collection, San Francisco Museum of Modern Art, 1998

Gebbers, Anna-Catharina, and Ellen Mara De Wachter, The Library of Babel/In and Out of Place, Zabludowicz Collection, London, 2010

Godfrey, Tony, Painting Today, Phaidon, London, 2009

Gregos, Katerina, Jo Anna Isaak, Lynne Tillman et al, Fusion Cuisine, Deste Foundation for Contemporary Art, Athens, 2002

Griffin, Jonathan, Paul Harper, David Trigg and Eliza Williams, The Twenty-First Century Art Book, Phaidon, London, 2014

Grubb (ed.), Nancy, Legacy: The Emily Fisher Landau Collection, Whitney Museum of American Art, New York, 2011

Grynsztejn, Madeleine (ed.), Dan Cameron, Jessica Morgan, Ralph Rugoff et al, Supernova: Art of the 1990s from the Logan Collection, San Francisco Museum of Modern Art, 2003

Heartney, Eleanor, Art & Today, Phaidon, London, 2008

Heartney, Eleanor, Helaine Posner, Nancy Princenthal, and Sue Scott, The Reckoning: Women Artists of the New Millennium, Prestel, Munich, 2013

Heiss, Alanna, Greater New York: New Art in New York Now, P.S.1 Contemporary Art Center, Long Island City, New York, 2000

Hermanns, Ralph, New York, of Course, Wetterling Gallery, Stockholm, 2007

Hessel, Katy, The Story of Art Without Men, Hutchinson Heinemann, London, 2022

Hixson, Kathryn, Youth Culture Killed My Dog (But I Don't Really Mind), Contemporary Arts Council, Chicago, 1995

Hixson, Kathryn, and Robert Hobbs, Presumed Innocence, Anderson Gallery, Virginia Commonwealth University, Richmond, University of Washington Press, Seattle, and Contemporary Arts Center, Cincinnati, 1998

Hodermarsky, Elisabeth, Helen A. Cooper, Linda Konheim Kramer and Marta Kuzma, On the Basis of Art: 150 Years of Women at Yale, Yale University Art Gallery, New Haven, 2021

Hoptman, Laura, and Crystalle Lacouture, A Plurality of Truths, Schick Art Gallery, Skidmore College, Saratoga Springs, New York, 2000

Hudson, Suzanne, Painting Now, Thames & Hudson, London, 2015

Huhn, Tom and Isabel Taube, Between Picture and Viewer: The Image in Contemporary Painting, Visual Arts, New York, 2010

Hunter, Sam, John M. Jacobus and Daniel Wheeler, Modern Art: Painting, Sculpture, Architecture, Harry N. Abrams, New York, 2000

Hunter, Sam (ed.), John Jacobus and Daniel Wheeler, Modern Art, Prentice Hall, Upper Saddle River, New Jersey, 2001

Hussey, Miciah (ed.), Isaac Alpert, and Sarah Willis, Drawing, Walther König, Cologne, 2020

Husslein-Arco, Agnes, and Anne de Boismilon (eds), Love Story: The Anne and Wolfgang Titze Collection, Verlag für Moderne Kunst Nürnberg, Nuremberg, 2014

Jansen, Charlotte, et al., Great Women Painters, Phaidon, London, 2022

Johnson, Rashid, Nate Lowman, Richard Prince, Sterling Ruby, Haim Steinbach, Ryan Trecartin et al, American Exuberance, Rubell Family Collection, Miami, 2011

Johnson, Ken, Are You Experienced? How Psychedelic Consciousness Transformed Modern Art, Prestel, Munich, 2011

Kamps, Toby, Lateral Thinking: Art of the 1990s, Museum of Contemporary Art San Diego, California, 2001

Karnes, Andrea, Marla Price, Emma Amos and Faith Ringgold, Women Painting Women, DelMonico Books/Modern Art Museum of Fort Worth, New York, 2022

Kertess, Klaus, 00: Drawings 2000, Barbara Gladstone Gallery, New York, 2000

King, Elaine A., The Figure as Fiction: The Figure in Visual Art and Literature, Contemporary Arts Center, Cincinnati, 1993

Klein, Richard, Dominique Nahas and Ingrid Schaffner, Pop Surrealism, Aldrich Contemporary Art Museum, Ridgefield, Connecticut, 1998

Lachman, Gary, Ina Blom, Michael Bracewell, Jan Verwoert et al, Secret Societies, Snoeck, Cologne, 2011

Lindemann, Adam, Collecting Contemporary, Taschen, Cologne, 2006

Logan, Kent, and Dean Sobel, Post Modern Portraiture from the Logan Collection, The Logan Collection Vail, Colorado, 2005

Lombino, Mary-Kay, Out of Shape: Stylistic Distortions of the Human Form in Art from the Logan Collection, Frances Lehman Loeb Art Center, Vassar College, Poughkeepsie, New York, 2008

Marcoci, Roxana (ed.), Diana Murphy and Eve Sinaiko, New Art, Harry N. Abrams, New York, 1998

Margolis, Nancy (ed.), Women's Work: Examining the Feminine in Contemporary Painting, Southeastern Center for Contemporary Art, Winston-Salem, North Carolina. 1997

Martin, Henry, et al, Great Women Artists, Phaidon, New York, 2019

Mayer, Musa, and Sally Radic (eds.), Philip Guston: Nixon Drawings 1971 & 1975, Hauser & Wirth, London, 2018

McCarthy, David, and Harry Philbrick, The Nude in Contemporary Art, Aldrich Contemporary Art Museum, Ridgefield, Connecticut, 1999

Molesworth, Helen, Open Questions: Thirty Years of Writing about Art, Phaidon, New York, 2023

Mullins, Charlotte, Painting People: Figure Painting Today, Distributed Art Publishers, New York, 2006

Napoleone, Valeria, Mark Hix and Jennifer Higgie, Valeria Napoleone's Catalogue of Exquisite Recipes, Koenig Books, London, 2012

Pagel, David and Heather Pesanti, Decade: Contemporary Collecting 2002–12, Albright-Knox Art Gallery, Buffalo, New York, 2012

Palczynski, Matthew, Haunting Narratives: Detours from Philadelphia Realism, 1935 to the Present, Woodmere Art Museum, Philadelphia, 2012

Patterson, Richard, Attention to Detail, The Flag Art Foundation, New York, 2008

Pincus-Witten, Robert, Naked Since 1950, C&M Arts, New York, 2001

Pissarro, Joachim, Then and Now: Art Since 1945 at Yale, Yale University Art Gallery, New Haven, Connecticut, 1998

Plummer, Johanna (ed.), Claudia Gould, et al, Forty Years at the Institute of Contemporary Art, University of Pennsylvania, Philadelphia, 2005

Poulter, Emma (ed.), All Too Human: Bacon, Freud and a Century of Painting Life, Tate, London, 2018

Richer, Francesca, and Matthew Rosenzweig (eds), No. 1: First Works by 362 Artists, Distributed Art Publishers, New York, 2005

Ricupero, Cristina (ed.), Alexis Vaillant, and Max Hollein, Secret Societies. To Know, to Dare, to Will, to Keep Silence, Schirn Kunsthalle, Frankfurt, 2011

Roselione-Valadez, Juan, Highlights & Artists' Writings Volume 1, Rubell Family Collection, Miami, 2014

Roselione Valadez, Juan (ed.), Tami Katz-Freiman and Anna Stothart, No Man's Land: Women Artists from the Rubell Family Collection, Rubell Family Collection, Miami, 2015

Rosenblum, Robert, The Charged Image: From the Collection of Douglas S. Cramer, University of Hartford, Connecticut, 2004

Rubbini, Alice, Adicere Animos, Galleria d'Arte Contemporanea, Bologna, Italy, 1996

Salvioni, Daniela, Looking at Ourselves: Works by Women Artists from the Logan Collection, San Francisco Museum of Modern Art, 1999

Scala, Mark W. (ed.), Emily Braun, Susan H. Edwards, and Richard Shiff, Paint Made Flesh, Vanderbilt University Press, Nashville, Tennessee, 2009

Schaffner, Ingrid, Project Painting, Lehmann Maupin and Basilico Fine Arts, New York, 1997

Schaffner, Ingrid, and Fred Wilson, Pictures, Patents, Monkeys, and More… On Collecting, Werner Muensterberger, Independent Curators International, New York, 2001

Schjeldahl, Peter, Let's See: Writings on Art from The New Yorker, Thames & Hudson, New York, 2008

Schwabsky, Barry, Valerie Breuvart, et al, Vitamin P: New Perspectives in Painting, Phaidon, London, 2002

Schwabsky, Barry, The Observer Effect: On Contemporary Painting, Sternberg, Berlin, 2019

Schwabsky, Barry, and Todd Bradway (ed.), Landscape Painting Now: From Pop Abstraction to New Romanticism, Thames & Hudson, London, 2019

Simon, Joan (ed.), Melva Bucksbaum, Ryan Frank, Steven Learner, Caitlin Smith and Elisabeth Sussman, The Distaff Side, The Granary, Sharon, Connecticut, 2014

Storr, Robert, 5th International Biennial SITE Santa Fe, Disparities and Deformations: Our Grotesque, SITE Santa Fe, New Mexico, 2004

Tovey, Russell, Robert Diament and Jerry Saltz, Talk Art: Everything you wanted to know about contemporary art but were afraid to ask, Chronicle Books, London, 2020

Tung, Lisa, and Ann Wilson Lloyd, Figuratively Seeing, Massachusetts College of Art and Design, Boston, 2009

Vaillant, Alexis (ed.), Jean-Philippe Antoine, J. G. Ballard, Craig Buckley, Will Holder, et al, Légende, Sternberg, Berlin, 2008

Wakefield, Neville, Somos Libres II: Works from the Mario Testino Collection, Rizzoli, New York, 2014

Wang Wei (ed.), Xiang Jing, Pi Li, Shirin Neshat and Jarrett Earnest, She: International Women Artists Exhibition, Long Museum, Shanghai, 2016

Wehr, Anne, and Lucas Zwirner (eds.), David Zwirner: 25 Years, David Zwirner Books, New York 2017

Weibel, Peter (ed.), Pittura/Immedia, Malerei in den 90er Jahren, Neue Galerie am Landesmuseum Joanneum and Künstlerhaus, Graz, Austria, 1995

Westheimer, Ruth K., The Art of Arousal: A Celebration of Erotic Art Throughout History, Abbeville, New York, 2022

Williams, Eliza (ed.), Zoo, Purple House Limited, London, 2001

Works on Paper 2000: An Exhibition in the Residence of the American Ambassador, The United States Embassy, Bratislava, Slovakia, 2000

Zeglin Brand, Peggy (ed.), Beauty Matters, Indiana University Press, Bloomington, Indiana, 2000

Zuckerman, Heidi, Conversations with Artists II, Aspen Art, Aspen, 2019

ILLUSTRATED WORKS

COMPARATIVE IMAGES

PUBLIC COLLECTIONS

ADDISON GALLERY OF AMERICAN ART, PHILLIPS ACADEMY, Andover, Massachusetts

ALBRIGHT-KNOX ART GALLERY, BUFFALO, New York

THE ART INSTITUTE OF CHICAGO

DENVER ART MUSEUM

FRANCES LEHMAN LOEB ART CENTER, VASSAR COLLEGE, Poughkeepsie, New York

GEMEENTEMUSEUM, The Hague

HAMMER MUSEUM, Los Angeles

HIRSHHORN MUSEUM AND SCULPTURE GARDEN, Washington, D.C.

INSTITUTE OF CONTEMPORARY ART, Boston

LONG MUSEUM, Shanghai

LOS ANGELES COUNTY MUSEUM OF ART

THE METROPOLITAN MUSEUM OF ART, New York

MUSEUM OF CONTEMPORARY ART, Los Angeles

MUSEUM OF CONTEMPORARY ART, San Diego

MUSEUM OF FINE ARTS, Houston

THE MUSEUM OF MODERN ART, New York

OKLAHOMA CITY MUSEUM OF ART

PENNSYLVANIA ACADEMY OF FINE ARTS, Philadelphia

THE ROSE ART MUSEUM, BRANDEIS UNIVERSITY, Waltham, Massachusetts

SAN FRANCISCO MUSEUM OF MODERN ART

SEATTLE ART MUSEUM, Washington

TAMPA MUSEUM OF ART, Florida

WALKER ART CENTER, Minneapolis

WEATHERSPOON ART MUSEUM, UNIVERSITY OF NORTH CAROLINA, Greensboro

WHITNEY MUSEUM OF AMERICAN ART, New York

YALE UNIVERSITY ART GALLERY, New Haven, Connecticut

PHAIDON PRESS LTD.
2 COOPERAGE YARD
LONDON E15 2QR

PHAIDON PRESS INC.
111 BROADWAY
NEW YORK, NY 10006

PHAIDON SARL
55, RUE TRAVERSIÈRE
75012 PARIS

PHAIDON.COM

First published 2025

ISBN:
978-1-83866-811-2
Signed Edition:
978-1-83729-120-5

A CIP catalogue record of this book is available from the British Library and the Library of Congress.

Commissioning Editor
Michele Robecchi

Project Editor
Caitlin Arnell Argles

Production Controller
Andie Trainer

Design
Melanie Mues, Mues Design, London

Layout
Cantina, London

Printed in the UK

PUBLISHER'S ACKNOWLEDGEMENTS

Special thanks to Claire Altizer and Gretchen Opiem at Lisa Yuskavage Studio, New York; Hanna Schouwink, Doro Globus, Kendall Cashmore, Allison Chipak, Anthony Gelfand and Sam Yehros at David Zwirner, New York and London. James Brown, Michael Cohen, Adela Cory, Kate Goldman, Melissa Larner, Violeta Mitrova, João Mota, Mary Simpson, Hans Stofregen, Tracey Smith, Zachary Townsend, Elaine Ward, Jonathan Whale.

We would also like to thank the following institutions: The Art Institute of Chicago; Musée d'Orsay, Paris; Greengrassi, London; Artists Rights Society (ARS), New York; Design & Artists Copyright Society (DACS), London.

Photographers: Kevin Landers, Ozier Muhammad, Jason Schmidt, Tony Prikryl, Laurie Simmons.

ARTIST'S ACKNOWLEDGEMENTS

This book is about going where the love is. It came out of a conversation about the artwork of my late friend Jesse Murry with Keith Fox, whom I met through our mutual commitment to keeping the memories alive of those who died of AIDS. Keith asked me to be part of Phaidon's Contemporary Artists Series and said it was a series that younger artists and students collect and covet. I no longer teach in school, but I loved the idea that this would communicate the kind of down to earth and clear insight into how I work that it seemed worthwhile, and I am grateful to be part of this special series.

The nice thing about the series is that it has a fixed format and has five sections: long essay, focused essay, interview, artist's writings and a studio visit. I connected the dots by asking people that I have had admiration for and felt their mutual support: Barry Schwabsky, Lena Dunham, Ariel Levy, and Jason Schmidt.

Barry was the first writer/critic to connect to what I was trying to do over 30 ago, and before that was one of the first people in the "art world" that visited to me in my studio, and the first one to write a review of my work. I am as always, grateful to him for being so generous to look so deeply and write so eloquently on the paintings.

I asked Lena if she would be willing to write the Focus essay and she replied yes and immediately asked to focus on Big Marie. Lena was an amazing 8-year-old who asked to come to my studio in 1994 after having seen and been inspired by my show of the "Bad Babies." We included a photo of her and her sibling in her essay of that studio visit taken by her mom, Laurie Simmons. I remember thinking it was funny and unusual for something as normal as a mom taking pictures of her kids to have those paintings of mine in the background. It has been an incredible experience to see Lena emerge as such a great talent and force in our culture. I'm so proud of her and grateful for her contribution.

When I thought of being interviewed, I decided that I wanted to share with the reader a lively conversation with someone that was new in my life, and it would be a real opportunity to share our fun and direct dialogues. During the worst of the Covid era I read Ariel's memoir, The Rules Do Not Apply. It provoked me to write her a fan letter and she responded immediately and we ended up having a super long conversation the next day in my studio with the door and windows open. We were both super fans of each other and I hope that the interview feels as good to read as it is to talk to her in person.

I hate having my picture taken but Jason is the one person who gets the best out of me. His genuine love of artists allows him to capture them in the studio and at work in a way that is very rare. I think these pictures are very special and reflective of the fun day we had together. I am very proud and appreciative of his friendship and his willingness to entertain to my ideas.

The last part being Artist's Writings—I can't thank anyone but the Tyler School of Art and Architecture for asking me to give the commencement speech that year. I hope it helps someone who needs those words of advice.

These books are so much work and I have so many people to thank. The secret sauce in all of these books is Michele Robecchi. Over many phone calls he patiently let me insert my opinion into things but kept it all on track beautifully. It has been a lovely collaboration. Also, thanks to Andie Trainer, the Senior Production Controller, who kept us all on track.

My team at David Zwirner deserves much thanks: Hanna Schouwink, my colleague and friend and giver of much wisdom. Kendall Cashmore, my gallery liaison, keeps it all together.

Thanks to Allison Chipak, the director of photography at Zwirner. I appreciate how much you don't mind the high standards I need for the photography of my work. Thanks to Marc Sapir, my color correction whiz who made sure to get the best color proofs for the book.

Thanks to my own team: Claire Altizer and Gretchen Opiem, my registrars. You are a gift from the universe. Thank you for your care of all of my archives.

To return to go where the love is: thanks always and for everything to my husband, Matvey Levenstein.

CONTEMPORARY ARTISTS:

Contemporary Artists is a series of authoritative and extensively illustrated studies of today's most important artists. Each title offers a comprehensive survey of an individual artist's work and a range of art writing contributed by an international spectrum of authors, all leading figures in their fields, from art history and criticism to philosophy, cultural theory and fiction. Each study provides incisive analysis and multiple perspectives on contemporary art and its inspiration. These are essential source books for everyone concerned with art today.

MARINA ABRAMOVIĆ KLAUS BIESENBACH, KRISTINE STILES, CHRISSIE ILES VITO ACCONCI FRAZER WARD, MARK C. TAYLOR, JENNIFER BLOOMER AI WEIWEI HANS ULRICH OBRIST, KAREN SMITH, BERNARD FIBICHER DOUG AITKEN DANIEL BIRNBAUM, AMANDA SHARP, JÖRG HEISER PAWEŁ ALTHAMER ADAM SZYMCZYK, ROMAN KURZMEYER, SUZANNE COTTER FRANCIS ALŸS CUAUHTÉMOC MEDINA, RUSSELL FERGUSON, JEAN FISHER, MICHAEL TAUSSIG UTA BARTH PAMELA M. LEE, MATTHEW HIGGS, JEREMY GILBERT-ROLFE CHRISTIAN BOLTANSKI DIDIER SEMIN, TAMAR GARB, DONALD KUSPIT MONICA BONVICINI ALEXANDER ALBERRO, JANET KRAYNAK, JULIANE REBENTISCH LOUISE BOURGEOIS PAULO HERKENHOFF (WITH THYRZA GOODEVE), ROBERT STORR, ALLAN SCHWARTZMAN MARK BRADFORD ANITA HILL, SEBASTIAN SMEE, CONNIE BUTLER CECILY BROWN COURTNEY J. MARTIN, JASON ROSENFELD, FRANCINE PROSE CAI GUO-QIANG DANA FRIIS-HANSEN, OCTAVIO ZAYA, TAKASHI SERIZAWA JORDAN CASTEEL LEGACY RUSSELL, ASMA NAEEM, KATHERINE BRINSON MAURIZIO CATTELAN NANCY SPECTOR, FRANCESCO BONAMI, BARBARA VANDERLINDEN, MASSIMILIANO GIONI VIJA CELMINS ROBERT GOBER, LANE RELYEA, BRIONY FER NIGEL COOKE DARIAN LEADER, TONY GODFREY, MARIE DARRIEUSSECQ RICHARD DEACON PIER LUIGI TAZZI, JON THOMPSON, PETER SCHJELDAHL, PENELOPE CURTIS TACITA DEAN JEAN-CHRISTOPHE ROYOUX, MARINA WARNER, GERMAINE GREER MARK DION LISA GRAZIOSE CORRIN, MIWON KWON, NORMAN BRYSON PETER DOIG ADRIAN SEARLE, KITTY SCOTT, CATHERINE GRENIER STAN DOUGLAS SCOTT WATSON, DIANA THATER, CAROL J. CLOVER MARLENE DUMAS DOMINIC VAN DEN BOOGERD, BARBARA BLOOM, MARIUCCIA CASADIO, ILARIA BONACOSSA JIMMIE DURHAM LAURA MULVEY, DIRK SNAUWAERT, MARK ALICE DURANT, KATE NESIN OLAFUR ELIASSON MADELEINE GRYNSZTEJN, DANIEL BIRNBAUM, MICHAEL SPEAKS ELMGREEN & DRAGSET LINDA YABLONSKY, MARTIN HERBERT, CONNIE BUTLER, JASON SCHMIDT CERITH WYN EVANS HANS ULRICH OBRIST, NANCY SPECTOR, DANIEL BIRNBAUM PETER FISCHLI AND DAVID WEISS ROBERT FLECK, BEATE SÖNTGEN, ARTHUR C. DANTO TOM FRIEDMAN DENNIS COOPER, BRUCE HAINLEY, ADRIAN SEARLE THEASTER GATES CAROL BECKER, LISA YUN LEE, ACHIM BORCHARDT-HUME ISA GENZKEN ALEX FARQUHARSON, DIEDRICH DIEDERICHSEN, SABINE BREITWIESER ANTONY GORMLEY ERNST GOMBRICH, JOHN HUTCHINSON, LELA B. NJATIN, W. J. T. MITCHELL DAN GRAHAM BIRGIT PELZER, MARK FRANCIS, BEATRIZ COLOMINA PAUL GRAHAM ANDREW WILSON, GILLIAN WEARING, CAROL SQUIERS SHILPA GUPTA ALEXANDRA MUNROE, NAV HAQ, ELVIRA DYANGANI OSE HANS HAACKE WALTER GRASSKAMP, MOLLY NESBIT, JON BIRD MONA HATOUM GUY BRETT, MICHAEL ARCHER, CATHERINE DE ZEGHER, NANCY SPECTOR SHARON HAYES JULIA BRYAN-WILSON, JEANNINE TANG, LANKA TATTERSALL THOMAS HIRSCHHORN BENJAMIN H. D. BUCHLOH, ALISON M. GINGERAS, CARLOS BASUALDO JIM HODGES JANE M SAKS, ROBERT HOBBS, JULIE AULT /JENNY HOLZER DAVID JOSELIT, JOAN SIMON, RENATA SALECL RONI HORN LOUISE NERI, LYNNE COOKE, THIERRY DE DUVE CAMERON JAMIE PHILIPPE VERGNE, RALPH RUGOFF, ELENA FILIPOVIC CHRIS JOHANSON CORRINA PEIPON, BOB NICKAS, JULIE DEAMER RASHID JOHNSON CLAUDIA RANKINE, SAMPADA ARANKE, AKILI TOMMASINO ILYA KABAKOV BORIS GROYS, DAVID A. ROSS, IWONA BLAZWICK ALEX KATZ ROBERT STORR, CARTER RATCLIFF, IWONA BLAZWICK, BARRY SCHWABSKY ON KAWARA 'TRIBUTE', JONATHAN WATKINS, RENÉ DENIZOT MIKE KELLEY ISABELLE GRAW, JOHN C. WELCHMAN, ANTHONY VIDLER MARY KELLY MARGARET IVERSEN, DOUGLAS CRIMP, HOMI K. BHABHA WILLIAM KENTRIDGE CAROLYN CHRISTOV-BAKARGIEV, DAN CAMERON, J. M. COETZEE JANNIS KOUNELLIS 'TRIBUTE', PHILIP LARRATT-SMITH, RUDI FUCHS YAYOI KUSAMA AKIRA TATEHATA, LAURA HOPTMAN, UDO KULTERMANN, CHATERINE TAFT CHRISTIAN MARCLAY JENNIFER GONZALEZ, KIM GORDON, MATTHEW HIGGS KERRY JAMES MARSHALL CHARLES GAINES, GREG TATE, LAURENCE RASSEL PAUL McCARTHY KRISTINE STILES, RALPH RUGOFF, MASSIMILIANO GIONI, ROBERT STORR CILDO MEIRELES PAULO HERKENHOFF, GERARDO MOSQUERA, DAN CAMERON WILLIAM MONK ISABELLE GRAW, TERRY R. MYERS, ÀNGELS MIRALDA WANGECHI MUTU ADRIENNE EDWARDS, COURTNEY J. MARTIN, KELLIE JONES, CHIKA OKEKE-AGULU YOKO ONO LAURIE ANDERSON, ERIKO OSAKA, THIERRY RASPAIL LUCY ORTA ROBERTO PINTO, NICOLAS BOURRIAUD, MAIA DAMIANOVIC JEAN-MICHEL OTHONIEL GAY GASSMANN, CATHERINE GRENIER, ROBERT STORR TREVOR PAGLEN LAUREN CORNELL, JULIA BRYAN-WILSON, OMAR KHOLEIF JORGE PARDO CHRISTINE VÉGH, LANE RELYEA, CHRIS KRAUS NICOLAS PARTY STÉPHANE AQUIN, STEFAN BANZ, ALI SUBOTNICK, MELISSA HYDE ADAM PENDLETON ALEC MAPES-FRANCES, ADRIENNE EDWARDS, ANDRÉA PICARD RAYMOND PETTIBON DENNIS COOPER, ROBERT STORR, ULRICH LOOCK RICHARD PRINCE ROSETTA BROOKS, JEFF RIAN, LUC SANTE NEO RAUCH INGRID MÖSSINGER, RALPH KEUNING, DAVID SALLE LILI REYNAUD-DEWAR ÉLISABETH LEBOVICI, DIEDRICH DIEDERICHSEN, MONIKA SZEWCZYK PIPILOTTI RIST HANS ULRICH OBRIST, PEGGY PHELAN, ELIZABETH BRONFEN UGO RONDINONE LAURA HOPTMAN, ERIK VERHAGEN, NICHOLAS BAUME, JASON SCHMIDT DAAN ROOSEGAARDE NICO DASWANI, FUMIO NANJO, CAROL BECKER STERLING RUBY KATE FOWLE, FRANKLIN SIRMANS, JESSICA MORGAN ANRI SALA HANS ULRICH OBRIST, MARK GODFREY, LIAM GILLICK DORIS SALCEDO NANCY PRINCENTHAL, CARLOS BASUALDO, ANDREAS HUYSSEN WILHELM SASNAL ANDRZEJ PRZYWARA, DOMINIC EICHLER, JÖRG HEISER THOMAS SCHÜTTE JULIAN HEYNEN, JAMES LINGWOOD, ANGELA VETTESE DANA SCHUTZ HAMZA WALKER, DAN NADEL, LYNNE TILLMAN /STEPHEN SHORE MICHAEL FRIED, CHRISTY LANGE, JOEL STERNFELD ROMAN SIGNER PAULA VAN DEN BOSCH, GERHARD MACK, JEREMY MILLAR LORNA SIMPSON KELLIE JONES, THELMA GOLDEN, CHRISSIE ILES, NAOMI BECKWITH NANCY SPERO JON BIRD, JO ANNA ISAAK, SYLVÈRE LOTRINGER SIMON STARLING FRANCESCO MANACORDA, DIETER ROELSTRAETE, JANET HARBORD FRANK STELLA ANDRIANNA CAMPBELL, KATE NESIN, LUCAS BLALOCK, TERRY RICHARDSON JESSICA STOCKHOLDER BARRY SCHWABSKY, LYNNE TILLMAN, LYNNE COOKE, GERMANO CELANT SARAH SZE OKWUI ENWEZOR, BENJAMIN H. D. BUCHLOH, LAURA HOPTMAN WOLFGANG TILLMANS PETER HALLEY, JAN VERWOERT, MIDORI MATSUI, JOHANNA BURTON LUC TUYMANS ULRICH LOOCK, JUAN VICENTE ALIAGA, NANCY SPECTOR, HANS RUDOLF REUST BERNAR VENET FLORENCE DERIEUX, BARRY SCHWABSKY, CLAIRE LILLEY ADRIÁN VILLAR-ROJAS HANS ULRICH OBRIST, CAROLYN CHRISTOV-BAKARGIEV, EUNGIE JOO JEFF WALL THIERRY DE DUVE, ARIELLE PÉLENC, BORIS GROYS, JEAN-FRANÇOIS CHEVRIER, MARK LEWIS GILLIAN WEARING RUSSELL FERGUSON, DONNA DE SALVO, JOHN SLYCE LAWRENCE WEINER BENJAMIN H. D. BUCHLOH, ALEXANDER ALBERRO AND ALICE ZIMMERMAN, DAVID BATCHELOR FRANZ WEST ROBERT FLECK, BICE CURIGER, NEAL BENEZRA JONAS WOOD MARK GROTJAHN, HELEN MOLESWORTH, IAN ALTEVEER YIN XIUZHEN HOU HANRU, WU HUNG, STEPHANIE ROSENTHAL LISA YUSKAVAGE ARIEL LEVY, BARRY SCHWABSKY, LENA DUNHAM, JASON SCHMIDT ZHANG HUAN ROSELEE GOLDBERG, YILMAZ DZIEWOR, ROBERT STORR